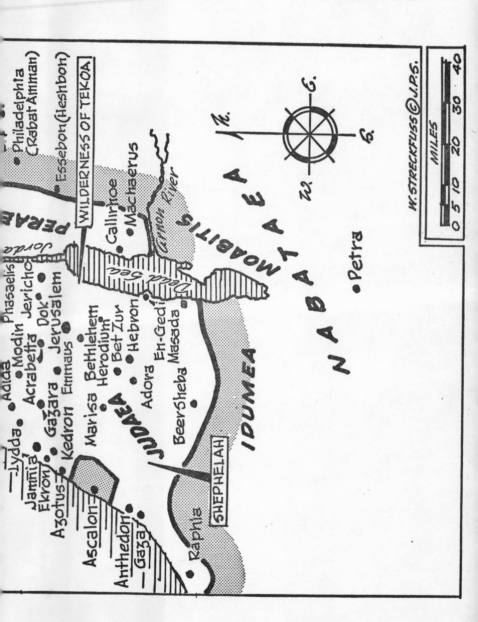

Philadelphia (Rabat Ammon)

Essebon (Heshbon)

WILDERNESS OF TEKOA

PERAE

Jordan

Callirhoe

Machaerus

Arnon River

Dead Sea

N A B A T A E A

Petra

Modin Phasaelis
Lydda Adida Jericho
Acrabetta Dok
Jamnia Gazara Jerusalem
Ekron Kedron Emmaus
Azotus Marisa Bethlehem
Herodium
Ascalon Adora Bet Zur
Hebron
Anthedon En-Gedi
Gaza BeerSheba Masada

JUDAEA

SHEPHELAH

IDUMEA

M O A B I T I S

Raphia

N.

W.   E.

S.

W. STRECKFUSS © J.P.S.

MILES
0 5 10 20 30 40

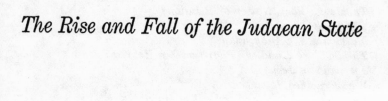

The Rise and Fall of the Judaean State

The Rise and Fall of the

JUDAEAN STATE

SOLOMON ZEITLIN

A Political, Social and
Religious History of the
Second Commonwealth

VOLUME TWO 37 B.C.E.-66 C.E.

THE JEWISH PUBLICATION SOCIETY OF AMERICA
Philadelphia/5729-1969

TO
HON. ZALMAN SHAZAR
President of Israel
In Affection and Esteem

TABLE OF CONTENTS

FOREWORD TO
FIRST EDITION

This volume was prepared as a structured history of the political, religious, social and economic life of the Judaeans from January, 37 B.C.E., when Herod became Judaea's *de facto* king, to the end of 65 C.E. when, with their victory over Cestius, the legate of Syria, they began the war against Rome. The victory over Cestius led to the end of the Herodian dynasty, to the establishment of a provisional government in Jerusalem, and to the fleeting independence of Judaea. The events embraced in this volume cover one hundred and three chronological years of continuous turmoil and suffering; it constituted a fiery ordeal, first under Herod and later under the procurators.

Those were fateful years in the life of the Judaean people; but, above all, they mark in retrospect a turning point in the history of the western world. For that comparatively brief period saw the foundations laid for the revolutionary idea of a supernatural messiah, who would be sent by God to save the Judaeans and smite their opponents. The Apocalyptists, who advanced the idea because of the agonies of that age and the political helplessness of the people, though an offshoot of the Pharisees, made few converts among them and even fewer among the Sadducees. Elsewhere, however, the idea of a supernatural messiah was destined to gain converts and grow into an overwhelming force.

In later eras of Jewish history, the idea of a supernatural messiah came to the fore among the Jews as well, even to the extent of being widely adopted as a religious tenet. The hope for a messiah gave them strength and courage during the Middle Ages, ages of degradation. For they believed that the supernatural messiah would come soon, redeem them from their misery and take them back to the Land of Israel, where they would live in peace under the scepter of the House of David. The expectation made their survival possible: they had but "to suffer and to hope." To be sure, the hope sometimes was a source of evil, when self-seeking opportunists took advantage of the conditions under which their fellows lived and proclaimed themselves the long-awaited redeemers—among the latest of them was Sabbatai Zevi in the 17th century. Nevertheless, the messianic expectation served as a tower of strength for the Jewish people from the age of the Apocalyptists, which is discussed in this book, down to our own. If historical development is to aid us in understanding ourselves, it is well to keep in mind, while reading this book, how vastly and variously this one idea helped revolutionize the western world as well as ourselves.

The writings of Flavius Josephus have served as the main source for the history of the Judaeans during the period covered by this volume. Josephus, unfortunately, was not a critical historian; he used in his own writing a variety of sources without recognizing that they were mutually contradictory. Facts are used in his *Antiquities* which are differently presented in his *War*. It was therefore necessary carefully to scrutinize his statements and reject one while accepting another. For example: in *Antiquities*, Josephus relates that the massacres of the Judaeans in Syria occurred before the victory over Cestius, while in his book, *Vita*, he places the massacres after the Roman legate's defeat. The second account seemed more likely since the slaughter of the Judaeans in Syria was due primarily to the fear that the victorious Judaeans would next turn on Syria and annex its cities. This fear was fortified by the belief which had penetrated that part of the empire that a ruler would come from Judaea to dominate the entire world. Fear, as is not unusual, turned to hate, and hate to murder.

The writings of the Graeco-Roman historians, essayists and poets served as another source for the history of the Judaeans in this period. No systematic history of the Second Jewish Commonwealth can be written without a comprehensive view of the Middle East when it was dominated by Rome. Judaea was of great importance in the wars betwen the East and the West—Parthia and Rome.

For the discussion of the religious and social life of the Judaeans the source used was early tannaitic literature. In this volume, as in volume I, individual *halakot* and various books of the apocryphal and apocalyptic literature were used to shed light on the religious and social life of the Judaeans. A separate volume of this series is to be devoted to the various types of Judaean literature, including *halakah*, apocrypha, and Josephus. For this reason, and because some of the books were written after the destruction of Jerusalem, they are not mentioned in this volume at all.

It was my intention to deal with the so-called Dead Sea Scrolls in this volume. Since, however, some protagonists of the antiquity of the scrolls have actually identified their authors with the Zealots-Sicarii [sic] and the early Christians, it seemed to me to be more appropriate to postpone to the next volume the excursus in which this subject, including these groups, will be treated. I hope there to set forth the reasons why the scrolls cannot be used as sources for the history of the Second Jewish Commonwealth or for the beginnings of Christianity.

The sections dealing with the Parting of the Ways and with Gnosticism likewise belong in the next volume.

In presenting the sketch of the life of Jesus, all the

Gospels were utilized. However, because of the contradictions among them, even among the synoptics, the various narratives had to be weighed one against the other. In a number of instances, upon careful critical examination, the non-synoptic John appeared preferable to the others, especially where he is supported by some of the early Church Fathers. While the sketch of Jesus' life is placed in Part I, which deals with the political life of the people, his controversies with the Pharisees was put in Part III, which deals with the religious life of the Judaeans.

I dedicate this book to my friend and classmate of my youth, Zalman Shazar, President of the State of Israel. Our discussions while students at the academy of Baron Gunzberg in St. Petersburg are still vivid in my memory. I was already then interested in the history of the Talmud and, to a lesser degree, in the history of the Second Jewish Commonwealth, while he was interested in the history of the messianic movements, especially that of Sabbatai Zevi. Labor Zionism had already enlisted his enthusiastic support, the ultimate goals being the establishment of an independent Jewish State in the land of Israel, and justice for all people. In a sense our paths have run parallel: I have tried truthfully to reconstruct a momentous period of our people's past; he has devoted heart and soul to the building of our people's future, while at the same time pursuing his scholarly researches. I consider myself fortunate and assigned to great merit to have lived to see the establishment of the Third Commonwealth with my friend as its President—an office for which he is uniquely endowed in heart and mind, in character and attainments. Let us hope that in his day Judah will be saved and Israel dwell securely.

I take this opportunity also to record the fact that the volumes which constitute *The Rise and Fall of the Judaean State* are being written largely because their writing was urged upon me by my friend, the late Mr. Sol

Satinsky, when he was President of the Jewish Publication Society. I have, during the past fifty years, published hundreds of articles and monographs in order to elucidate the numerous ambiguities, perplexities and obscurities which characterize the source material of that age. Sol Satinsky was a modest man; those who knew him well recognized that he possessed a fine intellect, broad culture and considerable learning. He had reverence for Jewish scholars. His interest in Jewish history was especially keen; he was convinced that to understand the Judaism of today one must know the Judaism of the past. Moreover his profound interest in the State of Israel led him to believe that knowledge of the history of the Second Jewish Commonwealth would serve as a guide to the leaders of the Third. In the early nineteen sixties he urged me to write a systematic history of the Second Jewish Commonwealth. May these volumes serve as a memorial to him.

My thanks are extended to Rabbi Eugene B. Borowitz for his careful reading of the manuscript of this volume and for his many thoughtful and interesting suggestions.

It gives me great pleasure to record my gratitude to my friend and colleague, Dr. Solomon Grayzel, for his part in editing the manuscript of this book. His linguistic gifts and historical insight were at my disposal. He succeeded in clarifying many a page without changing its meaning and intent.

I am grateful to the staff of the Dropsie College Library for having placed all the necessary books at my disposal, and to the staff of the Jewish Publication Society for its unfailing helpfulness.

A selected bibliography as well as a more elaborate index are deferred to the third volume.

SOLOMON ZEITLIN

Dropsie College
January, 1967

FOREWORD TO
SECOND EDITION

From tannaitic literature it is evident that the heads of
the *Bet Din*, later known as Sanhedrin, were sages. However, from the trial of Jesus, as depicted in the gospels,
it is correct to assume that the presiding officer of the
court was the high priest; and this contradicts what we
know from tannaitic literature. Many scholars have
followed the evidence of tannaitic literature, while other
scholars have followed the account given in the gospels.

Dr. A. Büchler (*Das Synedrion in Jerusalem*, 1902)
advanced the theory that there were two Sanhedrins,
each with different functions. He argued that one Sanhedrin exercised religious rights over all the Judaeans,
while the other Sanhedrin had exclusive jurisdiction as
far as the Temple was concerned. This latter Sanhedrin
was the governing body of the Temple and was headed
by the high priest and had the right to deal with criminal
cases. Jesus was seized, according to the gospels, in the
Temple. Thus, according to Büchler, he was seized by
the Temple Sanhedrin presided over by the high priest.
The term Sanhedrin in tannaitic literature refers to the
general Sanhedrin which administered the religious life
of the Judaeans and was headed by the sages. In
Büchler's opinion, both Sanhedrins were permanent institutions functioning side by side.

I rejected this theory for the following reasons. During the Second Commonwealth the court was designated by the term *Bet Din,* never by the word Sanhedrin. The word Sanhedrin applicable to the Jewish court came into vogue only after the destruction of the Temple. Furthermore, Jesus was not seized by the order of the Jews but by the order of the Roman authorities. It is true that there was a court called the *Bet Din shel Kohanim,* the priestly court. This court dealt only with matters which affected the priests. One of its special concerns was the examination of the genealogy of the claimants to the priesthood in order to ascertain whether they were *bona fide* of priestly stock. It held its sessions in the *lishkat haGazit,* in the Chamber of Hewn Stone. This court did not hold sessions in the house of the high priest. The *Bet Din shel Kohanim,* the priestly court, was never designated by the term Sanhedrin.

I propounded the theory that after the establishment of the Commonwealth there were two courts in Judaea. One was the *Bet Din,* later known as Sanhedrin. The *Bet Din* was a permanent institution which tried religious offenders. It was in session every day except on the Sabbaths, holidays and their eves. Its members were scholars. There was another institution which tried political offenders. It was not a court in the full sense of the word but a privy council, and its name was *synedrion.* The word *synedrion* had the connotation of a gathering of people. From Greek literature we know that the *synedrion* was not a permanent institution. It was invoked by the rulers of the state for advice and consultation when the need arose. In this sense it was used by the Greek historians Herodotus, Xenophon, Socrates, Thucydides, Polybius and Josephus. It is mentioned in II Maccabees in the same vein. Josephus also refers often to the privy council, *synedrion,* which Herod summoned from time to time. When Judaea became a province of Rome, the high priests were responsible for the tranquility of the country. In dealing with matters concerning the civil and political life of the people, the high priests summoned a council, *synedrion,* where cases were presented and advice was sought.

Thus there is no contradiction between tannaitic literature, the writings of Josephus and the gospels. The former refers to the *Bet Din,* the Sanhedrin, headed by scholars, while in the latter literature the references are to the *synedrion,* the council presided over by Herod and later by the high priests.

I have substantiated this theory in various articles and monographs, particularly in my book *Who Crucified Jesus?* but since the publications wherein I dealt with the institutions of the *Bet Din* and the *synedrion* are not readily accessible to the readers of these volumes I thought it expedient to present my views in succinct form in an Appendix to this second edition.

S. Z.

October, 1968

PART ONE

The Reign of Herod

1. HEROD, KING OF JUDAEA

In the year 37 B. C. E., the 10th of Tebet, a traditional fast day, fell on Wednesday.[1] That was the day Herod son of Antipater became King of Judaea in fact as well as in name. The Roman Senate had, upon the advice of Antony, already named Herod King of Judaea in the year 40.[2] However, in order to win his throne Herod had to defeat Antigonus, the rightful heir to the Hasmonean throne, and conquer Judaea. He could not accomplish this with his own resources, but when Antony dispatched a Roman army under Sosius, Herod was finally able to complete his conquest[3] and to request the death of Antigonus, whom Antony ordered beheaded. So the cunning, ambitious Herod achieved his goal at the early age of thirty-six.[4]

Yet Herod was not fully satisfied with this exploit; he felt his victory was not complete. True, the country had been subdued, but this had been achieved by the Romans. Antigonus had been Sosius' captive, not his—and the country was not yet entirely at peace. The Judaeans never acclaimed Herod king. Indeed, they always considered him a stranger and an outsider who had forced himself upon them, and who could maintain his rule only through force. More important, Herod knew that the Romans usually selected as king in a conquered country a member of the royal family in whom they had confidence.[5] Herod had no dynastic claim to the throne of Judaea. He was not a descendent of the royal family and the only right he had to the kingship was through his marriage to Mariamme, the paternal granddaughter of Aristobolus II and the maternal granddaughter of Hyrcanus II.[6] Herod's marriage into the royal family of the Hasmoneans, consummated shortly before his final victory, helped him to obtain the kingship.[7] These two factors—his dependence upon the Romans and his displacement of the Hasmoneans—shaped the life of Herod as a man and as king. In order to hold his throne, he had to guard against Hasmonean ambition, while serving Rome loyally by preventing any disturbances in Judaea which might affect Roman interests in Syria.

What began as a feeling of insecurity ended as madness. Herod became a psychopath and died a malevolent madman. His marriage to Mariamme became a nightmare. The thought that she gave him his claim to the throne of Judaea constantly haunted him.[8] Though he deeply loved Mariamme, he eventually killed her. He saw in the other members of the Hasmonean family conspirators who wanted to deprive him of his kingship, and he exterminated them too. Anyone suspected of opposition to him was put to death in an inhuman way, and often their families as well.[9] Mental disorder was also evident in other aspects of his private life. He was the only king during the Second Commonwealth who practiced polygamy and, like an Oriental monarch, he introduced eunuchs into his palace and practiced homosexuality.[10] After his death, the delegation which appeared before Augustus Caesar accused Herod of having been a rapist.[11]

Politically, however, Herod was a great success. Judaea attained the peak of its prosperity during his reign. He extended its boundaries further than they had reached during the reigns of David and Solomon. The Roman Emperor, Augustus Caesar, a shrewd and able statesman, valued Herod's administration and considered him the ablest client-king of the Empire. As a general, Herod was a courageous warrior, an inspired tactician in guerilla warfare as well as in open battle. He never lost the devotion of his army. As a builder of forts and cities he displayed great architectural taste. The Temple, which he rebuilt, was considered the most magnificent such structure in the East. As a man of culture he had an appreciation of learning, particularly Hellenistic, and his court was more Hellenistic than Judaean. Nicolas of Damascus was his court historian, and Herod himself wrote chronicles of his reign. Other Greek rhetoricians were in his retinue and he sought to give his sons a thorough Hellenistic training.

Yet despite all these outward evidences of his accomplishments, the people of Judaea hated Herod, and it was he who planted the seeds of the destruction of the Judaean State.

HEROD'S MANY PROBLEMS

The Problem of Hasmonean Loyalties

The early days of Herod's rule reflected the precariousness of his situation. His first problem was the Hasmonean family and their sympathizers. There were still Hasmoneans in the country—in Judaea there was Mariamme, his wife; Alexandra, her mother; Mariamme's brother, Aristobolus; and still alive in Parthia was Mariamme's grandfather, Hyrcanus II. There were others related to the Hasmonean family and many who sympathized with their cause. Knowing this, Herod began a reign of terror. He showed no mercy to the followers of Antigonus and killed forty-five of his chief supporters, confiscating their wealth. In order that no one should escape from Judaea and that no silver, gold or jewels should be smuggled out of the city, Herod stationed guards at the gates of Jerusalem's walls to examine coffins to see if they contained valuables instead of corpses.[12]

He appointed Costobarus, an Idumaean, as military governor. The latter's particular concerns were the guards at the gates and the investigation of all who were suspected of disloyalty to Herod. Costobarus did his job faithfully, with one significant exception. There was a family of prominence in Judaea, known as the Sons of Baba, who had been staunch supporters of Antigonus and who exerted great influence over the people. Though Herod was determined to kill them, Costobarus hid them and saved their lives. When Herod made inquiries concerning them, Costobarus assured Herod that he knew nothing of their whereabouts.[13] Perhaps he did this for the money the Sons of Baba gave him; but it is more likely that he did so because he was uncertain of the durability of Herod's reign. He hoped to rise in power and wanted these influential men on his side.[14]

Economic and Religious Problems

The requisition of his enemies' wealth did not end Herod's financial difficulties. His treasury was empty, and he needed great sums for bribes to Antony and his friends. He converted all the valuables which he had seized into money. Moreover, the economic life of the country was at a low point, as much of it had been devastated by the civil war. In addition, the year 37, when Herod became king, was a sabbatical year (38-37).[15] Since the Judaeans would not cultivate their land, their hardships were multiplied.

Herod's second set of problems was religious. The *Bet Din haGadol*, later known as the Great Sanhedrin, was the most important legal institution in the country. It exerted great influence on the life of the people. Herod showed honor to Sameas (Shemayah) and his pupil Pollion (Hillel) because, during the siege of Jerusalem, they had advised the people to admit Herod into the city.[16] But undoubtedly many members of the Sanhedrin were adherents of the Hasmonean family. To eliminate a potential source of rebellion, Herod purged the *Bet Din*

haGadol of many of its members and appointed as heads
of this institution the Sons of Bathayra who were natives
of Babylonia.[17] He purposely appointed men who were
not natives of Judaea, and thereby felt assured of their
loyalty. Perhaps, too, he sought by this friendliness to
Babylonian Jews to enhance the legend that his father,
Antipater, was not an Idumaean but, as Nicolas of
Damascus wrote, of the Judaean Babylonian nobility.[18]
He followed the same strategy in the far more important
appointment of a new high priest.

THE PROBLEM OF THE
HIGH PRIESTHOOD

Herod himself, not being of the priestly family, could
not succeed Antigonus as high priest. He felt it to be
politically dangerous to appoint a member of the Hasmonean family to a position of such great prominence
since this would pose a menace to his continued rule.
Therefore he ignored Aristobolus, Mariamme's brother,
the logical dynastic choice, and appointed instead Ananel
(Hananel), a priest from the Babylonian Diaspora, who
probably resided in Egypt.[19] This obscure priest, who
had no roots in Judaea, was completely dependent on
Herod for his position.

The appointment of Hananel as high priest was a severe blow to Alexandra. She had maneuvered the marriage of her daughter Mariamme to Herod with the
object of having her son Aristobolus made high priest.
She cherished the hope that her son would ultimately
succeed Herod as ruler. In her desperation, she sought
the aid of Cleopatra, knowing of Cleopatra's deep hatred
for Herod. Alexandra implored Cleopatra to exert her
influence over Antony to force Herod to appoint Aristobolus high priest.[20]

Josephus gives a romantic account of Alexandra's in-
trigues. He says that Dellius, a friend of Antony, visited
Jerusalem where he met Aristobolus and his sister,
Queen Mariamme. He was struck with their beauty and

assured Alexandra that, if she sent their portraits to Antony, her request would be granted. She followed his advice and did so. Upon receiving the portraits Antony was enchanted with the beauty of the two young Hasmoneans.[21] He could not ask Herod that Mariamme should visit him, since she was Herod's wife; but he did ask that Aristobolus should visit him. Herod, knowing that such a visit would harm his own interests, replied that the absence of Aristobolus from Jerusalem could lead to disturbances in the country.[22] This account is given in *Antiquities* but not in *War*. However, Josephus relates in another connection in *War* that Salome, the sister of Herod, accused Mariamme of immoral purposes in sending her portrait to Antony: "a man with a madness for her sex and powerful enough to resort to violence."[23] It is possible that this account of sending the portraits to Antony was maliciously invented against Mariamme to show her unfaithfulness to Herod, and it was spread among the people.

Herod was forced to yield to Cleopatra and Antony. Josephus writes that Herod decided to give the high priesthood to Aristobolus because Mariamme pressed him urgently to do so. Moreover, Josephus argues that Herod thought it would be to his advantage if Aristobolus became high priest, as he would then be unable to leave the country;[24] in other words, Aristobolus would be under Herod's watchful eye. This comment by Josephus is strange. Why, as high priest, could Aristobolus not leave the country? There was no prohibition against this, and in fact there was precedent to support it: the pious high priest Onias III went to Antioch to see Seleucus IV and complained against the intrigues of his brother Jason.[25] It is probable that Josephus copied this motive from Herod's biographer, Nicolas of Damascus, who insisted that Herod appointed Aristobolus as high priest of his own volition, because it was to his own advantage.

Wanting the people to believe that the appointment of Aristobolus was his own doing and not dictated by

Cleopatra, Herod called a council of friends, in which he included Alexandra. At the meeting of the council, he charged Alexandra with plotting the overthrow of his government with the help of Cleopatra. He claimed that he had always intended to make Aristobolus high priest and that he had appointed Ananel to this post only temporarily because Aristobolus was too young.[26] The council called by Herod and the speech he delivered were sinister deceptive maneuvers to cover his future acts. Despite the danger to his own rule, Herod knew he must appoint Aristobolus; but he intended nonetheless to destroy him—for reasons of self-preservation.

Herod then dismissed Ananel as high priest and appointed Aristobolus in his stead. Josephus claims that Herod's deposing of Ananel was unlawful, because no high priest had ever before been removed from office, except when Antiochus Epiphanes replaced Jason with his brother [cousin] Onias-Menelaus, and when Aristobolus II deposed his brother Hyrcanus II to assume the office himself.[27]

There is no analogy between the dismissal of Jason and that of Ananel. Josephus, or the source which he used, did not realize the significance of the historical changes which took place in Judaea. Before the establishment of the state, Judaea was a subject country, a part of the province Coele-Syria. At that time the high priest, besides his ecclesiastical authority, represented the people to the foreign rulers of Judaea in civil matters. The Persian authorities, later the Ptolemies and Seleucids, formally appointed the new high priest, though the office was hereditary in the Zadokite family. For this he had to pay tribute to the king as a token of subjection.[28] The foreign ruler also assumed the prerogative of dismissing any high priest who they thought did not act in accordance with their interests. Thus Antiochus Epiphanes dismissed Jason, whom he regarded as an obstacle to his plan to Hellenize the Judaeans, and appointed his cousin (brother) Onias-Menelaus, who he was confident would execute his policy. Similarly, during the wars of the Hasmoneans, Alexander Balas appointed Jonathan, the Hasmonean, who was not of the Zadokite family, as high priest. We may assume that Jonathan was not recognized as high priest by all the people but only by his followers.[29]

That situation changed radically with the establishment of Judaea as an independent state. A *Kneset haGedolah* (Great Synagogue), summoned on the 18th day of Elul, 141 B.C.E., conferred the high priesthood upon Simon and his family forever. That was how it came in time to Hyrcanus II. He was not deposed by his brother but may be said to have given up the office when, under Antipater's guidance, he fled Judaea and warred against Aristobolus II. Thus in Herod's day, the youth Aristobolus, grandson of Hyrcanus II, was the rightful successor to the office, since, though Hyrcanus II had no male issue, he sired one daughter, Alexandra, who was the mother of Aristobolus.[30] Thus Aristobolus was the grandson of both Aristobolus II and Hyrcanus II.

Under the law of the commonwealth, Ananel had no right to the high priesthood. Herod had acted as a foreign ruler would toward a subject country. His appointment of Ananel had been an unlawful act and therefore the dismissal of Ananel was not a violation of the law. It did, however, have dire consequences.

Herod had changed the high priesthood from a hereditary office into a political tool, first in his own hands and later in the hands of Rome. In the period of Roman hegemony over Judaea, high priests would be appointed and dismissed at the whim of the procurators, though they would retain certain political powers in the country.

Herod, knowing that Antony's support of Aristobolus was a response to Alexandra's intercession with Cleopatra, took measures to restrict his mother-in-law's ability to interfere with his purposes.[31] He virtually imprisoned her in her palace, and kept a strict watch on her every move.

Alexandra realized that Herod was determined to destroy her and her son. She appealed to Cleopatra, who advised her to escape with her son and come to Egypt. But it was not easy for Alexandra to leave Jerusalem unnoticed. She therefore had two coffins prepared in which she and her son were to be carried out of the city, whence a waiting ship would take them to Alexandria.[32] The plan was revealed to Herod by Aesop, one of Alexandra's personal servants, who wanted to ingratiate himself with the king.[33] The king allowed the plan to proceed and caught Alexandra and her son in the act of flight. His fear of Cleopatra kept him from punishing Alexandra, but his determination to remove Aristobolus grew stronger.

The Parthian Menace

In the autumn of 37, Antony married Cleopatra.[34] To the Romans his marriage to Cleopatra appeared bigamous, since Antony had previously married Octavian's sister. As a dowry, Antony gave Cleopatra the greater part of Phoenicia and Palestine, from the River Eleutherus, the original boundary of the Ptolemies, to Egypt. (Tyre and Sidon, however, remained free cities.)[35] He also gave her the kingdom of Chalcis and, upon her request, ordered the execution of its king, Lysanias, on the pretext that he had committed treason against Rome in the year 40.[36] He also turned Cyprus over to her.[37] In acquiring Cyprus and Chalcis, Egypt obtained the copper and timber it needed.

Cleopatra's dominating ambition—a major factor in the history of this period—was to restore the boundaries of Egypt as they had been at the time of her ancestor, Ptolemy Philadelphus. Coele-Syria had then been a part of Egypt, as were Judaea and Nabataea. Thus, she named the child, born after her marriage to Antony, Ptolemy Philadelphus.[38] Her ultimate goal was to cease being a client-queen and to rule over a mighty state, an Egypt even greater than it had been under the rule of the first Ptolemies. She therefore asked Antony for the kingdoms of Judaea and Nabataea; but these Antony refused her.[39] He had begun to organize his long-dreamed-of campaign to subdue the Parthians. He could not risk disturbances in Nabataea and Judaea in the rear of his army while he was invading Parthia.

Antony's expedition against Parthia was a catastrophe. At the outset he lost two legions with all their baggage and engines. In the campaign itself a fourth of his army was destroyed. His retreat, through the unfriendly countries of Media and Armenia, was a debacle, comparable to Napoleon's disastrous return from Russia in 1812. A Roman historian wrote that Antony considered his retreat a victory because he escaped with his life.[40] As a result, Herod feared that Parthia would invade Syria. The Hasmonean specter loomed in the background, for Hyrcanus II was in Parthia. Though held captive since the war against Antigonus, he was well treated by the king and greatly respected and honored by the Jews of Babylonia.[41] Now the Parthians might utilize Hyrcanus in a war and proclaim him king of Judaea as they had previously done with Antigonus. Though the mutilation of Hyrcanus[42] would prevent his becoming high priest, he might still serve as ruler.

Herod therefore began to weave a web to entangle Hyrcanus. He invited Hyrcanus to come to Judaea. He lured him by promises of honor in repayment for the beneficial services Hyrcanus had rendered him when Hyrcanus had been king of Judaea. His aim was to have Hyrcanus in his power and, when circumstances were propitious,[43] to put him out of the way. The Babylonian Jews implored Hyrcanus not to go, but to remain with them; but his nostalgic feeling for Judaea and for his kin, and his naiveté, made him give credence to Herod's words. He returned to Judaea. To go from Parthia to Judaea, Hyrcanus had to have permission to pass through Syria, which was Roman territory. It must be assumed that the scheme to bring Hyrcanus back to Judaea was carried out with the connivance of Antony, perhaps on his advice. To mask his treacherous designs,

Herod showed Hyrcanus great honor when he came to Judaea, calling him Father, as a title of respect.

The Consequences of Aristobolus' Murder

On the Festival of Tabernacles, in the year 36, Aristobolus performed his functions as high priest for the first time.[44] He was young, 17-18, and handsome; attired in the high-priestly robes, his appearance evoked great enthusiasm and affection from the people. They compared him to his grandfather Aristobolus. This evidence of Aristobolus' popularity brought Herod to decision: he must be put out of the way at once. After the Festival he invited Aristobolus and his mother, Alexandra, to a banquet in the summer palace at Jericho. Then, while Aristobolus was bathing in the pool, Herod's henchmen drowned him, making it appear to be an accident. Herod, who had welcomed him with signs of great friendliness, now made a display of profound grief. He ordered a lavish coffin and great quantities of perfume for the burial.

But Alexandra was not deceived. Great was her grief —for her plans of many years were shattered. For a while she contemplated suicide, but finally resolved to devote her life to revenge.[45] Aware of Cleopatra's hatred for Herod, Alexandra wrote to Cleopatra of the murder of her son, and implored Cleopatra to help her. Cleopatra urged Antony to move against Herod, on the grounds that Herod had been appointed king over a country to which he had no legal claim, and accusing him of having exhibited lawlessness toward the legitimate kings. While Antony wanted to please Cleopatra, he was apprehensive lest the killing of Herod would cause great disturbance in Judaea. He summoned Herod to come before him in Laodicea by the sea, southwest of Antioch.[46] Herod could not refuse and went to meet him, bringing lavish gifts for Cleopatra and Antony.

He had reappointed Ananel as high priest. He left his brother-in-law Joseph, the husband of his sister

Salome, in charge of the affairs of the realm,[47] with instructions to execute Mariamme should he fail to return. Herod was jealous and possessive of Mariamme, and feared that after his death Antony or someone else might possess her. Joseph was a simple soul. Knowing of the strained personal relations between Herod and Mariamme and wishing to impress her with Herod's love for her even beyond death, Joseph revealed Herod's instructions.[48] Mariamme became convinced that Herod would ultimately kill her.

While Herod was in Laodicea, a rumor spread in Jerusalem that he had been executed by Antony.[49] The rumor was false, but it indicated the real wishes of the people. Cleopatra undoubtedly demanded the death of Herod, but Antony could not afford to grant that wish. He was preparing another campaign, ostensibly against Parthia but in reality against the Armenians. He needed to secure his rear, and recognized in Herod a devoted ally. The rumors of Herod's death caused considerable disturbance in Jerusalem. Alexandra tried to persuade Joseph to join them in seeking refuge with the Roman legions near the city.[50] Julius Caesar had made Judaea one of the *civitates sine foedere immunes et liberae,* and so no Roman troops could be quartered in her territory without the consent of the ruler. Thus the legion encamped near Jerusalem was there at Herod's request, and their presence indicates that Herod felt insecure in Judaea.

Herod soon won Antony's confidence. He probably argued frankly that Aristobolus had to be removed because he was a danger to Herod's rule. Neither Antony nor Cleopatra were novices at political assassination.[51] Antony spared Herod, but to satisfy Cleopatra he gave her Jericho, the most fertile part of Judaea.[52] Its palm trees and the balsams of this region provided valuable exports whose revenue brought great wealth to Judaea. Antony also gave her a section of Nabataea, located east of the Dead Sea. It was rich in bitumen, an embalming essential, which was exported largely to Egypt.[53]

Upon Herod's return to Judaea, his sister Salome and

his mother Cypros told him of Alexandra's effort to get Joseph to flee the city when the rumor spread of Herod's death. Salome also accused her husband Joseph of immoral relations with Mariamme.[54] To prove that Mariamme was not faithful to Herod, Salome accused her of having had a portrait made of herself which she sent to Antony in order to arouse his lust.[55] Mariamme denied these accusations. Josephus relates that, while Herod and Mariamme were embracing "as is usual with lovers," and the king was telling her of his great love for her, she said, "It was not the act of a lover to command that, if anything serious should happen to him at the hands of Antony, I should be put to death too, although not guilty of anything." When Herod heard these words he became violently angry, crying out and tearing his hair. He felt that he now had clear proof that Joseph had betrayed him with Mariamme; otherwise he would not have revealed the secret to her. This account has a pathetic note. No one was present while Herod and Mariamme were embracing, hence the story must have been taken from Nicolas of Damascus or from Herod's own chronicles. Herod ordered the immediate execution of Joseph without giving him an opportunity to be heard. He wanted to kill Mariamme also, but, according to Josephus, he restrained the impulse because of his great love for her. He placed Mariamme's mother, Alexandra, under guard in chains because he believed that she was partly to blame for all his troubles. Josephus does not elaborate on what troubles she caused.[56] If Joseph did have immoral relations with Mariamme, no blame could be attached to Alexandra. Rather it would seem that Joseph was executed because of the disturbance in Jerusalem at the time of the rumor of Herod's death, and Alexandra did have a part in that.

The Intrigues of Cleopatra

Alexandra was not the only one to seek Cleopatra's help against Herod. Costobarus, Herod's military governor, also was not loyal to Herod. He was of the Idumaean nobility and his ancestors had been high priests of their national god Coze in the days before John Hyrcanus conquered Idumaea and its people accepted Judaism. He too intrigued with Cleopatra, seeking to have Idumaea separated from Judaea as an independent state.[57] Herod was suspicious of Costobarus and perhaps became aware of his intrigues with Cleopatra, but he did not dare to have him executed for fear of her, and also for fear of Costobarus' large following in Judaea, and particularly in Idumaea. Herod's sister Salome was now a widow, and deeply devoted to Herod. He therefore married her off to Costobarus,[58] hoping to gain Costobarus' loyalty as brother-in-law and to have Salome spy on all his actions.

Cleopatra accompanied Antony on his Armenian campaign early in the year 34 and went as far as the Euphrates. On returning, she stopped in Apamea and Damascus, which apparently had been presented to her by Antony. She intended going to Judaea to visit Jericho, her new possession. Herod feared her presence in Judaea, as he could not prevent her meeting with Alexandra, and this would undoubtedly make trouble for him. He also worried lest Cleopatra establish an Egyptian administration in Jericho. As a result, he met her at the border and made a financial deal with her. He leased the district of Jericho for two hundred talents annually and, not wanting the Egyptians as neighbors, stood surety for another two hundred talents which Malchus, King of Nabataea, was to pay as his share. Having made this deal with Cleopatra he entertained her lavishly and showered her with gifts. He then escorted her all the way to Egypt.

Josephus wrote that while Herod entertained Cleopatra she attempted to have sexual relations with him.[59] This story is probably an invention of Herod. Cleopatra, as pictured by historians, was not the kind of woman who indulged in sexual relations for mere pleasure; she employed sex for the purpose of attaining power.[60] To seduce Herod, whom she despised, would be no gain for

her. He was a client-king and she was a queen, the wife
of Antony. An affair with Herod would have been dangerous, since Antony, a violently jealous man, would
have killed them both.

Josephus further says that Herod was uncertain
whether Cleopatra was taken with his charms or whether
she wanted to trap him so that she could denounce
him to Antony. More likely, he wanted to kill her
while she was in his power to save Antony from her evil
influence, but Herod's friends dissuaded him from doing
this as Antony never would have forgiven it. Josephus
takes this story from the chronicles of Herod[61] who,
like all the Roman historians, portrayed Cleopatra as the
evil serpent of the Nile. Psychologically it is probable
that the one who wanted to do the seducing was Herod—
not Cleopatra. Since he could not seduce her, he conceived
the idea of killing her under the pretense of saving
Antony from her evil influence.

HEROD'S SEARCH FOR SECURITY

Masada

Herod sought to make his position more secure during
these early years of his reign by an energetic program
of fortress building and rebuilding. He strengthened the
Baris Fortress, which had been built by the Hasmoneans
on the northwest side of the Temple, renamed it Antonia,
in honor of Antony, and placed a garrison there. It
dominated the Temple: whoever held the fortress had
power over the Temple. Herod also recaptured Hyrcania,
which had been held by the sister of Antigonus,[62] fortified it and made it a political prison, a place of torture
and death:[63] few left it alive. He built a new fortress
south of Jerusalem, at the place where he had been defeated by Antigonus, and called it Herodion.[64] He built
another fortress named Herodion, in the south near
Nabataea,[65] as a protection against invasion by the
Nabataeans. Herod also rehabilitated Fort Machaerus,
situated east of the Dead Sea and north of the Arnon

River,[66] as a further protection against the Nabataeans. He rebuilt the Fortress Masada which had originally been erected by the Hasmoneans,[67] on the western shore of the Dead Sea, and made it almost impregnable. The feat deserves fuller discussion.

The location of Fort Masada made it a strong defensive bastion. On its east was the Dead Sea, while on the west it was difficult of ascent.[68] Herod had the entire summit on which the fortress sat enclosed with a wall of white stone, approximately eighteen feet high and twelve feet thick. Surmounting the wall, he erected thirty-seven towers about seventy-five feet in height. West of the fortress proper, extending toward the north, he built a palace surmounted by four towers approximately ninety feet high. In its interior were colonnades, apartments and luxurious baths. He stored there large quantities of corn, wine, oil, great varieties of pulse, and mounds of dates sufficient to last for years. There was some soil at the summit suitable for cultivation, and he set this aside for use in case of a shortage of provisions. To be assured of an ample water supply he had numerous tanks made as reservoirs. He hoarded great masses of arms of every description, sufficient for ten thousand men, and in addition laid in stores of brass, iron and lead.[69] Josephus notes that, when the Sicarii took possession of Masada in the year 65 C.E., they found all this material intact and the footstuffs in perfect condition due to the dry climate. These extensive preparations indicate that Herod was himself prepared to take refuge there when in peril.[70]

Border Wars

Ever since the victory over Brutus and Cassius at Philippi in October, 42 B.C.E., Octavian had been striving to eliminate Antony from power. One of his chief weapons was propaganda against Antony, and particularly against Cleopatra. In the year 32, contrary to Roman custom, he read to the Senate Antony's will, which had been deposited with the Vestal Virgins with all traditional confidence. In it Antony directed that, if he should die in Rome, his body should be borne in state to the Forum and then conveyed to Cleopatra in Egypt.[71] By reading the will Octavian wanted to show the Senate that Antony was more Egyptian than Roman, that he considered Cleopatra Queen of Egypt, Cyprus, Libya and Coele-Syria and wanted her to share her throne with Caesarion who, she maintained and Antony confirmed, was her son by Julius Caesar.[72]

When Antony returned from Armenia in the autumn of 33, he decided to make war against Octavian. He and Cleopatra spent the winter in Ephesus. About September in 32, his forces reached the coast of the Ionian Sea. In the beginning of the year 31, Octavian entered the third consulship and his position was greatly strengthened. In the spring, his fleet crossed the Adriatic to meet Antony. They confronted each other with tremendous forces. Antony mustered 100,000 infantry, 12,000 cavalry, and hundreds of fighting ships. Octavian had 250 ships and infantry and cavalry equal to his adversary's.[73] Antony had summoned to his aid all of his client-kings and their forces, with the exception of Polemon of Pontus, Herod, and King Malchus of Nabataea. These three, however, supplied Antony with men as well as provisions. The reason that Polemon did not join may be that he was charged with guarding the Armenian border.

According to Josephus, Herod did not accompany Antony because he was charged with the task of punishing Malchus for not paying the 200 talents rental he owed on Cleopatra's account.[74] The real reason for this unexpected fact of his absence from Antony's army is not difficult to surmise. Cleopatra's deep hatred for Herod was such that she was determined not to permit him to be near Antony. She prevailed upon Antony to make Herod undertake a war against Malchus, a war which served her interests well by weakening both kings whose territory she coveted.[75]

Herod invaded Nabataea early in the spring of 31, and was at the point of victory in the very first engagement. But Athenion, one of Cleopatra's generals, apparently stationed in the region to watch over her interests, suddenly attacked the Judaeans, killing many. The Nabateans took advantage of the weakened position of the Judaeans, attacked them and completely routed them. Herod tried unsuccessfully to reorganize his army. He then resorted to guerilla warfare and overran many parts of the country.[76]

At the same time, Judaea suffered a severe earthquake and about thirty thousand people perished in the ruins of their homes.[77] The army, however, which lived in the open, was not harmed. The defeat of the army and the calamity which befell the country compelled Herod to sue for peace, and he sent plenipotentiaries to arrange a peaceful settlement between Judaea and Nabataea. The Nabataeans learned of the calamity which had befallen Judaea and, confident that the entire country had been laid waste, murdered the envoys who were on a peaceful mission.[78]

Herod did not despair. According to Josephus, he tried to inspire his officers with courage and told his army that the catastrophe was due to natural causes and would have no further consequences. He declared that the murder of the envoys was not only an act against Judaea, but contrary to the universal law of mankind. He added that God was on the side of the Judaeans, for those who have justice with them have God with them. He appealed to them to defend their wives and children and to avenge the barbarous murders by the Nabataeans. He maintained that, if it had not been for Athenion, the Judaeans would have scored a complete victory in the first battle. Herod then offered the customary sacrifices and led the army against the Nabataeans.[79]

The Hasmonean rulers had not offered sacrifices before engaging in battle. It was not the custom among the Judaeans to do so. The Greeks and Romans did, and since the greater part of Herod's army consisted of foreign mercenaries, he offered sacrifices to inspire them and give them hope for victory. Since Judaean sacrifices could be offered only in the Temple, Herod either sent animals to Jerusalem to be sacrificed or, more likely, had altars built in the field and offered sacrifices according to the custom of the Greeks and Romans.

His army aroused, Herod crossed the Jordan towards Philadelphia (modern Ammon) and engaged the Nabataeans in a battle in which he completely routed them. They begged for peace, but Herod continued attacking until he totally crushed them. The Nabataeans thereupon proclaimed him Prostates, the protector of their nation,[80] in all likelihood only of the region near the Dead Sea which Antony had assigned to Cleopatra and for which Herod stood surety. Athenion did not intervene this time, because the war between Antony and Octavian was in progress and Athenion felt that it would be good policy to be neutral. Indeed, the story of his first involvement may be a fabrication of Nicolas of Damascus or perhaps Herod's own chronicle, designed to keep Herod's military prestige unimpaired.

The Execution of Hyrcanus

On September 2, in the year 31 B.C.E., a decisive battle was fought at Actium and the armada of Cleopatra and Antony was shattered. First Cleopatra and then Antony, powerless, fled to Egypt.[81] Herod, whose fortunes now hung in the balance, being a shrewd, cunning politician, deserted Antony. Receiving word of Herod's perfidy, Antony sent his trusted friend, Alexas the Laodicean, to persuade him to remain loyal.[82] Herod rejected his plea. This was not the first time that he shifted his allegiance. It was his only hope of gaining and staying in power in an unstable world. Nor was he alone. An army of trained gladiators had been held in readiness in Cyzicus for the games to celebrate Antony's victory over Octavian. When they learned of Antony's defeat, they were ready to march to his assistance, but

Quintus Didius, the governor of Syria, prevented them from doing so, an act which Herod zealously abetted.[83]

Cleopatra, too, was ready to transfer her love, but Octavian repulsed her. After the victory at Actium, Octavian departed for Rome to attend to national matters. Early in the spring of 30 B.C.E., he returned to the east to complete his victory over Cleopatra and Antony.[84]

Herod feared for his kingship; indeed, for his very life. Octavian was the adopted son of Julius Caesar whom Octavian revered as divine, and Herod feared that those loyal to the Hasmoneans would remind Octavian of his adopted father's action in giving the hereditary rule over the Judaeans to Hyrcanus. To remove this danger, Herod ordered that Hyrcanus be put to death on the grounds that he had conspired with Malchus, King of the Nabataeans. He produced before a *synedrion*, a council of friends and retainers, a letter supposedly written by Hyrcanus to King Malchus asking asylum, which the king granted. Hyrcanus was condemned by the council and strangled to death.[85]

Josephus gives two versions of the condemnation of Hyrcanus: the above, which he cites from the chronicles of Herod, and another taken from an anonymous author. The anonymous source implies that Herod, with characteristic trickery, invented these charges in order to remove the threat Hyrcanus' existence posed to his reign. Hence he forged the letter which convicted Hyrcanus of treason. Yet, there may be a kernel of truth in the version given in the chronicles of Herod.[86] Hyrcanus was a simple-minded soul, easily influenced by others. The presence of his daughter, Alexandra, that resolute, ambitious soul with her definite aims, cannot be dismissed.[87] The victory of Octavian over Antony gave Alexandra reason to hope for the restoration of rulership to her family. She might well have schemed to have Hyrcanus flee the country and place his claim to kingship before Octavian. She and her sympathizers could not appeal directly to him; Herod would not allow anyone to leave the country. Syria, to the north, was in the hands of a Roman general, an ally of Herod. The only possibility was to flee to the south, to the Nabataeans, who were unfriendly to Herod. From there she hoped Hyrcanus might find a way to reach Octavian and present his claims.

Changing Sides

On Octavian's return from Rome to invade Egypt, he stopped in Rhodes. Herod hastened to meet him there. He was perturbed, not knowing what kind of reception he would receive. He also feared that some disturbance might arise during his absence, since many of his adversaries were still active in Judaea. He sent his mother, sister and his children to the fortress Masada, and instructed his younger brother Pheroras to take charge of the government should anything happen to him.[88] He placed his wife Mariamme and her mother Alexandra in the fortress Alexandrion[89] and appointed Soemus, the Ituraean, a man he trusted, to keep them under surveillance under the pretext of showing them honor. Soemus was instructed to kill them if anything should happen to Herod. Josephus wrote that Herod had separated the two families because of the strained relations between them.[90] This cannot be taken as historical fact. Herod's family was sent to Masada which was strongly fortified for defense, while Mariamme and her mother were placed in Alexandrion as prisoners. It is significant that Mariamme's children were with Herod's family in Masada. Should Alexandra and Mariamme incite a revolt against him, his brother Pheroras could hold the children as hostages.

Josephus records in *War* that Herod said, in apologizing for his friendship with Antony, "Caesar, I was made king by Antony and I acknowledge that in all things I devoted my service to him . . . I sent him many such auxiliary troops as I could and many thousand measures of corn; nor even after his defeat at Actium did I desert my benefactor."[91] Josephus writes in the same vein in *Antiquities*, "I have not deserted him upon his defeat at Actium; nor upon the evident change of his fortune have I transferred my hopes from him to another."[92] Whatever source Josephus used for the address which Herod delivered before Octàvian Caesar, it does not square with what is known from other sources. Josephus, in having Octavian assure Herod of his security, has him say, "But you have already done me a service; for Quintus Didius writes to me that you have sent a force to assist him against the gladiators."[93] Hence Herod did desert Antony after Actium, and Josephus does not recognize the contradiction implicit in the address of Herod and the reply of Octavian Caesar.

Octavian Caesar confirmed Herod's kingship over Judaea, as well as the kingship of nearly all the rest of Antony's client-kings, including Archelaus of Cappadocia and Polemon of Pontus, who had supplied Antony with auxiliary forces.[94]

Once Herod was confirmed as ruler of Judaea, he presented Octavian Caesar and his friends with many gifts. When Octavian began his march from Syria to Egypt, Herod entertained him royally at Ptolemais, modern Acco. He escorted him and his army on the way south, and prepared a supply of water and wine for their desert crossing.[95]

In the summer of 30 B.C.E., Octavian Caesar was approaching the borders of Egypt. Without the knowledge of Antony, Cleopatra sent Octavian a golden crown and scepter, most likely to gain his favor. Octavian accepted the gifts, but made no commitments.[96] He took Pelusium, the nearest city of Egypt, without a fight. It was rumored that General Seleucus had surrendered it with the knowledge of Cleopatra. The fact that she gave Antony permission to punish Seleucus' treachery by executing his wife and children does not exonerate her.[97] History offers examples of even greater duplicity.[98]

On July 31st, Octavian's army reached Alexandria. Antony engaged him in battle, but his cavalry and infantry as well as Cleopatra's forces went over to Octavian. The following day, Cleopatra collected all her wealth and took refuge in her mausoleum. A rumor spread that she had died, and Antony stabbed himself. Cleopatra, believing him to be dead, asked that he be brought to her at the mausoleum. He was still alive when he was carried in, but died in her arms soon afterward. Plutarch wrote that Cleopatra rent her garments, beat and tore her breast with her hands, and wiped some of his blood upon her face, calling him master, husband and imperator.[99] It was self-pity rather than love for Antony. Plutarch wrote further that when Octavian Caesar learned of Antony's death, "He retired within his tent and wept for a man who had been his relation by marriage, his colleague in office and command, and his partner in many undertakings and struggles." He allowed Cleopatra to bury Antony.[100] According to the Roman historians, Octavian was anxious to capture Cleopatra alive, not only to obtain her wealth, but also to have her in his triumphal procession.[101] Cleopatra's first attempt at suicide failed and she was taken to the palace where she was kept under surveillance. It has been reported that she ended her life by putting upon her arm an asp that had been smuggled in to her in a basket of figs. Another report stated that she killed herself by poison that was concealed in a comb in her hair.[102] Before committing suicide she wrote a letter to Octavian, from which he inferred that she had killed herself. He at once sent a snake charmer called Psylli to suck the poison from her wound, but it was of no use.[103] How she committed suicide remains a mystery. Strabo, who lived during the period, already gives two versions[104] which later Roman historians repeat.

What drove this extraordinary young woman through her unprecedented career? Was it hunger for power, to be Queen of the Romans, or did she cherish the ambition of Julius Caesar, her former lover, to unite the world under one kingdom? The first hypothesis is the more plausible. She could not hope to overcome the Romans with armies and navies. Her only weapon was her seductive feminine charm. Though she succeeded in beguiling the two greatest dictators of Rome, Julius Caesar and Antony, she failed to entice Octavian Caesar. As the Roman historian, Dio Cassius, wrote, "By love she gained the title of Queen of the Egyptians, and when she hoped by the same means to win also that of Queen of the Romans, she failed of this and lost the other besides. She captivated the two greatest Romans of her day, and destroyed herself because of the third."[105]

Egypt, established as a powerful state by Ptolemy Lagus in the year 312 B.C.E., became a province of Rome in the year 30 B.C.E. Unlike other provinces, it was a personal state of Octavian Caesar, and he forbade any member of the senatorial order to set foot in it without his special consent.[106]

The question has also been raised regarding Octavian's feelings about Cleopatra's suicide. Was he chagrinned that he could not have her in his triumphal procession in Rome, or was he satisfied that by putting herself out of the way she had freed him from the necessity of killing her?[107] Probably he was more concerned with his triumph than with the problem of her execution.

Whether or not Octavian Caesar was glad at Cleopatra's death, Herod was, as one of his mortal enemies was removed. As long as she was alive and influential, he could never be certain of his kingship or even his life. His internal enemies had been encouraged by Cleopatra, and he could not deal with them harshly because of his fear of her. When he learned of her death, he hastened to congratulate Octavian Caesar.

Octavian Caesar, in Rhodes, received Herod cordially. He not only restored to him the territory which Cleopatra had annexed, that is, the region of Jericho, but he also added to his kingdom the cities of Gadara, Hippus, and Samaria, and the maritime cities of Straton's Tower, Jaffa, Antheton and Gaza. Octavian also presented Herod with a bodyguard of four hundred Gauls who had formerly served Cleopatra in the same capacity.[108] Later,

Herod escorted Octavian Caesar on his journey to Rome as far as Antioch; he then returned to Jerusalem.

THE EXECUTIONS OF MARIAMME AND ALEXANDRA

Mariamme's Trial and Death

Herod now had absolute, dictatorial power in Judaea. Hitherto his killings could have been ascribed to political necessity in the elimination of rivals. Now he began to kill to keep himself from being killed. This soon gave way to killing without any justification, political or otherwise. He killed for revenge or out of fantasy, perhaps even out of the joy of killing. Mariamme was the first victim of his new terror.

Herod had returned home from Rhodes victor, joyful over his success, only to be received coldly by Mariamme his wife. She knew that she and her mother had been virtually imprisoned in the Fortress Alexandrion and that Soemus had been given the same instructions which Herod had once given to his brother-in-law Joseph.[109] Herod was bitter at his wife's conduct. His mother and, particularly, his sister, who bore mortal hatred toward Mariamme, thought this an excellent opportunity to provoke Herod against her by new slander. Mariamme's death and Cleopatra's were almost to coincide.[110]

One day, when Herod made love to Mariamme, she expressed contempt for him and reproached him for the murder of her brother Aristobolus and her grandfather Hyrcanus. She said his love for her was not sincere. Herod was infuriated by her arrogant attitude towards him. His sister Salome, ever on the alert to destroy Mariamme, now falsely accused her of planning to poison Herod. Salome brought before Herod a cupbearer who told the king that Mariamme had given him many gifts and had requested him to prepare a love potion for the king. When Herod asked what the love potion contained, the cupbearer said it was a drug which Mariamme gave him and that since he did not know its properties, he had decided that the safe course would be to inform the king about it.[111] Herod never forgot that his father had been murdered by poison, and all his life he lived in fear of being poisoned. Herod became enraged and ordered that the eunuch who was most faithful to Mariamme be tortured to tell what he knew about the potion. The eunuch did not confess anything on this matter, but in his agony he said that Mariamme hated the king and that her hatred was intensified after she heard what Soemus told her. This made Herod violent, and he cried out that Soemus, whom he considered a most faithful friend, had betrayed him and that he would not have done this unless he had been intimate with Mariamme. He ordered Soemus arrested and executed at once, and called Mariamme to trial. He summoned a privy council of his friends, who, being aware of his anger against Mariamme, condemned her to death.[112] Upon the advice of some of the council, Herod first considered commuting the execution of Mariamme to imprisonment. But Salome and her friends successfully exerted counter-efforts and Herod ordered Mariamme executed. The grounds on which he did so are not known. Was she condemned for being an adulteress or because she tried to poison the king? She could not have been condemned to death for either of these crimes under Judaean law. There was no proof of either charge.[113]

The condemnation and execution of Mariamme were the results of frustration. Herod was continually wavering between a tender love for her and a resentment which sometimes turned to hate. When his rule was confirmed by Octavian Caesar, he felt that he had at last arrived at his throne by his own achievements and not through marriage. Mariamme, on the other hand, was a woman of great pride. She never forgot that Herod had attained the kingship through having married her, and that he kept it by murdering her family. She knew herself to be the daughter of kings and high priests and looked upon the family of Herod as commoners and usurpers. Mari-

amme was killed ultimately because she was a Hasmonean.

Josephus describes Mariamme as a most beautiful
woman, but cold and having in her nature something
at once womanly and cruel. She was not cold and cruel
by nature, but became so because of her marriage to
Herod. Married at a very early age, between sixteen
and seventeen,[114] she knew that she had been a political
tool of her mother's. She inherited neither her mother's
shrewdness and cunning, nor her grandfather's phlegmatic nature, but rather the resoluteness of her father
Alexander, and the pride and forthrightness of her
grandfather, Aristobolus II. Josephus concludes that
the enmity between them increased because she was
deeply distressed over what had happened to her nearest
kin, and that she did not refrain from expressing her
feelings and accusations.[115] Similarly, she carried on the
hatred and contempt which her family felt for Antipater,
his son Herod and the entire Herodian family. When
led to her death, she looked upon Herod with scorn, and
upon her mother Alexandra with disdain. She went to
her death calmly.[116]

In 29-28, when she was put to death, Mariamme was
twenty-six.[117] She had borne Herod five children. Three
were sons, one of whom (his name is unknown) died in
childhood and Alexander and Aristobolus. Her daughters, Salampsio and Cyprus, do not figure in history.[118]

At Mariamme's execution her mother Alexandra had
reproached her, crying out that she was wicked and
ungrateful to her husband and that she had suffered just
punishment for her reckless behavior.[119] What was
Alexandra's motive in this outburst? She had been living
for one purpose—to take revenge on Herod. As long as
Mariamme was living with Herod the time might come
when, through her daughter or her grandchildren, she
would wrest the kingdom from him. With the death of
her daughter, these plans were frustrated. More likely,
the scene was the result of a sinister deal between Herod
and Alexandra. They abhorred each other, but they

possessed qualities in common. Both were unscrupulous and ruthless. No act would have been too dastardly to deter them from a goal. Herod knew he had no proof of Mariamme's guilt and that the people would not believe his allegations against her. He thought that if her mother brought accusations against her and charged her with ingratitude to Herod, this would justify her death to the Judaeans. For making these accusations, Herod promised Alexandra immunity. In order to save her own life and keep alive her hope of revenge, she was willing to go along with Herod. The people, however, regarded Alexandra's actions as hypocrisy.[120] Herod did spare her life, but kept close watch on her at all times.

Josephus relates that after Mariamme's death Herod seemed inconsolable; he wept and called out her name unceasingly. He even commanded a servant to call out her name as if she were alive.[121]

Josephus' description may be somewhat exaggerated. Herod always did considerable play-acting, as when Aristobolus was drowned. After the execution of Mariamme, Herod fluctuated between relief from his dependence on her for status and his real longing for her. He was glad to be independent of the Hasmonean family, yet he ached physically for the beautiful, queenly Mariamme.

The Talmud records a ghastly tale about Herod—namely, that he had Mariamme embalmed and had intercourse with her corpse.[122] If this tale is true, Herod had already gone mad. Perhaps his relations with her after her death, if true, are not so much an indication of necrophilia as an insane determination still to bend this proud woman to his will. Josephus informs us that Mariamme had often refused to submit to Herod's sexual demands.[123] Herod could brook no independence in others, or tolerate anything less than total submission. Therefore he may have sought from Mariamme in death what he could not exact from her in life.

Some of Herod's remorse was genuine. He tried to

distract his thoughts with all kinds of festivities, but to no avail. Mariamme's image was always in his mind.

The Execution of Alexandra

A pestilential disease broke out in Judaea, and many who were stricken died. The people believed this to be God's punishment for Herod's crime in executing Mariamme. Herod, too, fell victim to the disease. He was in great pain, and developed an inflammation at the back of his head. At times he lost his reason, and his physicians advised him to go to Samaria. While he lay ill in Samaria, the people probably thought he was dying or that he might remain an invalid. Alexandra now made another bid for power. She tried to persuade the commanders of the two major fortresses of Jerusalem— Antonia which dominated the Temple, and the Upper Palace which controlled the residential sections, which together virtually ruled the whole city—to hand them over to her as regent of the kingdom. The commanders of these fortresses, however, particularly Achiab, a cousin of the king, refused her request. They informed Herod of Alexandra's schemes, whereupon he had her put to death.[124] So, shortly after the execution of her daughter Mariamme, Alexandra shared her fate. This was in the year 28, only ten years after she had maneuvered the betrothal of her daughter to Herod. The marriage, though a plague to all, cannot be considered as solely responsible for Herod's murderous acts. If he had achieved the kingship without marrying Mariamme, he still would have murdered the Hasmonean family, which was a threat to his security.

After Herod returned from Samaria and resumed control of the government, his sister Salome informed him that because of her loyalty to him, she had divorced Costobarus. She told him that Costobarus had kept his enemies, the Sons of Baba, in hiding for ten years.[125] Salome now revealed their hiding place, and Herod sent for them and executed them. She further informed Herod that Antipater, Lysimachus and Dositheus, who had been Costobarus' good friends, had joined him in plotting a revolt.[126] They too were speedily done away with, though Pheroras, Herod's brother, who was implicated, was spared. This purge took place in 28-27, soon after the execution of Alexandra.

Josephus comments that Salome, in divorcing her husband Costobarus, transgressed the laws of the country.[127] According to the Judaean law, only the husband has the right to divorce, and a woman cannot remarry unless she is given permission to do so by her husband when he divorces her. Josephus misstated the situation: Salome did not transgress Judaean law, since she did not remarry; however, her divorce was invalid. According to Judaean law, a woman cannot divorce a man. Salome was now not a divorcee, but a widow.

HEROD AS HELLENIZER

Violations of Judaean Law

Herod, secure with Rome by having gained the favor of Octavian Caesar, and secure at home by having purged the strongest of his enemies, now took steps to Hellenize the Judaeans. Thus he departed from cherished, well-established custom. In honor of his benefactor, Octavian Caesar, he introduced athletic contests and built a theater in Jerusalem and an amphitheater on the plains outside the city. He lavishly celebrated the quinquennial festival and invited people from the neighboring states to attend. Prizes were given to winners in the gymnastic games. Thymelikoi, people who engaged in music and dancing contests, were also invited to participate in the festival. Wild beasts, including lions, were brought in for combat, and men who had been condemned to death were sent into the arena to fight them.[128] This Roman custom was abhorrent to the Judaeans, who believed that even a condemned criminal shares something of the image of God and therefore must be put to death with a certain amount of dignity.

The theater which Herod built in Jerusalem was adorned with inscriptions to Octavian Caesar and trophies of all the nations which Octavian had conquered. The decorations were made of pure gold and silver. The Judaeans were not familiar with trophies; to them they appeared to be human images made for worship, a practice contrary to their most fundamental beliefs. To pacify the people, Herod had the ornaments which covered the trophies removed, showing that they were bare wood. However, this did not pacify all the Judaeans. A conspiracy was formed to assassinate Herod when he entered the theater, but an informer betrayed the plot to him. All the conspirators were caught and confessed, avowing that they were proud of their religious feelings. They were cruelly tortured and then put to death.[129] Herod here revealed his blood-thirstiness. Generally torture was inflicted only when the accused denied their guilt. The matter did not stop here. Next, the informer was seized by some of the people, torn limb from limb, and thrown to the dogs. Although this was done publicly, Herod could not discover who were the perpetrators. He had some women arrested and tortured until they revealed the identity of the men who had killed the informer. Herod not only put these men to death, but also their families.[130]

During the Roman civil wars and in consequence of them, brigandage had become rampant. The satirist Juvenal mentions that the Romans were afraid to walk in the streets at night. Octavian Caesar took strong measures to eradicate it.[131] Judaea had a similar problem with burglars. According to the law, if a thief was caught he had to pay a penalty double the value of what he had stolen. If he had already sold the loot, he had to pay four times its value.[132] If he had no money, the victim of his theft could sell the burglar into slavery to another Judaean. Such a slave could serve only six years; in the seventh he had to be freed by the owner.[133] Herod, however, sold those who had broken into houses to foreigners and sent them to other countries, hence into perpetual slavery.[134] The people were enraged at yet another transgression of fundamental Jewish law. Among the "housebreakers" there undoubtedly were some whom Herod considered his political enemies, and selling them into perpetual slavery to foreigners was a good way for him to get rid of them. The sages therefore enacted a law that, if a Judaean slave was sold outside of the country, he became a free man in the eyes of the law.[135] It therefore became the duty of every Judaean to ransom him, for the law prescribed the ransom of any Judaean who had become the slave of a foreigner.

Josephus records that those actions of Herod aroused enmity among the Judaeans. There was no open revolution, but outbreaks occurred from time to time. Whereas Antiochus Epiphanes forced Hellenism upon the people and punished those who maintained Judaism, Herod merely transgressed the laws of Judaea himself, never insisting that the people do so. Thus he erected temples to different gods, but did so outside of Judaea and excused himself by declaring that he acted under orders. At the same time, he told the Romans he was more interested in honoring Caesar than in observing Jewish law.[136] While in Judaea, he probably observed the Jewish laws. In Herod's later days, after he had murdered his own sons, Octavian Caesar is supposed to have remarked, "I would rather be a pig in the house of Herod than his son." If Herod had eaten pork, Caesar's remark would have lost its sting. Herod's building of theaters and temples in foreign countries and of his amphitheater in Jerusalem had the purpose of making him out to be a Hellene, and to gain him favor among the neighboring states and in Rome.

In Herod's days, there were no religious military leaders like Mattathias the Hasmonean and his five sons. The leaders of the Pharisees, such as Hillel, favored peace. The Pharisees devoted themselves almost exclusively to religion, seeking the best ways to keep religious law in consonance with life. They had learned the dangers of political action in previous generations, and they realized that Judaea, as a state, would not long be able to survive the claws of the Roman eagle. They felt that religion was an impregnable fortress against invaders, and they sought to keep it so against any Roman onslaught. Only a small group among them, known as the Apocalyptists, took an interest in politics.[137] Herod therefore felt favorably disposed toward the Pharisees.

Herod's Police State

Herod's organization of the state also served to deter mass outbreaks. He had a formidable army consisting of Gauls, Germans and Thracians, well trained by Roman officers, and he imposed a political surveillance which made Judaea a police state. No meetings of ordinary citizens were permitted, nor were persons allowed to assemble or even to walk together. All the movements of the people, rural as well as urban, were closely watched. Herod often disguised himself and mingled among the masses at night in order to learn what they thought of him. Anyone suspected of disloyalty faced arrest, torture or death.[138]

But the police state introduced by Herod could not give him security from his unhinged imagination. To strengthen his feeling of safety, he fortified his palace and strengthened Antonia. He also rebuilt the city of Samaria, surrounding it by a strong wall. He settled this city with people who had been his allies in previous wars and also with emigrants from many neighboring areas. They were all pagans. Herod reassured himself of their loyalty by making them prosperous and granting them a liberal constitution. He adorned the city in various ways, and erected a temple which gained renown for its size and great beauty. It took about two years for him to complete the city.[139] In the year 27 the Romans bestowed upon Octavian Caesar the title "Augustus," meaning "venerable, reverent," and signifying that he was more than human.[140] It was almost a deification. Octavian was proud of this title and adopted it as his proper name, and he was thenceforth referred to as Augustus Caesar. The Greek synonym of Augustus is Sebastos. This is why Herod named the new Samaria "Sebaste," in honor of his patron.

Herod still yearned to gain the loyalty of the Judaeans, and soon found an occasion to show them his benevolence. In the year 25-24, there was a severe drought in Judaea. There was widespread hunger, disease and suffering; and there was no seed for the next year's planting. Herod went out of his way to aid the people. Not having ready cash, he used the gold and silver of his palace to purchase large stores of provisions from Petronius, the prefect of Egypt.[141] Herod provided food for the poor and the aged and had clothing distributed to keep them warm during the winter. To the needy people of Syria he furnished seed for the following year's planting. He displayed great generosity, and his benevolence undoubtedly softened the attitude of the people towards him. Josephus remarks that the Judaeans thought that at heart Herod was really concerned for their welfare.[142]

The reasons for Herod's benevolence during this trying period were two-fold. First, he wanted their good will, no doubt in large part because the duty of a client-king was to prevent disturbances among his people. Augustus Caesar was firm in this respect, and Herod knew what was expected of him. Second, he wanted the praise not only of the Judaeans but of the people of the neighboring states. He remained, in his innermost being, fearfully insecure. Herod had not changed.

In the year 24, Augustus Caesar launched an expedition against Arabia Felix with the object of conquering it and Ethiopia. The army was headed by Aelius Gallus, the governor of Egypt. Herod supplied him with an auxiliary force of five-hundred picked men from his army. King Obodas of Nabataea sent an army under the command of his vizier Syllaeus.[143] The expedition was not successful, but this was not Herod's fault. The official version was that Syllaeus betrayed the Romans. It may, however, have been that the Romans placed the blame on the Nabataean commander. It is true that the success of the Romans would not have been to the advantage of the Nabataeans or of Herod, since the conquest of Arabia Felix and Ethiopia would have greatly diminished their revenues from caravans. But the real cause of the failure was probably the Romans' lack of knowledge of the climatic and physical conditions of the vast desert country in which the campaign was fought.

Herod's Loves

Herod, now nearly fifty, but physically vigorous and lustful, married another woman named Mariamme. Josephus tells how this came about. A well-known priest named Simon son of Boethus, originally from Alexandria, had a daughter Mariamme who was praised for her great beauty. Herod was eager to meet her and, when he did, became greatly enamored of her. Josephus says that, although Herod had the power to abuse her and satisfy his sexual desires without marriage, he nevertheless decided to marry her. Her father, although of an illustrious family, did not have the social standing to be the father-in-law of a king. Herod dismissed the incumbent high priest, Jesus son of Phabes (who had succeeded Ananel), and appointed Simon to this office. Then Herod married Mariamme.[144]

Josephus' account cannot be accepted. After the death of Herod, the Judaeans sent an embassy to Augustus Caesar and accused Herod of having been a rapist, of corrupting their virgin daughters and debauching their wives. The victims of his bestiality kept silent because they did not want to have their names revealed.[145] His marriage was not due to a determination to legitimatize his lust, but rather to his pursuit of political advantage. Since Herod himself could not be a high priest, he thought that having a father-in-law who was high priest would effectively make him master of the Temple.

When Herod married Mariamme II, he already had eight wives. Before he became king he had married a woman named Doris, of Jerusalem. He had also married Malthace from Samaria, Cleopatra from Jerusalem, Pallas, Phaedra, Elpis, and finally a niece, the daughter of his brother, and a cousin, whose names are unknown.[146] After he married Mariamme the Hasmonean, Doris, who had borne him a son, was dismissed from the palace, and Mariamme became the first lady. After her execution, he married Mariamme II, who then became first lady in turn. Herod still kept a palace harem in the Oriental style, including a group of eunuchs. As in Oriental courts, the eunuchs had great influence and were masters of intrigue. Though Josephus does not directly say that Herod was a homosexual, one may conclude from the passages in Josephus traceable to Nicolas of Damascus that Herod had strong homosexual tendencies. Herod indulged in homosexuality with his eunuchs, and Josephus' other source, Herod's own chronicles, emphasized that the king loved his eunuchs because of their beauty.[147] Josephus says that there were three eunuchs—one a butler, another a cup-bearer, the third his chamberlain—of whom Herod was especially fond.[148] When someone later informed Herod that Alexander, his son by Mariamme I, had carnal relations with these eunuchs, he was as enraged over his son's seduction of his beloved eunuchs as though someone had seduced one of his wives.[149] Josephus also states that a certain Karos was beloved of Herod.[150]

HEROD THE MAGNIFICENT

Building and Territorial Expansion

After Herod's marriage to Mariamme II he enjoyed a period of tranquility and glory. He built and rebuilt fortresses and cities in Judaea, in the neighboring states, and even in faraway countries. All client-kings vied with each other in the building of temples in honor of Augustus Caesar, but Herod outdid them all. In these endeavors he not only sought to gain the favor of Augustus Caesar as well as the good will of neighboring states and of the Hellenistic world, but also to show his ability and good taste, and to perpetuate his name.

He erected a royal palace in the upper city of Jerusalem and had it richly decorated with gold.[151] It was large enough to house his many wives and eunuchs and left ample space for the entertainment of his guests. He constructed in it two halls of immense proportions, one named in honor of Caesar and the other in honor of Agrippa, son-in-law of Augustus Caesar.[152] The palace was even more beautiful than the famous Temple he was to erect. In place of the ancient Capharsaba (ten miles northeast of Jaffa) he built a city which he named Antipatris, in memory of his father.[153] At Jericho he built a fortress in memory of his mother, Cypros.[154] North of Jericho, in the Jordan valley, he founded a city and named it Phaselis after his brother.[155] He reconstructed the city Antheton, which Augustus Caesar had ceded to him and named it Agrippium, in honor of Agrippa.[156] The two fortresses named Herodion (in honor of himself) have already been mentioned: one was for security reasons in the mountains near Nabataea, and the other was about seven miles south of Jerusalem. This second Herodion was richly decorated, contained royal apartments, with an abundant water supply brought from a distance. Herod built up the surrounding plain as a city with many dwellings for his friends.[157] He also rebuilt and fortified Alexandrion, which had been destroyed by Gabinius.[158]

Herod displayed great generosity towards foreign countries. He provided gymnasia for Tripolis, Damascus and Ptolemais, a wall for Byblos; halls, porticoes, temples and market places for Berytus and Tyre; theaters for Sidon and Damascus. He constructed an aqueduct for Laodicea on the sea, as well as baths and fountains. He paved the streets of Antioch, which had been shunned

because of its mud. He made contributions to the city of
Cos to pay the salary of the gymnasiarch. Since the temple of Rhodes had been destroyed by fire, he had it
rebuilt on a grand scale. He furnished aid in the construction of the buildings in the city of Nicopolis, near
Actium, which had been founded by Octavian Caesar in
commemoration of his victory over Antony.[159]

Judaea had but one port on the Mediterranean, Jaffa,
which had been in and out of Judaean hands during the
Roman civil wars. During Herod's reign Judaea's economy flourished, and exports and imports multiplied. The
port of Jaffa became increasingly inadequate. It had
always been a poor harbor, dangerous to shipping in
stormy weather. The southwest wind battered the vessels
there, and by washing up sand upon the shore made it
too shallow for easy landing. Even moderate breezes
dashed the waves against the cliffs to such a height that
their reflux spread turbulent commotion far out to sea.
Merchant ships often had to ride at anchor far off shore.
Herod therefore decided to build a magnificent harbor—
something like that at Piraeus or even larger. For the
new harbor Herod chose the village of Straton's Tower,
located considerably north of Jaffa, somewhat south of
Dor. He had materials assembled for the structure in the
year 22 and had the work begun in the year 20. He laid
out a circular harbor for large fleets to lie at anchor near
the shore. Tremendous blocks of stone, fifty feet long,
eighteen feet wide, and ninety feet in depth, were lowered
into twenty fathoms of water to support a mole two
hundred feet in width which was to serve as a break-
water. Half of the mole opposed the surge of the waves,
holding off the flow of the waters; the other half, supported on the stone wall, was divided at intervals by
towers (the largest called Drusus in honor of Augustus'
step-son), and contained vaulted warehouses and served
as a quay. He constructed another quay along the shore,
encircling the harbor, for a promenade. The entrance to
the harbor was from the north, the sheltered side. It was
adorned with three colossi: one standing on a tower, the

others on two huge obelisks. It was a gigantic undertaking.[160]

Straton's Tower, hitherto an obscure village, was rebuilt into a magnificent city. Its dwellings were constructed of polished stone. The streets were parallel, at right angles to the sea. It was provided with an elaborate drainage system of underground tunnels, so that rain water and refuse were easily carried off. A water supply was provided by aqueducts.

Herod built a theater and a temple of Augustus, and in it he placed statues of Augustus and Rome. The statue of the emperor was a replica of the Pheidian Zeus of Olympia, and the statue of Rome rivaled that of Hera of Argos. On the south side of the harbor he constructed an amphitheater for gladiatorial combats, athletic competitions and fights between wild beasts. It was large enough to accommodate a great mass of people.[161]

He named the city Caesarea in honor of Augustus Caesar. On its completion, in the year 10,[162] it became one of the most important ports of the eastern Mediterranean coast and the economic welfare of Judaea greatly prospered as a result. (The celebrations attending the completion of Caesarea will be dealt with later.)

Northeast of Judaea lay the troublesome districts of Hauran (Auranitis) and Trachonitis.[163] Originally they had been entrusted to the Iturean prince and high priest Zenodorus. When Zenodorus pillaged the properties of the neighboring peoples, complaints were sent to Augustus Caesar.[164] The emperor gave Hauran and Trachonitis and the rich plains of Batanaea, southwest of Trachonitis, to Herod, because he felt confident that Herod would subdue the brigandage and establish order. Thus Herod's kingdom was again enlarged.[165] Zenodorus was angered not only that part of his territory was taken from him, but that it was given to Herod. He went to Rome to prefer charges against Herod, but had no success. Zenodorus therefore tried to prevent Herod from gaining possession by selling Hauran for fifty talents to the king of Nabataea, who wanted it to secure his caravan route to Damascus. Augustus Caesar did not honor this transaction, and Herod took possession of the province.[166] Herod's relations with the Nabataean king, which had never been too good, now became worse.

In the year 23-22, Agrippa, Augustus' son-in-law, visited the Greek islands. While he was wintering in Lesbos, Herod came to meet him.[167] Some Gadarenes, meanwhile, came to Agrippa to complain against Herod's severity. Agrippa put the delegation in chains and sent them to Herod without giving them a hearing. Herod released them without punishment.[168] While Herod was severe with Judaeans and tortured and put to death anyone suspected of disloyalty, he was lenient with the non-Judaeans who inhabited the cities ceded to him by Augustus Caesar. For Herod considered himself the rightful king of Judaea, who also had the rights of conquest over its inhabitants, but he sought the good will of cities like Gadara and other territories inhabited by Hellenes, since these were his only by royal gift. This policy did not succeed. No matter how hard he tried to gain the good will of the pagans in his domain, he failed. They regarded him as a tyrant and looked upon him as one of the Judaeans, whose manners and ways of life differed greatly from theirs; they regarded Judaeans as barbarians. Thus, in the long run, the increase in the size of Herod's kingdom was not to the advantage of Judaea, as the Hellenes of the newly acquired territories always remained hostile to them.

Herod, Vassal of Rome

In the year 21-20, Augustus Caesar came to Syria and Herod met him there.[169] Inhabitants of Gadara again brought charges against Herod, accusing him of violence and of destroying their temples.[170] It may be assumed that these charges were untrue, as Herod would not destroy temples in the territories acquired from Augustus Caesar. On the contrary, he had new temples and statues erected and adorned the old ones. These charges were undoubtedly instigated by Zenodorus, but they were brought before Augustus Caesar and his council (*syne-drion*). When the Gadarene emissaries realized that the emperor did not believe their complaints against Herod, they committed suicide. At this time, Zenodorus suffered a hemorrhage and died. Augustus Caesar presented to Herod his entire territory which extended between Trachonitis and Galilee and included Ulatha, north of Lake Merom, and Paneas, east of Lake Huleh, including the sources of the Jordan. Augustus Caesar also appointed Herod a sort of counselor to the procurators of Syria; that is, he gave Herod the privilege of counseling the procurators in all their actions, which was a substantial privilege for one of their client-kings.[171]

Herod requested Augustus Caesar to give his brother Pheroras the tetrarchy of Peraea, Trans-Jordan, and Caesar granted the request.[172] Herod's purpose may have been to have his brother removed from Judaea, since Pheroras had been accused of plotting with Costobarus to poison him. Herod had also wanted Pheroras to marry Salampsio, Herod's daughter by Mariamme the Hasmonean; but Pheroras was in love with a slave girl, whom he married against Herod's wishes.[173] Herod allotted Pheroras a revenue of a hundred talents.

After Herod had escorted Augustus Caesar to the Mediterranean Sea, he built a magnificent white marble temple near his new city of Paneas, and consecrated it to the emperor.[174]

Upon Herod's return home in the year 20-19, he ordered the people to take an oath of allegiance to himself and to Augustus Caesar.[175] It is probable that at this time, too, daily sacrifices for the welfare of the emperor and Rome were instituted in the Temple.[176] Both were an expression of subjugation.

Those who refused to take the oath of allegiance were severely punished or put to death. But he made some exceptions. After Herod tried to persuade Pollion (Hillel) and his colleague Samias (Shammai) to take the oath and they still refused, he absolved them and their disciples from it because of his deep respect for Pollion (Hillel).[177]

Herod also absolved the Essenes from taking the oath of allegiance.[178] Josephus gives as the reason that one of the Essenes, Menachem, had prophesied during Herod's childhood that he would one day be king of Judaea. Josephus said that, when Herod became king and was at the height of his power, he sent for Menachem and asked him how long he would reign. At first Menachem did not reply, but on Herod's insistence foretold that his reign would last at least twenty, perhaps thirty years, but he did not specify how many more years after thirty.[179] Herod reigned thirty-four years. Thus Menachem's prophecy might be dated in the fourth year of Herod's reign, that is in the year 34 B.C.E.

Actually, there were no prophets during the Second Commonwealth. The Essenes were not prophets, though they prided themselves on possessing the gift of prophecy.[180] They were pious and ethical men respected by the people. The story of the Essene's prophecy was probably circulated by Nicolas of Damascus and accepted by Herod's adherents to show that he had been designated by God to be king of the Judaeans.

The reason Herod absolved the Essenes from taking the oath of allegiance was that he knew they regarded this as a violation of the pentateuchal injunction not to take the name of God in vain. However, they also held that anyone who became the ruler should be respected and obeyed because he attained his office by the will of God.[181] Herod, being certain of their obedience and respect, did not require them to swear their loyalty to him.

There was another group, numbering six thousand, a sect of Pharisees called the Apocalyptists, who also refused to take the oath of allegiance. They strongly opposed Herod, considering him a stranger and not properly of the royal family. They resented subjugation to Rome in any form, believing that God, by supernatural power, would free Judaea.[182] When they refused to take the oath, Herod imposed a fine on them, which was a mild punishment. Pheroras' wife paid the fine, but this was concealed from Herod. Josephus wrote that she followed the Apocalyptists in this because they had prophesied that Herod would lose the throne and that Pheroras and subsequently their children would inherit it. The Apocalyptic-Pharisaic sect thus strongly opposed Herod, and instigated Pheroras and his wife against him.[183] Similarly they instigated a plot against Herod in the inner circles of the court among the eunuchs. In order to obtain influence over them, the Apocalyptists prophesied that the eunuch Bagoas would have children. Later, when Salome informed the king of what had been taking place, he put to death most of the Apocalyptists who had led the plot as well as Bagoas and Karos, whom Herod had loved for his beauty. Herod also put to death all those members of his household who accepted the views of the Apocalyptic Pharisees.[184]

At the same time that Herod called for an oath of allegiance from the Judaeans, he lightened one of the burdens which had helped to make him so hated. On his return from the visit with Augustus Caesar in Syria, he remitted a third of the exorbitant taxes they were regularly required to pay.[185] He also turned his attention to a new and extraordinary project, the rebuilding of the Temple.

HEROD'S TEMPLE

The Temple in Jerusalem remained substantially the same structure since it had been built in 515 B.C.E. by Zerubbabel.[186] Though old in years and modest in dimension, it was an impressive building. Because of its Hasmonean fortifications, it was also strong. Its capture took Pompey three months, and Herod and Sosius four to six months.[187] The Judaeans were content with their Temple; but Herod thought that it did not have sufficient grandeur for his status. Knowing that the Judaeans might resent the destruction of the old structure in order to build the new, he called an assembly and laid his plan before them. He said that Zerubbabel's Temple was only sixty cubits high, much lower than that built by Solomon. Cyrus and Darius had prescribed the limited dimensions, and the Judaeans had not been able to enlarge the Temple under their Macedonian or Hasmonean rulers, for they were constantly engaged in wars. Now there was peace, and the Romans, the masters of the world, were his loyal friends. Now Judaea had a great opportunity to show its piety by rebuilding the Temple in full glory.[188]

At first the Judaeans were astounded to hear this unexpected proposition. They feared that he would tear down the Temple and not have sufficient means to rebuild it. Herod assured them that he had prepared a thousand wagons to carry the stones for the building and had selected ten thousand of the most skilled workmen. Moreover, since there were sections in the Temple where no ordinary Israelite could enter, he would select a thousand priests, some of whom would be trained as masons and others as carpenters, to carry on the work in the inner section of the Temple. He also promised the Judaeans that the construction would begin only after the most careful preparations.[189]

The building of the Temple was a stupendous undertaking which required great energy, skill and knowledge of architecture. Josephus gives us some idea of the monumental foundation required for this edifice:[190]

He (Herod) surrounded the Temple with very large cloisters, all of which were in proportion thereto, and he surpassed his predecessors in spending money so that it was thought that no one else had so greatly adorned the temple. Both (cloisters) were supported by a large wall, and the wall itself was the greatest ever heard of by man. The hill was a rocky ascent that declined by degrees toward the east parts of the city to the topmost peak. This hill the first of our kings, Solomon, by divine wisdom, surrounded with great works above at the top. He (Herod) also built a wall below, beginning at the bottom, which he constructed by a deep valley; and at the south side he laid rocks together and bound them one to another with lead. He cut off more and more of the area within as the wall became greater in depth, so that the size and the height of the structure, which was square, were immense and the great size of the stones was seen along the front surface, while iron clamps on the inside assured that the joints would remain permanently united. When the work reached the top of the hill they leveled off the summit and filled in the hollow spaces near the walls, and made the upper surface smooth and even throughout. Such was the whole enclosure, having a circumference of four stades (around 2428 ft.), each side taking up the length of a stade (607 ft.).

Elsewhere Josephus gives a more detailed description of the way in which the Temple area was expanded:[191]

Though the Temple, as I said, was seated on a strong hill, the level area on its summit originally barely sufficed for shrine and altar, the ground around it being precipitous and steep. But King Solomon, the actual founder of the Temple, having walled up the eastern side, reared a single cloister on this made ground; on its other sides the sanctuary remained exposed. In course of ages, however, through the constant additions of the people to the embankment, the hilltop, by this process of leveling off, was widened. They further broke down the north wall and thus took in an area as large as the whole temple subsequently occupied. Then, after having closed the hill from its base with a wall on three sides, and accomplishing a task greater than they could ever have hoped to achieve—a task upon which long ages were spent by them as well as all their sacred treasures, though replenished by tributes offered to God from every quarter of the world—they built, around the original block, the outer courts in the lower Temple enclosure. The latter, where its foundations were lowest, they built up from a depth of three hundred cubits; at some spots this figure was exceeded. The whole depth of the foundation was, however, not apparent, for they filled up a considerable part of the ravines, wishing to level the narrow alleys of the town. Blocks of stone were used in the building, measuring forty cubits; for lavish funds and popular enthusiasm led to the incredible enterprise, and a task, seemingly interminable, was through perseverance actually achieved.

In other words, when Herod decided to rebuild the Temple, he felt that the dimensions of the area would not be adequate and would have to be extended. He could not make changes or additions in the Temple precincts proper, since they were sacred ground. He therefore enlarged the *Har haBait*, the Temple Mount, that is, the hilltop which surrounded the Temple buildings. The Temple Mount originally covered five hundred cubits square,[192] approximately a quarter of a mile square. This area being less sacrosanct, additions could be made to it, and it was almost doubled. It was extended to twelve hundred feet from north to south and about nine hundred and ninety feet from east to west, assuming an oblong shape. The entire area was surrounded by a wall, with battlements at intervals.[193]

In the interior of the Temple Mount there were colonnades on all four sides. There were one hundred sixty-two columns, all with Corinthian capitals.[194] On each side were four rows of columns, making three aisles—each thirty feet in width, six hundred feet in length, and more than fifty feet in height. The center aisle was one and a half times wider and twice as high as the others. A number of the columns supported the royal porticoes. Besides those on the south side, there were porticoes on the east side known as Solomon's porches.[195]

The Temple Mount had five gates: two Huldah gates on the south for entrance and exit; the Kiponis gate on the west, which also served for entrance and exit; the Tadi gate on the north, which was not used; and the eastern gate, called the Shushan (because the palace of Shushan was portrayed on it), and the exit to the Mount of Olives.[196] There were four other gates on the west side: one led to the palace by way of a ravine called Tyropoeon (Cheese Makers'), which divided the upper from the lower city. Two other gates led to the Bezetha (the suburb). The fourth gate led to the Upper City (that is, west and southwest). The last four gates mentioned were used mainly as exits from the Temple Mount, while the five gates mentioned previously were for entrance to the Temple Mount and, further on, to the *Azarah*.

From THE WESTMINSTER HISTORICAL ATLAS TO THE BIBLE, rev. George Ernest Wright and Floyd V. Filson. Copyright 1945 by The Westminster Press. 1956 by W. L. Jenkins. Used by permission.

Caesarea: The remnants of the ancient amphitheater of Caesarea, built by Herod.

This slab was discovered in 1871, and is now in the museum in Istanbul.

Five Levites were stationed as watchmen at each of the
five gates.[197] Besides these sentries, four Levites were
placed at each corner on the inside. Everyone—Judaeans
and pagans—except those afflicted with leprosy or some
other contagious disease, had the privilege of entering
the Temple Mount.[198] But the Temple Mount enclave on
the south was separated by a *Soreg,* a balustrade,[199]
alongside which was placed a stone with an inscription
in Greek and Latin reading: "No foreigner is to enter
within the balustrade and embankment around the sanctuary. Whoever is caught will have himself to blame for
his death which will follow."[200] In addition to gentiles,
entrance was forbidden to those who had been defiled
through having had contact with a corpse. To the west
of this partition was the *Hal,* the Hill; it was nine feet
higher than the Temple Mount area.[201] Beyond the Hill
were the Temple precincts proper, its courts (the
Azaroth), surrounded by a wall. There were three
Azaroth: Azarah of the women, *Azarah* of the lay Israelite men, and the *Azarah* of the priests.[202] The first com-
partment reached was the women's *Azarah,* east of the
men's *Azarah.* There were in all ten gates leading to the
Azaroth: One in the east, one in the north, and one in
the south led to the *Azarah* of the women. Of the other
seven gates, three were in the north, three in the south
and one in the east. These led to the *Azaroth* of the Israelites and the priests. The last-mentioned gate led from
the women's *Azarah* to the men's *Azarah.*[203] All the gates
were plated with gold. They were forty-five feet high
and twenty-three feet wide, except the gate on the east,
called the Gate of Nikanor. Made of Corinthian brass,
it was an entrance to the women's *Azarah* and thus the
main entrance to the Temple. It was the largest gate,
being seventy-five feet high and sixty feet wide.[204] Each
gate had two doors. A flight of steps ascended to the
Azarah of the men.[205] Beyond the *Azarah* of the men
was the *Azarah* of the priests. This section was separated
from the *Azarah* of the Israelites by a flagstone wall.
At the entrance of the *Azarah* of the priests was the

Duchan, a platform. From it the priests blessed the Israelites, and here the Levites sang their daily hymns.[206] The *Azarah* of the priests was on a higher elevation than the *Azarah* of the Israelites; it contained the altar built of unhewn stone. This was the altar upon which sacrifices were offered. It was forty-six feet high and forty-six feet wide. Two apertures drained the blood into a channel which carried it off to the *Kidron*.[207] To the south of the altar stood a laver. Further to the left was the Gate of the Porch.[208] Another gate separated the Porch from the Sanctuary proper, before which hung a tapestry of fine linen embroidered in colors of blue, violet and purple.[209] Josephus gives the following description of the Temple building:[210]

The façade was of equal height and breadth, each being one hundred cubits (one hundred and fifty feet); but the building behind was narrower by forty cubits (sixty feet), for in front it had as it were shoulders extending twenty cubits (thirty feet) on each side. The first gate was seventy cubits high (one hundred and five feet) and twenty-five (thirty-seven feet) broad and had no doors, displaying unexcluded the void expanse of heaven; the entire face was covered with gold . . . The gate opening into the building was completely overlaid with gold . . . It had, moreover, above it those golden vines from which depended grape clusters as tall as a man; and it had golden doors forty-five cubits high (sixty-seven feet) and sixteen cubits (twenty-four feet) broad. Before this hung a veil of equal length of Babylonian tapestry, with embroidery of blue and fine linen, of scarlet also and purple, wrought with marvelous skill . . . Passing within, one found oneself on the ground floor of the sanctuary. This was sixty cubits (ninety feet) in height, the same in length, and twenty cubits (thirty feet) in breadth. But the sixty cubits (ninety feet) of its length were again divided. The first portion, partitioned off at forty cubits (sixty feet), contained within it three most wonderful works of art, universally renowned: a lampstand, that is, a Menorah (which had seven branches); a table (upon which were laid the twelves loaves of shew bread) and the altar (the golden one for incense) . . . The innermost recess measured twenty cubits (thirty feet), and was screened in like manner from the outer portion by a veil. In this stood nothing whatever: Unapproachable, inviolable, invisible to all, it was called the Holy of Holies.

The construction of the new Temple itself took a year and six months, while the entire complex of structures took eight years more.[211] (Actually some work continued until but a few years before the Temple was destroyed.[212]) The entire construction was supervised by Herod himself, except of course for the Temple proper, where no non-priestly Israelite was allowed to set foot. The structure stood at an elevation of 2,240 feet above sea level. Since its walls were of white marble, it gave the appearance from a distance of a mountain covered with snow. According to the Talmud it looked like the waves of the sea. The Roman historian Tacitus commented on its magnificence. There was a proverbial saying that he who had not seen the Building of Herod had never in his life seen a beautiful building.[213]

Both Josephus and the Talmud note that during the construction of the Temple, there was rainfall only at night.[214] This was taken as an omen that God was pleased with the rebuilding of the Temple. The day that the new Temple was formally finished is reported as coinciding with the anniversary of Herod's accession to the throne, thus giving rise to a double celebration.[215] It is not clear whether this date refers to that at the end of the year 40 when he became king *de jure,* or the one in 37 when he became king *de facto* after he captured the Temple.

Josephus says that when Herod completed the Temple, the people were filled with joy and gave thanks to God.[216] Herod himself offered hundreds of oxen to God and others made similar offerings. It might seem that Solomon and Zerubbabel had established the precedent in this regard. Josephus does not mention, and rabbinic literature does not refer to, consecration or dedication on the completion of Herod's Temple, as was the case in connection with the earlier ruler's celebrations. Moreover, during the Second Commonwealth the sages did not favor the offering of sacrifices to God, except such as were prescribed in the Pentateuch.

It is questionable whether the spiritual leaders and the rank and file of the Judaeans were happy over the Temple which Herod built. They knew from the Bible that King David was not permitted to build a Temple to God because he was a warrior and had shed blood.[217] Herod's hands were bloody, not only from the death of the enemies of Judaea, but from many innocent Judaeans as well. Thus rabbinic literature makes reference to Herod's building,[218] but never refers to it as a *Bayit*, a House. The Talmud speaks about the First House (Solomon's) and the Second House (Zerubbabel's), but never refers to a Third House—and this period is referred to only as the period of the Second House. Herod's Temple was beautiful, but, because it was built by Herod, the sages ignored it.

When Herod built the Temple he further fortified Antonia, making it utterly impregnable.[219] It is strange that he did not rename the fortress, since generally when deities were discarded the names of cities and shrines dedicated to them were often changed to honor new deities. Atop the fortress Antonia, Herod built a tower to give him better knowledge of whatever crowds formed in the Temple area. He also built a secret underground passage leading from Antonia to the eastern gate of the inner Temple, for protection in case of revolt, of which he was ever fearful. He ordered that the sacred vestments of the high priest be kept in Antonia,[220] thus assuring his domination over the high priests and the Temple. This practice was taken over by the procurators when Judaea became a province of Rome.[221]

Herod loved Jericho because of its mild climate, and spent the winter months there. As a result he erected a magnificent palace there between the fortress of Cypros and the old palace. Here he also built an amphitheater, and probably a theater as well, and a hippodrome where

gladiatorial contests were held. He built other palaces
in Sepphoris (Galilee), in Ascalon (on the coast outside
his domain), in Caesarea and Masada.

HEROD AND THE DIASPORA

Agrippa and the Judaeans

In the year 14 Agrippa came to Syria on the way to
attack the Bosphoran Kingdom.[222] Herod hastened to
meet him and, when Agrippa greeted him warmly, Herod
invited him to visit Judaea. It was a triumphal tour of all
the magnificent cities and fortresses Herod had erected.
Agrippa even visited Jerusalem, offered sacrifices and
feasted the people, who received him with great enthusiasm. He left to lead his expedition against the Bos-
phorans, who submitted without a struggle. Herod had
meanwhile assembled a small armada and caught up with
Agrippa's forces at Sinope, in Pontus. Agrippa received
him with affection, being deeply impressed by Herod's
supreme effort to assist him.[223]

While Agrippa and Herod were in Ionia, the local
Judaean community complained to Agrippa of mistreat-
ment by the Hellenes, who were the majority. They complained that they were prevented by the Hellenes from
observing their religious rites, from keeping the seventh
day, the Sabbath, for rest and study, and from sending
money to Jerusalem for the Temple. Nicolas of Damascus pleaded before Agrippa on their behalf.[224] This
talented man deserves special notice. He was a historian
whose history of the world includes references to the
Judaeans.[225] He was also Herod's court historian but,
even more, his monitor and his companion. He served
Herod as an adviser in foreign affairs and in many
instances as ambassador extraordinary and plenipo-
tentiary.[226] Since he was an accomplished rhetorician,
Herod used Nicolas to prosecute his enemies or to plead
his cause or those of his friends. Nicolas exercised great
influence over Herod, interesting him in rhetoric and,

particularly, in history. Nicolas of Damascus in turn was predisposed in Herod's favor in his own writings. Since Josephus made use of the works of Nicolas, his history of Herod is for the most part similarly tendentious.[227] After listening to Nicolas, Agrippa confirmed the right of the Ionian Judaeans to live in accordance with the religious customs, and forbade the Hellenes to hinder the Jews from sending money to Jerusalem for the Temple.[228]

While Agrippa was in Asia, he issued other decrees favoring the Judaeans of the Diaspora. He sent an order to the governing council of Ephesus, directing that the money collected by the Judaeans for the Temple in Jerusalem be regarded as sacred and that anyone who stole it be denied the right of sanctuary. He also decreed that a Jew might not be compelled to appear in court on the Sabbath. He sent a similar decree on Temple monies to the governing council of Cyrene.[229] No doubt the sending of money by the Judaeans to the Temple in Jerusalem was resented by the councils of the cities where they lived, as an unwarranted outflow of currency, gold and silver, to a foreign country. Agrippa's friendly attitude towards the Judaeans in this respect was reflected in parallel acts of Augustus Caesar. Thus a few years later Augustus Caesar issued a decree to the peoples of Asia in favor of the Judaeans.[230] In it he stated that the Judaeans were always well disposed towards the Romans, and had been so back in the time of his (adopted) father Julius Caesar, who favored the Judaeans when Hyrcanus was the high priest. He ordered that the money sent by the Judaeans to Jerusalem for the Temple should be inviolable; that no Judaean should be summoned to court on the Sabbath or after the ninth hour (three o'clock) on the day of preparation (Friday) ; further, that anyone caught stealing the sacred books or the sacred money from the Sabbation (where the Judaeans assembled on the Sabbath) should be regarded as sacrilegious, and have his property confiscated to the public treasury. Another Temple-money decree was issued by Augustus Caesar to the people of Sardes.[231]

In order to gain the good will of the Judaeans, Herod, upon his return to Jerusalem from his visit with Augustus, called an assembly of the people of the city as well as some from the country. He told them of his visit to Agrippa, and boasted that it was because of his good relations with Augustus Caesar and Agrippa that the Jews in the Diaspora would not be molested in the observance of their ancestral customs. Further, he announced a remittance of a quarter of all their taxes, thereby adding greatly to the joy.[232]

The Building of Caesarea

While Herod was in Rome with his sons in the year 12,[233] the people of Trachonitis revolted. Herod's generals succeeded in subduing the uprising, but some forty of the leaders of the revolt fled for asylum in Nabataea. When Herod returned to Judaea, he punished those suspected of rebellion and killed the relatives of those who had fled to Nabataea. This provoked the refugee rebels to revenge, and they organized a band which soon numbered a thousand. They invaded Herod's territory, harassing and ravaging the country for about two years.[234]

The domestic and military difficulties did not stop Herod from proceeding energetically with the building of Caesarea. The city and port were finished in the year 10, ten years after the work was begun. The dedication of the city was celebrated with great pomp and splendor. There were musical contests, athletic exercises, horse racing and fights by gladiators with wild beasts, both contestants being imported for the amusement of the people. Everything was done on an elaborate scale on a par with what was to be seen in Rome. He arranged that Olympic Games be held at four-year intervals. Augustus Caesar and his wife Livia sent many treasures from Rome further to beautify the city which bore the Emperor's name. Many cities and countries sent delegations who were enthusiastically welcomed and entertained. Josephus states they were provided with amusements, but does not specify their nature. If Herod imitated the

Roman celebrations, it may be assumed that he provided
prostitutes. Augustus Caesar is said to have remarked
that the extent of Herod's realm was not equal to his
magnanimity, by which standard he deserved to be king
of Syria and Egypt.[235]

The celebration, with its pagan overtones, displeased
the spiritual leaders of Judaea, causing them to declare
that Caesarea was legally outside the land of Israel, and
that such gentile lands outside Israel were in a state of
ritual uncleanness. By this decree they sought to destroy
the glory and importance of Caesarea, and to make it
impossible for any pious Jew, and descendants of priestly
families in particular, to dwell in Caesarea.[236]

Not long after the dedication of Caesarea, Herod completed the construction of the various buildings of the
Temple. He then had a large golden eagle placed over the
entrance of the Temple Mount.[237] This greatly angered
the Judaeans. Not only did such a symbol seem idolatrous,
but many of the spiritual leaders felt this to be an act
indicating the hegemony of Rome over the Temple. Still,
there was nothing they could do about it, so overwhelming was Herod's control of the country.

Herod had spent money so lavishly in his building
program that he was in great need of funds. Josephus
says that, when Hyrcanus I was in financial distress, he
opened the tomb of David where he found substantial
funds. Herod decided to do the same thing. One night,
Herod, accompanied by his most trusted friend and bodyguards, went secretly to the tomb of David, but found
no money there. He did find many ornaments of gold and
other valuable objects which he appropriated. When they
approached the coffins containing the bodies of David and
Solomon, a flash of flames consumed two of the soldiers.
To atone for this sacrilegious act, Herod built a wall of
white marble at the entrance to the tomb.[238]

The story that Hyrcanus I had opened the tomb of
David for the purpose of taking money is untrue,[239] but
there is good reason to believe that Herod did enter it.

Many Judaeans, who had been proscribed and feared confiscation of their wealth, hid their valuables in sacred places, such as the tomb of David, which they felt certain Herod would not dare enter. Nicolas of Damascus invented the tale about Hyrcanus I to justify Herod. Josephus, on the other hand, terms Herod's action reprehensible.

2. HEROD AND HIS FAMILY

THE SONS OF MARIAMME

The First Accusation

When Alexander and Aristobolus, the sons of Mariamme the Hasmonean, came of age, Herod sent them to Rome to complete their education. They stayed at the home of Pollio, a devoted friend of Herod who, although probably a pagan, was interested in Judaism. The lads also received invitations from Augustus Caesar to stay with him.[1]

In the year 17 B.C.E., Herod visited Rome to see Augustus Caesar and also to bring his sons back to Jerusalem. Augustus Caesar received him warmly as a friend; but the return home of Mariamme's sons brought new tragedy to the Herodian household. The young men had inherited the good looks and the aristocratic bearing of their mother. The people idolized them as descendants of the Hasmoneans and as the children of the martyred Mariamme. Their arrival therefore re-awakened the envious hatred of Salome, Herod's malevolent sister, and later also of Pheroras, Herod's brother, who coveted the throne.[2]

Before leaving to meet Agrippa, in the year 14 B.C.E., Herod arranged for the marriage of these two of his sons. Alexander was married to Glaphyra, the daughter of

Archelaus, King of Cappadocia. Aristobolus was married to Herod's niece Berenice, daughter of Salome by her husband Costobarus.[3] The marriage of Alexander was essentially a political alliance; the marriage of Aristobolus, an effort to unite the two branches of his own family, the Herodian and Hasmonean. Salome did not oppose the marriage, as it afforded her an opportunity to spy on Aristobolus and Alexander.

While Herod was away from Judaea, the surface tranquility of the household at home was shattered. Salome's lust for Hasmonean blood was not stilled by the death of Mariamme I. Her venomous hatred was now directed towards Alexander and Aristobolus, for the prevailing view in Judaea was that these two youths would be kings after Herod's death.[4] Salome was apprehensive that they would then avenge their mother's murder. They in turn did not conceal their hatred of Salome and all who had been involved in Mariamme's death, nor did they hide their unfriendly feelings toward their father.[5] And, as always, there were those who added fuel to the feud between Salome and the sons of Herod by exaggerating the words of the youths against their father and Salome, and reporting back the words of Salome against Mariamme.

When Herod returned, Salome and Pheroras warned him that he was in danger from his sons who openly threatened not to leave their mother's death unavenged. They also told him that Alexander, with the help of his father-in-law Archelaus, King of Cappadocia, was contemplating bringing charges against him before Augustus Caesar. Herod became alarmed, particularly because he had heard of his sons' hostility from other sources.[6] To keep Alexander and Aristobolus from too much presumption and to undermine their belief that they were his sole heirs, Herod recalled to his palace his eldest son Antipater, the child of Doris, whom he had married while still a commoner and dismissed when he became king.[7] Doris had cherished an abiding hatred towards Herod, and an even greater one towards Mariamme and her offspring. From Antipater's childhood, Doris had fostered in him a like hatred for his father and for his Hasmonean half-brothers. Antipater was as ruthless and barbaric as his father, and as cunning and treacherous as his aunt Salome. He possessed no moral scruples, was a master of intrigue, and adept in concealing his true feelings from his destined victims. Antipater would not have hesitated to murder Herod if the opportunity had come for him to become king. He was equally determined to remove anyone standing in his way, particularly Alexander and Aristobolus. They, though they knew that Herod had murdered their grandmother, their uncle and their grandfather as well as their mother, never harbored the thought of murdering their father. In contrast to Antipater, they were outspoken, even rash in expressing themselves, and this naiveté led to their downfall. Herod feared that the people loved Alexander and Aristobolus more than him, and was therefore equally suspicious of their behavior. Antipater was hated by the people, but he acquired supporters by bribery and promises of advancement when he became king.[8]

In the year 13, when Agrippa was returning to Rome from Asia, Herod took a further step. He brought Antipater to Agrippa and requested that Antipater be allowed to accompany Agrippa to Rome and be presented to Augustus Caesar. Alexander and Aristobolus thus were warned of having fallen into disfavor. Before Antipater departed for Rome he succeeded in having his mother Doris recalled to the palace.[9] This was less out of love for his mother than to provide Antipater with a source of information and a center for intrigue.

Herod's suspicions of Alexander and Aristobolus finally brought him to the point of bringing them before Augustus Caesar and making accusations against them.[10] In the year 12, Herod asked permission of the Emperor to speak with him on a subject which had caused him great anguish. He then charged his sons, not only with ingratitude, but with treason. He had brought them up in luxury, provided them with servants, and arranged brilliant marriages for them. He looked upon them as heirs to his throne. But they showed him only hostility and were plotting to murder him, more out of revenge than ambition.

Alexander and Aristobolus were horrified to hear that their father believed that they contemplated killing him. While Herod was speaking, they burst into tears. Noticing that Augustus Caesar was not impressed by Herod's accusations and by his expression semed to show compassion for them, Alexander arose to speak. According to Josephus, repeating Nicolas of Damascus, Alexander was a powerful orator. He opened his speech by admitting the gratitude he and his brother owed to their father, who had shown good will by bringing them to an impartial court before Augustus Caesar. As a father and a king, he could have executed them at once. True, they grieved over the death of their mother, but more so because after her death she was being slandered by unworthy people. As to the charge that they desired to reign and hence plotted to kill their father, he pointed out the absurdity of it. Would they be so foolish as to believe that by parricide they could gain the kingdom? Would the people suffer them to do so? Could a murderer of a king escape punishment from Augustus Caesar, the savior of mankind? Then Alexander replied directly to the charges. Had any poison been discovered in their possession? Had any conspiracy been uncovered? Had any letters written by them against the king been intercepted? All the accusations were based on hearsay. Malicious tongues had fostered these suspicions. He emphatically denied that they had had any intention of harming their father.[11]

Augustus Caesar was moved by the speech and convinced by the refutation of the charges. Herod, noting this, became sympathetic towards his sons, so that Augustus Caesar easily effected a reconciliation between them.[12] All, including Antipater, seemed contented. Herod presented Augustus Caesar with three hundred talents. The Emperor gave him half of the revenue from one half of the copper mines in Cyprus and entrusted him with the management of the other half. He again reaffirmed Herod's right, exceptional for a Roman client-king, to appoint whomever he chose to succeed him as king.[13]

While returning to Judaea, Herod visited King Archelaus of Cappadocia, the father-in-law of Alexander. Archelaus was delighted over the reconciliation and that his son-in-law Alexander had been cleared of suspicion.[14] Herod then made his way to Jerusalem. Upon his arrival, he assembled the people in the Temple and gave an account of Caesar's kindness to him. He announced that Antipater would reign after him and that Alexander and Aristobolus would in turn succeed Antipater. This meant that they would be subordinate kings to Antipater, or perhaps that he contemplated dividing his kingdom, giving Judaea proper to Antipater and the other provinces to them. He exhorted his family to live in peace and reminded them all that, being in full possession of his physical powers, the army and officialdom should look to him alone as king and master of the country.[15]

It was most likely at this time that he arranged the marriage of Antipater to the daughter of Antigonus,[16] the last of the Hasmonean kings. This match gave added status to Antipater and further undermined the prestige of the sons of Mariamme.

Rivals and Plotters

The arrangement made by Herod for his sons satisfied none of them. Alexander and Aristobolus were exasperated that Antipater, who was of common stock, was assigned to be king of Judaea and that they, true Hasmoneans, were relegated to a secondary position. Antipater was opposed to his brothers having any standing in the kingdom. His goal was to remove his rivals, and he proceeded to do so by political maneuvers. He adopted a policy of apparent friendliness to his brothers and of great concern for the welfare of his father. Simultaneously he organized a network of spies, posing as friends, who surrounded the brothers and reported to him and

Herod anything they might say that would incriminate them.[17]

Affairs in Herod's household worsened. Josephus ascribes this to God's punishment for Herod's sacrilege in entering David's tomb.[18] It was most likely due to the cunning maneuvers of Antipater and the unrestrained language of Alexander and Aristobolus. Antipater strove assiduously to convince Herod that he alone was guarding Herod's well being. Herod was impressed, and he recommended Antipater to the friendship of Ptolemy, his minister of finance.

The marriage of Alexander to Glaphyra daughter of King Archelaus, and that of Aristobolus to Berenice daughter of Salome, added basis for unrest. Glaphyra looked upon Salome and her daughter Berenice with disdain, because she herself was a descendant on her father's side of Temenus (one of the Heraclidae) and on her mother's side of Darius (son of Hystaspes), while Salome and her daughter were commoners.[19] Glaphyra's brother-in-law, Aristobolus, shared this view. In his wife's presence he complained that, while his brother married royalty, he had been married to a commoner.[20] Berenice carried this, like every other rash word, to Salome who duly reported it to her brother Herod. Alexander and Aristobolus openly declared that their stepbrothers were fit to be only village clerks and would be assigned to such positions when they came into power; as to their stepmothers, who were garbed in the apparel of their beloved mother, they would then be clothed in rags.[21] The campaign of accusation and slander against the two brothers continued in full force.

Herod also had difficulties with his brother Pheroras, the tetrarch of Peraea: he considered it a personal disgrace that Pheroras had married a slave girl. Twice Herod suggested that Pheroras should marry one of his own daughters. Pheroras at first promised to obey Herod and to leave his beloved wife, but later refused to do so.[22]

Salome now contrived a scheme to arouse Alexander to a drastic act against his father. She persuaded her brother

Pheroras, who also aspired to the throne, to tell Alexander that Herod had been intimate with Alexander's wife Glaphyra, thinking this would lead him to murder Herod. The machinations came to naught. Alexander, astounded at Pheroras' revelation, went directly to his father and tearfully related what Pheroras had said. Herod called for Pheroras. "But do you really suppose," Herod said, "that I do not see what your plan is? Because you brought these tales to my son, not merely with the view of slandering me, but to make them the occasion for a plot to use poison for my destruction. . . . Do you think that it is merely a word you have put in his mind rather than a sword into his hand to slay his father?" Herod's speedy agreement shows that he did indeed suspect Pheroras of plotting against him. Pheroras tried to absolve himself by putting the blame on Salome. She vehemently denied the accusation, insisting it was Pheroras' work alone, but her disclaimer prompted little credance. Angered at both, Herod summarily dismissed them.[23]

Another violent storm broke in Herod's household, again involving Alexander. There were three eunuchs of whom Herod was extremely fond because of their beauty. Someone, probably Antipater, informed the king that Alexander was having carnal relations with these eunuchs. When Herod questioned the eunuchs they confessed.[24] According to the pentateuchal law, homosexuality is a capital crime.[25] Herod ordered that the eunuchs be tortured, thinking that under torture he might exact from them whatever compromising statements might have been made by Alexander. The eunuchs were tortured in the presence of Antipater, yet all they said was that Alexander expressed hostility towards his father, saying he would not live much longer, that he was actually older than he looked, that he dyed his hair to conceal his age, and that upon his death Alexander believed that, with the army's support, he would be king despite Herod's arrangements.[26] Though there was no evidence that Alexander had plotted to kill Herod, the confessions filled Herod with alarm.

Antipater, always alert to Herod's fears and suspicions, further deepened his apprehensions by exaggerating the menace surrounding him and involving
many of Alexander's friends. They were thereupon arrested and tortured, but said nothing incriminating
about Alexander. Their silence further infuriated Herod
who believed that this was due, not to the absence of a
plot, but to loyalty to Alexander. One man did confess
that Alexander had complained of his father's en-
viousness, so that he was obliged to stoop when he
walked beside him in order not to appear taller than he.
He also said that when Alexander went hunting with
his father, he purposely missed some shots in order to
show less skill than Herod. Having extracted this much
information, Herod ordered the man to be tortured
further, thus finally making him confess that Alexander
and Aristobolus had been plotting to kill Herod while
hunting and then flee to Rome to claim the kingdom.
Letters were also found wherein Alexander complained
of his father's favoritism in assigning to Antipater
territory that brought in a revenue of two hundred
talents annually. Upon this evidence Herod arrested
Alexander.[27]

No judge or prosecutor would have accepted such
testimony. Alexander was not so naive as to think that,
after murdering his father, he could flee to Rome and
gain Augustus' confirmation as king rather than execution as a parricide. (Alexander had already said this
some time before in defending himself before Augustus
Caesar.) Even to Herod this accusation, exacted by
torture, did not seem entirely credible. Therefore he put
others to torture, and one man, under extreme torture,
told another story: that Alexander had sent messages to
Rome asking that Caesar summon him as he had some
damaging evidence against his father, namely, that he
had made an alliance with Mithridates the king of
Parthia against the Romans. He also said that Alexander
had a poisonous drug prepared in Ascalon with which to
kill his father.[28] The separate parts of this story actually

contradict each other, and the name of the Parthian king given by the witness was incorrect. It was not Mithridates who at that time ruled Parthia, but Phrataces.[29] However, Herod accepted the testimony and made every effort to find the poisonous drug. But there was no trace of it in Ascalon.

Alexander in his despair wrote a long letter on four papyrus rolls in which he confessed to a plot against his father, but wrote that in this he was aided by Pheroras and most of Herod's faithful friends. Among those mentioned were Ptolemy, Herod's trusted minister of finance, and a certain Sapinnius. He also stated that Salome had once forced her way into his chamber and had had illicit relations with him.[30] Was this letter written in the vengeful spirit of Samson's "Let me die with the Philistines?" If so, why did he not implicate Antipater in the plot? There may have been some truth in Alexander's accusations. Pheroras' plotting continued beyond this incident. It appears that Ptolemy was loyal to Herod, but the whole truth is not known. As to the accusation against Salome, the following reason can be given. Alexander had been accused of homosexuality which, according to the Pentateuch, is a capital crime. So is incest, which includes sexual relations between a father's sister, and his son.[31]

A reign of terror ensued, followed by frightful executions. Josephus gives a vivid description of the mood in *War*:[32]

The palace was given over to frightful anarchy. Everyone, to gratify some personal enmity or hatred, invented calumnies; many turned to base account against their adversaries the murderous mood of wrathful royalty. Lies found instant credit . . . The accused of a moment ago found himself accused and led off to death with him whose conviction he had obtained; for the grave peril to his life cut short the king's inquiries. . . .

Josephus wrote that Herod's mind was in such a state that he thought he saw Alexander coming upon him, sword in hand. In *Antiquities* Josephus gives a more lengthy description of Herod's state of mind:[33]

In his (Herod's) bitterness he was afraid that, in actual fact, a more powerful combination had been formed against him than he was able to escape. Whereupon he did not make any search openly, but sent out spies on the trail of those whom he suspected. His suspicion and hatred were directed against all, and since he regarded suspicion as a measure of safety, he continued to suspect those who were guiltless. . . . His courtiers, having no firm ground for hoping to be saved, turned upon one another in the hope that he who was before-hand in accusing another would thereby assure his own safety. . . . Some indeed pursued their private enmities in this manner, only to be caught and placed in the same predicament. . . . Herod's whole life became unbearable to him, so greatly was he disturbed; and because he trusted no one, he was greatly tormented by his anxiety. He imagined that he would often see his son advancing upon him or even standing over him with drawn sword. So intent upon this thought was his mind both night and day that he took on the appearance of suffering from madness. . . .

Attempts at Reconciliation

Archelaus, determined to intercede on behalf of his son-in-law Alexander, went to Jerusalem. He knew Herod well enough not to defend Alexander openly. He expressed sympathy with Herod over the unkindness and ingratitude of his son-in-law and said that he had come to take his daughter away from Alexander. His strong criticism of Alexander caused Herod to defend his son. Archelaus complimented Herod on his tolerance and goodheartedness and, when he noted that Herod was in a good frame of mind, suggested that Alexander was truly guilty, but that he was not the real culprit; that being young and innocent he was corrupted by skillful plotters. He further charged Pheroras with being the arch-schemer, thus turning Herod's attention to his conniving brother. Pheroras, upon learning what had taken place, became alarmed and urged Archelaus to go to Herod on his behalf. Archelaus promised to do so, but demanded that Pheroras must first make a complete confession of his activities to Herod. Pheroras took his advice and, garbed in black, went to Herod and confessed his misdeeds with tears in his eyes.[34] Herod did not punish Pheroras in any way, since he possessed no authority over him. Pheroras, as tetrarch of Peraea, was responsible directly to Augustus Caesar. Besides, Herod had no proof of his guilt except what he had heard from Archelaus, and this would not have been sufficient evidence for the emperor. It must also be borne in mind that, despite the scheming, Herod felt a particular affinity with his own family.[35]

The clever maneuvering of Archelaus succeeded in reconciling Herod and Alexander. He also prevailed upon Herod to forgive his brother Pheroras. Archelaus and Herod now contemplated going to Rome to give a full report to Augustus Caesar; but this idea was abandoned. Before Archelaus departed from Jerusalem for Cappadocia, Herod gave him gold and precious stones. He also presented him with eunuchs and one concubine. Evidently she was of some distinction, as Josephus gives her name, Pannychis.[36] Herod even accompanied Archelaus as far as Antioch.

But the reconciliation effected by King Archelaus came to naught. Difficulties were now raised by a certain Eurycles of Lacedemon (Sparta). He had become known to Herod from his participation in the Battle of Actium on Octavian's side. Though an adventurer and sycophant, he was well received in Jerusalem by Herod and his literary circle, having brought recommendations from King Archelaus. He thus enjoyed the confidence of Alexander, but did not hesitate to insinuate himself into Antipater's favor. In return for substantial sums of money, Eurycles told Antipater, no doubt in exaggerated form, of Alexander's continuing grief over the murder of Mariamme and of Alexander's resentment at Herod's hostility to him. Eurycles told all this to Herod as well, not failing to remark on Alexander's hatred of Herod. He charged that Alexander was contemplating flight to

Archelaus and planned to expose Herod's true character to Augustus Caesar. He urged the king to beware of Alexander, who was in such an emotional state that murder was a real possibility. When Eurycles left Jerusalem for Cappadocia, he told King Archelaus that he had been useful in reconciling Alexander with his father and so received substantial gifts from Archelaus.[37] (Eurycles continued his ill-doing in his own country, from which he was ultimately banished, dying in exile.)

Another Hellene in the court of Herod, Euraratus of Cos, who was friendly with Alexander, was interrogated, but swore that in his associations with Alexander he never heard him speak of a plot against his father.[38] Herod, however, was so paranoid that he accepted the words of Eurycles as positive evidence against his sons. Two of Herod's bodyguards, Jucundus and Tyrannus, whom he had dismissed, were later employed by Alexander. They therefore fell under suspicion; and Herod, to elicit the information he wanted, tortured them. Only when the torture became unbearable, did they break, saying that Alexander had tried to induce them to kill Herod while hunting, and make it appear an accident.[39] They also involved the hunt-master in this intrigue.

The commander of the Fortress Alexandrion was also arrested and tortured. He was accused of having promised to give Alexander and Aristobolus asylum and of supplying them with money; but even under torture he did not utter a word. His son, however, unable to endure the sight of his father's torture, implicated him and produced a letter supposedly written by Alexander which read, "When with God's help we have achieved all that we set out to do, we will come to you. Only take it upon you to receive us into the fortress as you promised."[40] Alexander protested that this letter was a forgery. It was forged by the king's secretary Diophantus at the instigation of Antipater. Diophantus was known to be a forger, and was later accused of similar forgeries for which he was executed.[41]

Herod brought his sons and those who had been tortured to Jericho, where he displayed them before the populace whom he had assembled. They were enraged, and lynched the alleged plotters with the connivance or even instigation of Antipater, who wanted no further investigation of the evidence. They were even ready to kill Alexander and Aristobolus; but Ptolemy, Herod's finance minister, and Pheroras, intervened to prevent this. The two princes were chained and imprisoned in separate cells.[42] They were confronted with a list of crimes which later was turned over to Augustus Caesar. Alexander and Aristobolus, on receiving the list, wrote that they had never plotted to murder their father, but having been in fear of their lives, they had planned to flee the country. When Ambassador Melas came from King Archelaus, Herod, who suspected Archelaus of being involved in the conspiracy, brought Melas before Alexander. Alexander admitted that he had intended taking asylum with Archelaus and with his support to make an appeal to Rome, but he categorically denied that either he or his brother planned any injurious act against their father. He repeated that he wished that Tyrannus and his other friends were still alive so that they could be carefully examined.[43] Not fully satisfied with Alexander's admission, Herod wanted to extract one from his wife Glaphyra. He confronted her with her husband Alexander in the presence of Ambassador Melas. He questioned her whether she was aware of Alexander's contemplated flight to her father, King Archelaus. Alexander said, "How is it possible that she, whom I love better than my own life, and is the mother of my children, should not be aware of what I do?" Glaphyra was ready to say anything that would help her husband, and she said that she was aware that Alexander had contemplated fleeing to her father.[44]

Herod now had the evidence against his sons which he had sought. Though confirmed, the tales related by Eurycles did not square with the confession of Tyrannus, that Alexander had planned murder and flight to the

Fortress Alexandrion. The two tales were contradictory, but Herod accepted both. He composed two letters, one addressed to King Archelaus, the other to Augustus Caesar, and gave them to his devoted servants Olympus and Volumnius. He ordered the envoys to stop in Cappadocia on their way to Rome and deliver his letter to King Archelaus. It accused him of hostility to Herod.[45] Archelaus admitted that he had promised refuge to Alexander and Aristobolus, but did so to protect Herod from himself, so that in his anger he should do no injury to his sons.[46] The letter to Augustus Caesar accused Herod's sons of planning to flee the country and of planning parricide, but he ordered the envoys to delay delivery of the letters until Nicolas of Damascus should succeed in placating the Emperor.[47]

THE EXECUTION OF ALEXANDER AND ARISTOBOLUS

The Nabataean Succession

Nicolas was in Rome on another urgent matter, the issue of which was influenced by Herod's family troubles.

In the midst of all the intrigues which raged in Herod's household, a love affair was being carried on in the palace. Syllaeus, the all-powerful vizier of the Nabataean king, Obadas, had once visited Herod, where he met and fell in love with Salome. She reciprocated his feelings, for Syllaeus was young, handsome, cunning and ambitious. Salome was a widow past fifty. The women of the palace began to talk about this unevenly matched pair, and accused her of intimacy with Syllaeus. In one place Josephus says that Salome actually entered into a marriage contract with Syllaeus.[48] Elsewhere, Josephus relates that, on one of his visits to Jerusalem, Syllaeus asked Herod for the hand of Salome and Herod consented, providing Syllaeus would agree to become a Judaean. This he declined to do, saying that if he did so, he would be stoned to death by the Nabataeans; the marriage plans were then abandoned.[49] Syllaeus' interest in Salome was probably due less to infatuation than to political ambition. Syllaeus wanted to become king of Nabataea and plotted to murder King Obadas.[50] Fearing the consequences and knowing of Herod's great power as the most trusted friend of Augustus Caesar, he thought that marriage with Herod's sister would protect his usurpation. Thus Syllaeus, in requesting Salome's hand, pointed out the political advantage for Herod, since the government of Nabataea was virtually his already and eventually would be even more so.[51] He did not stress a passionate love for Salome. It may be that Herod guessed Syllaeus' motives and therefore made the marriage conditional on Syllaeus' accepting Judaism. Herod knew that Syllaeus would not accept Judaism since, as a Judaean, he never could sit upon the Nabataean throne. Herod certainly did not want this crafty, energetic young man to succeed the inactive, phlegmatic King Obadas.[52]

Herod's attention was soon called to the increasing brigandage of the refugee leaders of Trachonitans and their band. They had increased their pillage to serious proportions, clearly with the encouragement of the rulers of Nabataea who were hostile toward Herod after Augustus Caesar had given him Auranitis, as this cut off the caravan route leading from Petra to Damascus. Syllaeus, who now harbored a personal grudge against Herod over Salome, was a leader in this antagonism.

Herod brought the matter up before Saturninus, the Roman legate in Syria, demanding that the Nabataeans surrender the brigands, and requesting the payment of a debt of sixty talents which Herod had loaned to Obadas through Syllaeus. Summoned before Saturninus, Syllaeus flatly denied that any of the brigands were Nabataeans; but the legate ordered the money repaid to Herod within thirty days and that each country return to the other those of its subjects who had taken refuge in the other's territories.[53] There were no political refugees from Nabataea in Judaea, so the decision was in Herod's favor. Syllaeus did not comply, but went instead to Rome.

Herod thereupon again brought the case before Saturninus, who gave him permission to take action. Herod led an army into Nabataea and beseiged and captured the fortress Rhaepta with its rebels. He also defeated the Nabataean general Nakabos who had come to their aid. To make certain that the Trachonitans should not rise in revolt again, he settled three thousand Idumaeans there.[54] This took place early in the year 8.

When Syllaeus heard that Herod was successful in his campaign, he managed to see Augustus Caesar. He appeared before him in black garments and tearfully told him that Nabataea had been ravaged and plundered by Herod, that twenty-five hundred of the leading Nabataeans had perished, and that all the wealth which was stored in the Fortress of Rhaepta had been appropriated by Herod. Upon hearing that Herod had invaded a neighboring state, the Emperor became infuriated. He then inquired of Herod's diplomatic representatives in Rome whether Syllaeus' facts were correct. When they sought to tell him that Herod had acted under the instructions of Saturninus, the Emperor refused to hear any further explanations. He believed Herod had been the aggressor and had disturbed the peace in Syria. He wrote him a harsh letter and said that their friendship was now at an end; and that Herod was merely a subject. Herod's humiliation gave courage to the Trachonitans, who rose up against the Idumaeans and overpowered them.[55] The Trachonitans apparently wanted freedom from Herod's rule, and were not the ordinary brigands, as Josephus makes them out to be on information derived from Nicolas of Damascus.

Herod could not suppress this revolt, having no sanction to do so from Augustus Caesar. Indeed, Herod's prestige had fallen in the entire Near East. He sent an embassy to Rome to plead in his defense, but Caesar refused to see them. On the other hand, Herod's arch-enemy Syllaeus enjoyed the confidence of the Emperor. To clear up his difficult situation Herod sent his most skillful diplomat, Nicolas of Damascus, to Rome.[56]

A turn of events in Nabataea soon gave Herod a much needed opening for a maneuver in Rome. The old king Obadas died, and a man named Aeneas, who had taken the name of Aretas, became king.[57] Aretas sent a delegation to Rome with a gold crown and other gifts for Augustus Caesar. The Emperor did not receive the delegation and refused the gifts. He was greatly angered because Aretas had made himself king without his sanction. The Emperor had the right to confirm the heir of a client-king or appoint a king of his own choosing. Another delegation, headed by Syllaeus, opposed King Aretas.

Nicolas of Damascus, who had come to Rome to reconcile the Emperor with Herod, thought that now was the opportune time for him to accomplish his mission. Instead of approaching the Emperor directly with a plea for Herod, he chose to become an advocate for the delegation of King Aretas. The King's emissaries gladly accepted Nicolas as their spokesman. Nicolas accused Syllaeus of many crimes, accusing him of responsibility for the death of King Obadas and of adultery, not only in Nabataea, but also in Rome. This last was a stinging charge, since Augustus regarded himself as a moral reformer.

When Nicolas of Damascus believed he had succeeded in turning the Emperor against Syllaeus, he thought it opportune to placate Augustus Caesar's anger toward Herod. He informed the Emperor that Syllaeus had lied to him by giving him false information regarding expeditions in Nabataea. The Emperor, refusing to listen any further, asked him whether or not it was true that Herod had led an army into Nabataea, killing twenty-five hundred people and plundering the country. Nicolas replied that it was true only in certain respects. Herod had led an expedition, but it was solely a punitive one, and the story of killing twenty-five hundred people and the plundering was false. In this he was supported by the Nabataeans of Aretas' delegation. Nicolas then proceeded in his accusations against Syllaeus, accusing him of not repaying a loan, even though he had sworn to do so by the genius of Caesar, and thus had committed sacrilege. He climaxed his denunciation by the revelation that the invasion into Nabataea had had the formal permission of Caesar's legate Saturninus. Syllaeus was forced to admit that his story regarding the killing of twenty-five hundred men was an exaggeration. This angered Augustus Caesar, and he ordered Syllaeus to repay the loan and said that punishment would come later.[58] Thus Nicolas succeeded in reconciling Caesar with Herod.

The Emperor, displeased because Aretas had assumed the throne of Nabataea without his sanction, considered transferring the country to Herod. However, Herod's envoys now delivered his letter of accusation against his sons. Reading it, Caesar changed his mind. An old man who had problems with his sons was not one to whom he should turn over Nabataea. He thereupon received the envoys sent by Aretas, accepted his gifts and confirmed him as king.[59]

This decision of the Emperor, apart from the denial of Nabataea to Herod, kept the latter from settling his problems with the Trachonitans. They continued to cause Herod great anxiety as they continually made forays into Judaean territory. They also harassed and robbed the pilgrims journeying from Babylonia to Jerusalem. Herod decided to build a stronghold on the eastern side of the Sea of Galilee from which to fight and subdue them. At this time a group of Judaeans, numbering five hundred horsemen, and other warriors, left their homeland, Parthia, under the leadership of a man named Zamaris, and crossed the Euphrates in the direction of Syria, which was under Roman rule.[60] Saturninus, the legate of Syria, welcomed them and assigned them a place named Ulatha[61] in which to dwell. What prompted the exodus of this group to a territory dominated by the Romans? Was this particular group or the whole Judaean community involved in strife with the Parthian authorities? The sources are silent, but the fact that

Saturninus assisted in settling them in Syria would indicate a political motive.[62]

When Herod learned of this, he invited these well-armed coreligionists to settle in his country. He promised to assign them Bathanea (Bashan), located to the west of Trachonitis, with the inducement that their land would be free from taxation and from any of the tributes that were exacted from the Judaeans. The group accepted his invitation and Bathanea became an effective buffer zone in the protection of pilgrims to Jerusalem.[63] This group became known as the "Babylonian Judaeans."[64] They remained loyal to the Herodian family and during the war against the Romans played a significant role.[65]

The "Trial" of the Princes

Augustus Caesar wrote to Herod (in response to the letter accusing his sons) that he was much distressed over the contents of his letter, and said that, if his sons were indeed plotting to kill him, they should be punished as parricides. If, however, they had planned only to flee, they should receive a severe reprimand. He advised Herod to call a *synedrion* at the Roman colony— Berytus —modern Beirut, of all the rulers of Syria, including Archelaus, King of Cappadocia.[66] Herod was pleased that Caesar had again become friendly, and that he had given him complete liberty to punish his sons. He assembled a *synedrion*, consisting of one hundred and fifty people, all the notables of the various cities of Syria and including his own kinsmen and friends, among them Pheroras and Salome. He excluded Archelaus, because he knew that he would argue further in favor of Alexander, his son-in-law.[67]

Alexander and Aristobolus were not permitted to appear before the council, being kept in jail in Platana, a nearby village. There were no advocates to argue the case in their defense. The *synedrion* was not even allowed to examine any documents. Herod accused his sons and produced some letters, but these made no mention of a plot to kill, not even of reproaches against their father, but merely that they were planning to flee. Herod said that he had the authority, both from his right as father and from Caesar, to act. He added further that, according to the law of his country, "if parents laid their hands on the head of him that was accused, the by-standers were bound to stone him and thereby slay him. This, he said, he was ready to do in his own country and kingdom, but still he awaited their determination."[68] Herod referred to the punishment of the "rebellious son" mentioned in Deuteronomy.[69] However, the law of the "rebellious son" had been so amended that during the Second Commonwealth a father did not have the right to kill his son, however rebellious he might be.[70] It is strange that Herod, who had transgressed every law of the Pentateuch, should invoke this law which had been rendered inoperative. Furthermore, the Pentateuch obliged him to go with his child to the elders of the city,[71] not to a *synedrion* consisting of notables of the pagan world. His procedure involved neither law nor fairness; it was a travesty on justice. When Herod asked those present to do their duty and condemn his sons, the verdict was a foregone conclusion. Saturninus, although he condemned Alexander and Aristobolus, appealed for clemency. He said that he himself was a father of sons and felt that it was terrible to put one's own son to death. His three sons, who were also sitting in the *synedrion,* also expressed this view. On the other hand, Volumnius, the procurator of Syria, advocated the death penalty, a sentiment echoed by most of those present.[72]

Herod was satisfied with the outcome. From Berytus he went to Tyre, taking along his sons, where he met Nicolas on his way from Rome. Here he learned of Caesar's feeling that, even if Alexander and Aristobolus were guilty, the king should exercise moderation and merely imprison them. From Tyre, Herod proceeded to Caesarea, accompanied by Nicolas and still taking along his two sons.[73]

The country was in a state of suspense. Would Herod really execute his sons? Sympathy for them ran high among the Judaeans as well as among the Greeks. Both sons were popular, but everyone was afraid to speak out. All were deeply distressed over the action of the king. One man, Tiro, who had been a comrade in arms of Herod, dared to voice the general feeling. He also had a son, a friend of Alexander and of the same age. Tiro had great respect for Herod and great affection for his sons. He secured a private audience with the king, telling him that he could no longer restrain his feelings. He asked how Herod could have allowed himself to be misled by evildoers. He further asked, "Are you going to put to death two youths who were born to you by a wife who was a queen, who are accomplished with every virtue? Will you in your old age entrust yourself to a single son (Antipater) who has ill repaid the hopes that you have given him?" To this he added that the entire army and its officers began to feel pity for the princes and were imbued with hatred of their accusers.[74] Herod first listened quietly, but when he heard that there was disaffection in the army he became incensed. He thought that there would be a mutiny. He ordered the arrest of Tiro and three hundred officers suspected of sympathy for the Hasmonean princes.[75]

While Tiro was being put in chains, Herod's barber, Trypho, told the king that Tiro had tried to persuade him to cut Herod's throat while shaving him, promising that Alexander would reward him. Herod put Tiro, his son, and the barber to torture. Tiro bravely withstood the torture without uttering a word. His son, however, unable to endure the sight of his father's agony, offered to make a full confession. He said that his father had indeed intended to kill the king while in a private audience with him.[76] The confession of Tiro's son, if not to save his father's life, was made to release him from the agony of torture. Nor was there any substance to the barber's statement. It is probable that the barber merely sought to gain Herod's favor by inventing a story. Herod re-

warded the barber's voluntary admission with torture—
an irrational response which indicates Herod's mental
unrest and perverted love of cruelty.

Herod called an assembly and brought before them the
officers, Tiro and his son, and the barber, all of whom he
accused of plotting to murder him. They were stoned to
death by the populace[77] and Herod ordered Alexander
and Aristobolus taken to Sebaste (Samaria) and
strangled. During the night their bodies were taken to a
crypt in the Fortress Alexandrion where their ancestors,
the Hasmoneans, were buried.[78] Their execution took
place in the year 7, at the same spot where a little over
thirty years before Herod had married their mother
Mariamme[79]—so far did Herod's vindictiveness go. Now
her sons would not be his heirs.

There is and was no evidence that Alexander and
Aristobolus ever plotted to kill their father. As their lives
became endangered, they contemplated fleeing the country. Their only fault was lack of caution. They trusted
everyone who showed them friendship and gave free
expression to their feelings. Believing themselves to be
the true heirs to the throne, they looked condescendingly
upon the other members of the court. True—they did not
love their father—how could they love a monster who
had murdered their mother, grandmother, uncle and
great-grandfather? Though they never planned to kill
him, he apparently could not stop until he killed them.
Each left progeny: Alexander had two sons, Tigranes
and Alexander; Aristobolus had three sons, Herod,
Agrippa and Aristobolus, and two daughters, Herodias
and Mariamme.[80]

Herod had other grandchildren and children as well
(not to mention his concubines and eunuchs). Doris was
the mother of Antipater; Mariamme II had a son, Herod;
Malthace, the Samaritan, had two sons, Antipas and
Archelaus, and a daughter, Olympias; Cleopatra had two
sons, Herod and Philip; Pallas had a son, Phasael;
Phaedra had a daughter, Roxane; Elpis had a daughter,

Salome. The other two wives were childless.[81] The number of his children by his concubines is unknown.

ANTIPATER'S MISCARRIED PLOT

Antipater and Pheroras

With the death of Alexander and Aristobolus, Salome, Pheroras and Antipater had achieved a major goal. Each had satisfied his personal motives. Salome had her revenge for her humiliations. Pheroras had eliminated the obstacles to his advancement. Antipater had made it almost impossible for Herod to change his mind about him as heir. But now a rift broke out among the conspirators. Salome alone was content. She was devoted to Herod. Only one incident had disturbed their relations —when Herod forbade her marriage to Syllaeus and ordered her to marry his friend Alexas. She had appealed to Livia, the wife of Augustus, to intercede with Herod in her behalf. Livia had advised her to obey Herod.[82] She then became reconciled with her brother and continued to be devoted to him.

Pheroras and Antipater, however, had not yet reached their goals. Herod was still alive. Pheroras felt no hatred against his brother; but he did want to be king, as it had been prophesied to him that he would be.[83] Antipater, however, hated his father for his treatment of his mother Doris. Like his father, Antipater never forgave an insult and always forgot the favors extended to him. Although recognized as heir to the throne, he feared that his father would live long enough to change his mind about the succession. Antipater therefore became obsessed with the thought of murdering Herod.

Uncle and nephew, cherishing no love for each other, joined in a plot to murder Herod, each for reasons of his own. They became very friendly with one another and spent much time in each other's company. A number of women joined them: Doris, Antipater's mother, who had long borne animosity towards Herod and who wanted her son to be king; and the wife of Pheroras, who had been humiliated by Herod when he wanted her husband to divorce her,[84] and who wanted her husband to be king. There were two other women who did not enter the plot, but hoped for its success. One was the wife of Antipater, the daughter of Antigonus,[85] who had been executed by the Romans at the insistence of Herod.[86] To her the murder of Herod by his son would be a fitting vengeance for the death of her father; besides, she hoped to be the reigning queen of Judaea as a descendant of the Hasmonean family. Mariamme II, Herod's wife, also was aware of the plot and hoped for its success.[87] She believed that Antipater, as a parricide and already the most hated man in Judaea, would meet with great opposition from the people and the army in his effort to take the throne. She thought that here would be a good opportunity for her own son Herod to become king,[88] particularly because he was the grandson of the high priest, Simon son of Boethus, the most influential man in Judaea.

Antipater's anxiety increased when Herod gathered his family and friends together and presented to them the orphan children of Alexander and Aristobolus. He embraced them and, with tears in his eyes, expressed the hope that the fate of their fathers would not overtake them. He then announced to the gathering his determination to arrange suitable marriages for the orphan children. Alexander, the son of Alexander, was to be wedded to Pheroras' daughter; Herod, the son of Aristobolus, was to marry Antipater's daughter; one of the two daughters of Aristobolus was to marry Antipater's son, and the other was to marry his own son Herod, by Mariamme II.[89] Antipater became fearful that the young Alexander, by marrying the daughter of Pheroras, would be a threat to his kingship. As the grandson of King Archelaus and son-in-law of Pheroras, Alexander would have the support of these powerful men against him. He implored Herod to make changes in the betrothals and succeeded in persuading him to do so; he wanted the daughter of Aristobolus to be betrothed to himself, while his own son should wed the daughter of Pheroras.[90] He hoped to strengthen his own position, not only by closer ties with Pheroras, but also by having two wives, both of Hasmonean descent.

The friendship of Antipater with Pheroras aroused the suspicions of Salome, who was spying on them. She now reported to Herod that in 20-19 B.C.E., when he had instituted the oath of allegiance, Pheroras' wife had paid the fine for the Pharisees, Apocalyptists, who refused to take it. Salome also told him of Pheroras' hopes based on the prophecies of the Apocalyptists.[91]

Herod immediately assembled a *synedrion* and brought charges against Pheroras' wife. He explained that her loyalty to him was suspect. Now he again appealed to Pheroras to divorce his wife and thus show his devotion to the king. Pheroras again refused to do so, saying that he would rather die than divorce his wife. Pheroras' refusal angered Herod; nevertheless, although he could have punished his brother's wife, he did not do so. He ordered Pheroras to leave for his tetrarchy and banished him from Judaea.[92] The reason he did not take retaliatory measures against them was probably that Pheroras had been appointed to the office of tetrarch by Augustus Caesar. He could take action against Pheroras and his wife only with Caesar's consent. Salome also reported to Herod her suspicions of Antipater, his wife and mother, because of their constant meetings with Pheroras. Herod forbade Antipater and his mother to be in the company of Pheroras and they promised to obey his order. Herod gave Antipater one hundred talents for complying with his request.[93]

Herod now made a will appointing Antipater as his heir and stipulating that the succession should next go to Herod, son of Mariamme II.[94] Although Antipater was only the officially appointed heir, he already acted like a king. Above all, he feared that Herod's longevity might thwart his ambitions. He tried to make friends among the powerful men in the various courts by bribery or gifts, as in the case of Saturninus.[95] Antipater became alarmed when Herod sent his two sons, Archelaus (by Malthace) and Philip (by Cleopatra), to Rome to be educated. He suspected that Herod did so in order that they could become friendly with Augustus Caesar and so succeed their father. Therefore, in spite of his promise to Herod, Antipater and his mother continued having clandestine meetings during the nights with Pheroras and their women fellow-conspirators. They continued plotting against Herod's life and went so far as to obtain poison which they planned to have administered to the king.[96]

Antipater vigorously expressed to Pheroras his complaints against his father. He feared that he might not survive his father. He argued that his father was already senile and unreliable, pointing out that in the will where he was made heir, Herod had appointed as successor, not one of Antipater's sons, but his stepbrother. Of course, had Antipater succeeded in attaining to the kingship, he would have killed off all the pretenders. The reason Herod did not appoint Antipater's son as successor was that he was a descendant of the Hasmonean family through Antipater's marriage to the daughter of King Antigonus. Herod hated any descendant of the Hasmoneans, and the thought that one of them would some day be king of Judaea was abhorrent to him.[97]

Antipater, aware of Salome's spying, found Jerusalem unsafe and thought it advisable to leave for Rome. He wanted to be away so that, should Pheroras succeed in poisoning Herod, he would not be under suspicion. He wrote to his friends in Rome, requesting that they write to Herod that it would be to his advantage for Antipater to visit Rome.[98] Before leaving for Rome, Antipater succeeded in obtaining the will which made him Herod's heir,[99] so that he might present it to Caesar for certification, and Herod might not change his mind about the succession while he was away. Antipater was given a royal send-off, and carried with him magnificent presents for Caesar. The journey took place in the early part of the year 5 B.C.E.

When Antipater arrived in Rome, he found another plotter against Herod's life. Syllaeus the Nabataean, still in Rome, had bribed Fabatus, a slave who managed Caesar's affairs in Nabataea, to work up a plan against Herod. But Herod gave Fabatus more money. Syllaeus thereupon accused Fabatus of acting in the interests of Herod, not of Caesar. Fabatus, in indignation, disclosed Syllaeus' plan for Corinthus, Herod's bodyguard, to kill him. Herod arrested Corinthus and two Nabataean friends of Syllaeus, as well as several other Nabataeans denounced by Corinthus. Under torture they confessed their guilt. Herod sent them to Saturninus who dispatched them to Rome for trial.[100] Syllaeus now received the punishment he had previously been promised for lying to Caesar about Herod.

Antipater, in Rome, continued to plot against his stepbrothers Archelaus and Philip. He bribed friends to write to Herod that the princes were complaining that the killing of Alexander and Aristobolus was monstrous and were expressing hostility toward Herod.[101]

Pheroras died while Antipater was still in Rome. During his final illness, Herod had visited him. Despite their previous difficulties, Herod had his brother's body brought to Jerusalem and gave him a magnificent state funeral. Josephus relates that, after the funeral, two of Pheroras' freedmen informed Herod of their suspicion that Pheroras had been poisoned. They said that he had supped with his wife the day before he fell ill and had partaken of an unfamiliar dish served to him, which they believed contained poison. They further informed Herod that it had been brought from Arabia by a woman who was an intimate friend of one of the mistresses of Syllaeus. Herod ordered Pheroras' women slaves tortured. One of the victims in her agony cursed Doris, the mother of Antipater, blaming her for all the evils. On hearing this, Herod pursued the inquisition until the secret meetings which had been held among Antipater, Doris and Pheroras came to light. Also it was revealed that Antipater had told Pheroras of the hundred talents which Herod had given him for promising not to associate with his uncle Pheroras. This disclosure gave credence to the confessions of the women, for Herod had made the gift in strict secrecy. He was now convinced of Antipater's disloyalty and duplicity. His first act was to banish Doris from the palace and to deprive her of all her royal raiment. He then began an interrogation of Antipater's servants.[102]

One of Antipater's stewards, a Samaritan also named Antipater, when placed on the rack, confessed that Antipater had given a box of poison to be delivered to Pheroras which was to be administered to Herod while Antipater was in Rome and beyond suspicion. The poison had been brought from Egypt by Antiphilus, a friend of Antipater who had passed it on to Pheroras. The poison remained in the possession of Pheroras' wife. When Herod asked her if this was true, she confessed and offered to produce it. On her way to fetch the poison she tried to commit suicide by throwing herself from the roof of her home, but she was only injured. Herod promised her immunity if she would tell the whole truth. She confirmed the account given by Antipater's steward and also stated that when Pheroras became ill and Herod visited him, Pheroras was overwhelmed by his brother's generosity. She said further that Pheroras had told her that he had plotted to kill Herod, but he realized that he was committing a great crime against his brother who was devoted to him. He therefore ordered the poison burned. This she had done, but retained a small portion to administer to herself should Herod put her upon the rack. She then produced the box which contained what was left of the poison. Antiphilus' mother and brother, when put to torture, admitted her tale was true and identified the box.[103] Mariamme II was also involved, having been privy to the plot. When her brother was arrested and put to torture, he denounced her. Herod divorced Mariamme, took away the high priesthood from Simon, her father, and in his place appointed Matthias the son of Theophilus. He also cut Mariamme's son Herod out of his will.[104]

Some matters in Josephus' account of the plot are obscure. Josephus does not mention the person who was to administer the poison to Herod. Antipater was in Rome; Pheroras had been banished from Judaea. Hence it may be assumed that the poison was to have been administered by one of Herod's wives, either Doris or Mariamme, most likely the latter. Her father probably also had knowledge of the affair, which would explain why his punishment was greater than the possibility of influencing his grandson's ultimate succession to the throne warranted.

The account of the attempted suicide of Pheroras' wife is difficult to follow. What prompted her to throw herself from a roof to commit suicide rather than take her poison? Was this not a theatrical act on her part, jumping from a low roof and taking care not to fall on her head so that she should only be injured? Josephus (or his source, Nicolas of Damascus, who hated Antipater) gave a theological explanation: by the providence of God, "whose vengeance was pursuing Antipater, she fell, not on her head, but on another part of her body and was not killed."[105]

Josephus further wrote that Pheroras' wife told Herod that Pheroras had ordered her to burn the poison, since he had repented of his evil plan to kill his brother, in view of Herod's generosity in visiting him. Now Pheroras had never hated his brother; he simply wanted to be king. As he lay dying, he realized he could not succeed his brother and had no personal reason for having Herod killed. Since Pheroras had not entered the conspiracy to benefit Antipater, he ordered his wife to burn the poison.[106]

Antipater's Trial

During the interrogation, new evidence came to light against Antipater. Bathyllus, Antipater's freedman, arrived from Rome with the letters from Antipater and his friends slandering Archelaus and Philip. Suspicion fell on Bathyllus, and he was put to torture. While on the rack he confessed that he had brought a more powerful poison to deliver to Doris and Pheroras to be administered to Herod should the first one fail.[107] Antipater's guilt was now indisputable and Herod was determined that he must be punished for plotting to kill him. He wrote to Antipater to hasten his homecoming. A rigid censorship was imposed on all letters going from Judaea to Rome, so that Antipater should have no inkling of the accusations that had been made against him. The only news that he received was that his uncle Pheroras was dead. At this he displayed great emotion—but his grief was not for the death of an uncle, but for the loss of an accomplice. Herod, being apprehensive that some news of what had occurred might reach Antipater, wrote him a letter in which he displayed friendliness in order to remove any suspicion. In it he noted that some minor charges had been made against Doris, but assured him that the charges and misunderstandings would be cleared up upon his arrival in Jerusalem.[108] This letter reached Antipater upon his arrival in Cilicia and disturbed him greatly. He became hesitant about proceeding further. Some of his friends advised him not to continue his voyage and to wait for more news. Others advised him that the best course would be to return to Jerusalem where he might easily regain his influence over his father. Persuaded by this argument, he decided to continue his journey. He set sail for Caesarea and landed at its port, Sebastos. There were no friends to greet him— no cheering crowds to welcome him. The people received him with curses. He sensed trouble, but could not turn back. He left for Jerusalem full of anxiety.[109]

At this time, Varus,[110] the legate of Syria, was visiting Herod. While they were together, Antipater arrived, still unaware of the accusations that had been made against him. He entered the palace attired in his purple robe. The doorkeepers admitted him, but did not allow his friends to enter. Herod denounced him violently, called him a parricide, and told him that on the following day Varus would hear the whole story and would be his

judge.[111] When Antipater left the palace, he was met by
his mother and his wife, and learned from them all that
had taken place and the testimony that had been brought
against him.[112] (Doris, who had borne venomous hatred
toward Mariamme I, had an entirely different feeling
toward her daughter-in-law, the daughter of Antigonus
the Hasmonean. Their friendship was cemented by the
common hatred they felt for Herod.)

The next day, Herod summoned a *synedrion*, Varus
at its head, to which he invited friends and relatives
(including his sister, Salome) before whom he paraded
the informers who, under torture, had given testimony
against Antipater. Arrived at the palace, Antipater
prostrated himself before his father, imploring him not
to pronounce judgment upon him until all the facts were
known. He said that he could establish his innocence.
Herod ordered him to rise and launched a bitter denunciation against him. He declared that, in spite of all the
favors which he had bestowed upon him, Antipater had
plotted against him. He had afforded him a princely
income; he had named him his heir and treated him
virtually as co-regent: and the reward he received was a
plot to kill him. He claimed that Antipater was responsible for the murder of his stepbrothers Alexander and
Aristobolus, saying "Whatever he (Herod) had done to
his sons had been done by Antipater's advice."[113] Antipater, in his defense, elaborated on the great services
he had performed for his father, arguing that he, who
had unmasked so many plots against Herod, would not
himself become a plotter against his father. Further he
argued that one who possessed half the realm without
danger to himself would be in a perilous situation if he
seized the entire realm, especially since he had witnessed
the punishment of his brothers whose denouncer and
accuser he had been. He produced letters from Augustus
Caesar praising him. Surely Caesar, lord of the universe,
also called Philopater (lover of his father) could not
have been deceived. He denounced evidence secured
under torture as unreliable. He finally offered himself

for torture, saying, "Let the fire be applied to me . . . for if I am a parricide, I ought not to die without being put on the rack." His arguments, accompanied by weeping, moved all but Herod to compassion.[114]

Nicolas of Damascus then began his speech of prosecution against Antipater. In answer to Antipater's claim that he had protected his father from the plotting of his stepbrothers, Nicolas said that Antipater's hatred of his stepbrothers was not for having plotted against their father, but because they had the right of succession to the throne. Nicolas appealed to Varus, "Will you not destroy this wicked beast whose pretense of affection for his father was meant for the destruction of his brothers, for when he was certain of obtaining the throne for himself alone within a short time, he showed himself to be a deadlier menace to his father than all the others."[115] When Nicolas wound up the case for the prosecution with fiery denunciations of Antipater, Varus ordered Antipater to defend himself. Antipater, lying prostrate, called upon God to show by some sign that he was not guilty, that he had never plotted against his father. Varus was not impressed by this. He then ordered the alleged poison to be brought before the *synedrion* and administered to a prisoner who was under sentence of death. Upon drinking the poison, the prisoner died instantly. The *synedrion* was then dismissed and Varus, after a private talk with Herod, left for Antioch. Herod imprisoned Antipater and sent an embassy and a letter to Augustus Caesar to inform him of Antipater's wickedness.[116]

Additional evidence of Antipater's schemes appeared, this time against Salome. A slave of Antiphilus arrived from Egypt with a letter to Antipater, which read as follows: "I have sent you the letter from Acme (a Judaean by birth, who was a slave to Livia, wife of Augustus Caesar) without considering the risk to my own life, for you know that I am in danger from two families if I be discovered. But I wish you luck in this affair." The letter alluded to was not found and the slave denied that he had received any other letters. One of Herod's spies noticed that there was a patch sewn on the slave's inner tunic. It was ripped open and two letters were found under it, one of which read as follows: "Acme to Antipater. I have written to your father the kind of letter you wanted, having also made a copy of the letter of Salome to my lady (Livia) that I composed. I know that when he has read it he will punish Salome as a plotter against him." The other letter ran: "Acme to King Herod. I have done my endeavor that nothing done against you shall be concealed from you, and so when I found a letter written against you by Salome to my lady, I copied it and sent it to you. This was dangerous for me, but was for your good. The letter was written by Salome because she wants to marry Syllaeus. Now please tear this letter in pieces, that I may not come into danger of my life."[117] Clearly, Antipater, in his anxiety to get rid of his aunt Salome, had bribed Acme to fabricate these letters accusing Salome of treacherous acts against her brother. Upon seeing these letters Herod burst into a violent rage and wanted to kill Antipater immediately. He summoned his son and, when he remained mute, Herod considered sending Antipater to Caesar to stand trial, but gave up the idea for fear that he might escape punishment through his friends in Rome. Herod again sent special envoys with letters to Caesar accusing Antipater and Acme. He also sent copies of the letters written by Acme which had been intercepted.[118]

THE LAST DAYS OF HEROD

Final Acts of Tyranny

Herod himself was now gravely ill. Realizing that his days were numbered, he wrote a new will, leaving the kingdom to Antipas, his younger son by Malthace. Despite the revelation of Antipater's intrigue against himself and Salome, Herod still gave some credence to Antipater's calumnies against Archelaus and Philip. He left a legacy of a thousand talents to Augustus Caesar, five hundred to Livia, and various sums to Caesar's friends and freedman. He also made ample provision for his sister Salome.[119]

Little more than two weeks before Herod's death, there occurred an outburst typical of those which had taken place from time to time when observant Judaeans could no longer tolerate Herod's disregard of Jewish laws and traditions. There were two sophists,[120] teachers, interpreters of the law, named Judas son of Sariphaeus and Matthias son of Margalothus, who attracted a large number of disciples. When word spread that Herod was approaching death, these two sophists exhorted their followers to tear down the golden eagle which Herod had erected over the great gate of the temple in violation of the laws of their fathers.[121] Convinced that they were performing a noble act, that they would achieve eternal fame and their souls immortality,[122] the disciples then tore down the eagle. In Antonia, where a cohort was stationed for the purpose of suppressing outbreaks in the Temple area, the captain heard the disturbance and hastened with his troops to quell it. He arrested more than forty men and also took the two sophists into custody. They were brought before Herod who interrogated them. He asked, "Who ordered you to do so?" They answered, "The law of our fathers." Then Herod said, "Why are you so exultant when you will shortly be put to death?" Their answer was that it was more important for them to observe the laws of Moses, which God had taught him, than to follow the king's decrees, and that they were not afraid of dying. "After death," they said, "we shall enjoy greater felicity."[123] Herod became infuriated and ordered them to be imprisoned. He called an assembly of Jewish notables in Jericho. He was carried into the theater where the prominent men were assembled. He was so ill he could not stand, but reclined on a couch. He bitterly castigated the men, recounting all his labors in the construction of the Temple. He boasted that the Hasmoneans in the one hundred and twenty-five years of their rule had been unable to build such a magnificent Temple. He complained that, even while he was alive, they had not hesitated to insult him, but that this act was, not only an insult to him, but more, a sacrilege, since he had erected the golden eagle as a votive offering.[124] Typically, he ignored the pentateuchal prohibition of images. The notables pleaded with Herod that they should not be punished, since the removal of the golden eagle had been done without their consent. He did not punish them, but removed the high priest Matthias from his post for his negligence and appointed Joazar, the brother of Mariamme II, to the high priesthood.[125] Joazar was probably the brother who had informed Herod that his sister Mariamme II was privy to the plot of Pheroras and Antipater, and this appointment was no doubt his reward. He also had the two sophists and their disciples burned alive and ordered the execution of those who had taken part in the action.[126] On that very night (the thirteenth of March, 4 B.C.E.) there was an eclipse of the moon, which the Judaeans regarded as a bad omen.[127]

Herod was approaching his end. His body was racked with burning pain and he breathed with difficulty. He was probably suffering from cancer of the bowels, with liver complications and gangrene of the genitals. He also had convulsions in his limbs and probably suffered from Hodgkin's disease. The doctors prescribed the hot baths of Callirhoe,[128] a medicinal spring northeast of the Dead Sea, and they also recommended immersion in a tub of oil; but nothing gave him relief. He was taken back to Jericho.[129]

Knowing that he was close to death, Josephus says, Herod summoned all the prominent men of the country and ordered them locked in the hippodrome. He told his sister Salome and her husband Alexas, "I know that the Judaeans will celebrate my death by a festival." However, he did not want to go to his death without lamentation and mourning. He therefore ordered that at the moment of his death those notables should be massacred, "so that all Judaea and every household might weep for me, whether they will or no."[130] Josephus comments on this order:[131]

He (Herod) took care to leave the entire nation in a state of mourning over the loss of their dearest ones, and gave orders to execute one member of each family, although they had done nothing wrong or offended him, nor had been accused of any other crime, though it is usual for all men who have any regard to virtue to forget their hatred at such a time even when it is directed against those whom they have a right to regard as enemies.

It is open to question whether Herod ordered that the assembled notables should be killed on the day of his death. It is more likely that they were to be held in the hippodrome as hostages to prevent any disorder after his death and to insure the succession of Archelaus. That is why the members of his family later blamed Archelaus before Augustus about freeing the notables from the hippodrome.[132] Josephus here made use of a source hostile to Herod and the motive it gives evinces the mistrust and hatred felt for him by the Judaeans.

This monstrous order, as related by Josephus, gave rise to the legend of the slaughter of the innocents in the Gospel according to Matthew.[133] Josephus' account had great influence on the founders of Christianity, for whom Herod was the Antichrist. Herod died a number of years before the birth of Jesus.[134]

Herod was somewhat consoled after receiving a letter from Augustus Caesar which informed him that Acme had been executed for conspiring against Salome. Caesar also left the punishment of Antipater to Herod's judgment.[135]

Herod's suffering increased from hour to hour. He asked for an apple and a knife and attempted suicide. His cousin Achiab seized his hand and prevented the attempt. Achiab, thinking that Herod had hurt himself, started to cry out, and soon lamentation filled the palace. Antipater, hearing the wailing, thought that his father was already dead and asked his jailer to free him,

promising to reward him on becoming king. The jailer
wanted to be sure that Herod was dead and went to find
out. Herod was still alive and, when the jailer informed
Herod of Antipater's promise to him, Herod ordered
that Antipater be put to death immediately and his body
dispatched to Hyrcania for burial.

Herod again revised his will. He nominated Archelaus
heir to the throne. He appointed Antipas tetrarch of
Galilee and Peraea. Philip he named as tetrarch of
Trachonitis, Batanea and Paneas. He gave Jabneh,
Azotus and Phasaelis to Salome. He also bequeathed sub-
stantial amounts of money to his relatives. To Caesar
he left ten million pieces of coined money, and to Livia,
Caesar's wife, five million pieces of silver.[136]

Herod died five days after Antipater's execution. He
was about seventy years of age. He had reigned thirty-
seven years from the time he was appointed king by the
Roman Senate, thirty-four years after he captured
Jerusalem.

Before Herod's death became known, Salome and her
husband Alexas, with the consent of Archelaus, freed
the prisoners from the hippodrome. She then announced
the death of Herod to the leaders of the army and the
people who were assembled in the amphitheater at
Jericho. She read his letters in which he thanked the
soldiers for their faithfulness and good will and besought them to transfer their allegiance to his son
Archelaus. Ptolemy, who had been entrusted with the
king's seal, read Herod's will, in which Archelaus was
proclaimed his heir. The officers and the army acclaimed
Archelaus as their king and promised loyalty. Ptolemy
pronounced a benediction over the deceased king and
delivered an exhortation to the people.[137]

What was Herod's intention in giving Judaea to
Archelaus while other parts of the country were assigned
to the brothers? Was it his desire that the brothers
should be subordinate to Archelaus, or did he want
Judaea to be divided? The questions must remain open.
There is no way to know.[138]

Archelaus arranged a magnificent funeral for his father. The body lay on a golden bier ornamented with precious stones and covered with purple. The dead king wore his diadem, above which a golden crown had been placed. His scepter was in his right hand. His sons and all his relatives followed the bier. The army came next: first his bodyguards, followed by the Thracians, the Germans, and finally the Gauls; all were equipped as for battle, led by their officers. After the army, five hundred slaves and freedmen carrying spices wound up the procession. The funeral cortège marched from Jericho to Herodion where Herod was buried according to his wish.[139]

Herod had been obsessed with the fear that the Judaeans would declare a festival on the day that he died, and the Judaeans declared the 28th of Adar, the day of his death, a semi-holiday. Megillat Ta'anit states that on the 28th of Adar, good news came to the Judaeans that they should not deviate from the Torah, the Law.[140]

Summary of Herod's Reign

Two themes of Herod's reign demand special consideration. One is the internal management of the kingdom. The second is the reaction of the religious groups to his rule.

Serving the Romans over a long period in many capacities, Herod learned how to organize his kingdom. In his palace there were always friends who were close to him and a picked bodyguard of the military élite. To make decisions in private as well as state matters he regularly called a *synedrion,* or council, which consisted of the officials, the friends, and relatives in whom he had full confidence. Nicolas of Damascus was his adviser in foreign affairs. His Secretary of State was Diophantus, a Hellene. The economic and financial management was entrusted to Ptolemy, who also was probably not a Judaean. The eunuchs in his court were not Judaean;

they were trusted slaves and close to him, and therefore had great political power.

Herod organized a formidable army and police force modeled after the Roman military system. It consisted mainly of non-Judaeans—Germans, Thracians, Gauls, Galatians and many Hellenized Syrians. Some Judaeans were also recruited. The officers of the army were Romans and such Judaeans as were loyal to him. Herod did not engage in foreign wars: as a client-king he could not go to war with foreign states; nor, with Rome dominating the entire Near East, could any neighboring state make war on Judaea. The strong army that Herod had organized was essentially for the suppression of any internal revolt.

For purposes of administration, the country was divided into toparchies,[141] that is, districts. The head of each district was a *strategos*, a governor who possessed military and civil authority and who was responsible directly to Herod. Every city had one man who was responsible for its management and tranquility. Every village had scribes with authority over the people. Herod was the autocrat to whom all these officials were responsible. It is understandable that they could retain their office only as long as Herod had confidence in their loyalty to him.

Herod's organization of the state, his army, his many buildings, his continuing gifts and bribes required an enormous amount of money. How did he obtain it? The main revenue undoubtedly came from taxation. When Herod ascended the throne, he made no change in the pattern of taxes the Hasmoneans had taken over from the Seleucids.[142] He only added new ones. There was a poll tax which everyone, men and women, had to pay, the amount of which is not known. In Syria this tax was collected from every male aged 14 to 65, and from every female aged 12 to 65. Younger children and those over 65 were exempt. It is probable that Herod followed the Syrian system of taxation. There was also a tributory tax which everyone had to pay to his sovereign. This tax was one of subjugation. In levying this tax Herod looked upon the people as his servants. It is not known how this revenue was collected. It is probable that the amount to be paid was levied upon each community, as was the custom among the Romans. There was a tax on the land—one third of the seed and one half of the fruit harvested. There was also a salt tax. It is reasonable to assume that they were farmed by revenue contractors, publicans; in Hebrew they were called *gabbaim,* collectors, tax collectors.[143] Another tax was on houses and real estate.[144] Herod introduced still another tax, the purchase tax: the seller and the buyer had to pay a fixed sum.[145] There were import and export duties on the borders of the country. The caravans passing through Judaea had to pay a tax. At the new port of Caesarea, which became of great importance for exporting and importing, an office was established for the collection of revenue.[146] There was also internal taxation on merchandise, and each important city had its customs. There was also a tax known as "presents," gifts presented to the ruler. Herod had another source of income in the colonists, those whom he had settled on the land.[147] They were his tenants and had to pay him a rental. When he rebuilt Samaria he settled it with non-Judaeans, and they became his tenants.[148]

Despite its value for taxation and other administrative purposes, no census was taken. The Judaeans dreaded a census, as the Bible already indicates, and Herod respected their feelings. The first census was taken in Judaea only when it became a province of Rome.[149]

The many different taxes and tariffs enriched Herod, but they did not benefit the population of Judaea directly. During his reign the people were for the most part more impoverished than during the time of the Hasmoneans. The erection of the numerous structures and cities did provide employment for many Judaeans and a strong Judaean proletariat came into being. Most of the labor force, however, was made up of pagans and slaves.

The vast income from these many sources did not go to the treasury of the state, which did not exist as such, but to Herod personally, who, as in almost all of the countries of that time, was in his person the state, and his personal treasury was the state treasury. Thus he could add to his resources by confiscating the money and the property of those whom he conscripted and executed,[150] the most significant example being his continuing appropriation of the funds belonging to the Hasmonean family. He also derived great profit from various enterprises and monopolies which he operated as a royal prerogative. Balsam, one of Judaea's most noted products, was highly profitable, particularly as he had greatly improved the area where it was cultivated. The export of dates was also lucrative.[151] He had different varieties of date palms developed, and named the groves Nicolaitans after his friend Nicolas of Damascus.[152] He was also engaged in pigeon breeding, and one species became known as Herodians.[153] Bitumen, extracted from the Dead Sea, continued to supply a substantial revenue; and, after his gift from Augustus Caesar, Herod derived a large income from the copper mines in Cyprus.[154]

Herod spent money on himself and his friends generously, almost to the point of abandon. He was no less free in his official spending, less on internal organization than on building and international relations. His funds and imagination made possible his many construction projects, among them fortresses, cities, beautiful palaces, the magnificent Temple, and the city of Caesarea and its great port, the most important in the Middle East. In the planning and construction of these buildings he displayed architectural genius and a rare understanding of art.

Money was required for the friendships on which politics in the Roman world depended. Herod knew how to acquire friends and hold their devotion. He had a keen understanding of Roman diplomacy and employed it for his benefit and even for the good of Judaea. Thus in his early years he was close to Sextus Caesar, Cassius the republican, and Cassius' mortal enemy, Antony—a feat of keen personal statesmanship.[155] Later, Augustus Caesar regarded him as one of his best friends, a *rex socius,* an associate king, and he retained a lasting relationship with Agrippa, the son-in-law of Augustus and second in power in the Roman Empire. He could not have accomplished all this had he been an ordinary person. Rather the record indicates that he was an extraordinary personality. His friendships, gifts and bribes were an important factor in making and keeping Judaea the most important and respected country in the Near East. At the same time he managed to retain such independence of action as the Empire permitted. The Romans did not interfere in the internal affairs of Judaea during his reign. No accounting was asked of him with regard to income and expenditures. He had absolute power over the life and death of his subjects and, when he occasionally consulted Caesar about his sons or the succession, it was to flatter the Emperor and show that he looked upon Augustus as his patron.

During the time of Herod, Judaea was superficially a great country and he could be called Herod the Great.[156] But the annexations to the country, with their foreign populations, were like a cancer gnawing at the state of Judaea. Herod never realized that in a non-democratic country, especially one that has a state religion, a minority of foreign people, of different religion and historical background, who are not assimilated but remain a homogeneous entity of their own, consciously different from and antagonistic to the majority of the people, are a latent danger to the state.[157]

The nation built by Herod during his reign of thirty-four years appeared formidable, but soon after his death it began to disintegrate.

The religious situation during Herod's reign is also of special interest, because it cannot be divorced from the politics of the time.

3. NEW TRENDS IN RELIGION.
HILLEL THE ELDER

NEW RELIGIOUS GROUPINGS

The Hasmonean kings were either Sadducees or Pharisees, and they enforced the religious laws and customs to which they adhered.[1] Herod was neither Sadducee nor Pharisee; he was a dissenting Judaean. In killing the chief supporters of Antigonus after capturing the Temple, he also destroyed the leaders of the Sadducees. Hence his political policy had great impact upon both these primarily religious groups.

The view held by the Pharisees, that only a descendant of the family of David was the rightful ruler over Judaea, was only an ideal;[2] but they cherished the hope that with the help of God it would someday be realized. They did not engage in open warfare against Herod as they had against Jannaeus Alexander, because the latter had sought to impose the Sadduceean religious law, while Herod did not interfere in such matters. Moreover, Herod was inclined to favor the Pharisees because of the support given him by their leaders, Shemayah and Hillel, during the siege of Jerusalem.[3] The Pharisees were therefore content to resign from all political activities and devote themselves to making religion the inner bastion of the Judaean nation. They became legalists, devoted to the interpretation of the Halakhah, the law, and its continued relevance to life.[4]

The Sadduceean ideology did not disappear, though the group itself tended to dissolve after the execution of its leaders. Rather, since its historical roots had not been eradicated, it became active again during Herod's reign, but in another garb. It was now called Boethusaean, after the high priest Simon son of Boethus, the father-in-law of Herod.[5] The Talmud uses the names Sadduceeans and Boethusaeans interchangeably. The Boethusaeans held that the high priest was the supreme religious leader and that in him alone was vested the authority of religious decision. They denied Providence, reward and punishment, and immortality of the soul—views held by their prototype, the Sadducees. For a while the Boethusaeans also kept away from any political activities.

The Sadducees and the Pharisees went through various changes in order to adjust themselves to the tyrannical rule of Herod. One group, the Essenes, was not affected. It consisted of ascetics who did not engage in political life nor seek to proselytize their fellow Judaeans. They held that any ruler should be respected and obeyed because he obtained his office by the will of God.[6]

Not all the Pharisees were quietists. There was a group that shared all the beliefs of the Pharisees with regard to the interpretation of the law and theology, but stressed that Judaea should be ruled by a scion of the Davidic family. They believed that Herod, being neither of the family of David nor a descendant of priests, had no right to the kingship of Judaea. They abhorred his Hellenistic attitude, detested the immorality which prevailed in the palace and deplored its bad effect. They continued their interest in political matters, advocating a real independence of Judaea to free it from the tyranny of Herod and the yoke of the Romans. Ultimately they trusted God to act to free His people by sending the Messiah who would be their future king. They maintained that they had foreknowledge of things to come, including these Messianic events, by divine inspiration. They were the Apocalyptic Pharisees.[7]

Apocalypse, as a literary style, can be traced to the last chapters of the book of Daniel, which were written during the persecutions by Antiochus Epiphanes. The Apocalyptists as a group came into being at the time of Herod. They brought forth the conception of the Messiah as a person endowed with supernatural power who would free the Judaeans from their oppressors.[8] This belief did not come as a development of the historical progress of Judaism, but as a specific reaction against Herod's tyranny, and the subjugation of Judaea to Rome.

Still another offshoot of the Pharisees was beginning to take form in this period. They shared the opposition of the Apocalyptists to Herod and to Rome, but they believed in achieving their aims by force. They held that terror should oppose terror. They emerged as a distinct group a decade after Herod's death, when Judaea became a Roman province.[9]

The impression should not be allowed to remain that all groups opposed or were passive toward Herod. Some Judaeans admired Herod for enlarging the boundaries of Judaea and raising its prestige in the entire Roman world. About sixty years after Herod's death the satirist Persius[10] could write:

But when Herod's birthday comes round, when the lamps wreathed with violet and ranged round the greasy window sills have spat forth their thick clouds of smoke, when the floppy tunnies' tails are curled round the dishes of the red ware, and the white jars are swollen out with wine, you silently twitch your lips, turning pale at the sabbath of the circumcised.

Apparently, despite the many years since Herod's death, some Judaeans still celebrated his birthday, adopting this Roman practice to Jewish needs. These Judaeans were so impressed by Herod's achievements that they strove for the continuation of the Herodian dynasty as rightful kings of Judaea under the protection of Rome. Undoubtedly the pagans who had been settled by Herod as colonists in Judaea also celebrated his birthday. (These were the Herodians mentioned in the Gospels, who asked Jesus, "Is it lawful to give tribute to Caesar or not?"[11]) The Judaeans who dwelt in the Diaspora and remembered in gratitude his intervention before Caesar in their behalf also joined the celebration. It was not celebrated in Judaea. The Judaeans never celebrated birthdays, and did not recall Herod's with joy.

HILLEL'S MIGRATION TO JUDAEA

His Rise to Influence

Herod's ambitions were wholly political. He did not personally head either of the major religious institutions of the country. He qualified even less for them than he did to be king. To be high priest and superior in the Temple he would have had to be of priestly descent. He also could not assume the title of *Nasi*, the head of the *Bet Din haGadol*, as its members had to be learned in the interpretation of the Law and in the traditions of the elders.

Herod's treatment of the high priests has been noted above. He paid far greater deference to the *Bet Din haGadol*. It was a body which had no jurisdiction over civil or political offenders. It tried only those who transgressed religious laws, and it legislated by interpreting the old *halakoth*, laws and biblical commands, and enacting new *halakoth* for all who followed the Judaean way of life throughout the world.[12] True, Herod tortured and killed anyone whom he suspected even if he was a member of the *Bet Din*. He killed many religious leaders. It is understandable that he could not allow leaders of the *Bet Din haGadol* to contemplate subversive acts against him.

Shemayah and Abtalion, who headed the *Bet Din* when Herod became king, continued their positions for a time. He particularly had confidence in Shemayah, who was friendly to him at the time of his war against Antigonus, and he was certain of his loyalty.

Between the years 34 and 32 B.C.E., the Bene Bathayra assumed leadership over the *Bet Din haGadol*, probably by Herod's appointment. They came from Babylonia and had no connection with the Hasmoneans.[13] In the spring of 31, Hillel the Elder, also a Babylonian, became head of the *Bet Din*.[14] Josephus calls him Pollion —the hoary, or venerable.[15] He was the greatest religious figure among the Judaeans since biblical times—perhaps the greatest of the entire rabbinic period which followed him.

Hillel was a man of peace, a lover of mankind, the antithesis of Herod. Humble in his way of life, he always had the interest of his fellow men at heart. He did not regard laws and doctrines as abstractions made for intellectual manipulation. He held that laws were made for men and not men for the laws. He strove to make Judaism a living religion, a treasure house of meaning and an impregnable citadel for refuge. He made the Judaean nation and its religion indivisible; the one cannot exist without the other. He broadened the horizon of Judaean belief and left it open for all who wished to embrace it. He left a great legacy for the Jews and, through his younger contemporary Jesus, who was influenced by his ideals, for Western civilization as well.

Neither the names of Hillel's parents nor the date of his birth are known. The only item recorded is that he had a brother named Shabneh who was a business man.[16] Hillel was a Babylonian who migrated to Judaea when he was a mature man, presumably to find solutions for three contradictions he found in pentateuchal laws. One verse says that unleavened bread is to be eaten for seven days during the Passover festival, and another says six.[17] One verse says that the paschal lamb should be brought from "the flock and the herd" and another says "the sheep and the goats."[18] One verse says of the cleansing of the leper "He is clean," meaning his disease ceases, and another verse says "The priests shall pronounce him clean,"[19] meaning that, though cured, he is not considered ritually clean until the priest so pronounces him. Hillel reconciled these contradictory pentateuchal passages to his own satisfaction as follows: unleavened bread is to be eaten for seven days when one eats unleavened bread made from the old, previous fall's harvest, but only six days when the unleavened bread is made from the new, spring harvest. His reason was that the grain from the new harvest could be eaten after the *Omer,* the new sheaf offering, was brought,[20] an act which took place on the second day of Passover, leaving only six days of the festival (including the second). As to the paschal lamb, the one verse meant that it had to be brought from the flock, and the other, which stated it should be brought from the herd, referred to the *hagiga,* the special festival offering sacrificed on the first day. The leprosy passages he interpreted to mean that both conditions are imperative: a leper must first be cured and then formally pronounced clean by a priest.

Hillel had reconciled the contradictory passages in the Pentateuch by his ingenious intellect, but he could not verify whether his interpretations were in fact Judaean law. In Babylonia, a Diaspora country, the paschal lamb was not sacrificed; and the laws of the new harvest and the laws of leprosy did not apply. When Hillel arrived in Judaea, according to this account, he learned there that his independent interpretations were all correct, well-established *halakoth.*[21]

He became a disciple of Shemayah and Abtalion, especially of the former, who held progressive views. Shemayah had laid down the principle not to seek "aquaintance with the ruling power,"[22] and Hillel faithfully observed this precept. He did not court the special favor of Herod nor did he engage in opposing him. He kept aloof from politics, since he believed that this was the only way religion could flourish and become an integral part of the people's way of living.

Hillel was reputed to be poor. Legend says that once,

on a Friday, when he had no money to pay the entrance
fee to the doorman of the academy where Shemayah and
Abtalion were lecturing, he climbed through an upper
window in order to listen to the sages. There was a
heavy fall of snow during the night and he almost froze
to death.[23] This charming legend fits Hillel well in representing him as accepting no barriers in his search for
knowledge.

Hillel's Hermeneutic Rules

Hillel achieved leadership among the Judaeans in an
interesting way. In the year 31 B.C.E., the fourteenth
of Nisan, when the paschal lamb had to be sacrificed,
fell on the Sabbath.[24] The Bene Bathayra (sons of
Bathayra), who were the heads of the *Bet Din haGadol*,
were from Babylonia, and did not have any precedent
with regard to this situation.

The issue involved more than Sabbath observance. A
critical principle of law was at stake. The Judaeans, like
all other peoples, had two varieties of law—the written
law, inscribed in the Torah, and the unwritten custom,
jus non scriptum. The written law could be interpreted
in order to introduce new laws; the unwritten law was
practiced, but as a custom, without the authority of
statutory law. New laws could not be introduced from
customs, though a number of the Pharisees held that
some customs should be made statutory, that is, have the
authority of written laws, in order that new laws might
be derived from them.

The slaughtering of the paschal lamb on the Sabbath
was a long-established custom among the Judaeans,
which had been practiced as recently as the year 35[25]—
but the Bene Bathayra did not have any tradition on
the subject. They were told that there was a man named
Hillel, who might know whether the paschal lamb could
be slaughtered on the Sabbath. When Hillel was asked,
he thought it an opportune time to make the slaughter
of the paschal lamb on the Sabbath statutory law. He

sought to argue that the law was implied in the Torah text, and to prove his case he employed hermeneutic rules. He reasoned first by the principle of *kal wa-homer*, inference *a minori ad maius*, from the less important application of a principle to its more important application. He argued that if the *tamid*, the daily sacrifice, which does not carry the punishment of *koret* (excision for not sacrificing it), takes precedence over the Sabbath, then the paschal lamb, which is significant enough to carry the punishment of *koret* for not sacrificing it, certainly should take precedence over the Sabbath. Then Hillel sought to prove it by inference based on analogy, both of verbal congruity and of equality of subject (in later tannaitic literature called *gezera shawah*, and *hekesh*). He argued that in the reference to the *tamid*, the daily sacrifice, the term *mo'ado*, "in its appointed time," is used. The same term is used regarding the slaughtering of the paschal lamb.[26] Hillel therefore argued: Since the slaughtering of the *tamid* takes precedence over the Sabbath, so the slaughtering of the paschal lamb, which is analogous as to appointed time, should also take precedence over the Sabbath. He also produced this further analogy: The *tamid*, which is a communal sacrifice, takes precedence over the Sabbath. The paschal lamb is also a communal sacrifice, and hence its slaughtering, too, takes precedence over the Sabbath.[27]

All these hermeneutic principles had been used by Judaeans before Hillel. (The argument *a minori ad maius* is pentateuchal,[28] though the term *kal wa-homer* was introduced by Hillel.) What was novel in Hillel's approach was the application of these principles to actual cases of statutory law, such as the slaughtering of the paschal lamb on the Sabbath.

Hillel's method was too radical for the Bene Bathayra and they rejected it. Only when he said that slaughtering of the paschal lamb on the Sabbath had been taught him as a tradition (an unwritten custom) by his mentors Shemayah and Abtalion was his decision accepted. The

Bene Bathayra then asked how the slaughtering knives were to be carried on the Sabbath, carrying being normally a forbidden act. Hillel replied that he had received the tradition concerning this, but could not remember it. In other words, he could not substantiate the permission for carrying the knives by hermeneutic derivation from the Written Law. However, he said "Leave it to Israel; if they are not prophets they are sons of prophets."[29] In fact, those who brought lambs for sacrifice did not carry the knives, but stuck them in the fleece of the lambs. The ordinary people, without study in the academy, knew the law.

Hillel's appointment as *Nasi* of the *Bet Din* was not opposed by Herod, who remembered his previous good will and surely knew of his rejection of politics and violence. Since the *Bet Din haGadol* was always headed by *zugot*, pairs, a man named Menahem was appointed as *Ab Bet Din*. There is no evidence that he was Menahem the Essene, who had foretold to Herod that he would some day be king.[30] On the other hand, because Menahem did not have a different view of the law, but subscribed to Hillel's interpretation of the *halakah*, he was required before long to give up his position as the *Ab Bet Din*. Before Hillel, one of the *zugot*, who headed the *Bet Din haGadol*, had always been a conservative, the other a liberal.[31] Shammai, who represented the conservative point of view, was appointed *Ab Bet Din* in place of Menahem.

Gradually two schools of thought arose concerning the area of freedom in and the appropriate manner of interpreting the pentateuchal laws and old *halakoth*. One, the House or School of Shammai, the Shammaites, represented the conservative; the other, the House or School of Hillel, the Hillelites, the liberal point of view. While these attitudes crystallized around the sages Shammai and Hillel, they had begun already with the first *zugot*, Jose ben Joezer and Jose ben Johanan;[32] but because Shammai and Hillel formulated and sharpened the principles on which these viewpoints took their diverging stand, the schools became known by their names, and almost every sage until the time of Jabneh classified himself as either a Shammaite or a Hillelite.[33] As these schools continued, questions and controversies multiplied and extended. New sages arose who could not agree with either school on certain points, although they continued to call themselves Shammaites or Hillelites. The emergence of a similar situation may be found in the Sabinian and Proculian schools of thought in the Roman jurisprudence of this period.[34]

It would be historically incorrect to lay down definite principles on the differences in the controversies between the Shammaites and the Hillelites. However, from what is known of the personal characters of Shammai and Hillel, it can be surmised that Shammai followed the established *halakoth,* while Hillel was the innovator disposed to introduce new *halakoth* so as to make the *halakah* consonant with life. He was a revolutionary in shaping Judaean law.

His basic principle was that new *halakoth* could be deduced from the Pentateuch by the device of hermeneutic rules, and that some of the unwritten laws could be made statutory thereby. At first Hillel faced great opposition, but later his hermeneutic principles became legally accepted, though with some limitations, and his three basic authoritative modes of interpretation were increased to thirteen.[35]

The Principle of Intention

Hillel introduced another new concept into the *halakah*—the principle of intention—which aroused the ire of Shammai. Hillel made a legal distinction between happenings which stem from volition and those which do not. For Hillel, the law may call an act only that which follows volition, while involuntary actions are to be designated as mere events or incidents. To illustrate: If a person falls from a bridge into the water, it is legally an incident, since there was no volition. However, if one jumps from the bridge into the water, it is legally an act since it followed upon volition. The question may then properly be asked, what prompted the person to do this act? Was it his intention to swim or to commit suicide by drowning? The consequence of the act—in this case, jumping—must be judged by the person's intention. Thus intention is a critical category with regard to the consequence of the act rather than to the act itself. To illustrate further: If a stone falls from a person's hand and in consequence some object is broken, it is legally an incident; but if he threw the stone, it is legally an act, since there was volition. If by throwing the stone an object was broken, the breaking was the consequence of the throwing and the question may now properly be asked, did the man have the intention of breaking the object? Suppose the person who threw the stone had the intention of breaking the object but, just as he threw it, someone passed by and was hit and killed by the stone; the man who threw the stone had no intention of injuring or killing this person. The injury or death of the victim was unpremeditated and therefore the person who threw the stone was not guilty of manslaughter. This new approach affected all branches of the *halakah:* ritual, civil and capital. It is understandable that Shammai strenuously opposed it.[36]

Four controversies are recorded between Shammai and Hillel.[37] In all tannaitic controversies recorded in the Talmud, the name of the person who adhered to the conservative point of view is given first.[38] Shammai's name, however, is given first in three of the disputes, while in the controversy on *Semikah*, that is, the transmittal of authority to introduce new laws, Hillel's name is given first.[39] This is due to the fact that this principle had already been accepted. Shemayah and Abtalion had already debated this issue, and the name of Shemayah, who adhered to this principle, was recorded first.

One controversy between Shammai and Hillel involving intention centered about the ritual purity of grapes gathered for pressing. According to pentateuchal law an object to be susceptible to levitical uncleanness must first have been immersed in a liquid.[40] Shammai maintained that if juice ran from grapes, the grapes were susceptible to levitical uncleanness, since this was the equivalent of immersion. Hillel rejected this thesis, since the owner had no intention of immersing the grapes but only of producing wine. This controversy over the grapes was a case designed to bring out the legal concept of intention, when the issue was put to a vote before the *Bet Din haGadol.* At that time Hillel's view was rejected. The Talmud states that it was a dark day for Israel. Although he was a superior officer in the *Bet Din,* Hillel sat before Shammai with bowed head, as if he were his pupil.[41]

Another debate revolved about the permissibility of eating an egg laid on a festival day. According to pentateuchal law, food may be eaten on a festival day if it has been prepared on the eve of the holiday.[42] The Shammaites held that, since the egg had been prepared before, by nature, it was permissible to eat it. The Hillelites, stressing intention, maintained that such preparation was without intention and the egg is forbidden on the holiday.[43] This debate actually took place— it summarized the arguments between the two schools on the subject of intention. Generally in the controversies between the Shammaites and the Hillelites, when the principle of intention was involved, the Shammaites were lenient and the Hillelites were strict. In other cases the reverse was true.[44]

Although the Shammaites strenuously opposed Hillel's introduction of the principle of intention, it eventually became an established part of Judaean law. To illustrate: A man could marry a woman by giving her money (later, a ring);[45] but giving money to a woman did not make her his wife. To make a marriage binding required an act with intention, giving her the money with the intention of marrying her as indicated by open declaration.[46] Hence, marriages of minors and lunatics are invalid since they cannot truly exercise intention.[47]

The Controversy on Semikah

Hillel became personally involved in another case. On holidays there were no sacrifices by private individuals, that is, no guilt-offerings or sin-offerings. The only sacrifices permitted were communal ones prescribed in the Pentateuch. However, any Judaean who made a pilgrimage on a holiday might bring a peace-offering and was required to bring a burnt-offering. According to the Pentateuch, the person who brought an offering had to lay his hands on the animal victim,[48] the reason being that by laying his hands on the sacrifice he transferred his iniquities to the victim and thereby the sacrifice became an atonement for his sins.[49] The Shammaites held that one could bring a peace-offering on a holiday, but should not lay his hands on it, and that no burnt-offering might be brought on a holiday. The Hillelites maintained that a person may bring both a peace-offering and a burnt-offering and lay his hands upon the sacrifices. Thus, according to the Shammaites, the bringing of a peace-offering was optional, but the laying of hands upon the sacrifice was forbidden. The Hillelites, aware of the psychology of the people, realized that, if people were not allowed to lay their hands on the sacrifices, they would not bring them and would not make pilgrimages. They believed that the laying of the hands on the sacrifice was a symbolic gesture that went back to great antiquity and could not be eradicated from the minds of the people. They therefore took a positive view so as to encourage pilgrimages, and make the Temple the religious center of the Judaeans throughout the world. The contention of the Hillelites that the Shammaite view would deter pilgrimages was proved correct: the Temple became deserted on the holidays. The view of the Hillelites then became the law.[50]

CONTRASTS IN LEADERSHIP

While generalizations are extremely difficult, it may be said that Shammai, as a conservative, tended to be rigid, holding that the law must take its course, making little allowance for human weakness. Hillel, by contrast, tended to be lenient in interpretations of the law and considerate of human feelings.

The difference in the characters of Shammai and Hillel is illustrated by several anecdotes concerning them. The most oft-told of these anecdotes concerns a heathen who came to Shammai and asked to be converted, but requested that he be instructed in the entire Torah while standing on one foot. Shammai ordered him away. The man then went to Hillel with the same request. Hillel welcomed him and said, "What is hateful to you do not do to your fellowman. This is the entire Torah and the rest is commentary; go and study."[51] Hillel did not refer to the love of God. When a heathen comes to be converted to Judaism, he has already given up his gods. This man would not have approached Hillel if he had not acknowledged the God of Israel as the one and only God of the universe. Nor was it necessary for Hillel to tell him to love his fellowman: one who confesses the universality of God must of necessity recognize the equality between man and man and therefore respect the interests of his fellowmen. This is the second great principle on which Judaism is based and implies that one should not harm his fellowman by robbing, murdering or otherwise doing him any injury. Later the rabbis put it succinctly by saying there were two kinds of precepts—those between man and God and those between man and man.

Hillel's statement to the convert was negative, "What is hateful to you do not to your fellowman."[52] The Pentateuch states that a person should love his neighbor.[53] Jesus, in the Sermon on the Mount, urged, "Love your enemies."[54] His admonition is ethical utopianism.

A person was not only forbidden to seek revenge for an injury done to him; he was asked even to restrain himself from bearing hatred towards his enemy. True, he may forgive, tolerate one who had injured him or a member of his family; but how can one expect a person to love an enemy who has harmed him or killed a member of his family? This is humanly impossible. The pentateuchal precept to love your neighbor as yourself is also unrealistic. It is not in the nature of a human being to love another as he does himself. Hillel, a realist who knew human nature, said that a person should not injure his fellowman, since he himself did not want to be injured by anyone else. Human beings can be educated up to this principle.[55] Hillel did not originate his Golden Rule: many sages among different peoples preached this; but Hillel emphasized it as a Judaean gospel.

Other talmudic tales stress Shammai's impatience and irritability as against Hillel's tolerance and meekness.[56] These stories are evidently from a later period, but they clearly reveal the reverence preceeding generations felt for Hillel.

Hillel's Enactments

Hillel apparently survived Shammai and became the sole leader of the *Bet Din haGadol*. During this period he promulgated two *takkanot*, executive enactments.[57] One of these is the *Prosbol*, from the Greek *pros boulé*, meaning "before the court." According to the Pentateuch, every seventh year "Every creditor shall release that which he has lent unto his neighbor; he shall not exact it of his neighbor and of his brother because God's release has been proclaimed."[58] This law hampered commercial transactions, as a creditor always feared that a debtor might not pay his debt before the sabbatical year. Fearing to lose the money they had lent, people did not want to make loans as the sabbatical year approached. To ameliorate the economic condition of the country, the sages prior to Hillel had interpreted the law of the

Pentateuch so that a creditor might deposit his promissory note with the local *Bet Din* and thereby maintain the right to collect his debt regardless of the sabbatical year. The sages reasoned as follows: when the creditor deposited the promissory note with the *Bet Din*, it assumed the responsibility for the repayment of the loan, and thus the money was as good as collected, and the sabbatical year was of no effect.[59]

This enactment was effective only if the debtor gave the creditor a promissory note, but not if the creditor merely made the loan in the presence of witnesses or trusted the borrower's word. Such a loan, unsecured by a note, was still subject to sabbatical cancellation. To encourage loans to the needy, Hillel extended the enactment of the sages. Hillel permitted a creditor, with no note from the debtor, himself to write a declaration stating "I declare before you, the judges in this place, that I shall collect the debt that I have outstanding with so and so whenever I so desire."[60] The creditor deposited this substitute note with the *Bet Din*. The document was therefore called *Prosbol*, the one presented before the court. The *Prosbol* had to be written and deposited in the court before the beginning of the sabbatical year, though there was an opinion that it was still valid if deposited before the end of the sabbatical year.[61]

Another *takkanah* has to do with real estate. During the Herodian period many Judaeans in Jerusalem were compelled to sell their houses because of economic pressures. The seller, however, according to pentateuchal law, retained for one year the option of repurchase at the sale price.[62] The law in the Pentateuch actually refers to Jubilee Years, and these were not observed during the Second Commonwealth.[63] The law of repurchase was a response to economic necessity and justified by this pentateuchal source. However, the buyer of a house, apprehensive that the seller might avail himself of the privilege of redemption, would absent himself in order to retain possession. To avoid such schemes, Hillel decreed that if the buyer is absent at the end of the first year, the seller may, if he wishes, deposit the purchase money paid him with the *Bet Din* and thus reclaim his house.[64] This enactment is based on the same principle as the *Prosbol*.

These *takkanot* illustrate Hillel's continuing efforts to make the law pliable so that it might improve and sanctify life. Thus, too, he did not hesitate to give legal status to documents written in the vernacular Aramaic, rather than in the official Hebrew, if this served a genuine human need.[65] During the Second Commonwealth, for example, a man could wed by sending a marriage contract to a woman through an agent or by proxy. Alexandrian Judaeans, who lived in Jerusalem, contracted such marriages. The Talmud records a case where the sages wanted to declare illegitimate the offspring of some men who had married women who had previously been wedded to Alexandrians by proxy via a marriage contract. Hillel requested these women to produce their original marriage contracts. There it was written, "When you will enter my house you will become my wife according to the laws of Moses and the Judaeans." Hillel ruled that, since they had not gone to the homes of these spouses, the marriages had never been legally concluded. Thus the offspring of the later marriage was legitimate.[66] Even in so important a matter as family purity Hillel would not be pedantic about legal form as long as legal principles were preserved.

Many aphorisms and sayings have been attributed to Hillel, but it is difficult to know which are authentic. Some are recorded in Hebrew, others in Aramaic. He used to say, "If I am not for myself who is for me? And being for my own self what am I? And if not now, when?"[67] "A name made great is a name destroyed . . . Who does not increase, decreases (i.e., his knowledge) . . . He who does not learn is worthy of death, and he who makes worldly use of the crown (of the Torah) shall perish."[68] It is recorded that, during the celebration of *Bet haShoebah*, Hillel used to say, "If I am here, everyone is here, and if I am not here, who is here?"[69]

He thus wanted to emphasize that man is a part of society and should never separate himself from it. He should consider himself one of his people and participate in their celebrations. He also used to say, "Do not withdraw from the assembly . . . Put no trust in yourself until the day of your death . . . Do not judge your fellowman until you have stood in his place."[70] It is said that once he saw a skull floating on the water and he remarked, "Because you caused someone to drown, you were drowned; and they who drowned you shall in turn be drowned."[71] His trust in retribution was complete.

Few aphorisms by Shammai have been transmitted. He is reported to have said "Make the Torah a fixed habit (i.e., study regularly). Say little and do much, and receive all men with a cheerful countenance."[72]

The Pentateuch states, "Remember the Sabbath and sanctify it."[73] Shammai followed this verse literally, always remembering the Sabbath. When he purchased a fine calf or fowl, or was presented with one, he immediately set it aside for the Sabbath. If later in the week he obtained a better one, he kept that for the Sabbath. Hillel followed the spirit of the Scriptures. He used to say that God should be blessed for all his benefits daily.[74] And so, rather than plan all week, he was confident that God would provide the best when the Sabbath came. Both were great teachers and jurists, but one was a great spirit as well.

After the collapse of the Hasmonean dynasty two persons dominated the life of the Judaeans: Herod and Hillel. Herod was vindictive and full of hate. He killed for the sake of killing and tortured people in order to extort information he desired. He was cognizant of the fact that, not only the existence of Judaea depended on the whim of the Emperor, but also his own kingship and his very life. He strove by his obedience to show his devotion to Caesar and to Rome. He vied with other client-kings in the erection of statues, temples and cities in honor of Augustus Caesar. He built fortresses and cities to perpetuate his name for posterity. He ruled over the Judaeans like a conqueror. Consequently, after Judaea ceased to be an independent state, nothing survived to commemorate his glory. It has been left only to archaeologists to discover the monuments which he erected. It is the irony of history that the city built by him in honor of Augustus Caesar, and which later became the symbol of Roman tyranny over the Judaeans, and was by them declared *hutz la'aretz* ("outside the Land of Israel"), is now a show place in the Third Commonwealth of Israel.

Hillel was the very opposite. He was a man of love who pursued love. He was fully aware that the eagle of Rome with its sharp claws would some day tear Judaea apart. He, too, built fortresses—not of stone and iron, but of the spirit—not to segregate the Judaeans from other peoples out of hatred, but for spiritual defense. He strove to make religion supreme and thus ward off the impending annihilation of the Jewish people. He knew that religion has no geographic boundaries, and so he sought to unite all those who adhered to the religion of Judaism and to the God of Israel. His lasting success is the continued existence of the Jewish people and its religious way of life; his monuments are to be found in every corner of the globe.

In the Talmud, Hillel is appropriately compared with Ezra,[75] who came from Babylonia and made the Torah the foundation of Judaean life. Hillel also came from Babylonia, and by his innovations and revolutions in Jewish law he made it the lasting constitution of the Jewish people wherever they might live.

PART TWO

Judaea as a Province of Rome

1. HEROD'S SUCCESSORS

THE INAUSPICIOUS BEGINNING
OF ARCHELAUS' RULE

The Popular Demands

Herod had ruled over Judaea with an iron hand for more than three decades. His death was bound to give rise to an outburst of indignation over the sufferings borne by the people, and a move to break the chains which had shackled them.

After *shivah*, the seven days of mourning, had passed, Archelaus furnished a funeral repast for the people, as was the custom in Judaea. He dressed himself in white and went up to the Temple, where the people received him with acclaim.[1] A platform had been erected upon which was placed a throne of gold. From this height, Archelaus acknowledged the greetings of the people and expressed gratitude that they bore him no ill will for the injuries which his father had inflicted upon them. He said he would refrain from taking the title of king until Augustus Caesar would confirm the will made by his father. He gave this as his reason for declining, while still in Jericho, to have the diadem placed upon his head, even though the army had been eager to do so. He thanked the people, saying he would reward them for their good will and make every effort to be kinder to them than his father had been. After offering a sacrifice, he departed and indulged in festivities with his friends.[2]

The people, hearing Archelaus belittle his father and admit that Herod had inflicted intolerable injuries upon them, became hopeful that Archelaus' rule would be mild. They sensed, too, that there was a strong conflict among the members of Herod's family as to who should rule and which of Herod's wills should be considered valid. Knowing that Archelaus had still to be confirmed by Augustus Caesar, they felt this to be an opportune time to make certain requests of him. They asked Archelaus to lighten their taxes, and to abolish the sales and purchase tax which was an especially heavy burden. They further requested that amnesty be granted to those prisoners who had been in chains for a long time.[3] He did not oppose these requests, as he was eager that tranquility should prevail. He felt that the good will of the people would greatly help him secure Augustus Caesar's confirmation.

With Passover approaching, many people came to Jerusalem from all over the country and also from foreign lands. Among them were devotees of the two sophists who were responsible for the tearing down of the golden eagle from the gate of the Temple and who had been burned alive by Herod and had had no funeral. Encouraged by Archelaus' mild words, the people organized a funeral march for these two martyrs, in accordance with the Judaean custom.[4]

The march of mourning was accompanied by piercing cries and funereal lamentations directed by a leader, and there were dirges and beating of the breast. These demonstrations incited the people to demand that the burning of the sophists be avenged, that the perpetrators be severely punished. They also called for the removal of the high priest Joazar son of Boethus, Herod's brother-in-law, the brother of Mariamme II, maintaining that the election of a high priest was a prerogative of the people.[5]

Archelaus could not grant these requests because of

their political implications. To punish those responsible for the burning of the sophists would antagonize Rome, whose symbol had been desecrated. To grant the people the right to select the high priest would be to surrender his hold on the Temple. Since he himself could not be the high priest, it was imperative for him to have the authority to put a man in that office whose loyalty to him was unquestionable. Archelaus therefore sent his lieutenant to the people to persuade them to cease from their demands. The lieutenant told them that the death inflicted on the sophists was in accordance with the law and that their entreaties were insolent. Furthermore, he said that this was not the time for petitions, but that they should wait until Archelaus returned from Rome as the acknowledged king.[6] At this the people became indignant and did not allow the lieutenant to continue his speech, demanding vengeance for the burning of their revered teachers. Since there was a large crowd at the Temple, Archelaus became apprehensive over the possibility of a grave disturbance and dispatched a cohort to the Temple to seize the leaders of the demonstration. This aroused the fury of the people who resisted the soldiers, throwing stones and killing some of them. To avoid the possibility of the riot becoming a revolt, Archelaus sent an army, the infantry penetrating the Temple area and the cavalry encamping outside the walls. The people were unprepared for such an attack and three thousand of them were slaughtered. Archelaus ordered all who had come to Jerusalem to leave the city and return to their homes.[7]

The savage slaughter struck the Judaeans like a thunder bolt and left the country dazed and uncomprehending. Only a few days before Archelaus had promised kindliness and understanding, and had spoken slightingly of Herod. Now he exceeded his father in brutality.

The Quarrel over Herod's Will

Archelaus was in a hurry to go to Rome and secure from Caesar the confirmation of his father's will. He took with him Nicolas of Damascus; Ptolemy, Minister of Finance to Herod, who held the seal; Ptollas;[8] Archelaus' mother Malthace; and Salome, his aunt, with her family. Archelaus left the management of the country to his half-brother Philip.[9]

Stopping in Caesarea, Archelaus met Sabinus, the procurator of Syria, who intended to go to Jerusalem to take charge of Herod's property and prepare an inventory of everything valuable in the country. Archelaus disputed the right of Sabinus to do so. Through the intervention of Ptolemy, P. Quinctilius Varus, the legate of Syria, came from Antioch in behalf of Archelaus and prevented Sabinus from carrying out his plan. However, after Archelaus sailed for Rome and Varus returned to Antioch, Sabinus nonetheless went to Jerusalem and took possession of the palace. He bade the commanders of the fortresses surrender the treasuries to him. They refused, claiming to be the guardians of the treasuries for Caesar and maintaining that they could not comply with his demands unless authorized by Caesar. Sabinus was thus momentarily frustrated.[10]

When Archelaus sailed for Rome, his brother Antipas also went there to claim the throne. He took with him Ptolemy, brother of Nicolas of Damascus, and Irenaeus, reputed to be a great orator and a brilliant advocate. Herod, in his third will, had designated Antipas as sole ruler of Judaea. Antipas declared that this will should be validated, while the fourth, naming Archelaus, was of no legal effect.[11] The family of Herod sided with Antipas against Archelaus. Malthace, their mother, apparently supported Antipas' claim against that of Archelaus, the older son. Salome played a double game. She secretly supported Antipas, but her intention was to foment discord between the two brothers in order to obtain a greater share in the division of Judaea. In the meantime Sabinus, who bore Archelaus a grudge for the rebuff in Caesarea, brought charges against him in a letter to Caesar.[12]

In Rome, the Emperor Augustus Caesar, after receiving Herod's will from Archelaus, the seal and the financial accounts of Judaea from Ptolemy, and the counterclaim from Antipas, together with reports from Sabinus and Varus, vacillated as to the decision he should make. He summoned a *synedrion* before whom the claims and counterclaims for the kingship over Judaea were to be argued.[13] Seated next to him was Gaius, his grandson by Julia and Agrippa, whom he had adopted as his son and intended to be his heir.[14]

The first to speak was Antipater, the son of Salome and Costobarus, who was considered the most eloquent speaker of the family. He argued that the last will of Herod, naming Archelaus as king, was drawn up a few days before Herod's death, when he was physically ill and not of sound mind. Therefore the third will, naming Antipas as his successor, should be declared valid. He further charged that Archelaus was unfit for the high office of king, that he had acted against the will of his father by releasing the nobles from the hippodrome where Herod had incarcerated them, and by liberating others whom his father had imprisoned for grave crimes. He accused Archelaus of being of villainous character, responsible for the slaughter of thousands in the Temple, not only natives but pilgrims from other countries as well. He indicted Archelaus for slighting the memory of his father, and called him hypocrite for mourning his father by day while at night he indulged in revelry, even on the night of Herod's death. He ridiculed Archelaus for coming to beg Caesar for confirmation of kingship when, in fact, he had already assumed the role of king, sitting on a golden throne, making changes among the officers of the army, and deciding lawsuits. When he finished speaking, Antipater produced many relatives as witnesses to support his charge that Archelaus was unfit for the office of king of Judaea.[15]

Nicolas of Damascus then rose in defense of Archelaus. To the charge that Archelaus had released the prisoners from the hippodrome, he retorted that the accusers of Archelaus had been in council with him over this matter.[16] The killing of the people in the Temple, Nicolas stated, was justified for they were not only rebels against Archelaus but also against Caesar. They had shown contempt for God and for the law of the festival. Nicolas ridiculed the assertion that the last will was made by Herod when he was of unsound mind. In it the decision was left to Augustus Caesar: Nicolas emphasized that Herod's reliance upon Caesar in his last will was proof that he had been in full control of his faculties.[17] The critical reader of this account cannot help but conclude that the last will was indeed drawn up when Herod was not of sound mind; and that it was composed by Nicolas and Ptolemy, friends of Archelaus.

Caesar dismissed the *synedrion*. He was well disposed towards Archelaus, but could not decide whether to appoint him king over the entire kingdom of Herod or to divide it in accordance with the last will.[18]

Before Caesar could reach a decision, Malthace, the mother of the contenders, died.[19] Also dispatches came from Varus about disturbances in Judaea. At the same time, a delegation of fifty men arrived from Judaea, to ask Caesar to abolish the kingdom of Judaea and join it to Syria, thus making Judaea a province of Rome. This plea was echoed by more than eight thousand Judaeans who lived in Rome.[20]

Caesar called another *synedrion* to hear the arguments of the delegation and their Roman brothers. Archelaus and his relatives were also present, including Philip who had come from Judaea to participate in these events.[21]

The Judaeans began by denouncing Herod as a ruthless tyrant who had killed many people in his cruelty. His rule had been worse by far than any the Judaeans had experienced since their return from Babylonia. He had adorned cities in foreign countries, while ruining the cities of Judaea by imposing burdensome taxation and extracting extra contributions from the people. He had conscripted many people in order to confiscate their property and had debauched their wives and their daughters. Instead of ruling for their welfare and in the observance of their ancestral laws, he had sunk the nation into poverty and consigned it to the last degree of iniquity. Now that Herod was dead, they had welcomed Archelaus in the hope that he would be a more moderate ruler. But Archelaus, the true son of his father, had killed three thousand of his own fellow Judaeans in the Temple precinct. The group appealed to Caesar to abolish the kingdom of Judaea and make it a part of the province of Syria.[22]

A familiar Sadducean note is echoed in this argument. There had always been a class in Judaea which believed that the country should be a theocracy ruled by a high priest, though politically subservient to a foreign power. Thus a group with a similar request had come before Pompey during the contest for the throne between Hyrcanus and Aristobolus.[23] The spiritual mover of this anti-Herodian delegation was undoubtedly Joazar son of Boethus. As high priest, he had the most to gain from reviving the old Zadokite ideology to abolish the monarchy in favor of a theocracy. The delegation also went to Rome with the blessing of Varus.[24] If the monarchy should be abolished, Judaea would come under his rule and he could enrich himself the more. One Roman historian wrote of him, "He entered the rich province (Syria) a poor man, but left it a rich man and the province poor."[25] He was insatiably greedy and ruthless in the exploitation of his domain.

The motives of the Judaeans of Rome who joined in this petition were more complex. (That over eight thousand were involved shows that there must have been a large Judaean community in Rome.) Many of them had been born in Rome, reared there, and had acquired Roman citizenship. They had their own Judaean institutions, particularly their houses of prayer and synagogues where they assembled for their communal interests.[26] They were surely aware that Augustus Caesar was in sympathy with Archelaus and that a plea for theocracy would incur Caesar's displeasure. Why should they then have intervened in the internal affairs of Judaea? The reason may be found in the constant tension between the West and the East, between the Romans and the Parthians. Only a few years later, in the year 1 B.C.E., there was an exchange of insulting letters between Phrataces, King of Parthia, and Augustus Caesar that nearly led to war.[27] Judaeans of Rome were apprehensive that, if a king were installed in Judaea, and should war break out between the two empires, a king of Judaea might well join the Parthians, as had Antigonus, and thus place them in great jeopardy. They might then be accused of sympathizing with or even of aiding their coreligionists, the Judaeans. Even without war, they were fearful that, if there were any disturbances in Judaea against Rome, they would be accused of dual allegiance. However, if Judaea were ceded to Syria and became a province of Rome, there could be no question of alliance with the enemy or of dual allegiance. Moreover, if Judaea were no longer independent, their sending of money and gifts to the Temple would be facilitated. In fact, they would then be united with Judaea politically as well as religiously.

When the theocrats concluded their argument, Nicolas of Damascus rose and taunted them with insincerity. He asked why they had not complained during Herod's lifetime, if Herod had been as cruel as just depicted.[28] Nicolas also accused them of being revolutionaries. After Nicolas finished his speech, Augustus Caesar dismissed the *synedrion*. He took the arguments under consideration and again postponed his decision for a while.[29]

Riots in Jerusalem

Augustus Caesar was influenced in his deliberations by news which came to Rome of outbreaks of violence in Judaea, amounting almost to full-scale revolution. Political authority had collapsed after the death of Herod, par-

ticularly as all the native leaders were in Rome vying
to be appointed king. New rulers appeared to fill the
vacuum, the Romans Sabinus and Varus, the procurator
and the legate of Syria. They ruled Judaea as though it
were already a province of Rome. The Judaeans were be-
wildered and embittered over the sudden change in
affairs. True, they had suffered under Herod, but they
had still felt Judaea belonged to them. The Roman take-
over, added to the distress remaining after three decades
of Herod's tyranny, made peaceful transition impossible.
Varus, who was at that time in Jerusalem, suppressed
the disturbances with vigor. Upon his departure for
Antioch, he left one legion to quell any uprising. Sabinus,
who remained in Jerusalem to govern, was fully responsible for the further bloodshed which occurred. He
tried to capture various fortresses and find the royal
treasuries. He took over the legion left by Varus and
armed his own slaves, using them to terrorize the Judaeans and to seize whatever they could get hold of. The
situation became grave.[30]

The Festival of Pentecost brought many Judaeans to
Jerusalem from all over the country; from Galilee, from
the South, from Idumaea, as well as from Trans-Jordan.
The people were determined to wrest authority from
Sabinus and punish him for his terroristic and murderous acts. The Judaeans formed three camps. One group
took possession of the hippodrome; another located itself
on the north quarter of the Temple facing south; the
third held the western part where the palace stood. Thus
they besieged the Romans from all sides.[31]

Sabinus was terrified at the numbers arrayed against
him and their apparent willingness to die for their cause.
He dispatched messenger after messenger to Varus
begging him for prompt support lest the entire legion
left in Jerusalem be annihilated. He himself mounted
the highest tower of the fortress, named Phasael (after
Herod's brother who had been slain by the Parthians),
and ordered the soldiers to attack the Judaeans. (Josephus comments wryly that Sabinus thought it perfectly

proper for others to die to satisfy his greed.) [32] A fierce
battle began. The Romans were well organized and
seasoned warriors. The Judaeans lacked discipline, but
they had the courage to fight for their cause. To attack
the Romans on more equal terms many of the Judaeans
mounted the porticoes which surrounded the outer court
of the Temple Mount. From there they threw stones and
missiles. The Romans suffered casualties, but were unable to stem the assault because the Judaeans were on
top of the colonnades. Then, unnoticed by the Judaeans,
the Romans set fire to the entire structure. The colonnades went up in a blaze; the gold decoration which had
been applied with wax added to the fury of the flames.
The Judaeans were trapped; most of those on the porticoes perished in the fire. Others who leapt to the courtyard, unarmed, were slain. None escaped. The Romans
now had a free hand and robbed the Temple treasury,
Sabinus taking four hundred talents for himself. [33]

The Roman victory in the Temple area did not crush
the spirit of the Judaeans. On the contrary, they became
more furious over the deaths of their friends and relatives, and the sacrilegious acts committed in the Temple.
They quickly besieged the palace where Sabinus resided
and threatened to set it on fire and kill all within. They
granted Sabinus permission to leave the palace with his
men and guaranteed him safe conduct if he would leave
Jerusalem. [34] Sabinus would have liked to do so, but he
mistrusted the Judaeans; he therefore delayed and sent
further requests to Varus for aid. A great number of
the royal troops had deserted and joined the Judaeans,
but two of Herod's generals, Rufus and Gratus, with
three thousand men, mostly from Sebaste, and with archers from Trachonitis, went over to Sabinus. Rufus
commanded the cavalry and Gratus the royal infantry.
The Judaeans laid seige to the palace and appealed to
the royal army not to interfere with them since they
now had the opportunity to recover their national
liberty. [35]

By this time government, order and discipline had

completely broken down and desertions from the army were a daily occurrence. Combat between Romans and Judaeans was continual. There were disorders throughout the country. Some of the leaders were sincere patriots and hoped that by organizing revolts they might regain their liberty. Others were self-seeking opportunists, who wanted to utilize the situation for their own benefit. Two thousand of Herod's troops, who had disbanded, now reorganized and plundered the country. Achiab, Herod's cousin, with a legion of the army, tried to suppress them, but was defeated and forced to take refuge in the hills.[36]

Judas son of Ezekias—Ezekias had been put to death by Herod when he was governor of Galilee at the time of Hyrcanus II[37]—assembled a force, seized the royal fortress in Sepphoris and confiscated for his cause the arms and money he found there. Josephus writes of him: "He became an object of terror to all men by plundering those he came across, in his desire for great possessions and his ambition for royal rank, a prize that he expected to obtain, not through his practice of virtue, but through excessive ill-treatment of others."[38] Josephus' description of Judas of Galilee is incorrect. He was by profession a sophist, a teacher. He and his followers were an offshoot of the Pharisees. Because Josephus had no particular party name to give the doctrines of Judas, he called them the "Fourth Philosophy"; popularly they were known as the Sicarii.[39] Judas and his followers were devoted to the achievement of national liberty. In the the eyes of the Romans, any Judaeans who fought for the independence of their country from Rome were brigands. Josephus echoes the Roman attitude towards Judas.

The plundering and ravaging of the country by different pretenders spread. The growing social chaos was due to two main factors. There was no central government or supreme authority in the country whatsoever. Moreover, the troops under Gratus, who had been called to suppress the uprisings, consisted of pagans from the regions of Sebaste and Trachonitis. They themselves by their arrogance, their anti-Judaean feelings and their greed, were a cause of provocation. So embittered were the people of Judaea that almost anyone who was ready to lead the fight against the royal army and the Romans found himself with willing recruits. A man named Simon, a former slave of Herod, encouraged by the prevailing chaos, declared himself king. He set fire to Herod's palace in Jericho and seized the arms in it. Gratus engaged him in battle and defeated him; Simon was killed. His surviving followers burned the palace of Betharamatha, near the Jordan.[40]

A humble shepherd named Athronges, who also had the ambition to become king, together with his three brothers organized a formidable army. Their aim was to wreak vengeance on the royal army and the Romans; but they never molested a Judaean. Once, near Emmaus they ambushed an entire Roman company which was carrying grain and ammunition. Forty men of the company were killed; the rest were saved by Gratus who succeeded in defeating Athronges. Two of Athronges' brothers were killed; however, his followers were still at large for some time and continued to harass the enemy.[41]

Varus, after assembling his forces, finally moved towards Judaea. He led two legions and four regiments of cavalry, and auxiliary troops which were supplied by various client kings. The city of Berytus supplied fifteen hundred men, and Aretas, King of Nabataea, who hated Herod and the Judaeans, sent a large army of infantry and cavalry. They assembled at Ptolemais and divided into three groups. Part of the army was assigned to Varus' son and another part to his friend Gaius. The rest remained with Varus. One force promptly attacked the Galileans who inhabited the region adjoining Ptolemais. Another force attacked Sepphoris, captured and burned the city and reduced the inhabitants to slavery. Varus with the main army marched towards Sebaste. He spared the city, since it had not taken part

in the disturbances. Varus and his army encamped in
a village called Arous[42] which had belonged to Ptolemy,
Herod's minister of finance. Arous had been burned
by the Nabataeans because of their deep animosity toward Herod. They also burned another village named
Sampho.[43] They pillaged and slaughtered wherever they
went, so that Varus found himself constrained to send
them back to their own country. In his advance towards
Judaea, he burned Emmaus as punishment for the killing
of forty men of the Roman army.[44]

The war which seemed imminent was never fought.
As Varus approached the outskirts of Judaea, many
Judaeans came out to meet him and beseech his good
will. They stated that it was the crowd that had come
to the festival who were guilty of the disturbances and
that they had had no part in them. Among the petitioners
were Joseph, cousin of Herod, and the two generals
Gratus and Rufus at the head of their troops. The
Romans who had been under siege in Jerusalem utilized
this opportunity to come to Varus. Sabinus, the center
of the disturbances, secretly left the city and was heard
of no more.[45]

Varus with his army subdued such resistance as was
left in the country. There were still ten thousand men
from Idumaea under arms; however, on the advice of
Achiab, cousin of Herod, they surrendered without fight-
ing. Varus pardoned them, but sent their leaders to
Caesar for punishment. Varus, however, crucified two
thousand Judaeans for their part in the uprisings.[46]
Crucifixion was a most cruel and hideous form of torture.
From the days of the Punic Wars, the Romans had re-
sorted to it as punishment for slaves and rebels.[47] Yet
Judaea, according to Roman law, was still an independent
state and Rome was deeply concerned that the Middle
East should be tranquil, since she feared the Parthians.
Varus' monstrous act can only be explained in terms of
his personal character. He regarded all who were not
Romans as no better than slaves, an attitude he later

manifested to the great distress of Rome when he became consul in Germany.[48]

Augustus' Disposition of Herod's Kingdom

Early in the summer of 4 B.C.E., Augustus rendered his decision concerning Judaea. He appointed Archelaus ethnarch of Judaea, Idumaea and Samaria. He also gave him Caesarea, Sebaste and Jaffa, with the promise of making him king should he prove worthy. Antipas received as his province Galilee and Peraea, which had no common borders. Philip was to rule over Batanaea, Trachonitis, Auranitis and the old domain of Zenodorus. The cities of Gaza, Gadara and Hippus were detached from the domain of Archelaus and annexed to Syria. Salome received what Herod had willed her; namely, the cities of Jabneh, Azotus (Ashdod) and Phasaelis; besides this, Caesar presented to her the royal palace in Ascalon as a gift. To Roxane and Salome, the unmarried daughters of Herod, Caesar gave a dowry in addition to what their father had left them and married them off to the sons of Pheroras, their uncle. Caesar declined to accept the large legacy left him in Herod's will. He distributed it among Herod's relatives who had not been given bequests in the will. He himself took only some works of art as mementoes of his friendship with Herod.[49]

On the whole, therefore, Herod's will was followed, but with several changes. Archelaus was not to bear the title of king, but of ethnarch. However, Augustus had not acceded to the request that Judaea become a part of Syria. His reasons for this were numerous. He wanted to carry out the provisions of the will of his friend Herod if he could. He was also influenced by Nicolas of Damascus whom he had known for a long time, and who was now writing his biography.[50] Caesar, however, detached a few cities populated by Hellenized pagans, making them independent of Judaea. His actions were quite in accord with the old Roman policy of making

native princes, in whom confidence was reposed, eth-
narchs or kings. The decisive factor was almost certainly
the disturbances in Judaea. He hoped Archelaus might
be able to placate the country, and spurred him to do so
with the promise that he would be king if he should
succeed.

The people, however, still longed for a descendant of
the Hasmoneans. This is shown by the fact that they
welcomed the claims of an imposter who bore a physical
resemblance to Alexander, son of Mariamme the Hasmonean. This man declared that he and his brother Aristobolus had never been executed, had been spirited away at
the last moment, two criminals having been executed
in their stead. The people believed this story and, when
the imposter went to Rhodes, the crowds greeted him
and showered him with gifts and money. From there he
went to Rome, where the entire Judaean population went
out to meet him. They felt it to be an act of God that
Alexander had escaped death, and rejoiced over the
miracle that a scion of the Hasmoneans was alive. Even
many who had met the real Alexander years before when
he was in Rome believed this man to be Alexander.[51]

Caesar refused to believe these claims. Having known
Herod well, he felt certain that Herod could not have
been deceived in such an important matter. He sent
Celadus, who had known the prince, to bring the man
to him, and saw for himself that this was not Alexander.
He told the man to tell him the truth in which case he
would spare his life. The man admitted he was an imposter, and Caesar sent him to be a rower on a sailing
vessel.[52]

When Archelaus returned to Judaea as ethnarch of
the country, he dismissed Joazar grandson of Boethus
from the high priesthood because of his support of the
delegation that had besought Caesar to abolish the monarchy. He appointed Joazar's brother Eleazar to the high
priesthood.[53] Archelaus assumed the name of Herod, but
not his tyrannical ways. Thus he followed his father's
policy to conform with Judaean law by not having the

coins of the realm engraved with his image. So, too, he gave a pledge of immunity to the brother of Athronges, the shepherd rebel, who was still at large—whereupon he surrendered.[54]

Archelaus' rule was undistinguished. He founded a village and, in the manner of his father, named it Archelais, after himself.[55] He rebuilt the royal palace in Jericho which had been destroyed during one of the disturbances. He continued his father's work of soil irrigation, extending it to the palm plantations in the Jordan Valley north of Jericho.[56]

Archelaus, who was married, fell in love with Glaphyra, who had been the wife of his half-brother Alexander. After Alexander's execution, Glaphyra married Juba, King of Libya. When Archelaus met and fell in love with her, he divorced his wife, Mariamme, and married Glaphyra. The marriage was contrary to Judaean law.[57]

The relations between Rome and Judaea were not as friendly as they had been during the time of Herod. In the year 1 B.C.E., a revolt broke out in Armenia. Augustus was apprehensive that the Parthians might take advantage of the revolt and march towards Syria. Because of his age, Augustus was no longer able to lead a campaign. He delegated his grandson, Gaius son of Agrippa, to do so.[58] When Gaius came to Syria he bypassed Judaea and, unlike his father, did not visit Jerusalem. Augustus commended him highly for this omission.[59]

The Judaeans and Samaritans bore no love toward each other. But in the year 6 C.E., a delegation of leading men from Judaea and Samaria complained to Augustus of Archelaus' cruelty.[60] Augustus immediately called the ethnarch to Rome. He gave him a hearing, but was not satisfied with his defense and exiled him to the city of Vienne, situated on the east bank of the Rhone.[61] Archelaus never returned to Judaea and died in exile.[62] Before his departure from Jerusalem he had dismissed the High Priest Eleazar and appointed Jesus son of See to succeed him.[63]

JUDAEA BECOMES A PROVINCE OF ROME

Judaea's Exceptional Status

After Caesar deposed Archelaus, he made Judaea a Roman province. He sent P. Sulpicius Cyrinius (Quirinius), the legate of Syria, to take a census. Whenever Rome annexed a country a census was taken of all the inhabitants, from the youngest to the oldest.[64] Rome also had a list made up of all the properties, public and private, in order to levy and exact tribute. Coponius was appointed procurator of Judaea;[65] he was of the equestrian order, as procurators generally were. The duty of a procurator was the management of the financial affairs of the country.[66] Originally he had no judicial authority, which was vested in the legate. When Caponius was appointed procurator, however, he received full judicial powers, including the *jus gladii*, the right to inflict capital punishment.[67]

Although Judaea was made a province of Rome, it was not added to Syria, perhaps because Judaea had no common border with Syria. Galilee, which intervened between them, remained the tetrarchy of Antipas. More important was the hard fact that Judaea could not be ruled by any but its own laws, which were religious. In any case, Judaea retained its identity. Its procurator was not subject to the legate of Syria. He was responsible solely to Caesar, appointed and recalled by the emperor.[68]

The essentials of Roman rule were three: tribute, conscription, and Roman laws. The tributes levied by Rome were *decumae*,[69] poll tax and the various kinds of *tributum capitis*, which means any personal tax. Another tax, *scriptura*,[70] was a tax on land, trade, shopkeepers and prostitutes. There was another tax, called *portorium*, on imports and exports.[71] Rome sold these revenues to a group of men known as publicans who resided in Rome. They, in turn, had publicans who collected the taxes for them in the various countries. The publicans, having the authority of the state behind their exactions, were much feared.

Conscription could not be levied on the Judaeans, since Julius Caesar had exempted them from serving in the Roman army because of their religious scruples.[72]

Nor could Roman laws be introduced into Judaea. The Judaean law which covered civil matters was also religious. Theft, robbery and injury, which in Roman society were considered civil or criminal matters, were prohibited to the Judaeans because God had forbidden them. The injunction against theft was on a par with the laws of sacrifice or levitical purity. Roman law was based on laws which had been formulated by able and gifted men. Judaean law was based on the Pentateuch, which was considered as the word of God and interpreted by wise men who were divinely inspired.

So Judaea remained a separate unit under its procurator. He had no real army, only some auxiliary forces consisting of Caesareans and Sebasteans. He resided in Caesarea, as it would have been offensive to the Judaeans to bring the soldiers with their Roman standards bearing the image of Caesar into Jerusalem.[73] Caesarea was essentially a pagan city—Herod had built a temple there to Augustus Caesar. It was also within easy communication with Antioch, where the legate was stationed, as well as with Rome.

During the festivals, particularly Passover, when Judaeans from all parts of the country and foreign lands came to Jerusalem, the procurator took up residence in Jerusalem in the palace of Herod.[74] He brought with him a few cohorts and an *ala*, that is, a regiment of cavalry, who were stationed in the colonnades of the Temple Mount to suppress any disturbances. The Roman standards carried by the soldiers were then sheathed to cover the image of Caesar in deference to the Judaeans. The *ala* was composed of Caesareans and Sebasteans who were violently anti-Judaean and gave great provocations to the populace.

While Rome eradicated all political authority, the Romans also made it a practice not to disturb religious authorities and allowed them to retain certain civil powers. The *sacerdos provinciae,* the high priest, was the head of the province, holding office for one year.[75] The *sine qua non* for appointment to this office was friendship for Rome, which meant a wholehearted willingness to follow Roman authority. In the days of the monarchy, the king would call a *synedrion* from time to time for counsel. So the high priest now summoned his own council, *bouleue.* The chamber in which they met was called *bouleuterion,* council chamber. Later this chamber was satirically called *parhedrion,* indicating that the high priests had become assessors, coadjutors to the Roman authorities.[76]

The religious authority over the Judeans wherever they lived remained the *Bet Din haGadol.* It had the authority to inflict punishment upon a transgressor of any command of the Torah, but it took no part in the political life of Judaea.

Josephus notes that, after Archelaus, the government of Judaea was an aristocracy, ruled by the high priests.[77] It would have been more accurate to say that the government of Judaea was a combination of timocracy—the love for the ruler—and nomocracy—the rule of law. The high priests who headed the community were lovers of Rome, while the daily life of the people was ruled by the *Bet Din haGadol* and its religious enactments.

The Early Procurators

When Coponius came to take over the rule of Judaea, he dismissed the high priest, Jesus son of See, and reappointed Joazar son of Boethus,[78] the staunch advocate of Roman rule. Joazar aided Coponius in taking his census by persuading the Judaeans to submit to the Romans. However, not all the people were persuaded.

Judas of Galilee, who had fought Rome during the time of Varus, called submission to the census a betrayal of liberty. He proclaimed paying tribute to Rome a sin, tantamout to slavery. He exhorted the people to fight for their liberty. His motto was: there is only one ruler—God.[79]

When the census had been taken and the collection of taxes proceeded, Coponius dismissed the High Priest Joazar and appointed Ananus son of Seth in his place.[80] Joazar's dismissal came about either because it was a policy to change the spiritual leaders of the provinces annually, or because Joazar had become too independent or influential.

Josephus relates an interesting if odd incident which occurred during the procuratorship of Coponius. On one of the days of Passover, when the gates of the Temple were usually opened by the priests before dawn, some Samaritans entered the Temple area unnoticed and threw human bones into the cloisters. Human bones could defile that section of the Temple. For this reason the Samaritans were thereafter no longer permitted to enter the Temple and a careful watch was kept of all who entered this area.[81] This incident, though seemingly minor, is related by Josephus as an important historical occurrence. It reflects the deep animosity which still prevailed between the Samaritans and the Judaeans, and may have some relation to the Samaritan hope, now that Rome ruled Judaea and Samaria (Sebaste), that they might receive permission to rebuild their own temple on Mount Gerizim.

When Coponius became procurator, he followed Herod's policy with regard to the high priest's vestments. Herod had kept them in Antonia and given them to the high priest a few days before the Day of Atonement.[82] Coponius similarly kept them in his custody. The Judaeans deeply resented this as an insult to their religion.

Shortly after the Samaritan incident, probably in the year 8 or 9 C.E., Coponius returned to Rome.[83] He was succeeded by Marcus Ambivius, whose administration lasted from 9 to 11. Salome, Herod's sister, the last surviving member of Antipater's family, died around the year 10. She bequeathed to her friend Livia, the wife of Augustus Caesar, her entire dominion, Phasaelis—Jamneh and its toparchy, and Archelais with its immense plantation of palm trees.[84] Rulers often gave away a territory with its population as a gift to foreigners, without considering the wishes of its inhabitants. Thus an important economic sector of Judaea passed into Roman imperial possession and was governed separately.

Marcus Ambivius was succeeded by Annius Rufus, whose procuratorship terminated with the death of Augustus Caesar on the 19th of August, 14 C.E.[85] Augustus Caesar had been strict in his rule, demanding obedience both from the population as well as from his administrators. He required faithful performance from his procurators, and would not condone provocation of violence nor transgressions against the religious feelings of the inhabitants. Hence there were no serious disturbances in Judaea during the tenure of the procurators as long as Augustus Caesar was alive.

Augustus Caesar was succeeded by his stepson Tiberius Nero, the son of Livia by a previous marriage.[86] Rufus was recalled from Judaea, and Emperor Tiberius appointed Valerius Gratus procurator; he ruled Judaea until the year 26. During his administration the high priests were changed frequently. He deposed Ananus and appointed as high priest Ishmael son of Phabi. Ishmael was later deposed in favor of Eleazar son of Ananus, who had previously been high priest. Gratus next appointed Simon son of Camith, who held the office for one year. The high priesthood was then given to Joseph Caiaphas, son-in-law of Ananus.[87] Gratus, of course, received a sum of money from each appointee. The office of high priest thus became a commodity for him to market, and it inevitably lost its prestige and influence over the people. Still, there were no serious disturbances in Judaea during the time of Gratus.

In the year 26, Tiberius appointed Pontius Pilate procurator.[88]

Pontius Pilate

The new procurator was portrayed by his contemporary, Philo, and later by Josephus, as a man of greed,[89] venality and cruelty, utterly lacking in human compassion. He resorted to robbery and oppression. Hence there were frequent clashes between the Judaeans and Pilate. At the very beginning of his term, he ordered his legions in Caesarea to march to Jerusalem with their standards uncovered, thus breaking with the custom of previous procurators. Pilate's actions aroused great indignation. A deputation went to Caesarea and for five days vainly pleaded with Pilate to remove these standards from Jerusalem. Pilate said that to do so would be derogatory to Caesar. The sixth day he surrounded the delegation with an army. He threatened them with death unless they returned to Jerusalem, but they threw themselves upon the ground, saying that they would rather die than allow their laws to be transgressed. Pilate yielded to this "obduracy" and ordered the standards back to Caesarea.[90]

Another clash occurred when Pilate dedicated a pair of shields in the royal palace of Herod, his official residence. Although the shields were not decorated with the likenesses of the Emperor, they bore inscriptions to him. The Judaeans protested, but Pilate refused to remove them. The sons of Herod joined in the protest to no effect. A letter bearing the signatures of the sons of Herod and other notable Judaeans was then sent to Tiberius and he promptly ordered the removal of the shields. The third of Kislev, the day when the standards were removed, was declared a semi-holiday.

Pilate began the construction of an aquaduct to bring a greater water supply to Jerusalem, which suffered periodic water shortages. To pay for this construction, he seized the funds from the sacred treasury known as *corbonas*.[91] The money in this treasury was not in the same category as the communal money of the Temple, but was considered private property held as a religious trust. It consisted of the sums deposited by the Nazarites for their sacrifices and was not to be used for any other purpose. The Judaeans protested strongly against this sacrilege, but Pilate refused to yield. To the contrary, he ordered his soldiers to garb themselves as civilians with their swords concealed under their clothing. When the Judaeans persisted in their protestations, he signaled his army to attack them. A fearful slaughter ensued; the Judaeans were forced to submit to Pilate's villainy.

In the year 35 C.E., Artabanus seized the throne of Parthia. He assumed the title King of Kings and boasted he would seize the territories once held by Cyrus and Alexander. Tiberius Caesar became alarmed, and appointed Lucius Vitellius, the father of the future Emperor Vitellius, as governor of the entire East.[92] Thus Judaea and its procurator, Pontius Pilate, now came under his jurisdiction. Vitellius was a man of great ability and supreme statesmanship. Later, his diplomacy effected a truce between Parthia and Rome.

The Samaritan incursion into the Temple was now followed by an equally bizarre event. An imposter bade the Samaritans assemble on Mount Gerizim, their holy mount, where he promised to reveal the sacred vessels which he alleged had been buried there by Moses. An immense throng gathered at the nearby village Tirathana. Pilate, apparently alarmed by the fanfare of the great mass of people, ordered his army to disperse them. They did so, but with violence. Many were killed, and others who were captured were subsequently executed. The Samaritans sent a delegation to Vitellius complaining of the murderous action of Pilate. Most likely the Judaeans joined the Samaritans in this complaint. Vitellius removed Pilate from the procuratorship and ordered him to go to Rome to stand trial.[93] It is not known what happened to Pilate when he returned to Rome. His despotic tenure in Judaea lasted from 26 to 36. Such fame as he acquired rests on his role in the trial and crucifixion of Jesus.

Vitellius appointed his friend Marcellus procurator of Judaea.[94] Vitellius himself went to Jerusalem during the Festival of Passover, probably in the year 36.[95] According to Tacitus, the Judaeans appealed to Rome to ease the existing burden of excessive tribute.[96] Vitellius had as his chief objective in the Near East the securing of a truce with the Parthians and, if not successful at that, engaging in a war to subdue them. Being a skillful strategist, he realized that he could not fight the Parthians if Judaea were in turmoil. He therefore sought to placate the Judaeans and they in turn received him warmly upon his arrival in Jerusalem. He released them from the tributes on agricultural sales and permitted the high-priestly vestments to rest in the custody of the high priest. This did not mean that Rome had relinquished its authority over the high priesthood.[97] Vitellius also removed Joseph Caiaphas as high priest and appointed Jonathan son of Ananus (who had formerly been high priest) in his stead.

The Emperor Tiberius died on March 16, 37 C.E.[98] During his reign—which lasted somewhat more than twenty-two years—there were only two procurators in Judaea. During the eight years of Augustus' rule when Judaea was a Roman province, there had been four procurators. During the time of Augustus the administration of the Empire was strictly centralized. Since legates and procurators, particularly the latter, were not of the aristocracy but of the equestrian class, Augustus was aware of their rapacity. He had, therefore, made it a matter of policy to keep a procurator in a province for only a short period; he did not want to provoke the people to rebellion. Tiberius, on the other hand, kept his officials in the provinces for long periods. He did not want too many ambitious men in Rome.[99] He too was aware of their greed, but he thought that if they were changed frequently, they would take advantage of their short tenure quickly to extract as much wealth as possible. Tiberius illustrated this by a tale: Once a man observed a wounded person lying helpless on the ground with a great number of flies gathered on his wound. Drawn by pity, he moved to chase the flies away. The wounded man begged him to desist, saying, "If you drive away these flies others will come and hurt me more. These flies have already drunk so much blood they are not capable of hurting me further."[100]

PHILIP AND HEROD ANTIPAS

When Judaea was divided by Augustus Caesar, in the year 4 B.C.E., Philip received the poorest share— Auranitis, Gaulanitis and Bathanea—the tetrarchy of Trachonitis. His realm was populated by Judaeans and pagans, the Judaeans being a minority. Philip's tetrarchy was peaceful. The Trachonitans, who had caused Herod trouble by piracy and ravage, now created no disturbances.

Philip, despite his poverty, emulated his father in building cities in honor of Caesar, some of great dimensions. On the site of the ancient city of Paneas, north of Lake Gennesaret, he founded a new city named Caesarea. To distinguish it from the older Caesarea, it was called Caesarea Philippi.[101] He gave it the right of self-government. He also rebuilt the village of Bethsaida on the north coast of Lake Gennesaret, where the Jordan enters the lake, and renamed it Julias, in honor of Augustus' daughter.[102] There was a small Judaean population in both of the new cities. As the population of Philip's tetrarchy was predominantly pagan, there was little complaint when he issued coins showing the head of Augustus, and later Tiberius, on the obverse. He was thus the first of the Judaean rulers to engrave the head of the emperor on coins; for he was a philo-Roman politically. Philip was a modest man. He spent his time in his territory, supervising the administration. He traveled from place to place. When anyone sought justice, he would set up his tribunal by the roadside and sit in judgment, giving his decisions and executing them without delay.[103] His people loved him. In his later years he married Salome, the daughter of Herod son of Mariamme II. Salome's mother was Herodias, the daughter of Aristobolus son of Herod.[104] They had no children.

Philip died early in the year 34 C.E., after a rule of thirty-seven years, in the twentieth year of the reign of Tiberius Caesar. He was buried in a tomb which he had constructed. Tiberius added his territory to Syria, but ordered that its revenue remain for its local administration.[105]

The territory of Antipas consisted of Galilee and Peraea, which had no common border. Although his territory was smaller than that of Philip, it was richer and more civilized. Galilee was thickly populated and fertile and brought Antipas vast revenue. The population was Judaean and freedom-loving.

Antipas built a number of new cities because they strengthened the security of his territory.[106] For the defense of Galilee he rebuilt the city of Sepphoris and surrounded it with strong walls. For the defense of Peraea he fortified Betharamphtha and named it Livias, after the wife of Augustus Caesar. He was successful in his policy with Augustus and even more so with Tiberius. He built a splendid city on the western shore of Lake Gennesaret which he made his capitol. He named it Tiberias in honor of his patron.[107] The city spread to the south to the village of Amathus, where there were warm springs. But part of the city was built on land where there had once been many sepulchres. Because of this, many Judaeans, those who were scrupulous about the laws of impurity and especially those of priestly families, would not settle there.[108] Therefore Antipas had to offer special inducements to the people to come to live there. He gave them free land on which to erect their houses, and release from certain taxes. He granted the city substantial autonomy through a constitution in which they had a council consisting of five hundred members. He adorned the city with magnificent buildings and built for himself a palace decorated with statuary of animals. He also induced some of his officials and forced others of his subjects to reside there.

Antipas, who also called himself Herod, was married to the daughter of King Aretas of Nabataea.[109] This was a political alliance, made to remove the hostility of the Nabataeans towards his father and to strengthen his position in Peraea. However, the marriage did not last. On one occasion, when Antipas went to Rome, he stopped on the way to visit his half-brother Herod son of Mariamme II. Herod's wife was Herodias, the daughter of his half-brother Aristobolus, and Antipas fell in love with her.[109a] She reciprocated his love and consented to marry him on condition that he divorce his Nabataean wife; and he agreed. When his wife learned of his plan, she suggested that she go to the Fortress Macharus,[110] situated east of the Dead Sea on the border of Nabataea. She secretly notified her father about the compulsory divorce and Aretas arranged for her flight to Nabataea. He was indignant over the humiliation of his daughter. Aretas and Antipas had already quarreled about the boundary of the territory of the Gebalitis, and with this new provocation a war broke out between them. Neither was on the battlefield; they entrusted their armies to their generals. Antipas' army was destroyed. It was held that this catastrophe was due to the treachery of the people, who were originally of the tetrarchy of Philip and were joined to the army of Antipas.[111] It is probable that the Trachonitans entered Antipas' forces and then betrayed him.

Antipas had by this time married Herodias. Josephus condemns Herodias for having transgressed the laws of the Judaeans in divorcing her husband and marrying his brother while her husband was still alive.[112] It is strange that Josephus should condemn Herodias but not Antipas, since pentateuchal law is directed to the man.[113] Josephus also states that some Judaeans thought that the destruction of Antipas' army was a punishment by God for having slain John, called the Baptist.

JOHN "THE BAPTIST"

Josephus characterizes John thus:[114]

> He was a good man and commanded the Judaeans to exer-
> cise virtue, both as to righteousness towards one another,
> and piety towards God, and so to come to baptism; for that
> the washing would be acceptable to Him, if they make use of
> it, not for putting away of some sins, but for the purification
> of the body; supposing still that the soul was thoroughly
> purified beforehand by righteousness. Now when many
> others[115] came to crowd about him, for they were greatly
> moved by hearing his words, Herod (Antipas), who feared
> lest the great influence John had over the people might put
> it into his power and inclination to raise a rebellion (for they
> seemed ready to do anything he should advise), thought it
> best, by putting him to death, to prevent any mischief he
> might cause and not bring himself into difficulties by sparing
> a man who might make him repent of it when it should be
> too late. Accordingly he was sent, a prisoner out of Herod's
> (Antipas) suspicious temper, to Macharus the fortress I
> before mentioned and was there put to death.

The genuineness of this passage has been questioned.
Josephus unquestionably wrote about John, but there
have been some interpolations in the passage as it stands
now, for example, the phrase, "John, that was called the
baptist."[116]

The Gospels also relate that Herod (Antipas) slew
John.[117] They give as his motive John's reproach to
Antipas for having married the wife of his brother. Mark
says Herodias wanted John killed, but that Herod
(Antipas) feared him, "knowing that he was a just man
and an holy, and observed him; and when he heard him,
he did many things and heard him gladly." Mark further
relates that, once on the birthday of Herod (Antipas),
the daughter of Herodias (Salome), an only child,
danced, which delighted Antipas so much that he promised to fulfill any wish that she might express. At the
instigation of her mother, Herodias, she asked for John's
head. Antipas thereupon beheaded John. Matthew gives

the same story with minor variations. Luke gives an account of the slaying of John, but does not connect it with Salome.[118]

The differences in the accounts by Josephus and the Gospels deserve notice. According to Josephus, Herod (Antipas) imprisoned John and later slew him because he was apprehensive that John might arouse the people to revolt. The authors of the Gospels say that Herod (Antipas) killed John because he rebuked him.[119] The latter reason is unlikely, as he had undoubtedly been rebuked by many of the Judaean spiritual leaders for his sinful act.

It would seem from the Gospels that the banquet in honor of the birthday of Antipas was given in the Fortress Macharus where John was imprisoned. The Gospels say Salome was young and unmarried; the chronology shows, however, she was already married to Philip.[120] That Herod (Antipas) ordered John beheaded to please her cannot be taken as historical fact. When John the Baptist became a Christian hero, this account explained his untimely death, and blackened further the name of Herod (Antipas) whom the Evangelists despised.

The most significant motive must again be found in the political realm. The slaying of John probably took place in the year 33-34 C.E., at a time when Tiberius was anxious over the designs of Artabanus, King of Parthia. It was therefore imperative for Herod (Antipas) to have no disorder in his territory. True, John did not preach revolt, but religious awakening. Nonetheless, Herod (Antipas) was aware of those who, like Judas of Galilee and the Apocalyptists, preached non-submission to the Romans in the name of religion. He therefore probably felt that it would be politically beneficial to him and the country for John to be imprisoned, particularly as John had concentrated his activities in Peraea where there was a melting pot of different peoples, easily incitable to revolt. But there is also some truth to the Gospel account. Herodias, like her great grandmother Alexandra, was an ambitious woman. She had left her husband Herod, a commoner, and married Herod (Antipas) because he was a tetrarch. John's taunting her as an adultress must have enraged her to the point where she persuaded her husband to kill him. Thus the stories in the Gospels supplement the account by Josephus.

The significance of John's baptism also receives divergent explanations which should be noted. Josephus gives the motive as "not in order to the putting away of some sins, but for the purification of the body." According to Mark, John's baptism was "of repentance for the remission of sins."[121]

Through the shrewd diplomacy of Vitellius peace was established between Parthia and Rome in the summer of 36. To demonstrate the equal status between the East and the West, a tent was erected upon a bridge over the Euphrates where Vitellius and Artabanus met. Artabanus even sent his son Darius to Rome as a hostage to seal the pact. Herod (Antipas) participated in the negotiations and entertained both parties royally; most likely he helped bring the two together. This was a triumph for the shrewd diplomacy of Vitellius. But Herod (Antipas) hastened to inform Tiberius of what had taken place. When Vitellius sent his report to Tiberius, the latter told him that he was already familiar with all details relating to the pact. Vitellius was deeply chagrined and felt that Herod Antipas had acted craftily towards him.[122]

After Herod's (Antipas') army had suffered defeat at the hands of the Nabataeans, he complained to Tiberius that King Aretas was an aggressor. Tiberius now ordered Vitellius to make war against Aretas. Vitellius was not enthusiastic about the expedition, since he entertained unfriendly feelings toward Herod (Antipas) ;[123] nevertheless, he could not disobey Tiberius' order. Early in the spring of 37 he marched with two legions and some auxiliaries towards Petra, the capital of Nabataea. He avoided Judaea, because of the problem of the Roman standards, and marched along the great plain. However, he personally went up to Jerusalem with Herod (Antipas) during the Passover and was received with acclaim. While there, he removed Jonathan from the high priesthood and appointed Jonathan's brother Theophilus in his stead.[124] On the fourth day of his stay in Jerusalem, he received word that Tiberius had died (March 16, 37). He ordered the Judaeans to take an oath of allegiance to Gaius Caligula and abandoned his expedition. The death of Tiberius saved the independence of Nabataea.

2. JESUS OF NAZARETH

THE CAREER OF JESUS

The Sources

It has been said correctly of the life of Jesus, "We do not have enough material to write a respectable obituary."[1] The reason is simple; there are no sources that can be called historical. The authors of the Gospels were not primarily interested in recording reliable historical data, but in presenting him as seen through the eyes of faith. What is historical in their accounts they swathed so completely in theological wrappings that it almost cannot be laid bare. Moreover, there are no other nearly contemporaneous accounts of him. No mention is made of the name of Jesus outside of Christian records. The well-known Christ passage in Josephus was interpolated in the fourth century by the Church historian Eusebius.[2] It reads as follows:

Now there arose about this time Jesus, a wise man, if indeed one ought to call him a man. For he was a doer of wonderful works, a teacher of such people as accepted the truth gladly. He drew over to him both many of the Judaeans and many of the Hellenes. He was the Christ. When Pilate, at the suggestion of the principal men among us, condemned him to the cross, those that loved him at the first did not give up their affection for him. On the third day he appeared to them, as the divine prophets had foretold this and ten thousand other wonderful things concerning him. And the tribe of Christians, so named from him, is not extinct.

The name of Jesus in connection with the death of James in Josephus is also a later interpolation.[3] The Roman historian Tacitus does make reference to Christus who was put to death by Pontius Pilate,[4] but he wrote his history during the close of the first and the beginning of the second centuries. Even then he does not mention Jesus by name. There are a few references to Jesus in the Talmud, but they are not earlier than the fourth century.[5]

Thus, to present a sketch of the life of Jesus one can draw only on the Gospels. Mark, Matthew and Luke are called the synoptic Gospels, since they are more or less in agreement. John is unsynoptic, for his narrative of events in the life of Jesus and his theology often manifest a distinctly different approach. The earliest Gospel is the one "according to Mark." Papias, who lived in the first part of the second century, said that Mark, a disciple of Peter, composed the Gospel from stories related to him by Peter.[6] The authorship of the Gospel according to Mark should consequently be placed in the period shortly after the destruction of the Temple, during the last quarter of the first century, or more than one generation after the death of Jesus.[7] Matthew, in writing his Gospel, made use of Mark and also of collections of the sayings of Jesus, *logia*.[8] The author of the third Gospel, Luke, was a disciple of Paul according to tradition. He was a physician and at the same time a man of culture who had genuine literary skill.[9] He endeavored to present an historical narrative of the life of Jesus and utilized the writings of Mark and possibly Matthew. John did not intend to present a biography of Jesus, but an essentially theological interpretation of his existence. Thus, he did not stress Jesus' descent from David, as the synoptics did, but that he was the Messiah, the Son of God, the Lamb of God which takes away the sins of the world. The book of John was probably written in the middle of the second century for Gentile Christians.[10]

His Birth

A biography usually begins with the date of birth, but in Jesus' case that is not known. Mark passes the birth of Jesus by in silence. Matthew says it occurred during the reign of Herod.[11] Herod died at the end of March, 4 B.C.E.[12] Luke says that Jesus was born when Quirinius (Cyrinius) took his census of Judaea, which was 6 C.E.[13] John says nothing on this score, and the early Church Fathers record different dates for the birth of Jesus.[14] It may be said that Jesus was born some time between the years 6 B.C.E. and 6 C.E. The exact month is more problematic. The Gospels did not record it and, while some Church Fathers placed it as early as November, others said it was March or April.[15]

Matthew and Luke identify the birthplace of Jesus as Bethlehem, which is south of Jerusalem, but still in Judaea, and state that the family moved from there to Nazareth which is not in Judaea proper but in Galilee.[16] Mark, on the other hand, does not mention that Bethlehem was the birthplace of Jesus. He always designates Jesus as "Jesus of Nazareth."[17] John, too, was not aware that Jesus was born in Bethlehem, but considered him a Galilean, as he wrote, "Others said: 'This is the Christ.' But some said, 'Shall Christ come out of Galilee'?"[18] Luke records the virgin birth and the manger scene in detail.[19] Matthew adds the homage of the Magi, the flight to Egypt and Herod's slaughter of the innocents.[20] After the death of Herod, Joseph and his family returned to the land of Israel but went to Nazareth, not Bethlehem, for fear of Archelaus. Matthew's explanation is unconvincing. If Joseph did not return to Bethlehem because of Archelaus, why did he return to Nazareth which was ruled by Herod (Antipas), called "the fox" in the Gospels?[21] The birth of Jesus in Bethlehem arose out of theological speculation, as further proof that Jesus was the messiah, the son of David. (David's family was from Bethlehem, and both Matthew and Luke take pains to trace the genealogy of Jesus back to King David.) Thus, Matthew quotes Micah as referring to the birth of Jesus, "And thou Bethlehem, in the land of Judaea . . . for out of thee shall come a ruler that shall rule my people Israel."[22] Matthew is likewise suspect, because his tale of the slaughter of the innocent babes has no historical foundation. Josephus, who was inclined to dramatize the cruelties committed by Herod, does not refer to a massacre of infants which he surely would not have failed to mention had there been one—a supposition confirmed by the silence of the early Church Fathers. Neither Mark nor John know that Jesus was born in Bethlehem, but regularly refer to him as Jesus of Nazareth, indicating that he was born there.[23]

Mariamme's son was circumcised on the eighth day and named Yeshu'a, Jesus in Greek.[24] His mother took him to Jerusalem to be redeemed, as he was her first born, and brought a sacrifice as prescribed by the Pentateuch.[25] That she brought two doves instead of a lamb shows that the family was poor. Mariamme bore four more sons, named Jacob (James), Joseph, Simon and Judas, and daughters[26]—at least two. Thus the family was of considerable size. Joseph, a carpenter, was the provider.[27]

According to Luke, Joseph and Mariamme went on a pilgrimage every year to Jerusalem for the Festival of Passover. They took Jesus along when he was twelve years of age.[28] According to the same Gospel, Jesus was enchanted by the discourse of the teachers in the Temple and had the intelligence to ask them various questions. It must be assumed that Jesus had received some kind of Judaean education in the small town of Nazareth. On the Sabbath he most likely attended the synagogue where the Torah was read and he listened to the discourses of the sages.

No further mention is made of Joseph after these stories of Jesus' youth. It is less likely that he was ignored than that he died early. Since it is recorded that Jesus pursued the trade of carpentry,[29] he probably took up the burden of supporting the family.

Jesus' Active Career

Nothing more is known of the life of Jesus[30] until he arrived at about the age of thirty when he met John the Baptist.[31] John began his ministry in the fifteenth year of Tiberius Caesar, that is, in 29 C.E.[32] Garbed in haircloth and with a girdle around his loins, John lived on dried locusts and honey. He besought the people to repent and be baptized in the Jordan.[33] The adult Jesus appears after his "hidden years," when he comes to John to be baptized. The various Gospels believe that John was the forerunner of Jesus the Messiah, or the Christ.[34]

The relationship between John and Jesus raises many problems. Jesus was not garbed like John the Baptist, nor did he subsist on dried locusts and honey. He was not an ascetic whose home was in the wilderness. He lived the same life that others did in Judaea, mingling with the people and visiting their synagogues.[35] While John appealed to the people to be baptized, Jesus never did so. John, the evangelist, says only that the disciples of Jesus practiced baptism.[36] Matthew's account of Jesus directing his eleven disciples to go and baptize in the name of the Father, the Son, and the Holy Ghost, places this after the resurrection.[37] According to Acts, Peter called for baptism in the name of Jesus Christ, and it is noted that Philip's converts were baptized.[38] Thus the evidence for baptism becomes clear later than the time of Jesus.[39]

Historically, therefore, the view that Jesus was not baptized by John carries great weight.[40] They ministered independently and there were even disputes between their disciples. The Gospel according to John records a sort of animosity against the disciples of John the Baptist.[41] The tale that Jesus was baptized is of theological origin, arising in the days when baptism became a fundamental symbol of the new faith. Since Jesus never practiced baptism, it was necessary for the early Christians to connect Jesus with John, who was regarded as his herald, and to assert that Jesus was baptized by him.[42]

According to Mark, Jesus began his ministry after the imprisonment of John the Baptist.[43] How long his ministry lasted is a matter of conjecture. It appears from the synoptic Gospels that it lasted less than a year.[44] According to John, it lasted several years. John says that during his ministry Jesus was in Jerusalem several times at the time of Passover. He also made a pilgrimage for the festival of Tabernacles, and visited during the days of Hanukkah.[45] According to the synoptic Gospels, however, he was in Jerusalem only once—during the festival of Passover, when he was tried and put to death by Pilate. The early Church Fathers had no definite tradition as to the length of Jesus' ministry, some following the synoptics,[46] others following John.[47]

There may be no contradiction between the accounts. John dates some of the events of Jesus' activity from the time when John the Baptist was still preaching, while the synoptic Gospels record them after the termination of John the Baptist's imprisonment (which lasted not quite one year). It seems likely that the ministry of Jesus did coincide for a few years with that of John the Baptist.

The synagogue of that day was not a house of prayer, with formal services, but a house of study and preaching, where the Torah and the Prophets were read and expounded. Both the reading and the preaching must have impressed Jesus deeply, and he followed this same method in his ministry. According to Mark, he entered upon his mission with an appeal to the people that, "The time is fulfilled and the kingdom of God is at hand; repent ye and believe the good tidings."[48] The Judaeans were suffering severly under Pontius Pilate. Some of them were eager to believe the good tidings proclaimed by Jesus that the kingdom of God was approaching. Jesus preached this gospel on the Sabbath day in various communities in Galilee. His preaching did not impress the people of Nazareth, who knew him as a carpenter's son. Thus he was led to exclaim, "a prophet has no honor in his own country."[49] His followers were mainly women, who were deeply impressed with his sincerity and simplicity. He mingled with the lower classes of society, publicans and sinners. When questioned as to why a man of piety should associate with such social outcasts, his answer was simple and to the point—the sick people, not the healthy, needed a physician.[50]

The Gospels attribute many miracles to Jesus; but such matters fall outside the historian's domain. Jesus is also said to have driven out evil spirits, particularly from women. Many people at that difficult time were distraught, psychically ill, and Jesus with his deep understanding and compassion was able to cure them because of their great faith. A similar power has been attributed to many great religious leaders and operates today in a different guise in psychotherapy. The followers of Jesus addressed him as "teacher," or "master."[51] It is recorded in the Gospels, particularly that of John, that Jesus was also addressed as "rabbi."[52] This is an anachronism, since that title was not introduced among the Judaeans until after the destruction of the Temple. Some of Jesus' enthusiastic followers who were cured, or expected to be cured of their ills, addressed him as "son of God."[53] Jesus, however, referred to himself only as *ben adam,* or in Aramaic *bar nasha.* Its original connotation is simply "a man," not the literal "son of man" as it was rendered in the Greek.[54] When Jesus acquired a considerable following, he appointed twelve men to whom he delegated his power of casting out evil spirits and healing the sick.[55] Twelve were required to symbolize all the tribes of Israel restored to their primal fullness. Jesus instructed his disciples to carry his message to the Judaeans. He ordered them, "Go not into the way of the Gentiles, and into the city of the Samaritans enter ye not."[56] However, he himself went to Samaria and to the cities of the Gentiles, Tyre and Sidon.[57]

There are numerous such contradictions and complications in the character of Jesus as recorded in the Gospels. Jesus preached love. According to Matthew, Jesus said in his sermon on the Mount, "Whosoever shall smite thee on thy right cheek turn to him the other also."[58] Yet Jesus bitterly upbraided the people of the cities who rejected his teachings. He was especially incensed against the people of Capernaum and said, "But I say unto you that it shall be more tolerable for the land of Sodom in the day of judgment than for thee [Capernaum]."[59] He also said that anyone who was not with him was against him.[60] He generally considered himself a Judaean, and felt deep concern for his own people. He said, "Think not that I am come to destroy the Torah or the prophets; I am not come to destroy, but to fulfill. For verily I say unto you, till heaven and earth pass, not an iota or one tittle shall in all wise pass from the Torah until all be fulfilled."[61] A similar patriotism is found in the story of the Canaanite[62] woman who besought him to cast out the evil spirit from her daughter. At first he declined and said, "For it is not meet to take the children's bread and to cast it unto the dogs."[63] Although Jesus believed it almost impossible for a man of wealth to enter heaven, and he associated with publicans and sinners, he did not hesitate to dine with the wealthy[64] or even with the Pharisees, whom he is alleged to have despised.[65] He was so obsessed with his mission that, when he was told his mother and brothers were outside waiting to see him, he said, "Who is my mother or my brethren? . . . For whosoever shall do the will of God the same is my brother and my sister and my mother."[66] Jesus thus ignored the presence of his mother and brothers; yet the law of Moses, the Torah, says, "Honor thy father and thy mother."[67]

It must therefore be emphasized: the sayings of Jesus as reported in the Gospels were not recorded during his lifetime. His disciples and followers had different traditions of his sayings and acts and these were not consciously collected until two generations after his death. Then the various accounts were incorporated into the Gospels and thus the contradictions. The historical Jesus is still an enigma.

The Messianic Claim

Did Jesus consider himself to be the Messiah, the Christ? Mark relates that when Jesus was with his disciples near Casarea Philippi, he asked them, "Whom say ye that I am?" and Peter answered and said unto him, "Thou art the Christ (Matthew adds, 'the son of the living God') and he charged them that they should tell no man of him."[68] According to Mark, there must have been some sort of discussion between Jesus and Peter, for Jesus rebuked him saying, "Get thee behind me Satan."[69] Matthew records the story differently. When Peter told Jesus he was the Messiah, Jesus praised him saying, "Blessed art thou, Simon bar-Jona, for man hath not revealed it unto thee, but my Father which is in heaven. And I say also unto thee that thou art Peter (rock) and upon this rock I will build my *ecclesia* (Church) and the gates of hell shall not prevail against it. And I will give unto thee the keys of the kingdom of heaven; and whatsoever thou shalt bind on earth shall be bound in heaven; and whatsoever thou shalt loose on earth shall be loosed in heaven."[70] Then he charged his disciples that they should tell no man that he was the Messiah (Christ). What was the underlying reason for Jesus to tell Peter not to divulge that he was the Messiah? Was this because Jesus himself did not think that he was the Messiah or only that it was premature to proclaim it lest he be persecuted by the authorities? No historical explanation can be advanced. His motives remain a mystery.[71]

Matthew relates that, when Jesus was in Capernaum, those who collected the half-drachma (half-shekel), the annual Temple levy, came to Peter and said, "Doth not your master pay the half-drachma?" Peter said, "Yes." Then Jesus said to Peter, "What thinkest thou Simon? Of whom do the kings of the earth take custom or tribute? Of their own children or of foreigners?" Peter answered, "Of foreigners." Jesus said to him, "Then are the children free."[72] This passage is ambiguous. The half-shekel had to be paid by all who embraced the Judaean religion regardless of where they resided. It was collected for the Temple and had no connection with earthly powers. Therefore Jesus is not understandable when he stated, "Then are the children free." In order not to give offense, however, Jesus said to Peter, "Go thou to the sea and cast an hook and take up the fish that first cometh up; and when thou hast opened his mouth thou shalt find money (shekel); that take and give unto them for me and thee." Although Jesus maintained that he was free from paying the half-shekel (he was not free), he did pay it in order not to offend the authorities.

Jesus' disposition to compromise in order not to antagonize the authorities is manifested in another, more famous, instance. When asked, "Is it lawful to give tribute unto Caesar, or not?" Jesus perceived that the questioners were trying to place him in a difficult position. "No," would make him a rebel against Rome; "Yes," would discredit him among the nationalists. To escape the net spread out for him Jesus said, " 'Show me the tribute money.' And they brought unto him a dinar. And he said unto them, 'Whose is this image and inscription?' They said to him, 'Caesar's.' Then said he unto them, 'Render therefore unto Caesar the things which are Caesar's; and unto God the things that are God's' "[73]

In the spring of 34, Jesus and his disciples went from Capernaum to Jerusalem. They did not go through Samaria, but crossed the Jordan and traveled by the east coast.[74] His disciples sensed that the trip to Jerusalem would be fatal. Again crossing the Jordan, they arrived in Jericho. From there they went to Jerusalem.[75] As they approached the city they stopped at Bethphage at the Mount of Olives.[76] From there Jesus rode on an ass to Jerusalem to demonstrate his humility or, more probably, to fulfill the prophecy of Zachariah who said, "Behold, thy king cometh unto thee, sitting upon an ass."[77] Thus Jesus' entry into Jerusalem may have been symbolic of his claim to kingship. According to the Gospels, when Jesus entered Jerusalem, many of the people spread their garments on the ground before him proclaiming, "Hosanna. Blessed is he that cometh in the name of the Lord."[78] John adds that the people took branches from the palm trees (an expression of victory and thankfulness) and called him "the king of Israel."[79] That night Jesus went with his disciples to Bethany.[80] Apparently he feared to remain in Jerusalem at night, feeling that a conspiracy was being fomented against him. Hence he spent every night away from Jerusalem.

On the following day Jesus went to the Temple. According to both Mark and Matthew, Jesus cast out the people that "sold and bought in the Temple and overthrew the tables of the moneychangers and the seats of them that sold doves."[81] The moneychangers, known in Hebrew literature as *shulhanim,* were a well-established and very useful institution. During the festivals many Judaeans from the Diaspora came on pilgrimage to the Temple. There they purchased from local farmers livestock for the sacrifices. This sale had to be transacted in Judaean currency, as the farmers would accept no other. Foreign money had therefore continually to be exchanged for the money of Judaea. The *shulhanim* served this purpose and charged a small percentage for their services. Most likely some of them occasionally made an excessive charge for the exchange of the various foreign moneys, the values of which were not well known to the average men of Judaea. It is doubtful, however, that Jesus could have thrown them out of the Temple area. They were well-entrenched and protected by the Temple guards. Luke and John do not mention moneychangers, but they do refer to the expulsion of those engaged in buying and selling—apparently the dealers in animals for the sacrifices.[82]

ARREST, TRIAL, AND CRUCIFIXION

The Course of the Arrest

The coming of Jesus to Jerusalem disturbed the Judaean leaders in Jerusalem. But a short while previously, Herod Antipas had put John the Baptist to death because he considered him a potential political problem—and some now believed Jesus was John, arisen from the dead to come to Jerusalem to preach his doctrine. Any disturbance was a peril to the Judaean authorities, who could maintain their status only if complete tranquility prevailed. The high priest in particular—then Caiaphas—was really a servant, or lackey, of Rome, appointed by the legate or procurator to ensure local control of malcontents. His sensitivity to the Galilean preacher is not difficult to imagine. Nor is Pilate's. As described above, Pilate was vicious to the people and hostile to their religion. He was cunning and treacherous. Due to his provocations, Judaea was on the brink of rebellion. The leaders of the people and High Priest Caiaphas, knowing his cunning and treachery, were fearful that if anything should happen Pilate would hold them responsible and wreak vengeance on the entire people. Thus John tells how even before the Passion week began a *synedrion* was called and it was argued that if Jesus continued his preaching, the Romans would come and "take away both our place and nation." High Priest Caiaphas elaborated on this and said, "It is expedient for us that one man should die for the people, and that the whole not perish."[83] Thus, the complex and stormy background of Judaea under the tyranny of Roman rule brought about Jesus' preaching and also his tragic death.

There is a fundamental discrepancy between the Passion narrative in the synoptic Gospels and John; but there are also contradictions, inconsistencies, and obscurities in the synoptics themselves. The problems of historical analysis would thus already be great. They are

further compounded by the intense theological significance of the events for the earliest witnesses and trans-
mitters of the traditions and for modern interpreters as
well. The historian who approaches this topic must call
upon all his resources of open-mindedness and ob-
jectivity.

Mark tells this story: Two days before the slaughtering of the paschal lamb and the Festival (of Passover),
the chief priest and the scribes sought to take Jesus and
to destroy him, "but they said, not on the feast day, lest
there be an uproar of the people."[84] Matthew says they
assembled in the house of High Priest Caiaphas, "and
consulted that they might take Jesus by subtility and
kill him. But they said, not on the feast day, lest there
be an uproar among the people."[85] Luke relates: "Now
the feast of unleavened bread drew nigh, which is called
the Passover, and the chief priest and the scribes sought
how they might destroy Jesus, for they feared the
people."[86] John knows of no plot among the high priest,
scribes and elders to kill Jesus—a departure of important
historical significance.

The synoptic Gospels describe the betrayal by Judas
Iscariot as follows: Judas went to the high priest and
offered to betray Jesus and in return was either promised
money or paid in advance.[87] John, on the other hand, does
not connect the betrayal by Judas Iscariot with the high
priest nor mention that he received money, but says that
he decided to betray Jesus because Satan had entered
into him after he had supped with Jesus. He writes, "And
after the sop Satan entered into him. Then said Jesus
unto him, 'That thou doest, do quickly.' "[88] This is another meaningful variation from the synoptic Gospels.

Jesus' betrayal by Judas Iscariot raises many perplex-
ing problems. Jesus trusted his disciples implicitly and
gave them the powers which he possessed. What then
prompted Judas to betray his master? The money, thirty
shekels, was of no significance. Only one other motive can
be substantiated by the sources, the Gospels, and that is
John's assertion that Judas became possessed. In other

words, John says that Judas was impelled to his conduct by a supernatural demonic force, over which he had no control. Where antiquity said Satan entered him, a modern would say he was not of sound mind. But why was Judas needed at all? Jesus could have been arrested without being betrayed. He was well-known and preached in the Temple every day. This enigmatic story may have been inspired by some theological speculation which is no longer known.

The Time of the Arrest

The synoptic Gospels say that on the fourteenth day of Nisan, when the paschal lamb was slaughtered, Jesus and the twelve apostles ate dinner together. He took the unleavened bread, broke and blessed it, and gave it to the apostles. He then took a cup of wine, drank of it, and passed it among his disciples. They sang a hymn, *hallel*, and went out on the Mount of Olives.[89]

John says that Jesus supped with his disciples, but does not make reference to the breaking of bread, the drinking of wine, or the chanting of the *hallel*.[90] According to the synoptic Gospels, Jesus was arrested on that night (according to the Judaean calendar, already 15 Nisan) and crucified on the following day,[91] the first day of the Feast of Unleavened Bread. Thus the last supper was on the first night of the festival, now known as the *seder*. That is not John's understanding. He relates that Jesus was arrested on the night of 14 Nisan and crucified on the following day (still 14 Nisan) when the paschal lamb was to be slaughtered.[92] Thus the last supper that Jesus shared with his disciples was an ordinary meal.

The discrepancy led to schism in the early days of Christianity regarding the fixing of the day of the *pascha* (called Easter in English-speaking countries) : between the Quatrodecimans and the anti-Quatrodecimans.[93] Some churches, following the date given by the Gospel according to John—that Jesus was crucified on the eve of the Passover festival, when the paschal lamb was slaughtered—celebrated *pascha* on the fourteenth day of Nisan. They were the Quatrodecimans. Other churches, holding that Jesus ate the paschal lamb and was crucified on the first day of the festival, as the synoptic Gospels say, celebrated *pascha* on the fifteenth day of Nisan. These were the anti-Quatrodecimans.[94]

The Investigation Before the High Priest

Although the Gospels are based upon common oral traditions, there are some discrepancies in their accounts of the arrest and trial of Jesus which cannot be explained. According to Mark, Judas came with a great, armed multitude from the high priest, scribes, and the elders, and he betrayed his master with a kiss. Jesus complained against them for coming with swords as if he were a *lestes,* a robber. Further, he said that he was in the Temple teaching and no one had ever molested him. He was then led away to the house of the high priest where all the chief priests, the elders and the scribes were assembled. All the disciples fled, except Peter, who followed his master. While Peter was in the courtyard, he was asked whether he was associated with Jesus of Nazareth. He denied that he was. They recognized him as a Galilean and therefore concluded that he must have known Jesus. He said, "I know not this man of whom you speak."

The high priests and all the members of the *synedrion* sought testimony against Jesus to put him to death, but found none. Some men testified falsely that they heard Jesus say that he would destroy the Temple that was made by human hands, and that he would within three days build another not made by human hands. The high priest asked Jesus what he had to say, but Jesus did not answer. Then the high priest asked him, "Art thou the messiah (Christ) the son of the Blest?" And Jesus said, "I am, and ye shall see the Son of Man sitting on the right hand of Power (God) and coming in the clouds of heaven." The high priest, on hearing these words, rent his clothes and exclaimed, "What need we any further witnesses? You have heard the blasphemy: What think ye?" And they all condemned him, as guilty of death. The following morning the chief priests held a consultation with the elders, the scribes and the whole *synedrion,* and delivered Jesus over to Pilate.[95]

Matthew gives the same account with slight varia-. tions.[96] Luke presents a different picture of the arrest. He does not say that the elders and the scribes were assembled in the house of the high priest when Jesus was arrested. He states that the morning after Jesus' arrest, "The elders of the people, the chief priests and the scribes came together and led him into their *synedrion* (their council)."[97] He was then asked, "Art thou the Messiah (Christ)? Tell us." Jesus answered, "If I tell thee, thou will not believe." This Gospel makes no mention of the high priest's accusation of blasphemy against Jesus. It says that when Jesus was delivered to Pilate he was accused of "perverting the people and forbidding giving tribute to Caesar, saying that he himself is a Messiah, a king."

There is a sharp disagreement among the synoptic Gospels themselves. According to Mark and Matthew, the scribes and the elders were assembled in the house of High Priest Caiaphas, and Jesus was examined and charged with blasphemy.[98] Jesus did not use abusive language against God. Even had he used such language, a person who does so cannot be condemned to death by a court according to Judaean law; he would be punished only by divine visitation.[99] Only a person "cursing God by the name of God" was liable to capital punishment.[100] Jesus did not curse God. His declaration that he would sit on the right hand of Power (God)[101] and come on the clouds of heaven cannot be considered blasphemy under Judaean law or even custom. Many a pious Jew then confidently anticipated a future world where they would sit in the company of God and enjoy the divine glory.

According to Luke, Jesus was interrogated on the first day of Passover, and was asked only whether he was the

Messiah. When the multitude delivered him over to
Pilate, they accused him of perverting the nation, of
forbidding the people to pay tribute to Caesar, and of
saying that he was the Messiah (Christ), the King.[102]
Luke does not mention that he was condemned to death
by the high priest and his council on religious grounds.
The accusation against him was political; he was accused
of subversion and charged with being a rebel.

The Trial Before Pilate

To continue Mark's account, when Jesus was brought
before Pilate, the procurator phrased his inquiry in this
way: "Art thou the king of the Judaeans?"[103] Mark says,
and the synoptics agree, that it was customary to release
a prisoner on the Festival of Unleavened Bread.[104] Pilate
asked the Judaeans, "Shall I release unto you the king of
the Judaeans?" But, the Gospels continue, the chief priest
instigated the populace to ask for the release of Barabbas
who, according to Mark, had stirred up insurrection
and had committed murder. Pilate then asked them,
"What shall I do to him whom you call King of the
Judaeans?" They cried out "Crucify him." Pilate then
released Barabbas. He scourged Jesus and ordered that
he be crucified.[105]

The other two synoptic Gospels give the same account, but again with some variations. Matthew says
that when the procurator asked Jesus, "Art thou the
King of the Judaeans?" Jesus answered, "Thou sayest."
Pilate asked, "What shall I do with Jesus who is called
Messiah (Christ)?" When Pilate pronounced sentence,
he washed his hands and said, "I am innocent of the
blood of this just man." To this the people replied, "His
blood be on us and on our children."[106] This account is
not recorded in any other Gospel. It must be added that
the washing of the hands, symbolizing guiltlessness, was
not a Roman custom, but a Judaean one. By no stretch
of the imagination can it be supposed that Pilate, who

despised Judaean customs, would at such a time have mocked one of their customs.

Luke remains political: When Jesus was delivered over to Pilate he called the chief priests, the leaders and the people and said to them, "You have brought this man unto me as one that perverteth the people; and behold I have examined him before you, have found no fault in this man touching those things whereof ye accused him."[107]

The Theological Interpretations

John's narrative presents a rather different picture. He states that Judas Iscariot had with him a cohort which he received from the chief priests and the Pharisees. When he arrived with the cohort, Jesus said, "Whom seek ye?" They answered that they were looking for Jesus of Nazareth. Then Jesus said, "I am he."[108] They arrested him and led him to the house of Ananus, the father-in-law of Caiaphas. John adds that this was the same Caiaphas who had counseled that it was better that one man should die than that all the Judaeans should die for one man.

Jesus was taken from the house of Annas to the house of the Caiaphas, and the following morning to the judgment hall (*Praeatrium*). The priests and the leaders did not enter it lest "They should be defiled, but that they might eat of the paschal lamb (Passover)."[109] On (for John it is clearly the morning of) the 14th day of Nisan the paschal lamb was slaughtered. This discrepancy as to the correct date cannot be explained as due to different oral tradition. The eve (more precisely, the afternoon before) of the Festival of Unleavened Bread was then a very significant day in the Judaean calendar; people made pilgrimages to Jerusalem from far distant countries for the solemn slaughtering of the paschal lamb. After the sacrifice, as darkness fell, the families gathered to eat of the paschal lamb and chanted hymns in commemoration of the deliverance from Egypt. That night and the following day was the first day of the Festival of Unleavened Bread. No one could have confused slaughtering day with the festival day. If Jesus had been crucified on the day and just at the hours when the paschal lamb was slaughtered, his followers would have been so impressed that no tradition could have arisen to place the crucifixion one day later, on the first day of the Festival of Passover. And the opposite is also true: If Jesus had been crucified on the first day of the Festival of Unleavened Bread, no tradition would place the crucifixion on the day the paschal lamb was slaughtered.

The explanation of this confusion of dates lies in a different direction entirely: it is not a confusion of dates, but a difference of theological accent. The synoptic Gospels conceived of Jesus as the savior, personifying the idea of salvation in the Passover festival.[110] He suffered death for the sins of the people and, in his death and resurrection, fulfilled the words of the prophet of Israel. Just as the Israelites were saved from Egyptian slavery on the first day of Passover, having smeared the blood of the paschal lamb on their doors as a symbol of unity between God and Israel, so the blood of Jesus served as a symbol of unity between God and the followers of Jesus. The Gospel according to John, on the other hand, presented the view of Jesus as the redeemer, personifying the paschal lamb. Just as the paschal lamb was sacrificed on the eve of Passover, so Jesus the Redeemer was crucified on the fourteenth day of Nisan to redeem the world from original sin. So the evangelist said, "Behold the Lamb of God which taketh away the sin of the world."[111] In his narrative of the crucifixion, John says that "when they came to Jesus and saw that he was dead already, they brake not his legs."[112] He was alluding to the paschal lamb, of which the Pentateuch says, "a bone of him shall not be broken."[113]

While there is a discrepancy between the synoptic Gospels and the Fourth Gospel as to the date of the crucifixion, they agree on the day of the week; both say that it was a Friday. Again, this has a theological mean-

ing. According to tradition, Friday saw the creation of
Adam; on Friday he committed the original sin and was
condemned to death.[114] He also died on Friday. So Jesus,
the redeemer from the original sin, had to be tried and
put to death on Friday.[115] It all had a theological rather
than a historical meaning.

John continues: since the chief priests would not enter
the judgment hall, Pilate himself went there. He called
Jesus in and questioned him, "Art thou the king of the
Judaeans?" Jesus asked Pilate if someone had told him
this or whether this was his own thought. Pilate retorted,
"Am I a Judaean?" and stated that the Judaeans and the
chief priests had delivered him. Then Pilate asked, "What
hast thou done?" Jesus answered, "My kingdom is not of
this world." Pilate did not comprehend this and asked
Jesus, "Art thou king then?" To this Jesus replied,
"Thou sayest that I am king."[116]

John then gives the same account as to the release of
Barabbas or the King of the Jews. After Barabbas is
chosen, he asked them concerning Jesus, and the chief
priests and their subordinates cried out, "Crucify
him!"[117] Pilate then told them to take Jesus and crucify
him themselves, since he found no fault with him. The
Judaeans answered that according to the Torah, he
ought to die because he had proclaimed himself "the Son
of God."[118] When Pilate heard this he was frightened and
again examined Jesus, but this time Jesus gave him no
answer. John states that Pilate again wanted to release
Jesus, but the Judaeans asserted, "If thou let this man
go thou art not Ceasar's friend." John adds that it was
on the day of preparation (Friday), on the sixth hour
(noon), that Pilate brought Jesus forth a last time and
said to the Judaeans, "Behold your king!" The people
cried out, "Crucify him!" Pilate again asked the
Judaeans, "Shall I crucify your king?" The chief priest
answered, "We have no king but Caesar."[119]

Pilate delivered Jesus to be crucified. He was crucified
between two other men, *lestaie*, robbers, one on each
side.[120] For the *titulus* which was put on the crucifix to

indicate the victim's crime, Pilate ordered inscribed in Hebrew, Greek and Latin the words "Jesus of Nazareth, King of the Judaeans."[121] The chief priest urged Pilate not to put this inscription up. Pilate answered, "What I have written I have written." After Jesus was crucified the soldiers divided his garments into four parts among themselves.[122]

The Course of Events

A historical reconstruction of the ministry of Jesus may now be given: During the reign of Tiberius Caesar, in the year 29, Jesus of Nazareth began his ministry. It was concurrent with that of John the Baptist. Jesus had a following in Galilee while John the Baptist was still actively occupied with his mission. The followers of Jesus believed him to be the Messiah, the Son of God and King of Israel; some of them wanted to proclaim him king.[123] Jesus felt that the time for this had not yet come and resisted their importunities.

During those years Jesus went to Jerusalem several times, particularly on the Festivals of Passover and Tabernacles. While Jesus visited Jerusalem he attended the Temple and preached his gospel of the imminent coming of God's kingdom. Undoubtedly he mingled with the Apocalyptists who actively awaited the advent of a messiah, a scion of David. These activities brought him into conflict with the effective civil leaders, the high priests and their followers. Moreover, his association with sinners, publicans, and women of low repute, and his laxness in the observance of traditional laws, antagonized the Sadducees and Essenes and brought about clashes between him and the Pharisees. Those who embraced the Fourth Philosophy, the followers of Judas of Galilee, looked upon him with contempt, as a dreamer and deceiver.

After the execution of John the Baptist, many of the disciples of Jesus wanted him to go to Jerusalem. Others were opposed to his going there as they feared that he would be imprisoned or executed. Nevertheless, Jesus decided to go to Jerusalem even though he felt certain he would share John's fate. With the approach of the Festival of Passover, in the spring of the year 34, Jesus went to Jerusalem.

At that time Judaea was ruled like a conquered country by a Roman procurator. The Romans punished severely anyone who incited the people against Rome's authority. They held the local Judaean leaders responsible— hostages, as it were—for the submissiveness of the entire populace. Under such oppressive circumstances many informed on the dissenters among their own people, thus saving their own positions and even their lives, hoping, at best, to have prevented more punitive measures against Judaea as a whole.

When Jesus arrived in Jerusalem his followers acclaimed him as the Son of David and King of Israel. The high priest and his associates, in order to save themselves and the country, thought it best to deliver Jesus to Pilate as a rebel. The chief priest assembled a *synedrion* of his associates, friends and retainers. (The term *synedrion* should not be confused with *sanhedrin,* which denotes a religious court. The latter term came into use only after the destruction of the Temple. During the time of Jesus the religious court was called *Bet Din*).

When Jesus was brought before the *synedrion,* he was interrogated about his teachings, especially whether he had claimed to be the messiah, and therefore King of the Judaeans, and he was asked if he was the messiah. The Judaean leaders were highly sensitive on this score. Judaeans from all over the country had come on pilgrimage to Jerusalem, and the civil authorities were fearful that if Jesus claimed to be the messiah he might trigger a rebellion against Rome.

The following morning, Jesus was delivered to Pilate. The *synedrion* charged him with perverting the people by prohibiting them from paying tribute to Caesar, and by claiming to be the messiah, the King of the Judaeans. It seems reasonable that Pilate did not think Jesus would be a source of danger to Roman rule and so tried to turn the accusation into one of religious character. The Judaeans claimed that Jesus was a political offender and thus they had no jurisdiction. Then Pilate took advantage of the custom of releasing a prisoner for the festival, and asked the Judaeans whether they wanted freedom for Barabbas, who was a murderer, or Jesus, their king. The Judaeans asked for the release of Barabbas, being fearful that Pilate was scheming to involve them as accomplices of Jesus in his claim to be king of the Judaeans. Again and again the term king occurs in the sources. Knowing the political situation, this cannot be a religious euphemism. Finally when Pilate again asked the Judaeans, "Shall I crucify your King?" the chief priest answered, "We have no king but Caesar." Then Pilate was satisfied and ordered the crucifixion of Jesus. Jesus was crucified in the Spring of the year 34.[124] In that year neither the 14th of Nisan, when the paschal lamb was slaughtered, nor the 15th of Nisan, the first day of Passover, fell on Friday or on Saturday.[125] However, if the year 34 was intercalated, that is, another month of Adar was added, the first day of the festival of unleavened bread did fall on Saturday. Thus, in accordance with the Fourth Gospel, Jesus was crucified on Friday, the eve of Passover.

Crucifixion was a regular, hideous, Roman punishment for political offenders accused of subversion.[126] The two men crucified with Jesus were executed by the Romans as *lestai*, or brigands. But this term also has a political connotation. They were almost certainly *not* common thieves, but rebels against Roman rule, probably of the group known as the Fourth Philosophy. They died for political reasons, and so did Jesus. His *titulus* described his crime. It should be taken in full literalness: *Iesus Nazarenus, Rex Iudaeorum*, "Jesus of Nazareth, King of the Judaeans." No wonder the chief priests requested Pilate to alter it to read, "He (Jesus) said, 'I am the king of the Judaeans.'" They feared that Pilate might even use a dead man's dreams as a pretext by which to oppress them. The Gospels further state that the soldiers divided the garments of Jesus. This need not be another effort to have the story fulfill Scripture. Since Jesus was executed as a political offender, his clothing belonged to the State.[127] Its minions took what they could.

One more fact deserves notice. Not all the Judaeans present at the trial approved of the execution of Jesus. When he was led to be crucified, Luke states, "There followed him a great company of people and women who bewailed and lamented him."[128] There is no good reason not to give credence to this testimony that many God and freedom-loving Judaeans were in distress on seeing Jesus led to Golgotha.

The historical Jesus died in the Spring of the year 34. He was born a humble Judaean and was crucified as a political offender against Rome for claiming, messianically, to be king of the Judaeans. The ideological Jesus, who revolutionized a large part of the world's thinking and changed the course of civilization, began with the crucifixion.[129]

3. JUDAEA UNDER THE PROCURATORS. AGRIPPA I

EMPEROR GAIUS CALIGULA

"Divine" Gaius

The accession of the young and well-educated Gaius Caligula[1] in the year 37 C.E. was received with gladness throughout the empire. The people hoped that the tyranny which had prevailed during the reign of Tiberius Nero would not return.[2] The Judaeans in particular were joyful when Vitellius announced the new accession, and they gladly took the oath of allegiance.[3] They were also pleased that he had almost immediately appointed Agrippa, son of Aristobolus and grandson of Mariamme the Hasmonean, as king over the tetrarchy which had been ruled by his uncle, Philip.[4] Thus when Gaius became ill the Judaeans brought sacrifices and prayed for his recovery.[5] During the first eighteen months their confidence seemed repaid. Gaius ruled the country with great magnanimity,[6] and the Judaeans hoped that they would enjoy such favors as they had under Augustus Caesar. A new procurator named Marcellus was appointed over Judaea in place of Pilate, and Petronius replaced Vitellius as legate of Syria.

As the second year of his rule ended, however, it was more and more certain that Gaius Caligula would become one of the cruelest caesars—not only towards the people but also to his friends and relatives—and one of the most self-centered, to the point of declaring himself a god, the counterpart of Zeus, and demanding worship from everyone.

Once Gaius was well-established in power his true nature revealed itself. The Roman historians wrote that he was cruel at heart and full of bitterness towards humanity.[7] Gaius had no feeling for friendship. Although Macro and Ennis had greatly assisted him in winning the throne and had been his intimate friends, he ordered them to take their own lives.[8] He killed Ptolemy, son of King Juba, who was his cousin. Suetonius wrote, "All these were rewarded for their kinship and their faithful services by a bloody death."[9] He also forced his grandmother, Antonia, who had brought him up, to take her own life.[10] (There was a rumor that he gave her poison.) It had been state policy in Rome for the caesars to adopt the cult of divinity, but they were deified only after their death. But Gaius took the role of divinity seriously while he was alive.[11] Many high officials who had worked under Tiberius and were afraid for their lives and positions added to his conceit by flattering him that he was indeed a god.

Thus Vitellius, who became one of the foremost statesmen of Rome, was according to Suetonius, the first to worship Gaius Caesar as a god. He always approached Gaius with his head veiled and prostrated himself.[12] When Gaius stated that he enjoyed converse with the moon and asked Vitellius whether he could see the goddess with him, Vitellius replied, "Only you gods, master, may behold one another."[13] Vitellius even distorted historical facts in his adulation of Gaius. Though the peace treaty between the Parthians and Rome had been signed in the last year of Tiberius' reign, Vitellius insisted it had been consummated during the reign of Gaius. He added that the Parthian King of Kings, Artabanus, was so anxious to win the friendship of

Gaius, that he sent his son Cyrus to Rome as a hostage and made obeisance to the Roman standards. The falsehood is recorded by the Roman historians Suetonius, Dio, and Tacitus; only Josephus preserved the truth.[14]

Gaius took his divinity seriously. He built a temple to his own godhood, with priests, animal offerings and a life-size golden statue of himself. Many of the Roman nobles vied with each other to secure the priesthood, and daily offered the sacrifices to him.[15] When his wife Caesonia gave birth to a daughter a month after their marriage, Gaius proclaimed this had come about through supernatural means. He took the child to the Capitol and placed her on the knees of Jupiter declaring that she had two fathers.[16] He even signed his official documents with the term god, and began living with his sister Drusilla,[17] following the custom of the Ptolemies who married their sisters. The Romans, unlike the Egyptians, considered this incest. When Drusilla died, he ordered that she too be deified.

A million Judaeans were living in Egypt at that time, most of them in Alexandria,[18] the bulk of them concentrated in the Delta district. Great animosity prevailed between the Greeks and the Judaeans. When Gaius declared himself a god, the heathens were able to accept him as such, and they erected statues of him and worshipped them.[19] The Judaeans, who believed in one God alone, could not do this. The Alexandrian pagans saw this as a great opportunity to destroy the Judaeans. The prefect of Egypt, Aulus Avillius Flaccus, an appointee and friend of Tiberius, welcomed the scheme. He thought that by showing zeal for the emperor's cult, he might rehabilitate himself with Gaius. Besides, he hoped by ingratiating himself with the Greek population to have them support him before Rome. When the Judaeans refused to allow the erection of statues in their *proseuche*, house of prayer, a disastrous pogrom took place in Alexandria.[20]

Petronius and the Statue

A similar outbreak took place in Jamneh, the city which Salome had bequeathed to Livia, the wife of Augustus Caesar, and thus had become the property of the imperial family. Although many of Jahneh's inhabitants were Judaeans, it had attracted many heathen settlers. As usual, there was no amity between these groups. The heathens wished to worship idols, which they could not do in Jabneh since it was regarded as part of Judaea and hence such worship would not be tolerated by the Judaeans. When the heathens of Jabneh learned that Gaius considered himself a god, they erected an altar to the emperor to avenge themselves upon the Judaeans, and the Judaeans promptly destroyed it.[21] Gaius became greatly enraged at this sacrilegious act. He decided to destroy the Judaean "superstition" and, if necessary, wipe out the entire people.[22] He ordered Petronius, the legate of Syria, to erect an enormous statue of himself in the guise of Zeus, and place it in the Holy of Holies in the Temple of Jerusalem, using force to crush any resistance.[23]

Petronius was not happy over this order. He knew that the Judaeans would not allow the erection of a statue in the Temple; that if it were done, it would bring about the decimation of the Judaeans. He was apprehensive lest the Parthian Judaeans, who lived across the Euphrates and were known as warriors, come to the aid of their coreligionists,[24] and he become embattled on two fronts. Moreover the peace treaty between the Parthians and Rome was still shaky. Should he withdraw his army from the Euphrates to fight the Judaeans, the *status quo* might no longer hold.

Gaius, moreover, was contemplating a visit to Egypt. This further disturbed Petronius. If the Judaeans rebelled, they would destroy the entire harvest, and the immense supplies of food needed for the emperor and his huge retinue would be unavailable. Petronius determined to delay the placing of the statue in the Temple as long as possible.[25] He commissioned sculptors in Sidon to make the statue, but instructed them that it must be of surpassing magnificence so that the length of time consumed in its execution was not important. He then took two legions[26] and a large auxiliary force to Ptolemais, probably in the winter of 39. The sources do not agree as to whether he informed the Judaeans of the decree of Gaius and asked their representatives to come to Ptolemais or whether the bad tidings were rumored throughout the land.[27] Thousands of Judaeans of all classes came to Ptolemais to implore Petronius not to violate the law of their forefathers, insisting they would rather be killed by his soldiers than submit to the violation of their law. Petronius angrily told them that he was not the emperor, and must carry out the emperor's decree. The Judaeans replied that just as he could not disobey the command of Gaius, they could not disobey the command of their God.

Petronius was profoundly impressed by the firm stand of the Judaeans and by the fervor of their mournful supplications. He called a *synedrion* of his friends and subordinates, who agreed that there should be no haste in carrying out the order of Gaius. They suggested that Petronius write a letter to Gaius explaining the reason for the delay, pointing out that a truly magnificent statue, in keeping with the dignity of the emperor, would require time. He also mentioned that it would be advisable to postpone the erection until after the harvest, so that the Judaeans should not destroy it. Gaius responded in a fury, acknowledging Petronius' prudence but commanding no further delay since the harvest would soon be completed.

In the Spring of the year 40, Petronius marched with his army to Tiberias[28] for reasons that can only be conjectured. Petronius, a reasonable man, probably received Gaius' new order with a heavy heart and went to Tiberias to seek advice from the family of King Agrippa—Agrippa being in Rome—who were friendly with Gaius, on how to prevent or delay the threatened catastrophe.

Petronius summoned the leaders to Tiberias and told them that every people subject to Rome erected a statue to Gaius in their cities along with their gods, and he deplored the fact that the Judaeans alone opposed such homage. It was a defiance tantamount to rebellion. The Judaeans declared that they were forbidden to place an image of God, and certainly not that of a human being,[29] not only in their Temple, but anywhere in their country. They would never transgress the laws that they had received from their forefathers, even if that meant all the Judaeans—men, women and children—would have to be killed. They said further that they did not contemplate revolt, but twice daily offered sacrifices in the Temple for the welfare of Caesar and the Roman people.[30] Aristobolus, the brother of Agrippa, other members of the royal family, and leaders of the city joined together and begged Petronius to inform Gaius that the Judaeans were loyal to Rome but that their religion forbade the erection of statues. Petronius agreed to write to Gaius in their behalf, although he was well aware of the risk to himself. He returned to Antioch and sent a report to Gaius, who wrote back that he deserved death for tardiness in executing an imperial order—in effect, that Petronius should commit suicide. Gaius also threatened to make Petronius an example of the fate deserved by one who dares disobey.[31] (The outcome of this harsh epistle is noted below.)

Agrippa's Intercession

King Agrippa, a close friend of Gaius, was in Rome when the emperor returned from Germany.[32] Philo was also in Rome at that time, as head of the delegation of Alexandrian Judaeans seeking Gaius' favor to ameliorate the anti-Judaean agitation in Alexandria.[33] Philo's account of what transpired is somewhat different from Josephus': Philo states that Agrippa was aware from

Gaius' facial expression that the Emperor was unfriendly to him. Agrippa was perplexed as to his offense and the emperor said to him, "Your noble fellow countrymen, who alone of every race of men do not acknowledge Gaius as a god, appear to be courting even death by their repugnance. When I ordered a statue of Zeus to be set up in the Temple, they marched out as a body from their city and country, nominally to make a petition but actually to defy my orders."

When Agrippa heard about the setting up of a statue in the Temple, he collapsed and was carried to his home in a coma, which lasted thirty-six hours. He then wrote a letter to Gaius appealing to him to rescind his order. The text which Philo gives reveals dignity and courage. Agrippa wrote as a Judaean whose native city was Jerusalem where the Temple of the most high God was situated and where his ancestors had been kings, some of them high priests. He considered the kingship inferior to the priesthood, for the office of the priest is to worship God while the king takes charge of men. Jerusalem was the holy mother city, not only of Judaea, but of all the Judaeans living in the Roman empire and beyond the Euphrates. He reminded Gaius of the good will which the Roman Caesars before him had bestowed upon the Judaeans. He stressed the friendly relations of Agrippa, Gaius' maternal grandfather, with his own grandfather Herod. He mentioned the good will that Augustus Caesar had shown towards the Judaeans and stressed Caesar's respect for the Judaean religion which was such that he had provided funds from his own treasury for the daily sacrifices offered in his honor. He acknowledged all the favors which Gaius had bestowed upon him, but said he would be a traitor to his own people if he did not make this appeal. He implored Gaius not to withdraw with this one stroke all the favors which Agrippa had received from him. Philo concludes that Gaius was greatly impressed by the letter and wrote to Petronius that if he had already put up the statue in the Temple, it should stand; otherwise, he should not carry out the order.[34]

Josephus, in *Antiquities*,[35] gives an entirely different account of how Agrippa succeeded in having Gaius rescind his order. He says that Agrippa once invited Gaius to a lavish banquet in the preparation of which no expense was spared. Gaius was impressed with the extravagance of his host and later, when in a merry mood, he made a speech in praise of Agrippa, saying he would grant any wish of Agrippa's to the limit of his ability. At first Agrippa refused to express any wish, but when Gaius pressed him he said, "My master, I will ask nothing relating to my own happiness, for what you have already bestowed upon me has made me superior, but I desire something which may make you glorious for piety and induce God to assist you in your designs . . . For my petition is this, that you will no longer have in mind the erection of the statue which you had ordered to be set up in the Judaean Temple by Petronius."

There is no doubt that Agrippa interceded with Gaius in behalf of the Judaeans to recall his decree. He did so not only because he was devoted to the Judaean religion, but out of self-interest. Should Petronius proceed to install the statue, the Judaeans would rebell and the country would be laid waste. His own kingdom would be reduced to ashes and his own life would be at stake, since his involvement was unavoidable. What means Agrippa employed in his intervention is not known. Neither the letter recorded by Philo, nor the speech preserved by Josephus is genuine.[36]

Agrippa's letter, reported by Philo, would not have placated Gaius, but would have infuriated him. The historians called Gaius a madman, who considered himself a god equal to Zeus; and in this letter Agrippa did not address him as god. On the contrary, he spoke of Jerusalem wherein a Temple was situated to the Most High God. To Gaius the insane, this would have been treason, *lèse majesté*. There are also some historical discrepancies in the letter. Agrippa could hardly have learned about the statue first from Gaius himself, since the Judaeans had been in an uproar over this for some time, after Petronius had informed them of it. It is inconceivable that, after the demonstrations at Ptolemais and Tiberias, the Judaeans had not informed Agrippa, an intimate friend of Gaius, of the calamity which threatened. The presumed Agrippa letter asserts that Augustus Caesar had provided revenue from his own treasury for the daily sacrifices. This is historically untrue, as Agrippa would have known, for these sacrifices were provided for by the Temple treasury.[37] The references in the letter to the good will of Augustus Caesar towards the Judaeans would not influence the attitude of Gaius. He had abolished the annual celebration of Augustus' victory at Actium and punished those consuls who celebrated it.[38] From time to time he even posed as a descendant of Antony (through his grandmother Antonia) rather than of Augustus.[39]

The speech of Agrippa as recorded by Josephus is simply inauthentic. In it he did not address Gaius as god, despite the fact that Gaius demanded that all address him thus. Agrippa's remark that, if Gaius would rescind his decree, God would render assistance to his designs, would have been an unthinkable blunder and put Agrippa's life in jeopardy, since Gaius considered himself a god and held the God of Israel in contempt. Josephus in *War*[40] gives the simple and undoubtedly correct explanation: only the death of Gaius prevented the statue from being erected in the Temple.

The bases for the fictions are easy to ascertain. Philo wrote the *Embassy to Gaius* and *Against Flaccus* as apologetic tracts. He composed the letter of Agrippa to point out that the Temple in Jerusalem was holy for all who adhered to the Judaean religion, wherever they lived, since it was dedicated to the Most High God. Yet, though Jerusalem was their mother city, the Judaeans were thoroughly loyal to Rome. Augustus Caesar had recognized the Judaean religion even in Rome, where he had banished all Oriental cults and given special privilege to the Judaeans, specifically the right to assemble in their synagogues and to send money to the Temple in Jerusalem. Thus Philo tried to maintain the integrity of Judaism while showing its place in the non-Jewish world.

Josephus probably had found a tradition that King Agrippa had intervened with Gaius. He then followed his usual method, derived from the Greek historians. Josephus, being certain that Agrippa spoke to Gaius, recorded the speech which he thought Agrippa should have made.

Gaius Caligula was assassinated by a group of republican conspirators, headed by Chaerea, on the twenty-fourth of January, 41 C.E.[41] Only thus were the Judaeans saved from the bloodshed which threatened. The news of Gaius' death reached Petronius twenty-seven days before the letter of Gaius implying that he kill himself.[42] The assassination saved Agrippa's life as well. Gaius would have executed Agrippa as he had so many other of his intimate friends. The day of Gaius' death, the twenty-second of Shebat, was declared a semi-holiday by the Judaeans.[43]

KING AGRIPPA 1

The Youthful Agrippa

Agrippa was the son of Aristobolus and the grandson of Mariamme the Hasmonean and Herod the Great. His mother was Berenice, the daughter of Salome and Costobarus.[44] He was born in the year 10 B.C.E., three years before the execution of his father. Both his grandmother Mariamme and his grandfather Costobarus had been put to death by Herod.[45] After the death of his father, Agrippa's mother sent him to Rome for his education. Agrippa married his cousin Cypros,[46] the daughter of Salampsio who was his father's sister. Cypros, like Agrippa, was partly Hasmonean since she too was a granddaughter of Mariamme.

Agrippa was an ambitious young man. Like his grandfather Herod, he knew that the fortunes of Judaea were
in the hands of the Caesars. But times had changed;
there was no more civil war. The empire was well-
established. One could not gain the favor of the emperor
by supplying arms and provisions for his army. Agrippa
therefore courted the friendship of the ruling family,
hoping to gain the kingdom of Judaea for himself, as
his grandfather Herod had done. He became a popular
figure in Roman high society which was already morally
quite corrupt, indulging in all sorts of excesses. To become intimate with them, Agrippa joined in their self-
indulgences. Through the friendship of his mother with
Antonia he became acquainted with her sons, Germanicus and Claudius.[47] Claudius was suspected of being
retarded and the brilliant Germanicus died suddenly in
the year 18, leaving a son named Gaius Caligula, whom
Agrippa also made his friend. After the death of Germanicus, it was generally held that Drusus, the son of
Tiberius, would succeed his father. Agrippa thereupon
cultivated the friendship of Drusus.

So long as his mother Berenice was alive, Agrippa
had sufficient funds to indulge in extravagant living.
Upon her death he had to borrow to continue his way of
life.[48] In the year 23 he received a severe setback—
Drusus, the only son of Tiberius, died. Agrippa had
built his future on his friendship with Drusus. Moreover, the death of Drusus so affected Tiberius that he
refused to see any of his son's friends.[49] Agrippa was
thus cut off from contact with Tiberius. Sejanus, the
praetorian prefect, now became the power in Rome. He
had great influence over Tiberius, and it was assumed
that he would succeed Tiberius. Sejanus was anti-
Judaean, and also schemed to eliminate any of the family
of Germanicus who might be his rivals.[50] Agrippa was
friendly with the imperial household, but he knew he
could expect no favors from Sejanus. No longer able to
remain in Rome, Agrippa departed for Judaea, leaving
behind him many embittered creditors.[51]

He settled in the Fortress Malatha, in Idumaea. He was so deeply depressed and disillusioned over the shattering of his life's dream that he contemplated suicide. His wife Cypros, who was devoted to him, wrote his sister Herodias, wife of the Tetrarch Herod (Antipas), to influence her husband in Agrippa's favor. Herod (Antipas), offered him a small position as overseer of the markets in his capital, Tiberias. Agrippa accepted it with reluctance; but he did not hold it long. A quarrel broke out between the two brothers-in-law at a banquet in Tyre. Antipas stated that Agrippa owed the very food he was eating to his generosity. Deeply humiliated, Agrippa gave up his position and went to Syria where he became attached to the legate, L. Pomponius Flaccus, with whom he had been very friendly in Rome. Flaccus received him warmly, but the friendship did not last long. The people of Damascus had a dispute with the people of Sidon over their boundary and the case was brought before Flaccus. The Damascenes, knowing that Agrippa was friendly with Flaccus, asked him to intercede for them. Agrippa took the side of the Damascenes and they won the case. His brother, Aristobolus, who was unfriendly to him, informed Flaccus that Agrippa had interceded for the Damascenes because he had been bribed. This infuriated Flaccus and Agrippa had to leave. He again found himself without means of support.[52]

In the year 31, Sejanus was executed for a conspiracy to seize the throne from Tiberius.[53] Agrippa now determined to return to Rome, but he had no resources. In Ptolemais there lived a freedman of his mother named Peter. Agrippa procured 17,500 drachmae from him. With this money he went to Anthedon and booked passage for Alexandria. While Agrippa was waiting to set sail, Herennius Capito, imperial procurator of his grandmother Salome's old domain, dispatched soldiers to arrest him for the unpaid debt of 300,000 drachmae which he owed to the imperial treasury from his previous years in Rome. Agrippa escaped Capito with great difficulty and arrived in Alexandria. He approached Alexander the Alabarch, the head of the Alexandrian Judaean community, for a loan of 200,000 drachmae. Alexander was unwilling to grant the loan, but due to the entreaties of Cypros, who assured him that it would be repaid, he gave Agrippa 50,000 drachmae and a draft on Puteoli (the main seaport for vessels carrying merchandise from Alexandria), for the remainder. Agrippa arrived in Puteoli, probably in the year 32. After cashing the draft, he wrote Tiberius Caesar, who was then living in Capri, asking permission to visit him. Tiberius replied that he was glad to learn of his safe return and would be pleased to see him. On the following day, Tiberius received a message from the procurator Capito informing him that Agrippa owed the imperial treasury 300,000 drachmae, and that when he sought to recover it, Agrippa evaded him. Tiberius then informed Agrippa that he would not see him until he had paid the debt. Agrippa found himself in a precarious situation; without the money he would lose the friendship of Tiberius. He then appealed to Antonia, mother of Germanicus and Claudius and grandmother of Gaius, for help and she advanced the money to him. Once the repayment had been made, Tiberius was again gracious to him.[54] He asked Agrippa to be friendly with his grandson Tiberius, the son of Agrippa's old friend Drusus, and to be constantly in his company. Knowing Roman society well and being an experienced politician, Agrippa neglected the young Tiberius, sensing that there was little likelihood that he would succeed his grandfather. Instead, Agrippa cultivated the friendship of Gaius, son of Germanicus and grandson of Antonia. It is probable that Antonia encouraged this friendship with Gaius Caligula. There was a far greater probability that Gaius would succeed Tiberius. Germanicus was a magic name for the Romans. Agrippa succeeded in obtaining a loan of a million drachmae from an imperial freedman. He repaid the 300,000 drachmae to Antonia and spent the remainder in the entertainment of Gaius. Thus the friendship between Gaius and Agrippa was cemented.[55]

Agrippa was indiscreet in his desire to see Gaius become emperor. Upon one occasion, when he was riding with Gaius and accompanied by his freedman Eutychus, he expressed the wish that Tiberius would die and that Gaius would succeed him. On a later occasion, he accused Eutychus of having stolen clothing from him and threatened to punish him. Eutychus fled, but was caught and arrested. He told the authorities that he had important information regarding the safety of the emperor. After a time, he was brought before Tiberius and he related what Agrippa had said. Tiberius believed Eutychus, since Agrippa had not cultivated his grandson Tiberius. Agrippa pleaded innocence and appealed to the emperor to recall his deep friendship with Drusus, but all to no avail. Tiberius ordered that Agrippa immediately be put in fetters and imprisoned. Antonia, who with Gaius was present in the palace, could not save him from imprisonment, but used her influence to make life more comfortable for him. He was permitted to go to the baths every day and to receive visitors. His devoted friend Silas and his two freedmen Marsyas and Stechus visited him regularly and brought him decent bedding and his favorite food.[56]

The news of the death of Tiberius in Capri soon spread to Rome. When Marsyas heard it, he hastened to the prison. He met Agrippa as he was coming out of the bath, and whispered in his ear in Hebrew, "The lion is dead." He was afraid of being overheard, since it was still only a rumor.[57]

Appointment to Kingship

Some days later Gaius sent official confirmation to the senate that Tiberius had died and that he had succeeded to the throne. Gaius' first act was to order Agrippa released from prison and allow him to live in his home under guard. Soon after the funeral of Tiberius, Gaius was ready to restore Agrippa's freedom, but Antonia told her grandson to delay it out of respect to Tiberius.

So it was a few days later that Gaius freed Agrippa and appointed him king over the tetrarchy of his uncle Philip, adding the tetrarchy of Abilene. Gaius also gave Agrippa a golden chain, of equal weight to the one with which he had been fettered while in prison. The senate, following the good will of Gaius, gave Agrippa the titular rank of praetor.[58] At the same time Gaius recalled Marcellus and appointed Marullus as procurator of Judaea.[59]

Agrippa was in no hurry to leave Rome for his kingdom, nor did Gaius want him to depart. They were intimate and constantly in each other's company. Both indulged in extravagant living.[60] After a year and a half had passed, Agrippa decided to depart for his kingdom. Apparently he had noticed a change coming over Gaius which boded ill. Agrippa left Rome in the late summer of 38, with the promise to return as soon as he had put the affairs of his kingdom in order.[61]

Upon his arrival in Alexandria, he met with a most outrageous reception. The leaders of the Judaean community received him warmly. They rejoiced that a scion of the Hasmonean family had become king. They hoped that through his friendship with Gaius Caesar he would champion their rights which the Greek inhabitants strove to curtail. The Greeks, knowing this, made a hostile demonstration against Agrippa. They dressed up a mentally deranged man, called Karabas, with a carpet for a royal robe and a papyrus crown on his head and acclaimed him *Marin,* Syrian for "my lord,"—all in mockery of Agrippa. Flaccus, the praefect of Egypt, did not intervene to disperse the mob and this greatly alarmed Agrippa. The leaders of the Judaean community informed Agrippa that Flaccus had not forwarded their letter of congratulation to Gaius, nor had he allowed their delegation to go to Rome to congratulate the Emperor. Agrippa promised to forward their address of loyalty to Gaius and then left in haste for his kinddom.[62]

Shortly after the departure of King Agrippa, the

riots over the statue of the Emperor took place in Alexandria. Many houses of prayer were burned and there
was great loss of life and property. It was the first
pogrom against the Judaeans. Flaccus not only con-
doned but even encouraged the violent actions against
the Judaeans, but the result was not what he had hoped.
In due course he was arrested and later put to death.[63]
His downfall was undoubtedly due to Agrippa's influence.

Agrippa's becoming king over the tetrarchy of Philip
aroused the envy of his sister Herodias. Like Agrippa,
she was very ambitious, which was one of the reasons
that had prompted her to leave Herod and marry Herod
(Antipas), whose tetrarchy was greater in extent and
provided more income than Philip enjoyed.[64] Now her
husband was only a tetrarch while Agrippa, who had
recently had no status and had been living in poverty,
was made king, a far superior title and one carrying
higher authority. She insisted that her husband Herod
(Antipas) go with her to Rome and use every means to
obtain the title of king from Gaius and thus end this in-
feriority. Her husband reluctantly yielded to her persua-
sions and they went to Rome. Agrippa then dispatched
Fortunatus, his devoted freedman, with a letter to Gaius
charging that his brother-in-law Herod (Antipas) had
been involved with Sejanus in the plot against Tiberius
Caesar and was now in league with King Artabanus of
Parthia. As evidence he stated that Herod Antipas had
sufficient arms for seventy thousand men.[65]

If Agrippa indeed accused Herod Antipas of having
been privy to Sejanus' conspiracy against Tiberius, it
was a slanderous lie. It is unthinkable that Herod
Antipas had any part in that plot. Tiberius had
been the patron and friend of Herod (Antipas), while
Sejanus was known to be anti-Judaean. Herod (Antipas)
could never have expected any favor from Sejanus.
Thus there could not have been the slightest basis for
such a charge.

The charge that Herod Antipas was in league with
Artabanus, King of Parthia, also cannot be accepted.

When Herod (Antipas) went to Rome in the year 39, there was no possibility of war between Rome and Parthia, though Armenia never ceased being a source of trouble. Hence a league with Artabanus made no sense. But undoubtedly Vitellius, who bore a grudge against Herod (Antipas), confirmed the charge.[66]

As to the statement that Herod (Antipas) had an equipment of arms sufficient for seventy thousand men, which he admitted, it is likely that he had assembled it in the years 35-36 when Parthia and Rome were on the brink of war. Herod (Antipas), following the policy and diplomacy of his father, King Herod, had most likely assembled large stores of arms in order to be able to join the victor.

Gaius removed Herod (Antipas) from his tetrarchy and added his territory to that of King Agrippa. He also confiscated all his wealth and exiled him to Lyons in Gaul. When Gaius learned that Herodias was the sister of Agrippa, he wanted to pardon her. Being a proud woman and knowing that she was responsible for the downfall of her husband, she gracefully accepted the immunity and joined her husband in exile.[67]

Thus Agrippa came close to realizing his full ambition. He had now added Galilee, populated· by Judaeans, to Philip's tetrarchy which was mainly heathen. His motives in seeking rule over all Judaea were patriotic. He wanted to make Judaea independent again, as it had been during the time of his grandfather Herod, and he wanted to be its king. To accomplish this he did not hesitate to slander his brother-in-law and uncle Herod (Antipas), even as he had ignored ethical niceties during his years in Rome.

The Restoration of Herod's Kingdom

It was about this time that the order was given to Petronius to have a statue of Gaius set up in the Temple in Jerusalem, as we have seen above, and it can be assumed that Agrippa received word of it from Petronius.

Agrippa saw this edict as a threat to his ambition to have Judaea become an independent state with himself as king. He left for Rome to see whether he could avert his personal misfortune and the national catastrophe. He arrived in the early autumn of 40, when Gaius had returned from his expedition to Gaul, Germany and Britain. Agrippa succeeded in preventing the imminent national calamity, but the full abolition of the decree of Gaius came only in January 41, when Gaius was assassinated.[68] The conspirators had republican sentiments and, as soon as word came of the assassination, the Senate was called to order by the consuls. However, the praetorians did not have republican sentiments; they wanted an emperor, particularly of the line of Caesar.[69]

While the soldiers were searching the palace, they found Claudius, brother of Germanicus, hiding in a closet in fear of his life. When they recognized him, they decided that he should be made emperor. As these forces were forming, Agrippa recognized that it would be to his advantage personally and also to that of Judaea if Claudius should become emperor. He knew he could expect nothing from the Senate if they should establish a republic. On the other hand, his mother Berenice was intimate with Antonia, Claudius' mother, and he himself had been friendly with Claudius from boyhood. He rushed from the palace and caught up with the praetorians who were carrying Claudius to their camp. Noticing that Claudius was vacillating as to whether he should accept the emperorship, Agrippa strongly encouraged him to do so.

Agrippa went from the camp directly to his home, where he found a summons to come to the Senate for a consultation, both because he was known to be close to the family of Germanicus and because of the high personal regard in which he was held. Before leaving for the Senate, Agrippa annointed his head with scent to create the impression that he had been at home with his wife. Upon his arrival at the Senate, he innocently inquired what the situation was.

He was informed that Claudius was proclaimed emperor by the praetorians, that two tribunes had been sent by the Senate to the camp asking Claudius to submit to the Senate and to a republican form of government, but that the tribunes had been sent back. Agrippa made a brief speech to the Senate, saying that he was ready to give his life for the honor of the Senate. He asked them to consider the situation with care; that if it should come to an open fight, they would be at a great disadvantage since they had only the support of the urban cohorts. The Senators replied that they had money in abundance and weapons with which to arm the people and free the slaves. Agrippa pointed out to them the unsoundness of their position: that an undisciplined and untrained mob could not be a match for the well-organized praetorians. He advised the Senate to send a delegation to Claudius to persuade him to follow their will, and offered to be one of the emissaries. Thus Agrippa became the intermediary between Claudius and the Senate. He secretly sent word to Claudius to be resolute; and Claudius rejected all demands from the Senate to submit. After the Senate lost the support of the urban cohorts, it yielded. On January 25, 41, the day following Gaius' assassination, Claudius, escorted by the praetorians, was recognized by the Senate and received the titles held by his predecessors—Imperator, Augustus and Pontifex Maximus.[70]

Soon after Claudius became Emperor, he added Judaea, Samaria, Trachonitis and Auranitis to the kingdom of Agrippa and confirmed the territory of Abila which had been given him by Gaius. Claudius also conferred the rank of consul upon Agrippa.[71] Thus, through Agrippa's shrewdness and keen diplomacy, Judaea became a united and independent state, a client kingdom in the Roman Empire. It had come almost as an unexpected surprise, though many years of conniving and manipulation made it possible. It was the totally joyous conclusion of a trip that had begun in great trepidation.

Claudius made Agrippa's brother, Herod, King of

Chalcis.[72] He also freed Alexander, the Alabarch of Alexandria, who had been imprisoned by Gaius.[73]

AGRIPPA AS KING

Agrippa, having accomplished his goal, left Rome. Upon his arrival in Jerusalem, which he made his capital, he offered sacrifices in the Temple in gratitude for his success. He hung the golden chain, which Gaius had bestowed upon him on his liberation from prison, in the Temple area over the treasury as a memorial of his faith, a testimonial of his accomplishment, and a symbol that God raises up the fallen.[74] Agrippa released the people from the tax on their houses.[75] This not only indicates his desire to gain the people's good will, but shows that the country was in such good economic condition that he could afford this gesture. He also defrayed the cost of the sacrifices offered by the Nazarites.[76] He removed the High Priest Theophilus son of Ananus, and appointed in his stead Simon son of the Boethus whose daughter Mariamme had been married to Herod.[77]

Jews and Pagans in Alexandria

The death of Gaius and the accession of Claudius to the throne caused disturbances in Alexandria. Upon the petition of Agrippa and his brother Herod, Claudius sent an edict to Alexandria in which he ordered the prefect to suppress any outbreak. In it he restored the privileges of the Judaeans of Alexandria, whom he termed Alexandrians,[78] the name bestowed upon them by Augustus and upheld by the Roman authorities until the time of Gaius who humiliated them when they would not acknowledge him as a god.

Agrippa believed that the responsibility for the welfare of the Judaeans throughout the Roman Empire lay upon him. Being friendly with the Emperor Claudius, he considered it his duty to intercede in their behalf as had his grandfather Herod with Augustus Caesar. Herod had done so to gain the good will of the inhabitants of the Diaspora. Agrippa, however, believed that as King of Judaea he had the responsibility to use his power so that his fellow Judaeans everywhere should not be molested in their religious customs. He petitioned Claudius to issue an edict similar to the one he had sent to Alexandria to all the authorities in the Roman Empire. Claudius issued the following decree:[79]

Tiberius Claudius Caesar Augustus Germanicus, High Priest, tribune of the people, consul the second time, ordains thus: Upon the petition of my friends King Agrippa and King Herod, that I should grant to the Judaeans who are in the Roman Empire the same privileges which I granted to those of Alexandria, I willingly comply therewith. And I make this grant not only for the sake of the petitioners but also because I think that these Judaeans for whom I was petitioned are worthy of those privilges on account of their fidelity and friendship to the Romans. . . .

In the edict he confirmed to the Judaeans throughout the Roman Empire the rights granted to them by Augustus Caesar to perform their religious observances without disturbance; but he advised them not to show contempt for the religious beliefs of others.

Claudius' admonition stemmed from a misunderstanding of the nature of the Judaean religion. As a Roman he thought Judaism was like any other religion of his time. These various polytheisms, worshipping several gods, could afford to be tolerant of those who worship still another god. But the Judaeans as monotheists, universalists, acknowledging one God as the only God of the entire universe, believed that the gods and idols of other peoples were false and valueless. Having been monotheists for centuries, the Judaeans could not but look upon the religious observance of the pagans with contempt and a sense of superiority. This unwavering Judaean belief that there was only one God, and that He was their own, brought misfortune upon them in the Diaspora. They were regarded by their neighbors as atheists, since they worshipped a God that could not be seen, and as misanthropes, since they refused intimate association with their neighbors. They were also regularly accused of disloyalty to local governments, because they did not take part in civic festivities which were always associated with the local deities. The edict of the Caesars always ameliorated the situation of the Judaeans for a while, but could not eradicate the basic religious cause of the hostility.

Thus, some time after the edict of Claudius, rowdies in the city of Dora, situated north of Caesarea, placed a statue of Claudius in a synagogue. This greatly provoked Agrippa, who complained to Petronius. Petronius angrily wrote a strong letter to the magistrate and council of Dora accusing them of disobeying the edict of Claudius Caesar. Placing the statue in a synagogue had made it impossible for the Judaeans to assemble there and perform their religious rites. Such sacrilege offended not only the Judaeans but the emperor as well. Petronius ordered them to surrender the culprits and warned against further disturbance, demanding that everyone be allowed to follow his own religious customs.[80]

Agrippa's Identification with the Judaeans

The year 40-41 was a sabbatical year, for which the Pentateuch enjoins a special ceremonial: "At the end of every seven years, in the set time of the year of release in the Feast of Tabernacles, when all Israel is come to appear before Adonai thy God in the place which He shall choose, thou shalt read this law before all Israel in their hearing. Assemble the people, the men and the women and the little ones, and the stranger that is within thy gates."[81] It was the first festival since Agrippa returned from Rome as King of Judaea. Judaeans came from all parts of the country and even from foreign lands to participate in the joyous celebrations and glory in the restoration of the kingdom of Judaea.

On the second day of the festival the rite of reading the

law was carried out. A wooden platform was erected in the Temple Court and the portion in Deuteronomy relating to the setting up of a king was read. The *hazzan*, the overseer, took the Torah scroll and handed it to the head of the assembly, who in turn presented it to the *segan*, who gave it to the high priest, who handed it to King Agrippa, who received it standing and read the prescribed portion,[82] including the words, "Thou shalt in any wise set him king over thee, whom Adonai thy God shall choose; one from among thy brethren shalt thou set king over thee; thou mayest not put a stranger over thee who is not thy brother."[83] The Mishne relates that when Agrippa read this portion, his eyes overflowed with tears; but the sages said to him, "You are our brother, you are our brother."[84]

The reason why Agrippa's eyes were filled with tears is found in the portion he read: "Thou mayest not put a stranger over thee." He felt he was a stranger, being a grandson of Herod whose ancestors were Idumaeans. That is why the sages acknowledged him as a brother. There is a possibility that there was still Boethusaean agitation that all authority should be vested in the high priestly family. They may have wanted to arouse the people in the Temple against Agrippa, but the sages and the people acclaimed him their brother and their king.[85] There is also a possibility that he was overcome with happiness that the kingdom of Judaea had been restored and he was its king. The Mishne does not state that he "cried" or wept, but that his eyes "flowed with tears," which could well have been due to joy.

Agrippa deposed Simon and once more offered the high priesthood to Jonathan, who asked that his brother Matthias be appointed instead; and this was done.[86] Whether the reason for the dismissal of Simon son of Boethus was that he had opposed Agrippa's reading of the kingly portion in the Temple or some other act or fault cannot be determined. Nor did the high priest Matthias long remain in his position; he was dismissed in favor of Elionaeus son of Simon Cantheras.[87] The frequent changes would indicate that the high priestly clan was not devoted to King Agrippa; they felt that they enjoyed greater authority when Judaea was under Roman rule. But the people at large were deeply devoted to him. That too would explain why Agrippa I appropriated the same authority over the sacred vestments as that exercised by his grandfather Herod and kept them in his, not the high priest's, custody.

The Talmud presents Agrippa as an example of devotion to Judaism and to the Judaeans. When, at the Festival of Weeks, the pilgrims brought their first fruits, they took the baskets with their offerings and put them on their shoulders as soon as they reached the Temple Mount, carrying them in this manner to the priests. King Agrippa is reported to have carried his basket on his shoulder like any ordinary pilgrim.[88]

Agrippa made himself known in nearby nations as had his grandfather. He erected a magnificent theater and amphitheater in Berytus (Beirut). He presented shows and gladiatorial combats there.[89] He even had statues made of his daughters and placed in Caesarea.[90] The Judaeans did not protest against this as they had during the reign of Herod. They realized that he was exercising good diplomacy in courting the goodwill of Rome. Agrippa showed his friendship for Claudius and Rome openly. He called himself *philokaisar* and *philoromaios* on the coins and inscriptions he made outside of Judaea.[91]

Josephus relates that a certain Simon, a sage, assembled a gathering of Judaeans once when King Agrippa was in Caesarea, accused him of sinfulness and said he had no right to enter the Temple. The King summoned Simon to Caesarea and, while sitting near Simon in the theater, asked him what he had done contrary to the law. Taken by surprise, Simon did not answer but begged the king for pardon. Agrippa not only absolved him but presented him with a gift.[92]

Silas, who had been most faithful to Agrippa when he was in prison, had been appointed commander-in-chief of Agrippa's army. Silas was lacking in culture, tact, and manners. He constantly reminded Agrippa of the hard times they had experienced together and of the many things he had done for Agrippa. He repeated this not only in private, but also at public functions, which humiliated and embarrassed Agrippa, and undermined his authority. Agrippa soon dismissed Silas from his post and imprisoned him. When, on a birthday, he offered amnesty to Silas, he chose to remain in prison.[93]

Around 40 C.E., Artabanus, King of Parthia, died. For a while there was a struggle for the kingship between his two sons, Vardenes and Gotarzes. Vardenes became King of Parthia in the summer of 42 and sought to recover Armenia. Vibius Marsus, the legate of Syria, threatened to invade Mesopotamia. At the same time Mithridates, King of Bosporus, dreaming of the glory of his ancestor, the great Mithridates, planned to free himself from dependence on Rome.[94] The plans of these two kings of the East to oppose mighty Rome undoubtedly had their effect on all the lesser nations of the Middle East. As the rumors spread that war would ultimately break out between the East and the West, their own ambitions to regain their freedom were aroused. They knew that Parthia had invaded Syria and Judaea less than a century before, and that Rome had not always been invincible.

King Agrippa took measures to prepare for any eventuality. The city of Jerusalem had grown, particularly toward the north where there were new settlements. Since there were no fortifications here, and Jerusalem was open to assault, Agrippa decided to build a strong wall north of Bethesda. He began the wall which, according to Josephus, would have been impregnable if completed and which no missile engines could have demolished. The foundation was constructed of stones closely joined, 20 cubits in length and 10 cubits thick (30 x 15 feet). When Marsus, the legate of Syria, heard about it, he informed Claudius, who politely sent word to Agrippa to discontinue the project. Agrippa reluctantly complied.[95] The wall, which was hastily completed during the later revolt, became known as the Third Wall, or the Wall of Agrippa.

Agrippa had other, more definite plans for whatever situation might arise between Parthia and Rome. He called a meeting of client kings in Tiberias. Five responded to his invitation: Antiochus, King of Commagene; Sampsigeram, King of Emesa; Cotys, King of Lesser Armenia; Polemon, King of Pontus, and Agrippa's brother Herod, King of Chalcis. When Marsus learned of the meeting he became suspicious of what had brought these kings together. Feeling that this assemblage would not serve the interests of Rome, he ordered the kings to return to their homes without delay. Agrippa considered this order a personal affront, but there was nothing he could do but comply.[96] His aim had undoubtedly been to unite the client kings in an entente which would have had a joint policy and thus have been able to withstand unreasonable demands from the Roman legates in the event of a Parthian war.

The followers of Jesus of Nazareth, the Nazarenes (not yet called Christians), were regarded as a seditious group for preaching that an independent kingdom of Israel would soon be restored.[97] They were persecuted by Roman as well as Judaean authorities. Chapter 12 of the Book of Acts states that James son of Zebedee, one of the apostles of Jesus, was put to death by the order of Herod (Agrippa), and that Peter was imprisoned by him, but miraculously escaped.[98] Josephus makes no mention either of the killing of James or of the imprisonment of Peter, and the story is historically questionable. Agrippa never called himself Herod,[99] only the sons of Herod—Archelaus, Philip and Antipas—added Herod to their names. Moreover, there is an account in Acts 5[100] that, when Peter was brought before the *synedrion*, a man named Gamaliel called the attention of the assembly to Theudas who had stirred up a revolt against the Romans and had been put to death. But Theudas was slain by Fadus who became procurator over Judaea after the death of Agrippa.[101] All that can be said is that the early Christians must have had a tradition about the killing of James, the brother of John, but it turns out to be anachronistic and historically vague.

In the summer of 44, Agrippa went to Caesarea where he celebrated the games in honor of Claudius Caesar. He appeared in the theater in a robe adorned with silver which, when the sun shone upon it, produced a dazzling effect. The people, seeing him in splendor, acclaimed him a god and immortal. Agrippa did not rebuke them nor did he accept their adulation.[102] He remained silent. He knew that the heathens deified their rulers. When he then felt severe pains in his belly, he remarked to his friends that he who was being hailed as an immortal was approaching death, and he was ready to accept what Providence had allotted to him. He was taken to the palace. The people prayed for his recovery, but Agrippa died.[103] His sudden death aroused suspicion that he had been poisoned, and there seems to be some justification for such suspicion. Relations between him and Marsus, the legate of Syria, had become hostile. Marsus suspected Agrippa of not being wholly loyal to Rome and was envious of Agrippa's influence over Claudius. Then, too, the inhabitants of Caesarea, mostly heathen, were also hostile to Agrippa. The effective way to remove his influence would be to kill him, and poison was a fashionable method.

Agrippa died at the age of forty-four, having ruled over Judaea three and a half years. Simultaneously, he held the title of king over the tetrarchy of his uncle Philip, which he had acquired four years earlier. He left one son, Agrippa, aged seventeen, and three daughters: Berenice who married her uncle Herod, King of Chalcis; Mariamme, and Drusilla. Mariamme was espoused to Julius Archelaus Epiphanes, while Drusilla was betrothed to the King of Commagene, with the condition that he be circumcised.[104]

Agrippa was a great king, versatile in friendship, astute in finding opportunity, able in administration. He realized the power of Rome, but was aware of its weakness in the Near East. He took into consideration the fact that Rome had not destroyed Parthia, which was still a threat to Roman domination of the Middle East. His life dream was to make Judaea viable and to strengthen her position in the Middle East, until she would be able to sustain her independence. To accomplish this, Judaea had to have the goodwill of Rome, and at the same time be on guard, ever watchful of the contentions between Rome and Parthia. No small measure of Agrippa's accomplishment was the confidence that his fellow client-kings of the Near East placed in him.

Agrippa was devoted to his people. He understood his fellow Judaeans and scrupulously followed the law and customs transmitted by their forefathers. He sought their welfare at home and, owing to his great influence in the Roman court, he safeguarded their religious and economic life in the Diaspora.[105] The words of the author of Lamentations, "Under his shadow we shall live among the nations,"[106] could have been applied to him. Though a king, he considered himself one of the people. In turn, he was beloved of his people. Outside the country he took the liberty of copying Hellenistic ways, but this gave no offense to the Judaeans. The heathens who inhabited Sebaste and Caesarea were hostile to him out of their long-felt hatred towards the Judaeans. As long as Agrippa lived, they flattered him. When they learned that he was dead, they openly showed their enmity. The soldiers carried the statues of Agrippa's daughters to the brothels. When Claudius learned that the inhabitants of Sebaste and Caesarea had abused the memory of his friend Agrippa, he was horrified.[107]

4. JUDAEA AS A PROVINCE OF ROME

THE LATER PROCURATORS

After Agrippa

The death of Agrippa was a tragic event for the Judaeans —a turning point in their history. If a historical comparison may be permitted, the death of King Agrippa can be paralleled with that of Josiah, King of Judaea. The tragic deaths of these two comparatively young kings were portents of the destruction of the kingdom of Judaea.

When Claudius received word of the death of King Agrippa, it was his intention to appoint Agrippa's son, Agrippa, king over the domain which had been his father's. He was dissuaded from doing so by his counselors, who had been dubious about the loyalty of King Agrippa I.[1] They felt he had been too independent, more devoted to Judaea than to Rome. Hence they believed it would not be to the interest of Rome to make his son king of Judaea. On the pretext that the son was too young —he was only seventeen—to be entrusted with such a strategically important country, they advised Claudius to cede Judaea to Syria. This Claudius did, appointing Cuspius Fadus procurator.[2] To honor the memory of his

friend, Claudius recalled Marsus, legate of Syria, who
had been at enmity with King Agrippa I, and replaced
him with Cassius Longinus.[3] He also wanted to punish
the soldiers of Caesarea and Sebaste who had so vilely
insulted the daughters of King Agrippa. He ordered them
sent to Pontus and intended to replace them with an equal
number of the Roman legion. A delegation was sent to the
Emperor asking that the soldiers of Caesarea and Sebaste be allowed to remain in the country.[4] The Emperor
granted this request, which eventually brought calamity
upon the Judaeans.

The year 44 must be seen as the beginning of the fall
of Judaea as a State. A wide gulf of misunderstanding
divided the Judaeans from the Romans. Neither appre-
ciated the culture of the other, their laws or the ethics
implicit in their respective traditions. The Judaeans regarded the Romans as oppressors. They considered the
Romans devoid of an understanding of the high ideals
of religion, since the Romans worshipped man-made
statues as gods. The Romans, on the other hand, looked
upon the Judaeans as barbarians and atheists, since they
had a God no one could see. However, the empire had
granted special privileges to the Judaeans. They were
free to observe their religious rites, and were exempt
from erecting statues in honor of the Caesars, though
they were expected to offer sacrifices for the welfare of
the Caesars and Rome, as did all subjugated peoples.
They enjoyed the right of trying religious and civil offenders in their own courts.[5] The Roman law was not imposed upon the Judaeans except in the case of political
offenders.

The cultural antagonism was intensified by bad government. The procurators sent to Judaea were not of senatorial rank; they were men of a lower status, generally
the equestrian. Their primary duties were, in theory,
to collect taxes and to keep the country tranquil. In fact,
most of the procurators were avaricious and their sole
concern was to enrich themselves by what they could extract from the inhabitants, legally or illegally.

When Judaea was annexed to Syria there was no open rebellion, but there were present in the country all the elements that ultimately produced it. First, there were patriots who agitated for the overthrow of Roman hegemony by armed force and the re-establishment of Judaea as an independent state. Then there were the Apocalyptists and other visionaries who preached the approach of the kingdom of God and maintained that Roman tyranny would be shattered by supernatural power, thus accelerating the hopes of the Judaeans for deliverance from the Roman yoke. There were, of course, many charlatans, taking advantage of the influence of the Apocalyptists upon the Judaeans, who presented themselves as men possessing supernatural powers, promising soon to deliver the Judaeans; they added to the unrest, and they not only aroused the people politically, but also socially and economically, since they were opposed to the accumulation of wealth and held to the principle of the equality of men before God. On the opposite side, the procurators did not understand or properly appraise the Judaeans and they doubted their loyalty to Rome. Their native pagan troops intensified the possibilities of revolt by their provocations of and aggressive attitude toward the Judaeans, often made the more serious as these were committed, in many instances, with the approval of the procurator.

In this historic crisis, Judaea had no true leadership. The high priests were mostly corrupt; they had purchased their positions with money and servility. In many instances they worked with the procurators against the interests of Judaea. The people not only had no confidence in them, but also looked upon them with disdain, regarding them as usurpers of the office. The new high priests were no longer from either the Zadokite or the Hasmonean families. While priests and aristocrats, they schemed their way into office and soon found themselves replaced. Probably after the time of Herod, and certainly after the death of Agrippa I, the high priests did not have the approval of the people.

Then, too, economic conditions went from bad to worse. There were years of famine, a particularly severe one in the year 48.[6] The famines affected the peasants most seriously, since their livelihood depended on the harvest. Many of them were deprived of their land by the wealthy; others lost their land to the moneylenders. They smarted under the whip of political and social degradation, and suffered even more keenly from inequitable economic pressure. The wealthy were generally content with Roman rule under which their social and economic interests were safeguarded. The masses, on the other hand, enthusiastically joined movements which preached the principle of equality, as did the Apocalyptists. Bandits under the guise of being Apocalyptists robbed the wealthy as well as the farmers, and thus wrought great havoc throughout the country, not the least resulting from the intervention of the Roman authorities who punished the guilty and the innocent alike. And to climax all the other internal difficulties, there was continual conflict among the various groups of Judaeans.

The twenty-one years from the death of Agrippa in the year 44 until 65, when open revolt against Rome ultimately broke out, were full of turmoil, suffering and bloodshed.

THE PROCURATOR FADUS

When Fadus, Claudius' new procurator, arrived in Judaea, he was immediately confronted with a difficult situation. The Judaeans of Peraea were fighting with the inhabitants of Philadelphia over a boundary. Fadus found the Judaeans at fault. He ordered their leader, Antibam, executed and his lieutenants, Amran and Eleazar, banished from the country.[7] Robbers also roamed the country, particularly in Idumaea and its environs. Fadus captured the ringleader Ptolemaus and executed him,[8] and for a while the country was pacified. Since Judaea was now annexed to Syria, Fadus demanded authority over the sacred vestments of the high priest. Knowing that the Judaeans would resist this demand, he summoned Longinus, the legate of Syria, who arrived with a powerful army prepared for any emergency. Longinus permitted the Judaeans to send a delegation to the Emperor Claudius and was willing to await his decision before acting. The Judaean delegation consisted of men named Cornelius, Trypho, Dorotheus and John. Upon their arrival in Rome, they were presented to the Emperor by young Agrippa. He and his uncle Herod, King of Chalcis, warmly supported the petition of the Judaeans which the delegation presented to the Emperor and, though they never had King Agrippa's close relationship with the emperor, Claudius issued a verdict in favor of the Judaeans. His decree addressed to the rulers of Jerusalem, the Senate (*Boulé*) of the people, and all the Judaeans, based his decision on Vitellius' similar generosity.[9]

King Herod of Chalcis, uncle of the young Agrippa, also asked Claudius for the authority to nominate the high priests and to supervise the Temple and the sacred treasury; the request was granted. King Herod deposed Elionaeus son of Catheras, and appointed as high priest Joseph son of Cami, who was shortly replaced by Ananias son of Nebedaeus.[10]

During the tenure of Fadus, a man named Theudas proclaimed himself a prophet and persuaded a great number of people to take all their possessions with them and follow him to the River Jordan, assuring them that the river would be divided and they would be able to cross. He wanted to demonstrate that he possessed divine powers and apparently had no desire to instigate a revolt against Rome. Fadus, however, felt that this adventure might be dangerous politically, as any pretension to divine powers implied messianism and thus kingship. Fadus sent a strong detachment of cavalry against Theudas and it slew both him and many of his followers.[11] What may have seemed purely religious to Theudas seemed political to Rome, and thus Theudas met the fate of John the Baptist and Jesus.

Procurator Tiberius Julius Alexander

Fadus was soon recalled by the Emperor.[12] Whether his tenure was short because of his cruelties, or because Claudius Caesar wanted to please the Judaeans by appointing one of their own people is not known. Fadus was succeeded by Tiberius Julius Alexander, the son of Alexander the Alabarch of Alexandria and nephew of Philo the philosopher.[13] Though a son of the most illustrious Judaean family in Alexandria and of a father who was a devout Judaean, he had forsaken Judaism and was a practicing heathen. His appointment as procurator of Judaea was another unfortunate step on the road to disaster. The Emperor did not understand the feelings of the Judaeans, who scorned converts to other religions. For a worshipper of the One God of the Universe to become a *mumar*, a "changer," to a religion in which one worshipped idols was to them inconceivable folly.

Tiberius Julius Alexander was uncomfortable in his new role. To show that he was a true Roman, he refused to tolerate any agitation against Rome. He crucified James and Simon, the sons of Judas of Galilee,[14] who apparently were the leaders of the Fourth Philosophy at this time. Josephus, despite his Roman bias, does not charge these two men with leading a revolt. Nevertheless, the renegade procurator, knowing that they were the leaders of a strong and rebellious group, executed them.

In the year 48, during the procuratorship of Tiberius Julius Alexander, Judaea suffered a severe famine. Queen Helena of Adiabene and her son Izates, who had embraced Judaism, were then in Jerusalem and sought to help those who were in want. At great personal sacrifice Queen Helena purchased produce in Egypt and distributed it freely among the needy.[15] The author of the Book of Acts also makes reference to this famine, and states that the disciples of Jesus sent relief to their brethren who dwelt in Judaea.[16]

Procurator Cumanus

Later that year Tiberius Julius Alexander was replaced by Ventidius Cumanus.[17] Subsequently Tiberius Julius Alexander was made governor of Egypt. He served still later as lieutenant to Titus during the war against the Judaeans and was responsible for declaring Vespasian Emperor of Rome.[18] Juvenal made reference to him in the verse, "Those triumphal statues among which some Egyptian alabarch or other has dared to set up his title."[19] In the year 48, too, King Herod of Chalcis died. Although he left sons, Claudius passed over them and gave his domain to Agrippa II.[20]

The procuratorship of Cumanus was troubled. The first disturbance was due to the outrageous conduct of a soldier during the celebration of the Festival of Passover. The procurators usually kept a cohort in the colonnades in the outer court of the Temple to check any disorders that might arise. One soldier indecently exposed himself to the people. This infuriated the Judaeans who cried out at the sacrilege and blamed Cumanus for this outrageous act. He attempted to dismiss the incident, but the Judaeans were so aroused that they insulted him. Realizing their fury, he called up the rest of his army to Antonia. When it arrived, the Judaeans were seized with fear and in the ensuing panic, many thousands were crushed and trampled to death. The returning pilgrims left for their homes in deep mourning for their relatives and friends, deeply embittered and vengeful. On the road from Jerusalem one group of young people encountered an imperial official, Stephanus, with his entourage. They attacked and plundered this small party. Cumanus, in reprisal, sent a punitive expedition against the neighboring settlements and ordered the arrest of the most eminent men. One of the soldiers in searching a house found several scrolls of the Torah. He brought

them out, displayed them before his comrades with scur-
rilous remarks, tore them into pieces and burned them.
The sacreligious act aroused violent indignation among
the Judaeans. A large group went to Cumanus in Caesarea demanding punishment for the offender for an act
which they considered not only an offense to them, but a
crime against God. Cumanus sensed from the attitude of
the Judaeans that this incident might lead to a general
uprising, and upon the advice of his counselors, he ordered the execution of the culprit. This, for a while,
placated the people.[21]

The tension in Judaea could not long be contained under such a procurator. Galileans on journeying to Jerusalem usually went by way of Samaria, whose convenient
road was lined with many populated cities—the alternate
road being the west shore of the Jordan. On one occasion
a Galilean pilgrim was slain by a Samaritan in the village
of Ginoa at the point where the road rises from the plain
of Esdraelon into the hills of Samaria. A leading Galilean
came to Cumanus and demanded justice. Cumanus, who
had been bribed by the Samaritans, failed to act. The
Galileans now appealed to all the Judaeans to take up
arms and revolt, saying, "Slavery in itself is bitter, but
slavery with injustice is intolerable."[22] The Judaean
notables recognized that such action, although justified
by the conduct of Cumanus, would bring about the destruction of the state and calamity to its people. They
knew Judaea was no match for Rome. They promised the
Galileans that they would endeavor to persuade Cumanus
to avenge the murder. The Galileans had no faith that he
would do so, and a group headed by Eleazar son of Dinaeus
determined to take the matter into their own hands.[23]
Josephus, typically, calls Eleazar *lestes*, a robber, but he
was a revolutionary. The Galileans, under the leadership
of Eleazar and a certain Alexander,[24] attacked many
villages in Samaria and plundered them. Cumanus assembled several cohorts of infantry and one squadron of
cavalry, armed the pagan inhabitants of Samaria, and
attacked the Galileans, slaying many and taking many

prisoners. The leaders in Jerusalem saw that a raging conflagration might easily ensue. They donned sackcloth, put ashes on their heads, and begged the rebels to desist, saying that their violent actions would bring about the destruction of their fatherland, the burning of the Temple, and the sale of their wives and children into slavery. They appealed to them to throw away their weapons and to return to their homes. The majority of the Galileans accepted these wise words and dispersed. Some of their leaders went to their fortified hiding places in the mountain.[25]

The pagans, however, were not satisfied. Thinking this a good opportunity to besmirch the Judaeans in the eyes of the Romans, they sent a delegation to Quadratus, the legate of Syria, who was then in Tyre, complaining of the depredations by the Judaeans, not for their sufferings but for the contempt the Judaeans had shown for Rome by taking action into their own hands. The Judaeans also sent a delegation[26] accusing the heathens who lived in Samaria—for convenience, the Samarians—of initiating the revolt. They also charged the procurator, Cumanus, of having been bribed by the Samarians. Quadratus went to Samaria[27] to investigate the situation and concluded that the Samarians were indeed guilty. To make the legate more lenient toward them, the Samarians informed him that many Judaeans were contemplating rebellion against Rome. Quadratus then ordered all the prisoners held by Cumanus crucified. He also arrested and beheaded five of the alleged leaders accused by the Samarians as organizers of the revolt. Quadratus then ordered the leaders of the Samarians and the Judaeans, and the procurator Cumanus, as well as Celer the tribune, who probably was the go-between of the procurator and the Samarians, to go to Rome and appear before the Emperor. He also arrested the High Priest Ananias and his son Ananus, who was the captain of the Temple, and sent them to Rome to give an account to Emperor Claudius. Quadratus then went to Jerusalem to assure himself that there no revolt was brewing. Finding the city relatively tranquil, he returned to Antioch.[28]

Cumanus and the Samarians had friends among Claudius' counselors who worked for a verdict in their favor. Agrippa II was in Rome at this time and intervened in behalf of the Judaeans. He spoke with the Empress Agrippina and, through her influence, Claudius was swayed to favor the Judaeans. The Emperor ordered the Samarian leaders executed and Cumanus banished. He ordered Celer, the tribune, taken to Jerusalem, carried through the streets of the city, and then executed.[29]

The Procurator Felix

Marcus Antoninus Felix succeeded Cumanus in the year 52.[30] A pleasant change took place in the fortunes of Agrippa II. Chalcis, which was small, was now taken from him and he was given the much larger tetrarchy of his granduncle Philip, and the old tetrarchy of Varus situated in the Lebanon district.[31] The authority over the nomination and disposition of the high priests was transferred to Agrippa.[32] Agrippa's sister Drusilla had been betrothed by his father, Agrippa I, to Epiphanes, son of King Antiochus, with the stipulation that he be circumcised and embrace Judaism. The bridegroom refused to change his religion, and Agrippa II then gave his sister in marriage to Azizus, King of Emesa, who did embrace Judaism.[33]

The appointment of Felix was irregular. He was not an equestrian but a freedman and hence of low social status. He was, however, a favorite of Claudius Caesar. Felix was the brother of Pallas, the freedman of Claudius' mother Antonia; and Pallas was, therefore, a power in the inner circle of the court. Felix adopted Antoninus as his middle name because his brother was a protégé of Antonia.[34] For some reason, the High Priest Jonathan son of Ananus, who was in Rome, also intrigued for the appointment of Felix as procurator of Judaea.[35] Tacitus, in characterizing Felix, wrote, "He practiced every kind of cruelty and profligacy, exercising the power of a king

with all the instincts of a slave."[36] He further wrote that
Felix freely committed crimes, feeling that, with his
brother's influence behind him, all of them would be considered venial.[37] Such a man, with the heart of a slave
and the power of a king, became the procurator of
Judaea.

Conscious of his low social status, Felix sought to improve it by marriage to a member of the royal family.
Suetonius wrote that he was the husband of three queens.
His first wife was the daughter of Juba II, King of Mau-
retania.[38] Josephus says that when Felix saw Drusilla,
the wife of King Azizus, he fell in love with her. Drusilla
divorced her husband, married Felix, and changed her
religion.[39] Both acts were completely repugnant to the
Judaeans over whom Felix was to rule.

Berenice, the sister of Agrippa II and widow of King
Herod, married King Polemos of Cilicia who on her account was circumcised and embraced Judaism. Later she
deserted him and was constantly in the company of her
brother.[40] She was active during the period of the great
revolt and became friendly with Titus, son of the Emperor Vespasian.[41]

On October 13, 54, Claudius Caesar died.[42] It was rumored that he had been poisoned by his wife Agrippina
whose son Nero, who had been adopted by Claudius, now
became Emperor of Rome.[43] As Emperor, Nero entrusted
Lesser Armenia to Aristobolus, son of King Herod of
Chalcis. He bestowed on Agrippa II certain parts of
Galilee and Peraea, the cities of Tiberias and Tarichaea
with surrounding territories, and the city Julius with
fourteen villages lying nearby.[44]

New legates and procurators were generally appointed
upon the accession of an emperor; Felix, however, continued his procuratorship under Nero because of the
great influence of his brother Pallas. Even after Pallas
was removed from office, in the year 55, he still wielded
great influence as a protégé of Agrippina. Felix was recalled only after Agrippina was murdered, in the year
59.[45]

Felix acted with extreme severity against those engaged in violence and brigandage and, an overlapping category, against the patriots who fought for the freedom of Judaea. Felix did not differentiate between a common robber and one who engaged in violence for political reasons. He was even more severe against those who pillaged the property of their political opponents; for the patriots confined their pillaging to those Judaeans who were friendly to Rome, considering such men betrayers of Judaean freedom.[46] Eleazar son of Dinaeus, the Galilean rebel who had eluded arrest by Cumanus, was seized by Felix through treachery. Felix assured him, as an official of Rome, that he would do him no harm; but disregarding his word of honor, sent him in chains to Rome to stand trial.[47] That was only one instance. Felix crucified an incalculable number of ordinary robbers as well as political offenders. Even ordinary citizens, suspected of complicity with the evil-doers, were crucified. Thus, his cruelties only furnished occasion for further outbreaks. As Tacitus said, Felix was fostering crime by his misconceived remedies.

Jonathan, the high priest, had intrigued for Felix's appointment, but their relationship speedily became strained. Josephus says that Jonathan took the liberty of admonishing Felix, who resented this and contrived a plan to kill the high priest. He hired bandits who went to the Temple as worshippers but had daggers concealed under their clothes. Mingling freely with the worshippers, they slew Jonathan without anyone noticing it.[48] There is a possibility that Felix had another, far more devious, motive in mind.

Tiberius Julius Alexander, who had crucified James and Simon, the sons of Judas of Galilee, did not thereby succeed in suppressing the Fourth Philosophy. The followers of this group continued to use terror against the Romans as well as against those in sympathy with Rome, whom they considered traitors to their own people. Only a small minority of Judaeans actively followed the Fourth Philosophy, so they could not afford open revolt against

Rome or its sympathizers. They therefore resorted to assassination. They concealed a curved dagger, *sica*, under their garments, which they used for their murders. Hence they came to be named Sicarii, a Latin term which carries the connotation of robbers.[49] There is a likelihood that Felix encouraged the Sicarii to murder Jonathan, the most influential man in Judaea at that time, in order to discredit them and turn the people from them in aversion.

The Apocalyptists also were active and attracted many followers. Their ultimate aim was the same as that of the Sicarii, but the methods of the two factions were diametrically opposed. The Sicarii utilized terror to accomplish their end, while the Apocalyptists opposed it. They believed God would work miracles and manifest His supernatural power on Judaea's behalf. Josephus called the Apocalyptists imposters and deceivers who pretended that God would display before the people spectacular signals of liberty. One of the most notable of the Apocalyptists was a Judaean from Egypt. He declared himself a prophet and led thirty thousand Judaeans to the Mount of Olives, promising them that the walls of Jerusalem would fall down for them so that they could walk into the city from any side. Felix became aware of the scheme and gave orders to his troops, infantry as well as cavalry, to attack the so-called prophet and his followers.[50] Four hundred were slain and two hundred were taken captive, but the prophet himself escaped.

The Book of Acts refers to this occurrence in the account of the arrest of Paul. The captain of the army asks Paul, "Art not thou that Egyptian which before these days madest an uproar, and ledest out into the wilderness four thousand men of the Sicarii?"[51] It does not call the Egyptian a prophet, but one of the Sicarii.

In the year 54, when Nero succeeded Claudius, news reached Rome that the Parthians had occupied Armenia, a signal for war. Rome immediately made preparations. The client kings, legates and procurators of the Near East received instructions to gather forces for the invasion of Parthia. Among them was Agrippa II, who received orders to supply men and arms. Corbulo, one of Claudius' distinguished generals, was appointed commander-in-chief of the campaign. Some legions from Syria were attached to his army. Quadratus, the legate of Syria, was jealous, feeling that, since the campaign was in his realm, he should have been placed in command. Nor did he relish having men in arms taken away from him to aid Corbulo.[52] All this was known to the extremists. With Rome occupied in Parthia, possibly to be defeated by the Parthians as they had been on a number of occasions, they thought this an opportune time to incite the people to revolt. With the Parthians on the border preparing to invade Syria, the revolutionists, particularly the Sicarii, intensified their propaganda.

During this period a serious conflict arose in Caesarea between the Judaean and the Greek-Syrian inhabitants over the question of citizens' privileges.[53] The Judaeans claimed special rights since their king, Herod, had built the city. The pagans argued that Caesarea was merely a reconstruction of the old city of Straton's Tower, whose inhabitants were Hellenes. Furthermore, King Herod had not built Caesarea as a Judaean city since he had constructed temples and statues which were prohibited in Judaea. Disorders led to rioting. When the Judaeans gained the advantage over their adversaries, Felix ordered his troops, consisting of Hellenized Syrians, to attack the Judaeans. They then plundered their houses. The city was quiet for a while and Felix sent delegations from both parties to Nero to argue their case. The verdict was in favor of the Hellenized Syrians.[54] While in Rome, some of the Judaeans accused Felix of brutality, but their accusations were overlooked, no doubt because of Felix's continuing influence at court.[55]

The men in control of the affairs of Rome under Nero were Afranius Burrus and Annaeus Seneca.[56] The former was the head of the praetorian cohorts and had powerful influence in the courts. Josephus states that the Hellenized Syrians bribed Burrus who, in consequence, sent an epistle in their favor to the authorities in Caesarea. This may or may not be true. Burrus was an intimate friend and collaborator of Seneca and was likewise a Stoic. The Stoics generally were hostile to the Judaeans. They saw them as competitors in their views on ethics and religion.

Nero's verdict did not establish peace in Caesarea. The Judaeans protested vehemently and clashes continued in the city until the outbreak of the great revolt against Rome.[57]

The truth of the matter was that while Caesarea was built as a part of the Judaean State, it was not, according to religious law, a part of the land of Judaea (Israel) where no temples and statues could be erected. The tragedy of Judaea was that when Herod built Caesarea, his ambition had been to attract Hellenized Syrians there so that he made it a Hellenistic rather than a Judaean city. Because Caesarea was the main port of the state for imports and exports and became an exceedingly prosperous city, many Judaeans settled there. They were always regarded as newcomers and interlopers by the Hellenized Syrians. The pagan cities were particularly envious of the Judaeans, who had attained great wealth there through their commercial ability. This jealousy added further fuel to the long-standing enmity between the two ethnic groups.

PAUL

The Visits to Jerusalem

In the last years of the procuratorship of Felix, Paul, whose Hebrew name was Saul, was arrested.[58] Paul had originally been among those who persecuted the followers of Jesus. He had obtained letters from the high priests to the leaders of the Judaean communities outside of Judaea with the authorization to do so.[59] In the year 44-45, while on such a mission to Damascus, he became converted in a miraculous way to the belief that Jesus was the messiah and that he had been resurrected after his death.[60] Just as he had been zealous in fighting the

Nazarenes, he now was even more intensely desirous of making converts to their belief.

In the year 47–48, the third after Paul's conversion, he made his first journey to Jerusalem.[61] He and Barnabas went there to bring to their brethren relief and sustenance in a time of famine. He also visited Peter, remaining with him fifteen days; but he saw none of the other disciples. He did however meet James, the brother of Jesus.[62] While there, he apparently did not try to make converts. His next trip was to Asia and the Mediterranean Islands, where he intensified his propaganda for converts. This brought him into conflict with the leaders of various Judaean communities in the Diaspora.[63]

Paul made his second visit to Jerusalem in the year 58-59.[64] He brought with him several of his converts and disciples from Caesarea and other places. The people in Jerusalem were aware of his propaganda and were incensed against him. James and the other leaders among the followers of Jesus were disturbed over his coming to Jerusalem. They told him that the people knew that he was persuading Judaeans not to follow the laws of the Torah,[65] and would resent his presence in the holy city. They suggested to Paul that he show his loyalty to the laws of Moses by purifying himself and the four men, "which have a vow on them," by having their heads shaved and going to the Temple to bring the necessary sacrifice. They told him that his doing so would make the people realize that the reports about him had been false.[66]

Paul and his friends followed these suggestions, but there were present in the Temple Court many Judaeans from Asia who knew about Paul's preaching against the laws of the Torah, and they started a disturbance. They called out, "Men of Israel, help! This is the man who is teaching everywhere against the people, against the Torah and this place. Moreover, he brought Hellenes into the Temple, and has defiled this holy place."[67] The incursion of pagans was a capital offense and the Roman authorities sanctioned it as such and applied it even to Roman citizens.[68]

A great disturbance resulted, not only in the Temple area, but in the city as well. The captain of the cohort, Lysias, rushed to the scene, arrested Paul and placed him in the fortress. The first question that the captain put to him was whether he was not the Egyptian who started the revolt with four thousand men of the Sicarii.[69] From Lysias' query, it can be assumed that he considered Paul a political offender who fomented sedition against the Roman State. Paul replied the he was a Judaean born in Tarsus and that he was "a citizen of no mean City." With this reply Paul dismissed the accusation leveled against him. As he was born in Tarsus, he could not be connected with the Egyptians, and since he was a citizen of Tarsus, a Roman province, he could not have been associated with the Sicarii, who were Judaeans fighting against Rome to regain the freedom of Judaea. He was not a Judaean patriot interested in the re-establishment of the Judaean State. His concern was the coming Kingdom of God which would benefit all who believed in Jesus, regardless of whether they were Judaeans or Hellenes.

Paul and His Judges

Lysias, anxious to discover the nature of the accusations leveled against Paul, ordered the high priest and the *synedrion* to assemble and Paul to appear before them.[70] When Paul learned that some members of the *synedrion* were Sadducees and some were Pharisees, he addressed them in the following words: "Brethren, I am a Pharisee, a son of Pharisees. I am on trial for the hope and the resurrection of the dead."[71] Paul's stratagem was brilliantly successful. A quarrel ensued between the Sadducees and the Pharisees along the usual lines over resurrection. The *soferim*, the scribes, the learned men of the Pharisees, openly declared that they saw nothing wrong in Paul's words. That he entered the Temple Court with a pagan was, according to their view, not a punishable transgression. Paul, a Judaean, certainly had every right to be in the Temple Court. Bringing pagans into the Temple Court made Paul only an accomplice and, according to the Judaean law of the time, an accomplice in a crime could not be punished.[72] A great dispute started between the Sadducees and the Pharisees. When the captain witnessed this argument, he ordered Paul taken back to the fortress.[73]

The fact that some members of the *synedrion* were Sadducees and others Pharisees undoubtedly proves that this *synedrion* was not a religious body but a state council, and that Paul was brought before them as a political offender. It is unthinkable that a religious court would consist of both Sadducees and Pharisees, since their views on the *halakah* and their beliefs were in direct conflict. What the Pharisees held to be a religious offense would not have been so considered by the Sadducees.

Lysias placed Paul in a military fortress because he was afraid that he might "be torn to pieces." Some forty fanatical Judaeans placed themselves under anathema (*herem*) that they would not eat and drink until they killed Paul, apparently considering him a renegade both to Judaism and to the Judaean people. He advocated the abrogation of the essentials of Judaean traditions— the Sabbath and circumcision—and was indifferent to the Judaean aspiration to freedom from the yoke of Rome.[74] Thus both the Sicarii and the Apocalyptists would regard him as a mortal enemy and, in that unstable and violent period, seek to destroy him.

The men who contemplated killing him asked the high priests and the elders to make a representation to the captain that Paul be sent for another examination, so that they might kill him on the way. Paul's nephew learned of the plot and informed Paul, who asked him to relay this information to the captain.[75] Lysias, perplexed by the case and not knowing how to handle it, since Paul was a Roman citizen, sent him with a heavy guard to Felix in Caesarea, and wrote a letter to Felix stating the facts of the case. Lysias also ordered the Judaean leaders to proceed to Caesarea to place their accusations against Paul before the procurator. The High Priest Ananias went to Caesarea accompanied by some elders and a pleader (*mufla*) named Tertullus.[76] In accusing Paul, Tertullus said he had caused sedition among the Judaeans throughout the world, and that he was the leader of the sect of Nazarenes,[77] but that his arrest was due to his seeking to profane the Temple. Paul flatly denied all the accusations. He argued that the only offense that the *synedrion* found against him during the examination was his belief in resurrection. Felix, after he heard the arguments, reserved judgment until Lysias would report to him personally. In the meantime, he ordered that Paul be held in prison.

Sometime later, Drusilla, Felix's wife, came to Caesarea.[78] Raised as a Judaean, she apparently was curious to learn what sort of man Paul was. He was, therefore, taken from the prison and brought before Felix and his wife. When he appeared, he began a harrangue about faith in Jesus the Messiah, the Christ. He also spoke to them "of righteousness, temperance, and of the judgment to come." These words meant nothing to Felix, as righteousness was not part of his life. He could not understand the meaning of judgment to come, being set in his attitudes and steeped in his crimes. Felix sent Paul back to jail where he remained for almost two years, until Festus, the new procurator, succeeded Felix in the year 60. It was suspected that Felix was waiting for a bribe to release Paul.[79]

In the year 59-60, Nero appointed Porcius Festus procurator of Judaea. King Agrippa II, who had avoided coming to Judaea because of his enmity towards Felix, came with his sister Berenice to visit Festus on his arrival in Caesarea. Perplexed over what to do with Paul, who had remained in prison, Festus consulted Agrippa, who expressed a desire to see Paul. He was brought before an audience comprising Festus, Agrippa, and his sister Berenice, the heads of the army, and the leading men of Caesarea.[80] Paul, instead of presenting his case, told the story of his conversion. Why, he asked, should it be incredible that God should raise the dead? It was for this belief, which the twelve tribes also held, that he had been brought to judgment.[81] Festus found Paul's statement beyond comprehension. He thought Paul's mind was affected, but that he was harmless.[82] Paul appealed to Agrippa to believe that Jesus was indeed the Messiah, who had arisen from the dead, as had been foretold by Moses and the prophets: "That Messiah, Christ, should suffer, that he should be the first that should rise from the dead, and should shew light to the people and to the Gentiles." Agrippa said to Paul, "Almost thou persuadest me to become a Christian." Agrippa said to Festus that if Paul had not appealed to Caesar, he should have been released.[83] Paul was dispatched to Rome.

Speeches recorded by ancient historians were often their own words put in the mouths of their heroes. That must be the verdict on this speech by Paul. It was almost certainly the creation of the author of Acts to convey his theological message. Paul could not have spoken of twelve tribes, as in those days there no longer were twelve tribes or any tribes. Agrippa could not have spoken of becoming a Christian as the term Christian had not yet come into vogue.[84]

5. APPROACH TO CONFLICT

HIGH PRIESTS AND POLITICIANS

Turbulent Rivalries

Agrippa II, who had the authority to appoint high priests, appointed Ishmael son of Phabi to that office.[1] A word must be said about the deterioration of the high priesthood and its relation to the worsening social situation. The appointments were made of members of aristocratic, wealthy families. In the jockeying for office, feuds developed between the contending families. There were numerous violent personal and family rivalries. The upper class led the general descent of the country as a whole into a state approaching anarchy. The high priests, once in office, sent their slaves to the farms to collect the tithes by force.[2] Some ordinary priests, who were supported by these tithes, actually died of starvation when thus deprived of their regular due. All this strengthened those groups who propagated religious and social revolution. Various patriots organized men to fight the Romans and their collaborators. These groups kept themselves underground for fear of severe retaliation by the Roman authorities. Unscrupulous men utilized this situation, organizing men who robbed and pillaged the populace for personal gain. The people were confused, not being able to distinguish between the patriots and the bandits. And even the high priestly families enlisted gangs in order to obtain the office of high priest.[3] These groups fought one another in behalf of their patrons, and this led to more disorder in the country as well as in the Temple area. All this contributed to a general contempt for the high priests and a lessened reverence for the Temple itself.

Agrippa also clashed with the high priests. When he visited Jerusalem, he lived in the Hasmonean palace located on a hilltop west of the Temple enclosure and connected to it by a bridge which spanned the intervening ravine. Agrippa erected a tower there which would afford him a full view of the Temple. The priests were indignant, insisting it was unlawful for anyone to be able to view what went on in the inner court of the Temple. They therefore erected a high wall on the top of the western colonnade of the inner court which cut off Agrippa's view. Festus was displeased even more than Agrippa, as the Temple was now screened from his troops in Antonia and the outer colonnades. He ordered the demolition of the wall, and the priests protested.[4] After a long dispute between them, the procurator agreed that the case be referred to Nero. With his permission a delegation of ten men, headed by the High Priest Ishmael and the treasurer Helcias, went to Rome. The delegation obtained a favorable verdict through the mediation of the Empress Poppea who was under the influence of Judaism.[5] However, Nero detained the High Priest Ishmael and the treasurer Helcias in Rome as hostages for the good behavior of the Judaeans.[6]

Agrippa did not have much influence in the court of Nero, though he styled himself a friend of Caesar and the Romans. Agrippa renamed the City of Caesarea Philippi—which had been built by Philip son of Herod —Neronias, in honor of the Emperor Nero. The city of Berytus having been favored by his father, Agrippa adorned it lavishly, and endowed it with a magnificent theater and beautiful statues. He also, at his own expense, bestowed upon its people large quantities of corn and oil.[7]

His generosity greatly displeased the Judaeans, who felt that the food should rather have been dispensed to them, for many of them were in want due to the great disturbances occurring in the country.

When Agrippa learned that the High Priest Ishmael was being detained by Nero in Rome, he gave the high priesthood to Joseph Cabi son of Simon, who formerly had been a high priest.[8] But he soon deposed Joseph and appointed Ananus son of Ananus.[9] In the year 62, shortly after his appointment, Festus died and Nero appointed Albinus as his successor.

Josephus states that the High Priest Ananus was a Sadducee and that, as such, was rigid in the judgment of offenders.[10] It would seem that a struggle had once again begun between the Sadducees and the Pharisees. The Pharisees had shunned politics since the time of Herod when the Sadducees had been crushed by him. In this period in which the Apocalyptists, the false prophets, and the Sicarii were active, both groups re-appeared on the political scene and renewed the struggle which had raged between them during the late Hasmonean period.

The High Priest Ananus, utilizing the interregnum—Festus had died and Albinus had not yet arrived—convened a *synedrion* of judges. James, the brother of Jesus, and his companions were brought before them, accused of transgressing the laws, convicted and stoned to death. The authenticity of these passages in Josephus, where the story is related is, however, open to doubt.[11]

The Judaeans were indignant over what Ananus had done. They petitioned Agrippa to order him not to be so harsh. Many Judaeans went to meet Albinus who was coming to Judaea from Alexandria. They complained to him that the High Priest Ananus had usurped the right of setting up a *synedrion* and done so without the consent of Albinus. Albinus was indignant and threatened to have him punished.[12] In the meanwhile, Agrippa dismissed Ananus and appointed Joshua son of Damnaeus in his stead, and he was soon succeeded by Joshua son of Gamala (abbreviation of Gamaliel).[13] It was said that while Joshua was still an ordinary priest he had married a widow of great wealth, named Martha, of the family of Boethus, and that she gave a large sum of money to Agrippa to appoint her husband to the high priesthood. This appointment made the deposed high priest bitter and led to a feud and finally violence between their families. Ananus, the previous high priest, who was a man of great wealth and possessed many slaves, took an active part in the brawls between these factions.[14]

The Procurator Albinus

Albinus, who replaced Festus, was responsible for even greater suffering by the people. His main object was to get money from whatever source, private or public. He also welcomed bribery in return for his favors. He accepted bribes both from Ananus, a friend of Rome, and at the same time from the Sicarii to free their partisans from prison. The Sicarii, encouraged by such actions, resorted to kidnapping and ransom. One of them kidnapped a scribe of Eleazar, the captain of the Temple who was the son of the high priest Ananus, and the Sicarii sent word to Ananus that the scribe would be released if ten men of their own group would be freed by Albinus. Ananus persuaded Albinus, undoubtedly with a substantial bribe, to accede to the request of the Sicarii. Albinus' behavior further emboldened the Sicarii and they intensified their activities.[15] Not only did the political parties terrorize and steal from those whom they considered friends of Rome, but the high priestly families as well as some nobles of the royal family, Saul and Costobar, also engaged in robbery and plunder.[16]

The situation in Judaea was indeed tense. Stirred by the propaganda of the Sicarii and the Apocalyptists, no small number became unbalanced. Many held that the destruction of the State and the Temple was inevitable. Josephus recounts a strange event which took place on the Festival of Tabernacles, in the year 62. Joshua son of Ananias, who was an ordinary, uncultured man, while standing in the Temple, suddenly cried out, "A voice from the East, a voice from the West, a voice from the four winds; a voice against Jerusalem and the Temple, a voice against the bridegroom and the bride, a voice against all the people." He continued crying out these words day and night, so that some of the notables, who were incensed at this ill-omened oracle, had him arrested. Although he was severely punished, he did not cry out and the people therefore felt all the more that he must be under some supernatural influence. He was brought before Albinus. Although he was flayed to the bone with scourges, he shed no tear nor did he beg for mercy, but continued to call out, "Woe to Jerusalem." When Albinus asked from where he came, he did not reply. Albinus concluded he was mentally deranged and set him free. Josephus further relates that the priests in the Temple also heard voices and saw bad omens. These accounts reveal the general state of mind.[17]

During the time of Albinus, the Temple reconstruction, which had been begun and partially consummated by Herod, achieved full completion. Eighteen thousand workmen now became idle. In order to avoid serious unemployment which might cause further disturbances in the country, the leaders of Jerusalem gave each workman, even if employed for only an hour, payment for a whole day's work.[18] They petitioned Agrippa to tear down and rebuild the eastern colonnade of the outer court, which dated from the pre-Herodian period. Agrippa opposed this plan, arguing that, though it might be easy to demolish a building, it was hard to build it up again. Apparently he was not sure that the Roman authorities would permit this. He suggested another method: that the employment problem be relieved by paving the streets of Jerusalem with marble.[19] In the meantime, the underpinnings of the Temple foundation began to collapse. Agrippa, with the consent of the chief priests, decided to bolster the structure anew and to raise it twenty cubits higher. For this work he spared neither labor nor expense. An example of the scale of his enterprise was his importation of huge timbers from Mount Lebanon.[20]

The Levites, in this period, were held in low esteem and the priests tried to suppress them even further. Their activities had remained largely the same over the years. Some of them chanted the hymns during the services, others supervised and guarded the gates of the Temple, while still others performed all kinds of manual work necessary for the maintenance of the Temple. But the Levites were not permitted to wear the sacerdotal, simple linen garb worn by the priests. They besought Agrippa to call a *synedrion* to permit them to do so. His *synedrion* granted them this privilege, and also allowed the Levites who were engaged in manual labor or who guarded the gates the privilege of participating in chanting the hymns. The priestly families, who had always looked down on the Levites, were greatly displeased. Josephus, who was of an aristocratic priestly family, expresses their sentiments in his writings and says that this action of the *synedrion* was an open transgression of the laws. He even intimates that the burning of the Temple was due in a measure to this sin, for whenever the Judaeans broke the law they suffered.[21]

After Albinus had been in office for two years, he was replaced by Gessius Florus. When Albinus learned that Florus was coming to succeed him, he ordered that all prisoners who had been condemned to death for major crimes against the State be executed, and that those who had been imprisoned by local consuls or previous procurators for minor offenses, such as robbery, should be released upon payment of a fine. Hence when Albinus left the country the prisons were empty and the country was even more unsettled.[22] Ordinary robbers felt that they could always escape punishment by bribing the procurator.

The Procurator Florus

Florus assumed the procuratorship in the early part of the year 64. He was the last procurator. Josephus says that in comparison with Florus the Judaeans considered Albinus righteous. Florus was the perverse climax of a long line of corrupt and vicious officials.[23]

The clashes between the Judaeans and the Hellenized Syrians in Caesarea had grown in gravity, since Nero Caesar's decision favoring the Greeks. An incident occurred in the early part of 64 which inflamed the passions of the feuding inhabitants. The Judaeans owned an assembly house where they gathered, particularly on the Sabbath, to read the Torah. The adjacent plot was owned by a Hellene. The Judaeans had made many offers to purchase it and were willing to pay a price far in excess of its value. The Hellene stubbornly refused the offers and insisted on building a workshop on it in order to inconvenience the Judaeans. Many of the Judaean youths tried to interrupt its construction and even attacked the workmen. Florus, who had his seat in Caesarea, took measures against those who interrupted the construction. Some of the Judaeans under the leadership of John, a tax collector, gave eight talents to Florus as a bribe to side with the Judaeans. He accepted the money, but the following Sabbath when the Judaeans went to their house of assembly, they found at the entrance a pot with its bottom up upon which birds had been sacrificed. They considered this a fearful outrage and the question of appropriate reaction rent the Judaean community. The elderly people wanted to take the matter before the authorities, but the younger element, passionate youths, were eager for a fight, and a clash ensued. The commander of the city intervened, removed the pot and endeavored to quell the riot, but could not succeed because of the violence of the pagans. The Judaeans took the scroll of the Torah from Caesarea to Narbata, which was in Judaean territory, for safety. Twelve leading Judaeans, headed by John, went to Caesarea where Florus was stationed. They complained to him about the outrages committed by the Hellenes and asked for his assistance, politely reminding him of the eight talents which they had given him. He arrested them and placed them in fetters on the charge that they had carried away the Torah scroll from Caesarea.[24] This was surely their right under the edict of religious freedom given to them, but Florus disliked the Judaeans and had contempt for their religion. He schemed to make life unbearable for them, and thus arouse them to open revolt against Rome in order to have them decimated and their land laid waste. In the meantime, he enriched himself with plunder from every source.

The Middle East was still smoldering. The peace between Parthia and Rome was far from stable, with Armenia still the trouble spot. Already in the year 61, Tigranes of Armenia had plundered Adiabene, whose king was Monobazus, the successor of his brother Izates.[25] The royal family, and most likely a substantial segment of the population, had accepted the Judaean religion.[26] Adiabene was a feudatory of Parthia and so Vologases, King of Parthia, felt compelled to intervene.[27] He mobilized his forces and made it appear that he was threatening to invade Syria. Corbulo, the legate of Syria, took all possible measures to put the country in a state of defense. In the meantime, Nero had adopted a new policy with regard to Armenia. This country hitherto had been ruled by a client king, a vassal of Rome. Now Nero decided to annex it and appointed L. Caesennius Paetus commander-in-chief of the army for this purpose. But he was decisively defeated by the Parthians.[28] It was one of the great military disasters that befell Rome. As Seutonius wrote, "A shameful defeat in the Orient, in consequence of which the legions in Armenia were sent under the yoke and Syria was all but lost."[29] He said that songs were posted and circulated in Greek and Latin, containing the phrase: "While our ruler his lyre twangs and the Parthian his bowstring . . ."[30] Paetus was then recalled and Corbulo appointed commander-in-chief with extraordinary authority, similar only to that given to Pompey. Gaius Cestius succeeded him as legate of Syria in the year 63.[31]

The humiliating defeat of the Romans in Armenia undoubtedly raised the hopes of the revolutionary groups in Judaea. They now knew that Rome was not invincible, and held that the peace re-established between Rome and Parthia would not be lasting. They realized that the original Armenian attack on Adiabene had been made with the consent of Rome, and that should war break out between Judaea and Rome, Adiabene, partly Judaized, would come to their aid and stir up disturbances in the Middle East. They may even have calculated that Parthia, with its large Jewish communities, might aid them to further her own political interests.

The High Priest Joshua son of Gamala, despite his short tenure, succeeded in improving the education of Judaean youth by making school attendance compulsory for all young children and establishing schools for them.[32] Agrippa removed him from office and appointed Matthias son of Theophilus. He was the last high priest appointed by Agrippa.[33]

In the year 64, Josephus, then twenty-six years of age, made a journey to Rome in behalf of his friends, the priests, who had been arrested and sent to Rome in bonds by Felix when he was procurator. Here Josephus formed a friendship with the actor Aliturus, who was a Judaean and a favorite of Nero. Through Aliturus, Josephus was introduced to the Empress Poppea, and he thus secured the liberation of his friends.[34] This journey shaped Josephus' future life. During his stay, he had occasion to mingle with the aristocracy and was indelibly impressed by Roman culture. He was charmed by the metropolis of the world and its culture. He was deeply awed by Rome's military power.

The political situation in Judaea became graver from day to day. When the Judaeans heard of the outrages perpetrated in Caesarea, they tried to restrain their feelings. Florus, on the other hand, made efforts to fan the flames of revolt. He gave orders that seventeen talents should be taken from the Temple treasury to be paid into the imperial treasury of Rome.[35] It is possible that this money was requisitioned for the payment of tribute that was in arrears, but his action was provocative and aroused violent indignation. The people gathered in the Temple area, and loudly invoked the name of Caesar, imploring him to liberate them from the tyranny of Florus. Many young people passed around beggar's baskets, ironically appealing for alms for the unfortunate Florus. He was deeply insulted and marched with an army of cavalry and infantry to Jerusalem. Those Judaeans who abhorred riots and bloodshed went out to meet him, prepared to give him an obsequious reception. He, however, ordered them to retire to their homes. On the following day, June 3, 65,[36] he summoned the chief priests and the leaders of the city and ordered them to hand over the men who had insulted him. The leaders declared that the people were peaceful and well-disposed, that those who had caused the disorder and insulted him were a few reckless, foolish youths, and that they were unable to identify those who were responsible. The meek speech of the Judaean leaders only exasperated Florus and he gave orders to the soldiers to sack the "upper market" and to kill anyone whom they encountered. According to Josephus, three thousand six hundred people —men, women and children—were killed. Florus even ordered men with the rank of equestrians scourged and crucified.[37]

At this time Agrippa was in Alexandria, where he had gone to congratulate Tiberius Alexander on the occasion of his appointment as governor of Egypt. Berenice, his sister, was in Jerusalem at the time to discharge a vow which necessitated a residence of thirty days. She had shaved her head and abstained from wine for the prescribed period before she could offer the sacrifice. She witnessed the slaughter of the people and sent her lieutenant to Florus to implore him to stop it, but he paid no attention. She herself went to him begging him to take a merciful attitude. He met her appeal with contempt and insult.[38] On the next day, June 4, a great multitude flocked to the upper market and lamented the death of their relatives and friends. They were so aroused that violence seemed imminent. The chief priests and the leading men became alarmed over the situation, and organized their own demonstration for peace. The chief priests dressed in their sacerdotal garments, rent their clothes, and throwing themselves on their knees, implored the people to restrain themselves and not provoke Florus. The multitude complied out of respect for the wishes of their leaders.[39]

Florus was not mollified. He told the leaders that two cohorts were now marching from Caesarea to Jerusalem and they should show their respect by going out to greet them. At the same time he sent word to the centurions that they should not return the salute of the Judaeans, but should treat them with contempt. The high priest assembled the people in the Temple and besought them to go out to meet and salute the oncoming troops; but many Judaeans could no longer bring themseives to do this. The chief priests again made a dramatic appeal. They formed a procession and in full attire carried the holy vessels, while the harpists and the choristers bore their musical instruments. They fell on their knees and appealed to the people to be conciliatory, and the Judaeans now complied. When the cohorts made no response, many Judaeans, filled with resentment over the insult, raised a clamor against Florus. The troops, again under his orders, now struck out against them and in the ensuing fight many Judaeans were killed. Florus sought to occupy the Temple, but the Judaeans drove the troops back. To prevent its seizure, they cut off communication by breaking down the porticoes of the Temple Court.

Florus became alarmed over this resistance, and recognized that he was not strong enough to subdue it. He sent for the leaders and informed them that he intended to leave the city. He asked them how many troops they would require to maintain order. The leaders, familiar with the bad behavior of the Roman troops, felt that they would be a liability rather than an asset. They said that one troop stationed in Jerusalem would be enough. Florus withdrew with his troops to Caesarea and sent a report of the revolt to Cestius, the legate of Syria.[40] The capture of Antonia by the Judaeans and the withdrawal of Florus from Jerusalem occurred on the 14th day of Sivan, the 8th of June, in 65, a date later declared a semi-holiday.[41]

The chief priests and Berenice sent a report to Cestius, the legate of Syria, in which Florus was accused of provoking the riots in Jerusalem. Cestius decided to send the tribune Neapolitanus to investigate. He stopped in Jabneh where he met King Agrippa who was returning from Alexandria. The chief priests and the Council also went to Jabneh to welcome Agrippa, and to enlist his support against Florus. Agrippa and Neapolitanus proceeded to Jerusalem where they were received with acclaim. The leaders of the people showed them the upper market which was a scene of desolation, and the many houses which had been plundered. Neapolitanus, at the request of Agrippa, made a tour through the city and satisfied himself that there were no signs of revolt against Rome; then he returned to Cestius to report his findings.[42]

Agrippa's Failure

The populace appealed to Agrippa to send an embassy to Emperor Nero to complain of Florus' brutality.[43] Agrippa found himself in a quandary. If he should decline the appeal, he would be considered an enemy and, perhaps, be held responsible for allowing the flames now smoldering in the hearts of the people to burst into open revolt. On the other hand, he believed it unwise to send a delegation to Emperor Nero.

It is difficult to understand the reason for Agrippa's hesitancy. Perhaps he was afraid to go over the head of Cestius, or he had other misgivings. Agrippa knew his people well. Though they all, including the aristocracy, were united in denouncing Florus, he could count on the aristocracy remaining loyal to Rome in any event. On the other hand, he knew that a great segment of the people, the revolutionaries, were for the independence of the Judaean State and a new social order. Nothing less would satisfy them. Hence the dismissal of Florus and his punishment would not change their attitude.

Agrippa summoned the people to the Temple area and, with Berenice at his side, delivered a speech which Josephus presents in all its length.[44] According to Josephus, Agrippa presented the following arguments: He knew that many of the people were of sound mind and opposed to a revolt. He also knew that the young people, not realizing what sufferings war brings, were propagating rebellion, pointing to the insolence of the procurators and pronouncing panegyrics on liberty. This was only a device. Would the change to a good procurator satisfy them? What they wanted was to throw off the yoke of Rome and it would make no difference to them even if the procurator were a good one. Hence, he had nothing to say to them. He was appealing to the vast majority of the people. No doubt some procurators were bad, but this was to be expected in so vast an empire as Rome. The Emperor wished the best for his subjects, but could not know what was happening in the far corners of his realm. Even if some of the Roman procurators were intolerable, this did not mean that all the Romans, particularly Caesar, were harsh. A war cannot be against the procurators alone, but also against Rome and Caesar. Many Judaeans grieved over their bondage and sought liberty. They should have striven not to lose their liberty. This was the fault of their forefathers who, by their strife, made it possible for Pompey to conquer Judaea. Further, Rome's power was invincible. The Athenians and the Macedonians, who had enjoyed imperial greatness, were richer and far more numerous than the Judaeans and were great warriors, yet they became servants to Rome. Rome ruled all the countries of the world—Gaul, Germany, Iberia (Spain), and Azov. Egypt, too, with its great population of seven million five hundred thousand persons, exclusive of Alexandria, was subject to Rome. The tribute Egypt paid to Rome in one month exceeded that paid by Judaea in an entire year, and besides money, Egypt supplied Rome with its corn for four months of the year. The Judaeans could not expect their coreligionists in Adiabene to come to their aid. The Parthians would not permit this, since they had a truce with Rome. What hope had they for victory? Stronger and wealthier nations had been conquered by Rome and were now at peace with her. It may be that the Judaeans believed that God would come to their assistance, but it must have been by God's will that Rome became such a great empire. Furthermore, if the Judaeans made war upon Rome, they would have to transgress the laws of their ancestors by fighting on the Sabbath. They should rather have pity on their wives and children and save the holy city for, if they made war, it would be burned to the ground and the entire population would be exterminated. Not only would their lives be endangered, but those of all their coreligionists in the Diaspora who would be slaughtered in all the cities where they dwelt. With tears in his eyes he appealed to them to spare the Temple and the holy city. Concluding, he called the sanctuary and the angels to witness that he had endeavored to persuade the Judaeans to keep the peace; but if they should decide to make war, he would have no part in it.

Undoubtedly Agrippa did deliver a strong speech to the Judaeans to dissuade them from revolting against Rome, but the version Josephus presents could not have been delivered by Agrippa. Agrippa could not have known then how many legions the Romans had stationed in each country to keep the peace. Josephus, in writing the speech, made use of Roman archives wherein he learned the details about the various countries, the number of legions stationed in each, and the amount of tribute exacted. Moreover, Agrippa's warning to the Judaeans that, should they declare war against Rome, their coreligionists would be exterminated was a *post factum* statement based on what happened later.

Agrippa's appeal made a deep impression on the people and had a sobering effect. While persisting in their protests against Florus, they declared their loyalty to Rome. Taking advantage of their reaction, Agrippa told them that their words were not enough; their deeds were rebellious. The Fortress Antonia belonged to Caesar, not to Florus, and the tribute too was paid to Caesar. To show loyalty to Rome, they should reconstruct the porticoes and pay the tribute. They followed his advice and reconstructed the porticoes. The *boulé,* the council of Jerusalem, dispatched men throughout the city and its environs to collect the tribute.[45]

For a while it appeared that Agrippa had succeeded in softening the anger of the people, and that the peace party had won a victory. But Agrippa had also appealed to them to submit to Florus until Caesar should send a successor. In this he blundered. The outrages Florus had perpetrated were such that even the moderates, hitherto influenced by Agrippa, were no longer under his influence. In fact, he had antagonized them by his insistence that they tolerate Florus. Recognizing that conditions in Jerusalem were getting beyond his control, Agrippa decided to leave the city. Before leaving, he arranged to have the leaders of Judaea go to Florus in Caesarea in order to see to the collection of the tribute from the rest of the country.[46]

THE REVOLT AGAINST ROME

Discontinuance of the Imperial Sacrifice

When Agrippa departed from Jerusalem, no one at all was left who could exercise influence over the populace. Without strong leadership in Jerusalem, conditions went from bad to worse. One band went to the south and made an assault on the Fortress Masada. They overpowered the garrison, slew the Romans and stationed their own men in the fortress.[47]

Since the time of Augustus sacrifices had been offered in the Temple in behalf of the Emperor and of Rome. A group of extremists under the leadership of Eleazar, captain of the Temple and son of High Priest Ananias, proposed that a law be enacted that no sacrifice be offered in the Temple for heathens and that no gifts to the Temple be accepted from them. The leaders of the Judaeans were aware this meant that no sacrifices would be offered for Caesar, an act tantamount to open revolt. Thereupon they and the most notable Pharisees, probably of the school of Hillel, appealed to the people not to follow the advice of Eleazar and his adherents. They produced historic precedents to show that the Judaeans had always accepted gifts from heathens and offered sacrifices for foreign rulers. They maintained that the adoption of this law would not be in accordance with the traditions of their forefathers. Eleazar and his followers were of quite another mind. They held that the daily sacrifice for Caesar was offered not because of friendship but because of subjugation. Not wanting a direct break with Rome, Eleazar sought to introduce a general law whose effect would be no less drastic. The Pharisees did not succeed in persuading the people, and when the ordinary priests adopted Eleazar's position, the sacrifices for Rome and Caesar were discontinued.[48]

The Talmud gives some details of this event. It records that a conclave was held in the house of Ananias—not in the house of Eleazar—and that eighteen decrees were promulgated, among them the decrees not to accept any sacrifices nor gifts from heathens. At this session the Hillelites were outnumbered. The Palestinian Talmud records that the session was stormy and that six Hillelites were killed. It comments that this was a dark day, similar to the day when the Israelites made the golden calf.[49]

With the cessation of sacrifices for Caesar, the revolt may be said formally to have begun. The tribute to Rome was also no longer paid. In commemoration, this day, the 25th of Sivan, the 19th of June 65, was declared a semi-holiday.[50]

Defeat of the Peace Party

The leaders of the peace party, perceiving that it was beyond their power to subdue the revolutionary group,

decided that the only course left to them was to seek
military aid. They dispatched a delegation, led by Simon
son of Ananias, to Florus. Another delegation, headed by
three men, Saul and his brother Costobar, and Antipas,
who were of the royal family, were sent to Agrippa asking for troops to quell the rebellion. Florus paid no attention to the request of the delegation. He was even glad
that a revolt was taking place, hoping that now he would
be able to destroy the people. Agrippa, on the other hand,
promptly brought in an army, two thousand men from
Auranitis, Trachonitis and Batanaea, and a thousand
cavalry.[51] With the aid of these troops the people who
were for peace were able, under the leadership of the
high priest, to occupy the upper city. But the lower city,
as well as the Temple, were in the hands of the rebellious
group.

The objective of the royal troops was to capture the
Temple and expel the rebels. Under Eleazar's leadership,
the rebels fought to capture the upper city. There was
bitter fighting between the opposing forces for seven
days, and it resulted in great slaughter for both sides.
Neither group would surrender its position. The eighth
day, the 10th of Elul (the 14th of the month Lous), the
2nd of September, was a day when the people regularly
carried wood for the altar to the Temple.[52] Sicarii entered
the Temple unnoticed among the humble people carrying
wood and joined Eleazar's group. Together they greatly
outnumbered the royalist troops entrenched in the upper
city, who were thus forced to retreat, entrenching themselves in the palace, the Roman troops present accom-
panying them.[53]

The Sicarii, whose aid made Eleazar's victory possible,
were beyond his control. They plundered and destroyed
the palace of Agrippa and Berenice, and the house of
Ananias, the father of Eleazar. They set fire to the
archives where promissory notes were kept, making the
collection of debts impossible. By thus freeing the poor
from their indebtedness, the Sicarii hoped to win their
favor.[54]

Eleazar and the leader of the Sicarii held diametrically opposing views as to the purpose of the revolt. Eleazar was a nationalist. His goal was to restore the political independence of Judaea. On the other hand, the philosophy of the Sicarii was to revolutionize society. They were not interested in the independence of Judaea as such, but in forcing their views that all men were equal before God and that there be no rule of men over men. The Sicarii were like many sincere idealists who, when they gained power, brought calamity upon their people. They were in large measure responsible for the catastrophe which befell Judaea.

After the forces of Eleazar captured the upper city, they laid siege to Antonia. The siege began on the eleventh of Elul, the 3rd of September. After two days they succeeded in capturing Antonia and they put the Romans in the fortress to death. Then they proceeded to besiege the palace which was occupied by the royal troops and the aristocracy, the leaders of the peace party.[55] Many who were for peace now went into hiding. Among them was Joseph son of Matthias, later known as Josephus Flavius. When Josephus had returned from Rome, he worked against war, which he termed reckless, a madness that would bring about incredible catastrophe. After the fall of Antonia, he sought refuge in the Temple, since he feared for his life.

The siege of the upper palace made little headway until assistance came to the besiegers. Menachem son of Judas the Galilean was, like his father, a sophist, a teacher, and the leader of the Sicarii. With some of his followers, Menachem went to Masada. There he broke into King Herod's armory and seized all the arms; with these he equipped his forces. Menachem thus became the leader of a well-armed force. He then marched to Jerusalem— in the words of Josephus, like a king—and joined Eleazar's forces. The besieged in the royal palace had no alternative but to capitulate. But the privilege of surrender was granted only to the royal troops and the Judaean aristocracy.[56] This event occurred on the 17th of Elul, the 9th of September, 65 C.E., and the day was declared a semi-holiday.[57]

The Romans, deserted by the royal army, were now left alone in the palace. Their position was no longer tenable, and they retreated to the tower Phasael Mariamme Hippicus, located on the north side of the palace enclosure. Menachem and his men captured the upper palace and slew all the Romans who remained there on the 22nd of Elul, the 14th of September.[58]

A siege of the towers was now begun and eventually the Romans agreed to surrender on the condition that their lives be spared. The leaders of the revolt agreed to this. However, when Metilius, the commander of the garrison, led his men out unarmed, the populace fell upon them and slew them. The people were so embittered that they disregarded the word of their leaders and committed this treachery. Only Metilius escaped by embracing the Judaean religion.[59]

No Romans were now left in the city and the royal army of Agrippa had likewise been required to leave. Thus the yoke of Rome was broken and, beginning with the third of Tishri, the 24th of September, no documents in Jerusalem were dated to the year of the reigning emperor.[60] It is likely that at this time, too, new coins were issued with the legend, "The first year of the redemption of Israel." The symbol thereon was in consonance with the character of the approaching Festival of Tabernacles, the four species of the *lulab* on one side and, on the reverse, a representation of a *sukkah*.[61]

Menachem's army excelled Eleazar's in discipline as well as in number. He had little difficulty in establishing a reign of terror, murdering the aristocrats and all whom he considered potential enemies. On the 4th of Tishri, the 25th of September, he hunted out Ananias, the high priest, father of Eleazar, and had him and his brother Ezechias executed.[62]

Eleazar, who had welcomed the aid of Menachem and his followers in his battle against the royal army and the Romans, now recognized the danger. He felt that not only was Menachem a threat to his own life, but to the established social order. A conspiracy was formed by Eleazar and those who advocated peace. They thought that, by killing Menachem, the social revolution would collapse. One day when Menachem and some followers were in the Temple, the conspirators fell upon them. Most of the party were killed, but he escaped and hid. The pursuers found him, tortured him, and put him to death along with his lieutenant Absalom. Many of the Sicarii then fled to Masada, among them a relative of Menachem, Eleazar son of Jairus, who subsequently became their leader.[63] Menachem was assassinated early in the autumn of 65. From that time until the burning of the Temple nothing was heard of the Sicarii. Throughout the years of the war between the Judaeans and the Romans they furnished no aid.[64]

Defeat of Cestius

After the death of Menachem, Josephus and the other members of the aristocracy came out from their hiding. They saw that the populace was armed and determined, to the point where they were powerless to check the revolution. They decided to bide their time and do nothing to aggravate matters. They awaited the coming of Cestius, the legate of Syria, with his powerful army.

The defeat and slaughter of the Roman army in Jerusalem was a signal for the slaughter of the Judaeans in Caesarea. Over twenty thousand Judaeans were massacred,[65] apparently with the blessing of Florus. Another immense massacre occurred in Alexandria.

The revolution against Rome, which started in Jerusalem, spread throughout the country. Cestius moved to quell the revolt, undoubtedly with the encouragement of Agrippa and the aristocracy. He left Antioch with the twelfth legion, strengthened by the addition of six thousand men taken from his other three legions. In addition, there were six cohorts of infantry and four squadrons of cavalry. His client kings supplied auxiliary

troops. Antiochus, King of Commangene, provided him
with three thousand infantry and two thousand cavalry.
Soaemus, King of Emesa, supplied two thousand archers
and two thousand cavalry. Agrippa gave him three thousand infantry and nearly two thousand cavalry, and
accompanied Cestius to aid him by his knowledge of the
terrain. More auxiliaries were added to his army as it
passed through the country.[66]

Cestius, in marching towards Jerusalem, thought it
necessary to pacify Galilee. He sent his lieutenant Gallus
with a force to restore order there. Sepphoris, the
strongest city in Galilee, welcomed Gallus and the men
who favored the revolt fled to the mountains. Seeing no
signs of revolt in Galilee, Gallus went on to meet Cestius
in Caesarea.[67] From Caesarea the army went to Antipatris, northeast of Jaffa, and from there to Lydda.
Cestius reached Lydda about the 20th of October. The
residents of Lydda, who had gone to Jerusalem for the
Festival of Tabernacles, knowing of the approach of war,
remained there. Cestius found only fifty Judaeans in
Lydda and put them to the sword.[68]

The Judaeans in Jerusalem, aware of the approach of
Cestius, did not celebrate the Feast of Tabernacles, but
supplied the populace with arms. No thought was given
to the Sabbath traditionally set aside for rest. Cestius'
advance force reached Bet Horon, about twelve miles
northwest of Jerusalem and here the Judaean army
barred the way. In the clash the Judaeans were victorious. For, while the Judaeans made a frontal attack on
the army of Cestius, others, under Simon son of Gioras,
attacked the Romans from the rear as they were ascending towards Bet Horon. The Romans lost four hundred
infantrymen and one hundred and fifteen cavalry. The
Judaeans lost only twenty-two men.[69] The Judaean victory was attributed to the military genius of the leaders
Monobazus of Adiabene and Cenedaeus, his kinsman.
The other leaders were Niger of Peraea and Silas, one of
the Babylonians whom Herod had settled in Batanaea,
now a part of the domain of Agrippa. Silas had deserted

Agrippa and joined the revolutionary group. The leaders responsible for the victory at Bet Horon were thus not natives of Judaea. They had joined the revolt to help make Judaea an independent state.

Agrippa still felt that a majority of the people in Jerusalem were for peace. Thinking that the power of Cestius' full army would have a sobering effect on those who were vacillating, he decided, with the consent of Cestius, to make a last appeal to the Judaeans. He sent two of his best friends, Borcius and Phoebus, who were well known in Jerusalem, to offer on behalf of Cestius pardon to all those who had been engaged in the revolt if they would lay down their arms and resume allegiance to Rome. The revolutionaries, apprehensive that the offer of amnesty would have a pacifying effect, did not give them an opportunity to speak to the people. Phoebus was slain and Borcius was wounded but escaped.[70]

Cestius now decided to march on Jerusalem with full force. He pitched his tents on Mount Scopus north of the city. For three days he remained inactive, still hoping that the Judaeans would surrender. He knew that a large segment of the people opposed the revolt and he believed that the display of the might of the army so near the city would weaken the morale of the revolutionaries. During these three days he sent his men to the surrounding villages to forage for corn, indicating that his supply of food was limited. On the fourth day, the 29th of Heshvan,[71] 17th of November, Cestius marched on the city. The populace made no attempt to resist. Cestius occupied the upper city and set fire to the district Bezetha and the timber market. He then encamped opposite the royal palace. The rebels held the lower city and the Temple.[72] At this time some of the leaders of the peace party, led by Ananias son of Jonathan, made an offer to open the gates to the Romans; but before the negotiations could take place, he and his confederates were thrown over the walls of the city to their deaths. Cestius then attacked the walls of the lower city. He continued the attack for five days, but without success. He then

attacked the north wall of the Temple but without ef-
ect.[73] Cestius finally determined that he could make no
progress this way. He now saw that his hopes that the
might of the Roman army would weaken the morale of
the people and that the loyalists would gain the ascend-
ency were not being realized. He decided to retreat.

Josephus says that the reason Cestius did not press
his attack was that Tyrannius Priscus and other cavalry
commanders were bribed by Florus to advise Cestius not
to do so.[74] If this is true, it was probably because Florus
was apprehensive lest Nero place the onus of the revolt
upon him, and he wanted to shift blame for the war
upon Cestius. He may also have wanted to let the situation deteriorate so that Judaea would be wiped out by
the Romans.

The more likely reason for the retreat of Cestius was
that he was not prepared for a lengthy campaign. He
did not have sufficient provisions for the army, and it
was clear that the majority of the Judaeans supported
the revolutionists resolutely. The country was not entirely subdued, and Cestius may have feared that, while
fighting in Jerusalem, he would encounter attacks from
the inhabitants of the country at large. The time of the
year also worked against him. It was the end of Heshvan
and the beginning of Kislev, the rainy season. Cestius
feared that, if he continued the attack against the walls
and the Temple, he would be at the mercy of the Judaeans. To save his army, the wisest thing was to return
to Caesarea.

Cestius' decision to retreat was disastrous. As soon as
the rebels saw the Romans withdrawing from Jerusalem,
they plucked up their courage and attacked the army
from the rear. They harried the Romans with guerilla
warfare tactics in which they were adept. The rear ranks
of the army of Cestius suffered severe losses, and their
wounded were left as they continued the retreat. Many
commanders of the army, among them Priscus, were
killed. Much of the equipment had to be abandoned.
Cestius halted when he arrived at Gabao; he remained

here two days taking counsel as to further action. On the third day, he decided to continue the retreat. The Judaeans, swarming from all sides, harassed his retreat, and their strength increased by every delay. His retreat became a rout.[75] He led his army to the Bet Horon road. On the open ground the army was less harassed by the Judaeans, but when the army began to descend (upper Bet Horon has an altitude of 1,730 feet, while the lower altitude is 1,240 feet), it was attacked from the front and the rear. Becoming desperate, Cestius laid plans for secret flight at night under cover of darkness. At daybreak, the Judaeans, discovering that the Roman quarters had been deserted, hastily organized a pursuit. The Romans in their terror had abandoned most of their equipment, which the Judaeans appropriated. Eleazar son of Simon succeeded in seizing the entire treasury of the army and all the money which the Romans had confiscated from the Judaeans. Thus the Romans suffered a severe defeat. They lost 5,300 infantry and 480 of the cavalry. The Judaeans returned to Jerusalem in triumph, singing hymns.[76] The victory over the Romans occurred on the 7th of Kislev, 25th of November, in the year 65, and the day was declared a semi-holiday.[77]

SLAUGHTER OF THE JEWS IN SYRIA

The Judaean victory over the Romans created panic throughout Syria and the Syrians fell upon the Judaeans and slaughtered them. In Ascalon two thousand five hundred Judaeans were slain; in Ptolemais two thousand were killed, and the rest put in chains.[78] In Hippus and in Gadara, many Judaeans were put to death. The slaughter of the Judaeans spread as far away as Damascus where, according to Josephus, ten thousand five hundred Judaeans were killed.[79] The Judaeans of Judaea reacted with reprisals. They attacked Gadara, Hippos, Ptolemais, Philadelphia, Pella, Gaba, Sebaste and Ascalon. They also attacked and set fire to Gaza and Anthedon. The environs of these cities were pillaged and the inhabitants slaughtered by the Judaeans.[80] All Syria was a scene of frightful disorder. In many cities the Judaean inhabitants fought by the side of their Greek-Syrian neighbors, in some cases because they were forced to do so, while in others they fought willingly to protect their cities from the Judaean invaders. Thus Judaeans fought against each other.

Josephus relates the following pathetic tale: When the Judaeans attacked Scythopolis, they found that they had to fight their own coreligionists, as the Judaean inhabitants had arrayed themselves on the side of the Greek-Syrians. Later, when the Scythopolitans were no longer in danger from the invaders, they proceeded to slaughter their Judaean neighbors and allies. One man, Simon, of a distinguished Judaean family, who was a leader in fighting off the invaders, now, when the Judaean community was about to be slaughtered, delivered a very moving farewell:

Justly am I punished for my crimes, men of Scythopolis, I and all who by such a slaughter of our kinsmen have sealed our loyalty to you. Ah! well, let us who have but naturally experienced the perfidy of heathens, us who have been guilty of the last degree of impiety towards our own people, let us, I say, die as accursed wretches, by our own hands; for we are not meet to die at the hands of the enemy. This, God grant, shall be at once the fit retribution for my foul crime and the testimony to my courage, that none of my foes shall be able to claim having slain me or glory over my prostrate body.

Upon finishing his speech, Simon killed his entire family —parents, wife, children—and then himself.[81] Josephus was not in Scythopolis and this speech is mainly a statement of his own invention. He could not hide the perfidy of the traitorous Greek-Syrian inhabitants of Scythopolis and other cities towards their Judaean coinhabitants.

The slaughter of the Judaeans in the Syrian Diaspora was only partially due to the deep hatred felt towards them by the Syrian-Greeks. The more immediate cause of the sudden outbreak must be found in religious and political considerations. There being substantial Judaean populations in the Syrian Diaspora,[82] the views of the Apocalyptists and Christians had penetrated throughout Syria. The Syrian-Greeks learned that there were Judaeans who believed in one who had been anointed, who had been crucified by the Romans as king of the Judaeans, who had been resurrected and would establish a kingdom, which they called the Kingdom of God, over the entire world. Rumors permeated the Middle East that a king would come from the East who would rule the world, and they reached as far as Rome.[83] Many of the heathens throughout the cities of Syria believed these rumors and were greatly disturbed because they might become subject to Judaea. Substantial segments of the population, particularly the women, had become Judaized, and some had become converts to the Judaean religion. Thus when the Syrian-Greeks planned to slaughter their Judaean fellow townsmen, they had to keep the matter secret from those whom they suspected of having become Judaized. The victory of the Judaeans over the Roman army aroused fears that the Judaeans would conquer their cities and that a Judaean king would rule over them.

It is to be noted that the defeat of the Romans by the Judaeans did not lead to retaliation upon the Judaeans in Rome. Rome did not suspect the Judaeans in their midst of being in sympathy with their co-religionists in Judaea. There were no riots against them, nor were the Judaeans on the islands of the Mediterranean disturbed.

There was a threat of extermination of the Judaeans in Batanaea, a part of the kingdom of Agrippa. After the defeat of Cestius, Agrippa went to Antioch to discuss the situation with him. While absent from his realm, he placed Noarus in charge of its administration. Noarus was a relative of the King of Emesa, and saw an opportunity to supplant Agrippa. He thought that Agrippa, a Judaean, would be put to death by the Romans and that he, a scion of a royal family, would be chosen as his successor. He made vigorous efforts to show his loyalty to Rome. He executed leading Judaeans of Caesarea Paneas to ingratiate himself with the Greek-Syrians. He summoned twelve distinguished citizens of Caesarea Paneas and gave them instructions to go to Batanaea and inform the Judaeans, the so-called Babylonians, that he had received word that they were preparing to rebel against Agrippa. He ordered them to lay down their arms and send seventy of their most notable men to him as hostages to demonstrate their loyalty. They sent the twelve men and the hostages, and Noarus executed all but one of the hostages, who escaped. Noarus was now ready to march against the Judaeans of Batanaea, since they were now leaderless and without arms. However, the hostage who had escaped informed his compatriots of Noarus' intentions. The Judaeans equipped themselves with arms, and withdrew to the Fortress of Gamala with their wives and children, leaving behind large stores of supplies and cattle. Noarus marched to Batanaea and not finding them there, seized everything they had left behind. The Judaeans were eager for revenge and contemplated marching against Noarus. This would have suited him very well, but Philip son of Iacimus, and grandson of Zamaris, the original leader of the Babylonian Judaeans, arrived on the scene. Philip had been the commander of the royal troops in Jerusalem. When they surrendered to the insurgents, he had remained in Jerusalem. Fearing that he would be assassinated by Menachem, Philip, aided by compatriot Babylonians of Batanaea, escaped from Jerusalem in disguise and made his way to his own territory and hid in one of the villages of Gaulanitis where he contracted malaria. From there he sent letters to Agrippa, which were intercepted by Noarus. When he arrived in Gamala, he took command of his subjects, the Babylonians of Batanaea, and persuaded them to keep the peace. Thus the scheme of Noarus was frustrated.[84]

Agrippa, learning of Noarus' actions, dismissed him

and sent Aequus Modius to take his place. The Fortress of Gamala and the surrounding district was now under the supervision of Philip and preserved its allegiance to Rome. Later Philip was accused before Vespasian of having betrayed the royal forces as well as Rome when he surrendered the royal palace to the rebels. Vespasian sent him to Nero to give an account of his act. When Philip arrived in Rome he found that Nero had died in the meantime. He then returned to Agrippa and took charge of his forces.

ORGANIZING FOR WAR

After the victory over Cestius, the rebels took the Fortress of Cypros which dominated Jericho. They also captured the Fortress of Machaerus. Jerusalem and a great part of Judaea were now free of Rome. The moderates in Jerusalem were confronted with a crucial problem as to what action they should take. They knew that the victory over the Roman army had been won because of the Roman contingent's modest size. Rome had vast forces at her disposal, and could not allow the Judaeans to establish an independent state. If the Judaeans succeeded, they would kindle a fire of liberty which would rage throughout the Near East. The client kings of the Near East would also revolt and the Parthians, ever troublesome, would surely take advantage of the situation. The moderates felt certain therefore that the Romans would concentrate their power to crush the rebellion and wipe out Judaea. On the other hand, they could not openly oppose the revolution. Not only the extremists, but the entire population of Jerusalem were intoxicated by the triumph over Cestius and the twelfth legion. They had even captured the eagles— the emblems borne by the twelfth legion—a severe blow to the prestige of the Roman army. The Judaean leaders knew that, if they came out now for peace with Rome or even expressed skepticism as to the ultimate victory of Judaea, they would be slaughtered.

Many distinguished people fled Jerusalem. Josephus is more blunt: swimmers deserting a sinking ship.[85] Among them were members of the royal family; Costobar and his brother Saul went to Cestius. Cestius dispatched Saul and his companions to Nero to make a report and to place the onus of the revolt upon Florus. Cestius himself sent a report to Nero and suggested that a legate with extraordinary power and a large army be sent to Judaea to crush the revolt.[86]

The leaders of the moderate group thought that to save Judaea it would be advisable for them to remain in Jersusalem so that by shrewd diplomacy they might avert a complete casastrophe. Openly they strongly advocated continuance of the revolt and expressed their willingness to assume leadership in prosecuting the war against Rome. Thus they thought they would succeed in becoming the leaders. Secretly they were for peace. The populace of Judaea, believing the words of the leaders of the moderates, were ready to entrust them with the reins of government. On the 28th of Tebeth,[87] the beginning of January 66, a great assembly was convened in the Temple for the purpose of establishing a government to carry out the necessary preparations for the war. It chose as head of the government the High Priest Ananus, a Sadducee who inherently was for peace. Josephus (Joseph son of Gorion), who had Sadduceean leanings, was also included in the administration. Another member was Simon son of Rabban Gamaliel, a Pharisee.[88] Sadducees and Pharisees thus once again became members of a government. Even the Essenes were attracted to the government. All combined for the purpose of making the government appear to represent all the groups which existed in Judaea. Yet those who had distinguished themselves by their heroism in the defeat of Cestius—men like Niger and even Eleazar son of Simon, who began the revolt, were not so chosen.[89]

This government turned out tragically for the State of of Judaea. It played a double role. It thought it would achieve its goal by shrewdness. Speaking openly for war, inwardly it was for peace. It wanted to disarm the extremists so that it should have all power concentrated in its hands, and thus be allowed to make peace with Rome.[90] It failed utterly. This government was greatly responsible for turning a revolution into a civil war. All of its members were assassinated later by the very extremists whom they had sought to undermine. This tragic story and the events of the war with Rome will be treated in the next volume.

PART THREE

Social and Religious Developments:

First Century B.C.E. and

First Century C.E.

1. THE PHYSICAL BACKGROUND OF JUDAEAN LIFE

THE CHARACTER OF THE LAND

Geography

The many shifts of border and political rule which befell Judaea in the century from the beginning of Herod's reign until the rebellion against Rome have already been noted. In general in this period, the boundaries of the State of Judaea extended from the district of Tyre in the northwest to the territory of Trachonitis on the northeast, and in the south from Idumaea, extending to the coastal city Raphia on the southwest. Mount Carmel and Dora were not a part of Judaea during the time of Herod and Agrippa, as they had been in the time of Jannaeus Alexander. So, too, the cities of Scythopolis and Pella were detached from the State and belonged to Decapolis, which formed much of Judaea's eastern border.

In the tannaitic literature, the State of Judaea is described in terms of three regions:[1] Judaea, Galilee, and Peraea. Josephus adds a fourth, Samaria, never included by the sages. Galilee is further divided into Upper and Lower Galilee. Ptolemais and Mount Carmel are the western limits of Upper Galilee. On the east it touches Gaulanitis, Hippus, and Gadara. Lower Galilee

extends from Tiberias south to the district of Samaria.[2]
Samaria lies between Galilee and Judaea, beginning at
the village of Ginaea (Gema) and terminating at
Acrabatene.[3] Peraea is entirely east of the Jordan River,
but goes no further than Philadelphia (modern Ammon).
It extends from Pella on the north to Machaerus on the
south.[4] The northern reaches of the Judaean region
began south of Sebaste, and the territory extended to
Idumaea in the south, the Jordan on the east, and the
Mediterranean Sea on the west. The city of Jerusalem,
located in the center of Judaea, was called the navel of
the country.[5]

Of the four districts, the Galilee was the most fertile.
The soil was rich for pasture or produce, and many
varieties of trees grew there. The area was well watered
by the Jordan's tributaries, and every inch was cultivated through the use of irrigation. Galilee was therefore densely populated, with many towns and villages.[6]

Southeast of the Sea of Galilee is Mt. Tabor. Farther
south is the hill of Moreh. To the west of Mt. Tabor and
the hill of Moreh is the Valley of Esdraelon, or the Valley of Jezreel. To the north is the Belus, a small stream
flowing five miles along the lower slopes of Mt. Carmel
and emptying into the Mediterranean Sea, not far from
the city of Ptolemais.[7] The sand on the banks of this
diminutive river was used in the making of glass.[8] Farther to the south of Galilee is Mt. Gilboa; and still farther
south, in Samaria, are Mt. Ebal and the well-known Mt.
Gerizim. To the west is the Plain of Sharon, located in
the center of Samaria.

The districts of Samaria and Judaea were similar in
topography. Both consisted mainly of hills and plains
most of whose soil was fertile, with southern Judaea
the most fruitful part. The areas were well wooded with
an abundance of fruit, both wild and cultivated. The
many springs of sweet water and large areas of grass-
land were particularly suited for pasturing herds of
cattle, especially goats.

The hills in Judaea are not as high as those in Samaria.

Toward Jerusalem the hills descend, so that Jerusalem is only about 2,600 feet above sea level, but north of Hebron they are as high as 3,346 feet above sea level. Toward the west and the Mediterranean Sea lies the fertile plain called the Shephelah, the Lowlands, where there were many vineyards and olive groves. From the south of Hebron the hills of Judaea descend to the Negev, the Southland—a semi-arid area extending from Beer-Sheba to Kadesh-Barnea. East of Jerusalem, on the west coast of the Dead Sea, is the wilderness of Tekoa. Farther south is En-Gedi, and below it the Fortress Masada. The district has many caves which were regularly inhabited by people, sometimes for refuge and hiding.[9]

The district of Peraea (including Decapolis) is more extensive in area than the other districts. It was rugged or desert for the most part, but some sections had good enough soil to produce crops of many species, while olive, pine and palm trees grew on the plains. This district was divided by rivers into four sections. North of the Yarmuk River, to the east of the Sea of Galilee, the soil was rich and there were many cities. South of the Yarmuk to the Jabbok River there were a number of springs and streams. This section had a large population and a number of important cities. The Jabbok River rises above Philadelphia, and flows north and then east, emptying into the Jordan. South and east of this river is a dry region beyond which stretches the great desert. Southeast of the River Arnon was Nabataea, with its capital Petra in the south.

No description of Judaea can exclude mention of the Jordan, its main river. It first becomes visible in Panion,[10] but its sources are in Mount Hermon. Josephus states that Philip, the tetrarch of Trachonitis, had a shaft thrown into the pool of Philae, located south of Caesarea Philippi, and it eventually surfaced at Panion. This, according to Josephus, indicates that it must flow underground from a point much further north.[11] From Panion the Jordan, running above sea level, traverses the marshes and lagoons of Lake Semechonitis, Huleh. The river then flows directly south and, as it skirts the pleasant town of Bethsaida-Julias on the east, it enters Lake Gennesaret, the Sea of Galilee (in the Bible, the Sea of Kineret). When it reaches Lake Huleh it is also at sea level. On the west side of the Lake is Tiberias with its salubrious hot springs. The entire region is blessed with natural beauty and a bland climate. The soil is fertile; walnut and palm trees abound, and fig and olive trees flourish. From Lake Gennesaret the Jordan wends its way increasingly below sea level through a desert region and flows into Lake Asphaltitis, the Dead Sea (in the Bible, the Salt Sea).[12] On the northeast bank is Callirrhoe, celebrated for its hot springs.[13]

The water of the Dead Sea is bitter and undrinkable, since a quarter of its content is a variety of salts and minerals. Rich in bitumen and asphalt, it was given the Greek name Asphaltitis; because of its high saline content, no life is found in it.[14]

There are other rivers in Judaea. The Yarmuk, Jabbok and Arnon are tributaries that empty into the Jordan from the east. The Kishon and the Yarkon empty into the Mediterranean.

The religious boundaries of the land were somewhat different. Caesarea was not considered a part of the Land of Israel and did not share its sanctity.[15] On the other hand, Scythopolis (originally Beth Shean), was included within the land religiously, although a city of the Decapolis.

For purposes of administration the State of Judaea was divided into toparchies: Jerusalem, Gophna, Acrabatene, Thamna, Lydda, Emmaus, Pella, Idumaea, En-Gedi, Herodian, and Jericho. The cities of Jabneh and Jaffa had jurisdiction over the surrounding localities, while the territories of Gamala, Gaulanitis, Batanaea, and Trachonitis retained their integrity and were part of Agrippa's kingdom.[16] At the head of each toparchy was a governor who bore the title of strategos, and was responsible to the Judaean king or the procurator. In each village scribes were appointed as supervisors of the census of men and cattle in order to collect taxes.[17]

Two cities had special privileges. When Antipas built Tiberias, he gave the city the privilege of self-rule as a polis, in order to attract people to settle there. Tiberias was therefore governed by a *boulé,* council, as were the free cities of Greece.[18] Agrippa I also granted Jerusalem the privileges of a polis, so that its *boulé* had authority over the city and its environs. The council of Jerusalem was responsible for the collection of taxes, and thus it, and not the procurator, appointed the tax collectors.[19] Both cities were, of course, under the control of the king or the procurator.

The entire area of the State of Judaea, excluding Batanaea, Auranitis, and Trachonitis, which are northeast of Galilee, was a little more than 10,000 square miles. Neither Herod nor Agrippa ruled a state as large as that of Jannaeus Alexander.

The Population

The population of Judaea before its fall cannot be given with any precision, as no census has survived. It has been estimated that it was between four and five million, but this is only informed speculation.[20] Josephus cites various statistics which can be used as a basis for such estimates. He mentions that shortly before the destruction of the State, Cestius, the legate of Syria, wanting to know how large was the population of Judaea, asked the high priest to count the paschal lambs, and these amounted to 255,600.[21] Since the number of people who partook of a paschal lamb was at least ten, the number celebrating was estimated at 2,556,000.[22] The figure is compromised by the fact that many Judaeans who lived outside of the State of Judaea made pilgrimages to Jerusalem for the Feast of Unleavened Bread, while many natives throughout the country did not, being unwilling or religiously exempt. Hence, this account cannot be taken as a criterion of the population of Judaea.

Josephus also states that there were two hundred and four cities and villages in Galilee, the smallest containing about 15,000 inhabitants.[23] This would bring the population of Galilee alone to over 3,060,000. Galilee, it is true, was thickly populated, but the district of Judaea was not sparsely settled. Thus the population of Galilee, Judaea and Peraea should come to more than 6,000,000. However, it is to be assumed that Josephus' estimate of the population of Galilee is inflated.

Josephus further gives an account of the losses sustained by Judaea during the war against Rome. In the early days, over 30,000 Judaeans were killed in various cities by their Syrian fellow-citizens.[24] When Jerusalem was taken by the Romans, though 40,000 had fled the city to the Romans, 97,000 were still taken prisoner.[25] Yet Tacitus records a report that there were 600,000 people in the city when the siege began.[26] Josephus also relates that 1,100,000 perished during the war.[27] But it should be noted that not all the Judaeans were for the war, and many a city, such as Sepphoris, the largest in Galilee, surrendered to the Romans without a struggle. Thus, the number of four or five million, which is usually given for the population of the state of Judaea, is but a guess, though it is a good one.

THE ROMAN PRESENCE

There is a statement in Seder Olam that the kingdom of the house of Herod lasted one hundred and three years, which is the period from Herod's accession to the throne in January 37 B.C.E., until the victory over Cestius in November 65 C.E.[28] During this period, as described in detail above, the political fortunes of Judaea varied greatly and it was in part or entirely ruled by procurators. Judaea, even during the reign of its kings, was not an independent state. No part of the Empire had true self-government in the Roman world.

Judaea was supposedly autonomous as to internal affairs, but that was true only so long as they were not in conflict with the interests of Rome. Roman officials had no scruples about interfering in the internal affairs of the allied peoples. In foreign affairs, it goes without saying that they had no right to an independent policy or to make war. Under the procurators, or later when Judaea was part of the Syrian jurisdiction, it had even less freedom.

The Roman army of occupation consisted of five cohorts, or regiments, each made up of between five and six hundred infantry and one *ala,* a cavalry regiment of five hundred men.[29] These regular forces were supported by auxiliaries recruited from the natives of the provinces and officered by Romans. The auxiliary forces in Judaea, particularly of the *ala,* were made up of Sebastians and Caesareans. (Judaeans were excused from service in the Roman army, an exemption dating back to the time of Julius Caesar.[30]) The seat of the procurator, and therefore the headquarters of his troops, was in Caesarea rather than Jerusalem, for economic, political and especially religious reasons. In Jerusalem, technically the capital of Judaea, there was only one cohort, stationed in the Fortress Antonia and commanded by an officer. Stationed there, the army had constant supervision over activities in the Temple. At the main festivals, particularly the Festival of Unleavened Bread, when Judaeans made pilgrimages to Jerusalem, the procurator with additional forces came to Jerusalem, residing in the palace of Herod.[31]

It was Rome's policy to dissolve all political assemblies when countries were made provinces of Rome; this happened in Greece, Macedonia, and Sicily. Later, assemblies were permitted to function for religious purposes, particularly as centers for the worship of the emperor. The head of such assemblies was the high priest, *sacerdos provinciae,* elected by assembly members of equestrian rank and holding office for a year; but the legate had complete authority over him. He authorized his election and removed him from office if he thought the high priest did not serve Rome fully. In Judaea, no assembly could elect a high priest. The high priesthood was either hereditary or limited to priestly families. So from the year 6 to 41, the procurators appointed the Judaean high priests, who were consequently their tools. Besides being the heads of the Temple, they necessarily assumed a political function. They were responsible for the tranquility of the country and were supposed to forestall any subversion against Rome. It was their duty to hunt out the malcontents and report them to the procurator.

The procurator could inflict capital punishment on political offenders suspected of agitation and subversion against Rome.[32] He also exercised this right in relation to bandits, since this affected the social and economic life of the country. But he did not interfere with the religious life of the people. Persons who transgressed religious laws such as incest, adultery, and homicide, were tried in the Judaean court, the *Bet Din*. This institution should not be confused with the *synedrion*, the private council which the high priests summoned from time to time to consider political cases which then had to be presented to the procurator. It is within this political context that the accounts of the arrest and trial of Jesus must be understood, as noted above. The trial of Paul must similarly be seen within the frame of the political authority of that day.[33] After the year 44, when Agrippa I died, Judaea became a part of Syria and, unlike the period before Agrippa, the legate of Syria assumed authority over the procurator of Judaea.[34] Although the procurator had absolute power to inflict capital punishment on any inhabitant of the province, the offender, if he was a Roman citizen, had the right to demand that his case be tried in Rome.[35] Since Agrippa had granted a *boulé* to Jerusalem, many Judaeans acquired the rank of equestrian, although Florus, in his unprecedented cruelty, did not hesitate to scourge and crucify them.[36]

Paul was tried as a political offender during this

period. His first offense was that of bringing gentiles into the Temple, which was not only a religious transgression, but also an offense against the state, since it guaranteed the sanctity of the *Hel*, the Temple Mount proper. Paul was also accused of fomenting sedition among the Judaeans, and of being a leader of the Nazarene sect which at that time was forbidden by the Roman authorities.[37] The Judaeans could only arrest Paul. They had no authority to try him. And when Paul as a Roman citizen appealed to Caesar, the procurator had no right to try him and so sent him to Rome.[38]

James, the brother of Jesus, however, was tried by Jews. In the interegnum between the death of Festus and the arrival of Albinus, the high priest Ananus summoned a *synedrion* of judges which charged James with unlawful conduct. James was condemned and stoned to death. Josephus does not say what his unlawful conduct was, nor whether James had transgressed religious or political laws. It is probable that James was charged with being seditious as a leader of the Nazarenes.[39] The opposition the Judaeans expressed against Ananus to Albinus on his arrival was not that he had appointed a *synedrion* of judges without the procurator's consent, but that he had inflicted the punishment for a State offense. The explanation for this unprecedented step lies in Josephus' identification of Ananus as a Sadducee and thus strict in the application of all laws, religious or political.[40] From this perspective, sharpened by the zeal to demonstrate to the new procurator loyalty to Rome, it was easy for Ananus to see in James a menace to the State.

2. ECONOMIC LIFE

THE ECONOMIC RESOURCES
OF JUDAEA

Agriculture

Judaea was depicted in the Pentateuch as a land of milk and honey. It had both of these products in abundance. The milk came from the many flocks of goats, Samaria being the richest in this respect. The goats were plentiful as they could graze not only on pasture land, but even on the sparse grass growing between the rocks in arid areas. Honey came from bees, and also in the form of the syrup from dates which were pressed by foot. Honey was vital to the economy of the ancient world, playing a more important role than sugar does today. Honey was used in the preparation of the main part of the diet as well as for confections.

In Ptolemaic Egypt, bee-keeping was an important industry. Many landowners kept thousands of beehives, and many beehives belonged to the king. They were protected by high duties on imported honey.[1] It may be assumed that in Judaea also many were engaged in bee-keeping, and that the Egyptian duties were directed against the honey imported from Judaea. It is not known, however, whether a local tax was imposed on the bee-keepers in Judaea.

With the abundance of milk, cheese-making was important for both domestic needs and export. There was a special place in Jerusalem, south of the Temple, called Tyropoeon Valley,[2] from the Greek word *tyropoios*, cheese-maker, where cheese was sold.

The territory surrounding Lake Gennesareth, rich in palm trees, fig and olive trees, and grapes, produced wine and oil for the domestic and foreign markets. The wines from this region, as well as those of Mt. Carmel, were renowned for their flavor and provided a good commodity for the foreign market.[3]

Natural Products

Judaea did not have the resources essential for industry. She possessed neither gold nor silver; these metals had to be imported. Copper and iron were present only in small quantities. Josephus mentions an Iron Mountain stretching from the south into Moab, but it is not known whether Judaea in the Second Commonwealth produced copper or iron, or whether this was merely a name.[4] During the time of Herod, copper was brought from Cyprus where Augustus Caesar had granted Herod the management of the copper mines.[5] Lumber was also scarce in Judaea, the trees not being suitable for extensive use in construction; lumber had to be imported from the Lebanon Mountains.[6] There was an abundance of stone and rock. The homes were built of stone, and masonry therefore became an important occupation in Judaea.

The greatest single source of wealth in Judaea was the balsam tree which was cultivated in the area surrounding Jericho. These trees were considered to be the best in the world, so that Judaea in effect had a monopoly on this material. Oil was produced from the balsam, as were medical ingredients for the treatment of headaches and cataracts. Perfumes were also manufactured from the extract of the balsam. These and other products were exported to many countries.[7] Some estimate of their value may be gained from Pliny. He states that during the war against the Romans, since the groves were Caesar's, "the Judaeans vented their wrath upon this plant (balsam), as they also did upon their own lives; but the Romans protected it against them, and there have been pitched battles in defense of a shrub." He further relates that five years after the conquest of Judaea, the branches and shoots of the balsam trees brought in 800,000 sesterces (approximately $35,000 of the gold standard)—and this was a small residue saved by the Romans from what had been destroyed by the Judaeans![8]

Bitumen, extracted from the Dead Sea, was another important source of revenue. It was exported in enormous quantities, particularly to Egypt, where it was used in embalming. Asphalt, also taken from the Sea, was widely desired for caulking ships and as an ingredient in many medicines.[9]

The opening of the port of Caesarea in 10 B.C.E. made a great change in Judaea's economic life. Dora and Jaffa, the ports used till then, had poor harbors. Caesarea, on the other hand, was magnificent in every way and became second in importance to Alexandria in that part of the world. Through Caesarea merchandise was conveniently exported and imported to Rome, Egypt, and the Greek islands. Foreign ships paid tariffs to dock and a maritime industry developed among the Judaeans.

Fish in abundance from the Mediterranean Sea and Lake Gennesareth not only supplied an important article of diet, but also provided an industry. The fish from the lake was excellent for pickling. The city of Tarichaea, on the west side of the lake, many of whose inhabitants were occupied in the trade, derived its name from the Greek word *taricheiai*, factories for the pickling of fish.[10]

Pigeons figure prominently in the economy of the Ptolemaic as well as the Roman periods. Pigeons were a significant item in the diet of the people, so much so that Herod occupied himself with their breeding and raising.[11]

During this period a new industry developed: the manufacture of glass, and glass blowing. The sand on the banks of the stream Belus furnished the raw material. Since the wealthy preferred glass to earthenware pottery, the economy was greatly stimulated by this new commodity.

Economic Drawbacks

Nevertheless, there were many reasons why the Judaeans faced economic difficulties. The State of Judaea was small in area and, on the whole, of limited fertility. In this period it may justifiably be called over-populated. The absence of wars and natural disasters kept the death rate relatively low. The laws of hygiene observed by the Judaeans made for a longer life span. Accordingly, the population growth probably exceeded the mortality rate.

The laws of inheritance exacerbated the problems of land distribution. A farmer's acreage had to be divided at his death among all his sons, which made for very small holdings. The difficulty was increased by the law of primogeniture, by which the first-born son received twice as much as his brothers.[12] Hence, unless an estate was large, the younger sons might easily find themselves with less land than could sustain their families.

The water situation further complicated the agricultural economy. Judaea was not endowed with many rivers and streams, the people depending mostly on rainfall for water. Some sort of irrigation system existed, but it was inadequate. Thus, years of drought brought great suffering, particularly for the farmers. Two severe famines in this period seriously disrupted the old structure of many small private farms. It is a phenomenon of economic development that, in such crises, the rich swallow the poor. Many lost their farms and a whole new class of semi-farmers or tenant farmers came into being. Land tenancy on the royal domain had been common. Now private landlords multiplied. Many a farmer became an *aris*, a tenant, for a certain share in the harvest; but if there was a loss, he bore a share of the loss. There was another type of tenant who paid the landlord a definite rental in kind, irrespective of the yield.[13] Men also hired themselves out for particular periods or for particular work; others were unskilled laborers, handymen. A large proletarian class thus came into being. The matter deserves further comment.

During the Hasmonean period there were two main economic groups, the military and the farmers, the *ame ha-aretz*.[14] In the Herodian period, armies were composed mainly of mercenaries, and not Judaeans. As a group, the *ame ha-aretz* did not involve themselves in the political or economic problems of the country. However, with the general economic progress of the country, the number of artisans greatly increased. Their ranks were swelled by the agricultural distress. Many of the dispossessed farmers became workers or entered into commerce. The manual workers were seafarers, fishermen, iron workers, masons, carpenters, tanners, shoemakers, tailors, weavers, glass makers, dyers, launderers, bakers. Painters engaged in the ornamentation of objects, but did not portray living creatures. Scribes copied books and wrote documents and letters. Physicians prepared drugs; blood-letting was a common therapy. This group enhanced the life of Judaea, for no highly developed society could have existed without such artisans.[15]

Many other Judaeans engaged in internal commerce, the selling of merchandise. Farmers brought their cattle to sell in Jerusalem. There was also a market in the city for the sale of such items as wool, clothing and braziers, and stores throughout the country likewise selling general merchandise. Peddlers went from city to city, cosmetics for women being a favorite item.[16]

The economic difficulties of Judaea may be seen from the problem facing Agrippa II upon the completion of Herod's Temple reconstruction. Workmen by the thousands were thrown out of employment, an enormous number for one section of a small country. Agrippa II engaged the men to pave the streets of Jerusalem,[17] probably the first instance in history of the conscious use of public works to overcome an economic crisis.

With a changing balance of economic power and con-flicting class interests, there was continual strife be-tween the farmers and the urban population, between the poor classes and the wealthy. After the reign of Herod, this strife became more intense among the vari-ous factions as their economic, social, and cultural dif-ferences became more marked. A large number of Judaeans migrated to Egypt, particularly to Alexandria with its large Judaean population, and to Rome, Cyprus, Cyrenaica, and the islands of Greece. Some went to Parthia, which had strong communities of their core-ligionists. The real Judaean Diaspora, it is fair to say, began after the Hasmonean and during the Herodian period, as the outcome of a substantial emigration from Judaea. This fact should give a deeper understanding of the close relationship of the Diaspora communities to Judaea, the literal motherland of many of their resi-dents and the source of the message of the universality of God that they brought with them.

SLAVES

Number and Treatment

Both the artisans and the merchants of Judaea employed handymen to assist them, and also slaves. Slaves were customarily acquired by a country through wars in which the victor either appropriated the vanquished or sold them into slavery. During this era, the Judaeans were not engaged in wars of conquest, and thus had no slaves by direct seizure. Judaea did not even have the stone slave-block for selling slaves which was a promi-nent market-place feature among other nations. The Judaeans, however, bought slaves from other peoples.

There were many gentile slaves in Judaea. The wealthy class employed a large number of slaves, and the high priest generally had a small army of them.[18] Simon son of Gioras freed a large number of slaves in order to raise a formidable army.[19] Thus, too, no fewer than five hundred slaves, it is reported, carried all kinds of spices at the funeral of Herod.

In imperial Rome slaves were in the power of their owners. By the *ius gentium,* the master was vested with the power of life and death over his slaves. The prevailing treatment of the slaves, particularly during the period of the Roman Republic, was brutal, sadistic, and expressed itself in acts of extreme cruelty. Cato the Elder (c. 234-149 B.C.E.), who owned many slaves, maintained the principle that it was good management to feed slaves and animals well in order that they might have sufficient strength to work hard; but for the slightest disobedience, the slave was to be flogged.[20] Ben Sirah, a contemporary of Cato the Elder, also held that slaves were chattel. He wrote,[21]

Fodder, a wand and burdens are for the ass; and bread, correction and work for a slave. If thou set thy slave to labor, thou shalt find rest; but if thou let him go idle, he shall seek liberty. A yoke and collar do bow the neck; so are tortures and torments for an evil slave. Send him to labor that he be not idle; for idleness teaches much evil. Set him to work, as is fit for him; if he be not obedient, put on more heavy fetters. But be not excessive toward any; and without discretion do nothing. If thou have a slave, let him be unto thee as thyself because thou hast bought him for a price. If thou have a slave, treat him as a brother.

Proportionately the Judaeans did not have as many slaves as the Romans, and fear of their slaves was not felt by the Judaean masters. Slaves were not crucified in Judaea, nor were they made gladiators as in Rome.[22]

Judaean and Gentile Slaves

The Bible already refers to different classes of slaves. The Hebrew slave of the Pentateuch should really be considered a bondsman, since his service was limited by time. He served only six years, and had to be freed in the seventh year. A master could sell his Hebrew slave only to a coreligionist, but even then not to one outside of Judaea. The Pentateuch speaks of two possibilities for such servitude: a father who sells his daughter and an impoverished man who sells himself into limited bondage.[23]

There was one other class of Hebrew slavery. If a person was convicted of larceny, he had to make restitution of the property and pay a fine in addition. If the thief could not pay, he was sold into slavery,[24] the sale price being used for his indebtedness. Or as Josephus puts it, "He that hath no means to defray the imposed amount shall become the slave of those who have him condemned." Thus, in the book of Genesis, when Joseph's goblet is supposedly stolen, he says to his brother Judah, "He with whom it (the silver goblet) is found shall be my slave."[25]

Theft, robbery, and injury were considered private wrongs: a case between the injured person, the one who suffered the loss, and the thief. It was not a case for the state; the injured person had the right to fix the punishment. He could absolve the thief, enslave him, or sell him into slavery. The latter was the extreme satisfaction that the plaintiff might demand.[26] During the Second Commonwealth, he might enslave or sell the culprit if he did not pay the fine, although he had paid the principle. The talmudic law enacted after the destruction of the Temple limits such sales only to the case where the thief could not pay the principle, but does not allow it if he merely could not pay the fine.[27]

The pentateuchal law binding a Hebrew slave for six years service does not apply to the man enslaved for robbery. He served just long enough to earn the principle and fine on the stolen property.

Besides the classes of slave just mentioned, there were the debtors, known in Roman law as *nexi*. If one borrowed money and could not pay his debt, the creditor had the right to take him or his children into bondage. This type of slavery was abolished during the Hasmonean period. The debtor could no longer be enslaved; the creditor's sole right was to seize his property.[28]

Philo and the Gospel according to Matthew seem to give a contrary picture.[29] Their testimony has been explained on the theory that the new law was not practiced in Egypt and Syria, whose archaic patterns the authors record. It can be better explained in terms of their purpose, which was not to depict the law as it prevailed, but to present an ethical message to the people. Philo emphasizes that, since slavery is a degradation to human beings, Judaean law tries to allay its severity. Matthew preaches the religious principle that God will forgive the iniquity of a man if he will forgive his fellowman the wrong committed against him.

The gentile slave is distinguished from the Hebrew slaves in the Pentateuch only in the following: the Hebrew slave was freed after six years, whereas the gentile slave's service had no limitation. Indeed, if a Hebrew slave wanted to remain a slave, his ear had to be pierced as a sign of punishment.[30] There was no regulation regarding a gentile slave who refused freedom; there was no law forcing him to accept freedom. He was the permanent possession of his owner, and as such inherited by his children upon his death.

A gentile slave was acquired as real property, either by purchase or by deed of transfer from a previous owner so that the new owner gained possession: that is, if the previous owner relinquished his rights over the slave.[31] Anyone could acquire a slave by possession, like real property. The slave existed only for the master; all products and activities of the slave were the property of the master,[32] including children. If a female slave was sold while she was pregnant, the child belonged to the purchaser. If a female slave was sold after she had borne her child and was still suckling it, her child was still the property of the previous owner.[33] The child of a female slave had no father in the eyes of the law, no more than the child of a prostitute. Only children of a lawful marriage were so recognized; and marriage among slaves had no legal status, since it would have abrogated the master's power of absolute control.

Slaves were chattels like pieces of property. A debtor could offer his slave as a hypothec for a loan.[34] If the loan remained unpaid, the slave could be seized by the creditor as if he were real estate. If the debtor sold his property or his slave after he received a loan, the sale was not valid and the creditor had the right to seize the property or the slave from the buyer. In the case where the debtor placed the slave as a hypothec for his debt, then manumitted him and then defaulted on his loan, the hypothec ceased to exist and the creditor had no right to seize the ex-slave.[35] It was in the same category as if a debtor placed his house or field as a hypothec for the debt which later a storm or flood swept away— the hypothec was gone, and the creditor sustained the loss.

A slave could gain his freedom if his master freed him and gave him a writ of manumission. If the master made the slave his heir, he also became a freedman.[36] If a slave were taken captive and someone ransomed him—if he was ransomed as a slave, he remained a slave; but if he was ransomed as a free man, the person who ransomed him could not make him serve as a slave, but he still had the status of a slave.[37]

Private property could become a *res nullius*. If the owner publicly relinquished his right over it, anyone could acquire it and it became his property by possession. Since a slave was considered property, if an owner merely relinquished his rights over him, he became a *res nullius* and any person could take possession. The owner who relinquished his rights over his slave did not thus make him free; it simply meant that his owner no longer had the right to employ him as a slave.[38]

A slave who had gained his freedom could nonetheless never attain the status of the freeborn. A freedman was subject to various social, religious and political disabilities, and remained bound by special obligations to his previous master and the family of the manumissor.[39]

Some freedmen, however, had great influence in politics in Rome by reason of their intimate attachment to eminent families and the confidence their previous masters had in them. Whereas in Rome some freedmen were the tutors of the children of their manumissors, in Judaea tutorship was never entrusted to gentiles. Thus, Herod sent his sons Alexander and Aristobolus to Rome to get a Greek education.[40]

Liberalizing the Slave Laws

The status of the gentile slave and the rights of his owner over him are not clearly stated in the Pentateuch. The sages strove to elevate the status of the gentile slaves by interpreting two conditions concerning the service of Hebrew slaves to include gentiles as well. The Pentateuch says,[41] "If a man smite his man slave or female slave with a rod and he die under his hand, he shall surely be punished. Notwithstanding, if he continues a day or two, he shall not be punished; for he is his money." They also included gentile slaves in the command,[42] "And if a man smite the eye of his man slave or the eye of his female slave and destroy it, he shall let him go free for his eye's sake." By extending punishment to an owner for intentionally killing his slave and making freedom possible to a slave who was maimed, the sages showed their belief that a gentile slave is fully human. That is why his owner is made responsible for unwarranted action toward him. This, indeed, was revolutionary for their time.

This process of liberalization lies behind a controversy between the Sadducees and the Pharisees in regard to gentile slaves recorded in a Mishne. The Sadducees deride the Pharisaic position which was: if an ox or an ass has done injury, the owner is liable, while if a slave has done injury, the owner is not liable. Sadducees sought to refute this position by an analogy. They argued that an animal is not in the category of those who are obliged to perform *mitzvoth* (commandments). Nevertheless, if an animal committed an injury, his owner was responsible. Now a slave is obligated to perform certain commandments. Since he is more responsible than an animal, should not his owner be responsible for his acts? The Pharisees replied that there was no comparison. An animal has no understanding, but is like an object. Therefore if it has committed an injury, its owner is liable. However, a slave has understanding, and, furthermore, may even be provoked by his master to commit an injury. Therefore, the Pharisees held the slave, not the master, responsible.[43] The controversy really concerns the status of the gentile slave. The Sadducees considered him an object, the property of the owner, and thus with neither rights nor liabilities. The Pharisees free his master of responsibility because they want to recognize the slave as a human being, one who is responsible for his own acts.[44]

Partnership, where two or more owners shared one property, was highly developed during the latter part of the Second Commonwealth. Each partner had the privilege of relinquishing his rights in a property or of selling it. If two men shared the ownership of a gentile slave, one partner had the right to manumit his share in the slave. If he did so, the slave became half free. According to the School of Hillel, the half-slave had to serve his master one day, and was free the next. The School of Shammai objected to this since it would place the half-slave at a disadvantage. He could not marry the daughter of an Israelite, because he was half slave; he could not marry a female slave because he was half free.[45] The Hillelites recognized the soundness of the Shammaite view and followed it.

Thus, during the later period of the Second Commonwealth, the conditions of the gentile slave greatly improved, because the Judaean sages, like the Stoics, believed that slaves were human beings and should be accorded human treatment.[46] Neither group advocated the abolition of slavery which was the foundation of the economic and social structure of the times. The Judaean sages were, however, able to shape Judaean law so that slavery became more humane.

CRAFTSMEN AND ARTISANS

The status of craftsmen and artisans was not much higher than that of the slave. Ben Sirah, who portrayed the life of the Judaeans of the Hellenistic period, wrote:[47]

So every carpenter and workmaster that labored night and day; and they that cut and engraved seals, and are diligent to make great variety and give themselves to counterfeit imagery and watch to finish a work. The smith also, sitting by the anvil, and considering the iron work, the vapor of the fire, wasted his flesh, and he fighteth with the heat of the furnace; the noise of the hammer and the anvil is ever in his ears, and his eyes look still upon the pattern that he makes. He setteth his mind to finish his work, and watcheth to polish it perfectly. So does the potter, sitting at his work and turning the wheel about with his feet, is always carefully set at his work by number. He fashioneth the clay with his arm, and boweth down his strength before his feet. He applieth himself to lead it over; and he is diligent to make clean the furnace. All these trust to their hands; and everyone is wise in his work. Without these cannot a city be inhabited; and they shall not dwell where they will, nor go up and down. They shall not be sought on council, nor sit high in the assembly; they shall not sit on the judge's seat, nor render the sentence of judgment; they cannot declare justice and judgment; and they shall not be found where parables are spoken by the wise. But they understand the work they have wrought, and their thoughts are on the practice of their craft.

This attitude towards craftsmen prevailed throughout the entire period of the Second Commonwealth, with some flexibility as to the recognition of the value of craftsmen and their importance to society. The sages held that parents should instruct their sons in a craft that could sustain them, and though it would not gain them great wealth, it would be insurance against poverty. They emphasized that the sons should be trained in a dignified craft. Thus they advised against instruction to become camel drivers, shopkeepers or barbers, in the belief that the former two are constantly tempted to deceit and cheating, while barbering was undignified.[48] The sages took great pains to assure honest weight and prevent cheating. They ordained that scales should not be made of lead or cassiterite, but of glass;[49] both lead and cassiterite become oxidized, thus adding to their weight. They also ordered shopkeepers to clean their measures twice a week, and their scales after every weighing.[50]

A craftsman was held responsible for any goods that he received. For example, if wool was given him to be dyed and the material was stolen from him, he was held responsible for its cost. If a wooden chest was given to a carpenter to be repaired and he spoiled it, he had to make restitution.[51] Naturally, the man who hired a craftsman was equally held to his agreement, so that should either abrogate it, he was at a disadvantage in the eyes of the law.[52]

Craftsmen were superior both socially and economically to the free hand-laborers. As the number of Judaeans who became large landowners grew in the economic crises during which the small landowners lost their holdings, and since the Judaeans did not own many gentile slaves, the number of men who found employment by selling their services increased. Varro (116-27 B.C.E.) in his book on agriculture had already propagated the idea of hiring free hands for cultivation.[53] The social status of such agricultural laborers was low. Cicero regarded them as next to slaves. "Vulgar are the means of livelihood of all hired working men whom we pay for mere manual labor, not for artistic skill; for in their case the very wage they receive is a pledge of their slavery."[54]

Most laborers were only seasonably employed, the summer and particularly the harvest season being the time of greatest demand. They were particularly needed for the pressing of olives and grapes. They had from earliest times done this with their feet, but in this period the screw board was introduced for the purpose.

The hired hand was generally paid a dinar for his day's work, from early morning until sunset.[55] Food, provided by the employer, was meager, consisting of bread and pulse. This was not a fixed rule, however, as each locality had different customs.[56] The laborer also had the right to partake of anything growing in the field where he worked, such as figs or grapes. To avoid the rise in the cost of labor because of competition during the harvest, it was established that members of a community had the right to fix a price for laborers. Anyone in the community who tried to pay more could be fined.[57] So that the laborer should do an honest day's work, he was not allowed to work for himself during the night.[58]

Laborers were hired by the day, week, or even the month. Still they were often unemployed. To sustain themselves then, they had to depend on alms and many went begging from house to house.[59] The craftsmen, too, faced periods when there was a lack of work and when they were dependent on the community for their survival. After Herod, Judaea had a class of poor people, and another who were quite wealthy.

3. SOCIAL AND COMMUNAL LIFE

THE ORGANIZED TOWN

Charitable Institutions

The leaders of Judaea abhorred the idea of Judaeans going from house to house seeking food; they held this to be a degredation of their fellowmen. To ameliorate this condition and discourage beggary, they instituted in each community organizations to deal with the needs of the poor.[1] If a poor man came to a city, the *tamhuy*, soup kitchen, was to give him food. If he should stay overnight, the *kuppah*, fund for sustenance, was to give him what he needed for the night. If he stayed for the Sabbath, he should receive enough food for three meals; he usually received pulse, herbs, oil and fish. The local poor received their sustenance from the *kuppah*, but if a poor man went begging, he was not entitled to any sustenance from the community, neither from the *kuppah* nor the *tamhuy*.

These charitable institutions, which might be termed a "federation of Judaean charities," were financed by a tax imposed on the members of the community. One who lived in a city for thirty days had to contribute to the sustenance of the poor; one who lived in a city for six months contributed for the clothing of the poor; one living in a city for a year contributed to the maintenance of the city.[2] (Later, when education for children became

universal, such a newcomer was also liable to the fund
for education.) The money for the *kuppah* was collected
by two men called *gabbaim*. Two men were assigned so as
to avert suspicion that the money might be embezzled.
The money for the *tamhuy* was collected by three men.
Both the *kuppah* and the *tamhuy* were distributed by another committee of three.[3]

Officials and Obligations

It is certain that there was a general organization to collect and administer the charities, apparently called *Heber
Ir*.[4] It will be recalled that some city dwellers who were
cultured, and careful in the observance of the laws of
levitical purity, called themselves *haberim*.[5] Therefore it
may be assumed that when a city institution came into
being to supervise the charities and other affairs of the
city, it was called *Heber Ir*. It can further be postulated
that it had seven members. When Josephus was appointed
by the provisional rebel government of Judaea to supervise Galilee, he appointed seven men in each city to over-
see its affairs.[6] In a later period, when Babylonian Jewry
organized its communities, they too had a seven man
supervisory council, called in the Talmud the "seven of
the best of the city."[7] The sources do not reveal whether
the members of the *Heber Ir* were elected by the local
citizens or appointed by the religious authorities (the
Bet Din) or by the civil authorities (the Judaean royal
family or later, during the time of the procurators, by the
high priests). In the case mentioned above, Josephus, a
civil authority, appointed the *Heber Ir*. In a later period,
Rabbi Judah the Prince, a religious authority, appointed
the *gabbaim*,[8] charity collectors; and still later, the exil-
arch of Babylonia appointed them. Thus it is reasonable
to assume that the members of the *Heber Ir* were appointed during the period of the Second Commonwealth,
but by whom is not known.

The cities had some sort of constitution which the inhabitants were careful to have enforced. No tannery

could be built within the city limits, but had to be located at least fifty cubits beyond the city; nor were cemeteries allowed within the city. Non-fruit-bearing trees were not allowed to be planted within the city. If someone planted such a tree within the city, he was obliged to cut it down. If, however, the tree had been planted before the city was founded, the owner was entitled to compensation for having it cut down.[9]

Most large cities had public baths, but these were particularly essential to the Judaeans who had to observe the laws of levitical cleanliness. A bath-keeper, called *balan* or *oliar* (*olearius*), received a small compensation for taking care of the bathhouse and the clothing of the bathers.[10] There were also public barbers. If there was only one barber and one bathhouse-keeper in the city whose families lived elsewhere and who, on the approach of the holidays, wanted to go to visit them, the inhabitants had the right to prevent their going unless there had been a previous agreement to permit it. The same rule held if there was only one food-shop owner in the city. The barber, the bathhouse keeper, and the food shopkeeper,[11] despite their low social status, were obviously essential to the city.

To participate in the affairs of the community, one had to live in the city for at least one year.[12] If, however, a person bought a house for the purpose of living in it (but not of renting it out), he was called a *ba'al bait*, and he immediately became a member of the community, a house owner. Houses were regularly rented by the week, month, or year. If a person rented a house for a year, and that year was intercalated by the addition of another month, the tenant had the benefit of the additional month.[13]

HOME LIFE IN JUDAEA

Dwellings

There was a marked difference between the dwellings of the poor and of the wealthy class. The poor lived in homes made of perishable materials, even in huts and caves. The houses of the wealthy were well constructed, and many possessed architectural beauty.

Houses in the city were generally built around a court, the entrances facing the courtyard. The houses were usually of one story; but the wealthy also had an upper story (occasionally two) consisting of one or two rooms for social gatherings and the entertainment of guests. If the guest was a person of prominence, he was lodged in the upper story.[14] Most single-floor houses consisted of one room. The Hellenes, whose women did not participate in dinners with men, had a special quarter for women called *gynaeconitis,* the women's quarter,[15] but the Judaeans generally dined together with their wives and children, except during the time of menses when the wives were separated. There is a possibility that the wealthy class, who may have practiced polygamy, as Herod did, had a separate women's quarters in their houses called *bet nashim,* women's dwelling.[16] Such households, which would not have been forbidden by Judaean law, were almost certainly an insignificant minority in the country.

Houses were built either of stone or brick. Wood was scarce and used only where absolutely necessary—in doors, door frames, and window frames. Generally the interiors were plastered. The roofs were flat, and after a rainfall the water had to be swept off.[17] Many houses, however, had roof spouts by which the water was drained and collected for personal use and irrigation.[18] The houses of the poor, living in villages and on farms, were of more perishable material, such as dried clay. Some of the wealthy had cellars under their homes in which there was equipment for pressing olives and dates, and this was called the *bet habad.*[19]

Light and Heat

Candles were used for lighting the home and the courtyard. They were usually of tallow, with a wick of pith; a kind of wax extracted from honeycomb was also used.

The wealthy class also had lamps and candelabra in their homes. A lamp consisted of a dish holding oil and a wick. The wick was of flax or cotton fiber; the flax wick was considered superior as it provided a brighter light. Wood, tar and bitumen were also used as fuel.[20] Naphtha was probably used only by the very wealthy as it had to be imported from Babylonia. The best fuel for lamps was olive oil. Lamps were often placed on tables and window sills; some were hung from chains.[21] Portable lamps, lanterns (made of pottery or of glass) were carried by men walking on the roads and city streets. Lanterns were also placed in the courts, some hung from posts.[22] Torches were used to notify the people of special events such as the announcement of the new moon;[23] when triumphs were celebrated, the people marched in the streets bearing torches. People generally borrowed fire from one another, though kindling by iron and flint was well known.[24]

The heating of houses was done by braziers made of metal or pottery. The wealthy also placed braziers in the courtyards where the people could warm themselves out-of-doors.[25] Ovens for baking and cooking, in the homes as well as out-of-doors, were also made of metal or pottery.[26] The ovens were open at the top and had an opening on one side into which bread and food were placed;[27] the ashes were removed from an opening below. Some out-of-door ovens were placed in a hollow in the earth, while in the homes they were elevated on a stand.[28]

House Furnishings

The floors of the poor were hard-packed earth, usually covered with straw. The floors of the wealthy class were of stone or brick, in many cases covered with linen fabric of the same type as that used for draperies at windows and doors.[29]

The houses were furnished with chairs, benches and tables. Beds were made of rope attached to bedsteads,[30] and were portable so that on journeys people carried their beds with them.[31] The beds of the wealthy had frames of wood or metal.[32] Some beds were flat on the floor; others were attached to bedsteads. The mattresses of the poor were of straw; those of the wealthy were of wool or flax, as were their pillows.[33] Most people slept in the garments they wore during the day, and therefore had no need for bedcovers. Many slept in the nude.[34] The well-to-do used bed clothes usually of linen or wool.[35] The bedcovers were often painted various colors, and some were elaborately embroidered. The houses of the wealthy had bathtubs.[36] Water was heated and then poured into the tubs for the family to bathe in. Some of the wealthy homes had mirrors, made of metal or silvered glass, framed and attached to a wall.[37]

Water

Water for domestic use as well as for irrigation was provided by cisterns and wells. Some wells were the private property of their owners and no one else had the right to their use. The wells in common courtyards were the property of all those who dwelt there. Some wells were city-owned, and only inhabitants had the right to use them. They could prevent any outsiders passing through the city from making use of these wells for their caravans. Wells on the highways were the property of the State, and any passing travelers had the right to their use. These wells were called "of those who return from Babylonia"; that is, when the Judaeans returned from Babylonia it was agreed that the wells on the highway were to be common property.[38]

The water was carried in buckets on the heads or slung from a shoulder. Men also carried water on their backs in skin bags. In irrigating the land, where large quantities of water were required, it was carried in skins on the backs of donkeys.

When Herod built Caesarea, he constructed for its inhabitants a drainage system which emptied into the Mediterranean.[39] In the Temple, a similar if smaller system drained the blood from the sacrifices into the Brook

of Kidron.[40] It is therefore to be assumed that Jerusalem
and other large cities had drainage systems like that of
Caesarea.

Food and Dishes

There was a vast difference between the classes in their
diet and their dress. The diet of the poor consisted mostly
of vegetables: pulse—of which there was an abundance
in Judaea—cabbage, pumpkin, cucumbers, lentils, beans.
The bread was made from barley, spelt corn, and wheat,
the latter two providing the best bread.[41] The diet of the
wealthy class consisted of eggs, fish and meat, particularly calf. At their tables there was often wine and cold
water to mix with it.[42] The popular Judaean food was
fish, which was caught in the Mediterranean and in the
Sea of Galilee. Fish was eaten with an egg on top, or was
mixed with egg and fried.[43] Fish was inexpensive; one
did not have to take care of it as is the case with domestic
animals. In slaughtering a goat or lamb, the owner lost
income from its milk, and wool in the case of a lamb. In
the case of an ox, its slaughter would be deprivation of
help in farming. The ox shared with the farmer in the
toil of cultivating the land.

A meal usually consisted of one main dish, except when
the Sabbath began, when there was a minimum of two
dishes, one of which was fish.[44] Even the very poor were
supplied by the community with two such dishes to welcome the Sabbath.[45] The ordinary meal usually com-
menced with *parpereth,* a salad consisting of vegetables
with a vinegar sauce; or radishes; or fruit pickled in salt.
At the end of the meal there was a sweet dessert or a dish
of peppers mixed with wine.[46] The main meal was usually
eaten at noon,[47] but an early substantial breakfast was
considered important. On the Sabbath there were three
meals,[48] and the community was obliged to supply that
number to the poor. Near to the table there was a utensil
containing water which was kept warm, similar to the
samovar of the Russians.

People usually sat at a table while eating. Many of the wealthy class were accustomed to recline on cushions while they ate, in the Roman style.[49] The servant, *shammash*, served the food[50] and, at the close of the meal, napkins were used to wipe the mouth and hands, since vegetables and lamb, if served, were greasy. The napkin was placed on the cushion.[51]

A variety of utensils were commonly used in the kitchen; sieves, ladles, grilles, knives, forks, and spoons. Pots were usually of metal, iron, copper or zinc for those who could afford it. Tableware, forks, knives, and spoons, were of wood, and plates of wood or pottery.[52] The prosperous had metal utensils and plates of glass, blown glass, or even of silver or gold.[53] To have goblets of silver or gold was a mark of wealth and distinction.

The Judaeans, particularly the Jerusalemites, were hospitable. People from every part of Judaea, as well as from other countries, on pilgrimage to Jerusalem, were entertained by their coreligionists. The repast consisted of meat and drink, and also had a spiritual character. The sages had ordained that, if three people dined together, a special blessing, called "the blessing of *Zimmun*," had to be recited at the end of the meal by one of those present. The Jerusalemites had a custom of hanging a strip of linen at the door to indicate that guests were welcome. When the strip was removed, it was understood that no guest could come in.[54] Since it was the custom to entertain many guests, preparations for the repast were often assigned to a caterer, called *tobbach*, literally "butcher." A law was instituted that, if the food was not satisfactory, the caterer had to pay a fine because of the humiliation of the host, the amount he was assessed being in accordance with the status of the host.[55]

Dress

Men wore loose garments. The *talith* was a cloak similar to that worn by the Greeks, the *pharos*, a mantle without sleeves. A kind of trousers was also worn. Men generally worked with uncovered heads;[56] they wore a head-covering only in the blistering sunlight. The women also wore loose garments. For the sake of modesty, the sages ordained that the women should wear a kind of belt or trousers called *senar*.[57] Two types of footwear were worn: urban dwellers and the more prosperous wore shoes covering the entire foot, made of black or white undyed leather; the rural folk and the poor wore sandals of wood or straw.[58]

Men wore rings, and men of stature had signet rings.[59] Canes were carried; they were symbols of dignity,[60] as in the Greek, but not Roman fashion. Some canes were hollowed out and used to hide jewels in order to evade the payment of duty while transporting them from one city to another.[61] The poor carried staffs, a sign of poverty.[62] They were of practical use in walking from city to city to obtain alms and thus were occasionally hollowed out to hold water for the slaking of thirst.[63]

Women wore rings,[64] and some, apparently those with thin hair, wore wigs.[65] They usually carried spice boxes or perfume flasks.[66] Jewelry was worn: necklaces, earrings, and nose rings.[67] A person with a decayed tooth might have it encased in gold.[68]

The women always had to have their heads covered. If a woman walked with uncovered head, her husband had the right to divorce her without paying her the *ketubah* which, at the time of their marriage, he had obligated himself to pay her in case of divorce.[69]

Parental Authority

The father was the head of the household. In Rome, the father had the *patria potestas*, authority of life and death over his children.[70] Judaean law did not give the father such rights. According to the Pentateuch, a rebellious son could be put to death; but the father first had to bring his son before the Elders. If he was found guilty he was put to death by the people, not by the father.[71]

The father was master of his home. He had limited

rights and obligations to his wife and children. His pentateuchal right to sell his children into slavery while they
were minors was curtailed in this period. The pentateuchal provisions concerning inheritance were circum-
vented by a new legal device. Traditionally he could not
favor the sons of a loved wife against the sons of an un-
loved wife, and the firstborn was entitled to a double
share.[72] In any case the estate had to remain in the family
and was not transferrable.[73] The Pentateuch simply does
not recognize testamental succession. The Pharisees,
however, introduced a new law of inheritance; a person
could make a will, *daitheke,* whereby part of his property
could go to whomever he designated. He gave it to them
as a gift through a document stating that his property
belonged to whomever he designated, from that day and
after his death.[74] The property then belonged to the
designee, but his right to benefit from or use it began
only after the decease of the donor. Some sages were
unhappy over the fact that a father could thus disinherit
any of his sons, but others were of the belief that a father
had the right to disinherit a prodigal son.[75]

Among the obligations of a father towards his children
was that his sons receive instruction in the Torah, and
also training in a craft, which should preferably be a
respectable one.

A father had the authority to give his minor daughters
in marriage without their consent. Upon his death the authority passed to the hands of the eldest son, their
brother. In any case, however, the sages ordained that,
when she arrived at maturity, she could reject this match
and the marriage would have to be annulled, without need
for a formal divorce.[76] Such a girl was not formally considered a divorcee.

MARRIAGE AND THE STATUS
OF WOMEN

With marriage, a girl's father no longer had any authority over her; it all passed to the husband. The wife be-

came his property, legally, as previously she had been the property of her father. All of her earnings, even if she found something of value, became the property of her husband.[77] On the other hand, the husband had certain legal obligations towards his wife. He had to provide her with food and clothing.[78] If she was kidnapped or captured, it was his obligation to ransom her. At her death he had to give her an honorable burial and hire mourners.[79] If his wife possessed wealth and brought slaves and handmaidens with her, she could be absolved from household duties and the work delegated to her handmaidens, even the suckling of her babies. However, an opinion was expressed that regardless of the slaves a woman brought with her, her husband should compel her to do some work, as idleness leads to unchastity.[80]

Marriage Customs

The following is a picture of the customs and ceremonies of marriage in vogue during the latter part of the Second Commonwealth as presented above.[81] There were different stages in the marriage ceremony. The first was a kind of betrothal called *erusin,* signifying a binding of the girl to the man after the fashion of civil procedures. According to pentateuchal law, if she then had an amorous affair while thus spoken for by another man, it was considered an act of adultery and she was punished by death.[82] During the Second Commonwealth, the betrothal, called *kiddushin,* consecration, was regarded as a religious bond. The terms *erusin* and *kiddushin* are interchangeable in tannaitic literature. Yet the betrothed woman, while bound to the groom, was not actually considered his wife. If a *kohen* betrothed an Israelite, she had the right to eat *terumah,* the priestly food. The law, however, was later amended, and this right was revoked.[83] If a betrothed woman died, the *hatan,* the groom, was not obliged to arrange for her burial.[84] A man could arrange to send an agent to betroth a woman for himself. The agent had to fulfill the conditions delegated to him. The conditions made by the groom or his agent had to be honest. If the conditions were fraudulent, the *kiddushin*, the betrothal, was not valid.[85] The groom wrote a *shtar erusin*, later called *shtar kiddushin*, a writ of betrothal, in which he signified that the bride was betrothed to him, and also fixed the date for the marriage.[86] There was a custom among certain groups whereby the groom added a clause to the *shtar* (also called *ketubah*, a writ) stating that when the bride entered his house, the *huppah* (bridal chamber), she would become his wife.[87]

It was the custom for the groom to present gifts to his bride and to his father-in-law.[88] To celebrate the betrothal, there was an elaborate repast. In some localities, as in Judaea, but not in Galilee, the groom resided in the home of his future father-in-law between the time of the betrothal and the marriage. In such a case the groom could not later claim that his wife was not a virgin at the time of the marriage;[89] nor could he demand the return of the gifts presented to his father-in-law and to the bride if the *erusin* relationship was broken off before the marriage was consummated, as he could in the case of the early death of the bride-to-be.

Originally the writ of *kiddushin* did not require the signature of witnesses.[90] Later a law was introduced requiring that a writ of *kiddushin* must bear two signatures. This law was promulgated to protect the purity of the family, as without the attestation of witnesses either party might claim that they had not been married to each other and that, therefore, she was free to marry his brother, and he was free to marry her sister. Since the offspring of such a second union would bear the stigma of full legal illegitimacy, the attestation of two witnesses on the writ of *kiddushin* was made an indispensable condition of the marital procedure.[91]

There were some restrictions on marriage. A high priest could not marry a widow.[92] If an ordinary priest, however, became betrothed to a widow and later was appointed to the position of high priest, he was allowed to conclude his marriage to her.[93] An ordinary priest could not marry a divorcee.[94] Strangely, if an ordinary priest transgressed this law, he was allowed to continue as a priest and perform his functions in the Temple; his offspring, however, were not allowed to perform the services in the Temple.

The wedding proper was an occasion for great festivity. If the bride was a virgin, her hair was worn flowing over her shoulders. Robed in white, she wore a tiara of gold or silver, as did the groom. The bride was borne to the groom in a curtained litter, in a procession during which singers chanted bridal hymns.[95] The bridegroom set forth from his home attended by his close friends, *shoshbinin,* bearing torches. It was the custom for the *shoshbinin* to present gifts to the groom with the intent that the groom would reciprocate on a similar occasion.[96] It was also the custom for the father of the bride to provide a minimum dowry for his daughter of fifty *zuz.*[97] If the bride was poor or an orphan, the community of the city was obliged to provide this minimum dowry.[98]

At the marriage ceremony, the groom gave the bride a writ, *ketubah,* in which he declared his obligation to support her, and her right to continue living in his home in case of his death. He further specified that in case of a divorce or his death, she would collect the amount of two hundred *zuzim* if she was a virgin when he married her, or a hundred *zuzim* if she was a widow or divorcee. These amounts were the minimum obligatory under the law. The groom could, however, add to this sum any amount he wished to show his good intent and to protect his wife in any future contingency. The *ketubah* was a legal document introduced by the sages to protect the wife financially.[99] It was legally less a marriage contract than a hypothec which made the property of the husband subject to the wife. In case of his death, it gave the woman the right to seize property from his estate in the amount specified. If the property was sold subsequent to the marriage, she had the right to repossess it from the purchaser.[100] When a man divorced his wife, and paid the amount specified in the *ketubah,* he generally obtained a receipt from her as in any business transaction.

Weddings usually took place on Wednesday evening, as court sessions were held on Thursday.[101] In the case where the newly wedded husband maintained that the bride had deceived him, not being a virgin and therefore not entitled to the two hundred *zuzim,* he could present his case to the court the following day, Thursday. Two *shoshbinin* attended the bride and bridegroom, with the special task of protecting the interests of both in the case of any accusation against the bride's virginity. The wedding ceremony was elaborate, and celebrated with a banquet. Men danced around the bride while chanting her praises. The festivities lasted for seven days.[102]

The Foundation of the Home

Although the marriage bond has been described thus far in its legal aspect as a civil contract, it also had deep religious significance for the Judaeans. The prophets referred to marriage as a covenant of God[103] and Genesis makes it God's own command: "Therefore shall a man leave his father and his mother, and shall cleave unto his wife, and they shall be one flesh." During the festivities, the parents and friends pronounced blessings on the joyful event and prayers for the future welfare of the newly wedded pair.[104] During this period the blessings were not yet standardized as they became after the destruction of the Temple.

After the groom had taken his bride to his father's house and the marriage was consummated, she became his legal wife. He assumed sole authority over all of her property and all that she might receive.[105] Although polygamy was sanctioned by pentateuchal law, the Judaeans adhered to monogamy with but modest exceptions. Even most of the kings, as in the cases of Jannaeus Alexander and Agrippa, had but one wife.

The relationship between husband and wife was characterized by affection and tenderness. Despite the legal arrangements, she was on the personal level more his friend than his subject. The ardent feeling between husband and wife is portrayed in the "Song of Songs," which was compiled during the Second Commonwealth. And the Psalmist speaks of the wife as the fruitful vine in the innermost part of the house.[106] Women also had an important effect on the destiny of the people. During the biblical period there were prophetesses like Deborah and Huldah; the Second Commonwealth knew such influential figures as Alexandra, her granddaughter Alexandra, and Berenice daughter of Agrippa I—all of whom played critical roles in the affairs of Judaea. So it is not surprising that the author of the book of Judith, portraying God watching over His people, chose a heroine, Judith, to save the Judaeans.

The chastity and faithfulness of the wife were the foundations of the family. In Rome, Caesar's wife had to be above suspicion;[107] in Judaea, it was true of every wife, no matter how humble her husband's status. Thus, among the grounds for divorce and the forfeit of the *ketubah* was the wife's transgression of the customs of Judaea; for example, walking in the street with uncovered head, or speaking with men indiscriminately.[108] Some held that even noisy demeanor was ground for divorce and forfeit of the *ketubah*.

If the husband was jealous and suspected his wife of having an amorous affair with a man, but had no witnesses and the wife denied the accusation, he had to bring her before the priest who made her drink the "bitter waters" mentioned in the Book of Numbers. If she had committed adultery, it was believed, her belly would swell and her thighs fall away. This procedure was in effect during the Second Commonwealth.[109] The giving of the bitter water must be considered symbolic, intended to frighten the wife into telling the truth. However, if a man brought this accusation against his wife, he had to divorce her, and if his suspicion was directed against a particular man, that man was not allowed to marry the divorcée.[110]

Divorce

It must be emphasized that the institution of marriage was intended to create a spiritual union. The pentateuchal phrase, "They shall be one flesh," was understood to set forth the ideal of full harmony between husband and wife. Nevertheless, divorce was permitted. According to the Pentateuch, the husband had to write a writ of separation, and send her away from his home. In the Hasmonean period, divorce was apparently easy in Judaea. The husband could divorce his wife at any time that she displeased or angered him. That, as noted, was why Simon ben Shetah introduced the *ketubah*, with its financial obligations on the husband.[111] In the Herodian period the Hillelites argued that if a person no longer cared for his wife, he could divorce her. The Shammaites, however, held that a divorce should be granted only in the case of adultery.[112]

Divorce took the form of a civil transaction. Originally the husband wrote a writ of divorce (*get*), which freed his wife from him, and she could marry anyone she wanted. Since no signature of witnesses was required to validate the writ, the husband could later claim that he never wrote it and his wife was still married to him. To eliminate such abuses, the signatures of witnesses was required on the *get,* and the document itself was to be deposited in the archives of a court. Further, if the husband or wife had aliases, these aliases and the names of the cities where they had dwelt had to be recorded in the *get.*[113]

The Child and the Home

One purpose of marriage to which the Bible makes reference was childbearing. Judaean law put pregnant women in a special category, entitling them to receive tender care, even dispensing with many pentateuchal prohibitions in their favor. A pregnant woman was permitted to eat on the Day of Atonement if she so desired; a doctor or midwife was permitted to travel on the Sabbath to attend her in childbirth.[114]

If the child was male, he was circumcised on the eighth day, the law of the Sabbath being superceded. (The term *brith*, the covenant of Abraham, was used to describe this operation only after the destruction of the Judaean State.[115]) Some women took their infant to the Temple when they went there to bring the prescribed sacrifices.[116] If the child was a firstborn son, when he was thirty days old, he had to be redeemed from the priest. His father had to pay five shekels to the priest in accordance with the pentateuchal law.[117] The day that the child was redeemed was a festive one.

As already stated, it was the duty of the father to train his son in a craft. However, the first instruction which the child received was in the oneness of God. Every child was early taught the declaration made morning and evening by every Judaean, "Hear, Israel, Adonai is our God, Adonai is One." Thus the child learned that the God he worshipped, Adonai, is the one God, the God of the universe. If the father was a learned man, he also gave his son instruction in the Torah; if not, he engaged a teacher.[118] Later, classes were established for the instruction of children. Shortly before the fall of Judaea, education became universal and was supported by the community.[119] If the child was gifted, he attended the *Bet Midrash* where the sages gave instruction in legal matters.

Levirate marriage, as required by the Pentateuch, was also practiced. If a man died without issue, his eldest brother had to marry the widow. If he refused, then he and the widow had to appear before a court where the man performed the act of *halizah;* that is, after the brother-in-law confirmed that he did not want to marry her, she took off his right shoe and spat on the floor saying, "Thus shall be done to a man who does not build the house of his brother." After the act of *halizah,* the widow was permitted to marry anyone she desired.[120]

JOYS AND SORROWS

Sabbaths and Holidays

From the time of Herod until the fall of the State, the life of the average Judaean was not an easy one, with the tyranny of Herod and the procurators giving way only to the disturbances that accompanied political change. Only the very rich and the well-connected had an easy life. Yet one day in the weekly calendar was enjoyed by every Judaean: the Sabbath. The farmers rested from their toil. The artisan did no work. The day was divided between eating and going to the assembly house to listen to the interpretation of the Torah. Even the poorest man enjoyed that day, since the community provided him with three meals. To add to the enjoyment, the sages permitted a Judaean to walk through his city and two thousand cubits beyond it.[121] Candles and lamps were lighted on the eve of the Sabbath for celebration and pleasure. Some Judaeans had lamps especially set aside for this Sabbath custom;[122] specimens have been discovered of brass and of beautiful design. The lighting of the Sabbath candles was the duty of the mistress of the household.[123]

The Judaeans also celebrated the holidays of their calendar as they had during the Hasmonean period. No significant changes in their observance took place in this period prior to the destruction of the Temple.[124]

Death and Burial Customs

The Pharisees and the Essenes, but not the Sadducees, held that death is not final; only the body dies, but the soul is immortal and is destined to be reborn. Rewards were in store for those who lived righteously, and punishment for those who sinned.[125] The Judaeans buried their dead; the bodies were not cremated.

When a person died, his eyes were closed, the body was washed and anointed,[126] and wrapped in a shroud[127] of very expensive material, by a special group or society. Professional wailers, women engaged to cry at funerals, clapped their hands, smote their breasts, and cried aloud; some went to the extreme of tearing their hair.[128] At some funerals a director was engaged who led in a dirge. This was followed by piercing shrieks.[129] The corpse was borne to the grave on a bier usually made of wood;[130] but people of wealth had it overlaid with silver and Herod's was covered with gold.[131] Coffins were introduced because many Judaeans who lived outside of Judaea wanted to be buried in the motherland, while most local Judaeans wanted to be buried in the same place as their parents.[132] Thus what began as transportation eventually became the accepted practice for everyone. The coffins were made of pottery or wood, the wealthy again using metal, even silver.[133]

The immediate members of the family followed the body as it was borne from the home to the "place of graves." Originally, in the case of the wealthy, the face of the dead person was left uncovered, whereas that of the poor was covered. It may be surmised that, in the case of the rich, the face was fixed so as to look well, while the poor could not afford it. It was accordingly ordained that the faces of all the dead be covered.[134]

People were buried where their parents had been interred, often in caves.[135] There was a special burial place for paupers.[136] The wealthy had monuments erected on the graves, some of such large dimensions that there was room for relatives to assemble there when they visited the grave.[137] At the end of the burial, a stone was set on the grave and the mourners stood in line, the people passing by them and offering condolences.[138] The mourners stood there with uncovered heads, but when the condolence line had passed they again covered their heads.[139] Whether this custom originated before or after the fall of Judaea cannot be ascertained. Plutarch relates that among the Greeks and Romans it was the custom for the sons of the deceased to cover their heads during the burial of their parents, since their parents were considered gods.[140] The Judaeans did not regard their deceased parents as gods, although reverence for their ancestors was strongly marked among them. When the Judaeans prayed to God, they covered their heads, as did the priests while performing services in the Temple. It is probable that this was a late custom. By uncovering their heads at the graveside they showed respect to the dead as well as to those who came to offer condolences.

The children of the deceased had to observe seven days of mourning.[141] They rent their garments, lowered their beds, did not wear shoes, did not bathe, and wore black garments.[142] Upon returning from the cemetery, a meal of comfort was served to all who came to the home. Many who called to condole brought gifts: the poor brought vegetables; the wealthy fish and meat.[143] The meal of comfort was a banquet. Wine was served during it and to accompany the special blessing which followed it: "Blessed art thou Lord, the good, who doest good to all."[144] Josephus, describing the funeral banquet of Archelaus after Herod's burial writes, "A Jewish custom which reduces many to poverty, such entertainment of the people being considered obligatory, and its omission an act of impiety."[145] The Talmud too speaks with disdain of the extravagance of the Judaeans at funerals—for shrouds, mourners and pipers. Gamaliel the Elder left a will in which he directed that his funeral be simple. Thereafter, many Judaeans followed his example.[146]

4. JUDAISM IN AN AGE OF CRISIS

THE TRIUMPH OF PHARISAISM: GAMALIEL

The small State of Judaea was surrounded by hostile nations and empires. From the time of the Restoration, the political leaders had but one aim—to make and keep Judaea an independent nation. But Judaea's independence was short-lived. The power of Rome was not to be denied. Eventually, Judaea fell.

Judaea was conquered and ceased to exist as a political state. Yet Judaean culture and religion did not die. The Judaeans, as a people, as adherents to monotheism, were a tiny minority in the midst of the polytheistic peoples of the world. How could polytheism fail to be victorious? Indeed, many small nations were destroyed by the Ptolemies, the Seleucids, and later by Rome. They are known today only in the historical records of ancient times or from relics excavated by archeologists. But the Judaean religion did not die; rather, in the course of history it overcame polytheism. Through it the Jewish people has survived and even succeeded in establishing a Third Commonwealth.

This survival was due to the evolution of their religion which was molded during the period of the Second

Commonwealth by their spiritual leaders, the Pharisees.
The initial critical stage of this development from an
ethnic to a universal yet national religion has been related
in detail in volume I. Here it should be noted that it
continued and became dominant in the Judaean way of
life.

The Sadducees and the Pharisees who originally were
religious groups later became political parties. The
Pharisees recognized that their involvement in the civil
wars which ended in bringing Herod to power had been
tragic for Judaea, and they now determined to devote
their energies solely to the teaching of religion. They were
therefore not molested by Herod. In fact, he accorded
their leaders honor. It is an irony of history that during
the tyrannical rule of Herod, the Pharisees flourished
and, just as the economic and political situation of Judaea
deteriorated, their ideas of Judaean religion attained
supremacy under the leadership of Hillel and his son,
Rabban Gamaliel the Elder. The views of the Pharisees
became normative, the standard way of living for the
Judaeans. The Judaean State developed from a priestly
theocracy to a more democratic nomocracy. The Judaean
religion itself became nomistic: a religion of law. When
the state fell and the people soon was scattered, the law
survived and functioned—and with it the Judaean religion and the Judaean people.

During the Herodian period, there were no controversies between the Sadducees and the Pharisees, for
Herod suppressed the former. Hillel and Shammai were
at the head of the *Bet Din,* but they were the last of the
zugot, the pairs, the *duumvirate.*

After Hillel's death he was succeeded as *nasi* by his son
Gamaliel,[1] and the position of *ab Bet Din* was abolished.
Gamaliel was called "Rabban," the master,[2] the very title
signifying his supremacy.

Rabban Gamaliel, like Hillel, gave the law a liberal
interpretation. For example, he introduced laws to
protect the interests of women. Previously, though a
woman could remarry upon the death of her husband,

there had to be reliable evidence concerning it; hearsay was not sufficient. Since divorce, the analogous circumstance, was a civil matter and required two witnesses, two were needed here as well to testify to the death of the husband. Rabban Gamaliel, to ease the difficulties in the way of the widow's remarriage, ordained that the testimony of one witness was sufficient.[3] In a similar matter, a husband had formerly had the right not only to divorce his wife, but then to annul the divorce at his pleasure. Thus his wife might be held in suspense as to her marital status. To ameliorate this situation, Rabban Gamaliel prohibited husbands from withdrawing a divorce once it had been formalized.[4] Moreover, since divorce as well as marriage could be accomplished by a writ being served by proxy, further uncertainties were introduced. Rabban Gamaliel required the writ of divorce to have the signature of two witnesses.[5]

A similar liberalization is recorded concerning witnesses who saw the birth of the new moon. They were allowed to travel to Jerusalem even on the Sabbath, but after testifying before the *Bet Din*, since they were not in their home community, they had not been permitted to walk in the city of Jerusalem on the Sabbath, but were confined to one place, called Beth Yazek. In order to keep the Sabbath enjoyable for such travelers and to encourage the witnesses to come to Jerusalem, Rabban Gamaliel now gave them the same Sabbath privileges as the inhabitants of Jerusalem.[6]

The author of Acts records that Paul (Saul of Tarsus) had studied under Gamaliel;[7] but this is open to question. In his Epistles, Paul does not betray a knowledge of the law as propagated by the Pharisees. His information on Judaean customs and beliefs reflects the practice of the Diaspora communities. In his reasoning however, he shows himself to be a dialectician who uses a form of argument similar to that of the sages in Judaea.[8]

The author of Acts gives an account of Gamaliel in connection with the arrest of Peter.[9]

Then stood there up one in the (*synedrion*) council, a Pharisee, named Gamaliel, a teacher of the law, had in reputation among all the people, and commanded to put the apostles forth a little space: and said unto them, Ye men of Israel take heed of yourself with regard to these men what you are going to do. For before these days rose up Theudas boasting himself to be somebody; to whom a number of men, about four hundred, joined themselves, who was slain and all, as many as obeyed him, were scattered and brought to naught. After this man rose up Judas of Galilee in the days of taxing, and drew away much people after him; he also perished; and all, even as many as obeyed him, were dispersed. And now I say unto you, refrain from these men and let them alone, for if this counsel or this work be of men it will come to naught. But if it be of God, you cannot overthrow it lest haply ye to be found to be fighting even against God.

This account cannot be accepted as historical. First, Gamaliel refers to Theudas as preceding Judas of Galilee, but that is incorrect. Judas of Galilee incited the people to revolt in 6 C.E. when Augustus Caesar appointed Coponius procurator of Judaea. The activities of Theudas took place in Peter's own day, but after the death of King Agrippa I when Fadus was procurator, 44-45 C.E.[10] Second, there is an undeniable anachronism in the speech of Gamaliel. King Agrippa I died in 44 C.E. though he is supposed to have persecuted Peter. Hence, when Gamaliel spoke of the council, King Agrippa I was still living. How then could Gamaliel have referred to Theudas who led his revolt after the death of King Agrippa I?[11]

Finally, Gamaliel said Peter should be let free lest the council be fighting against God, *theomachoi*. This expression could not have been used by any Pharisee.[12] The idea of engaging in war or fighting against God was foreign among the Judaeans, but was a widespread notion among the Greeks. The source of this account is probably a tradition among the early Christians that Rabban Gamaliel, a liberal person, was tolerant of the followers of Jesus.

Rabban Gamaliel became president of the *Bet Din* in

the year 10 C.E., and served until he died, near the mid-century mark.

JUDAISM AND ITS NEIGHBORS

Criticism and Hostility

The Judaean religion was national and also universal, for the Judaeans believed that their God was the one and only God of the universe. This idea of the univeral and exclusive sovereignty of God was revolutionary in the polytheistic world. Monotheism's claim of one God only involved intolerance of other gods as false. The Judaeans, in fact, held the gods of other peoples in scorn, calling them idols. On the other hand, polytheism was tolerant. Where two or more different gods were being worshipped, if syncretism did not amalgamate them, their worshippers still could tolerate one another. If polytheists suppressed other religions, it was done for political reasons, as in the case of Antiochus Epiphanes.[13] The belief that the God of the Judaeans was the only God was a fundamental challenge to the Graeco-Roman world and evoked great hostility. The denial of all other gods was to the peoples of the Empire tantamount to atheism, particularly when coupled with the idea of a God who dwelt in heaven and could not be depicted by any image. This friction over theory was reinforced by practice, since no pagan could worship his gods during a visit to Judaea, while the Judaeans on visiting other countries did not worship their gods.

The Roman practice provides an instructive contrast. Republican Rome was tolerant of other religions, non-Roman cults and religions being permitted in the city. Nor did Rome interfere with the religions of subject peoples. With the establishment of the monarchy under Augustus, Maecenas advised Augustus against tolerance of other religions in Rome.[14]

Augustus Caesar followed his advice, himself assuming the title of *pontifex maximus*. The Roman religion became more of a state-religion, a support for the monarchy. No longer was Rome as tolerant, particularly toward the oriental cults. With the exception of the Judaean religion, foreign cults were no longer tolerated in the city of Rome. Philo, however, relates that some time later the Judaeans, who lived on the other side of the Tiber in Rome, still had their own houses of prayer where they assembled on the Sabbath and received instructions in their ancestral philosophy, namely, religion.[15] There is no reason to doubt his testimony.

The heathen, particularly the Stoics, abhorred the Judaean religion. Cicero considered it a barbaric superstition: "Even while Jerusalem was standing and the Judaeans were at peace with us, the practice of their sacred rites was at variance with the glory of our empire, the dignity of our name, the customs of our ancestors. But now it is even more so, when that nation by its armed resistance has shown what it thinks of our rule; how dear it was to the immortal gods is shown by the fact that it has been conquered, reduced to a subject province."[16] The historian Justin, describing out of what seems almost total ignorance the origin of the Judaeans, displays a similar attitude:[17] "After Moses, too, his son Arvas was made a priest to celebrate the superstitious rites they had learned from the Egyptians." Tacitus, of all the classical authors, was probably the most hostile towards the Judaean people and most venomous against their religion:[18]

The Judeans regard as profane all that we hold sacred; on the other hand, they permit all that we abhor. They dedicated, in a shrine, a statue of that creature whose guidance enabled them to put an end to their hunger and thirst, sacrificing a ram, apparently in derision of Ammon. They likewise offer the ox, because the Egyptians worship Apis. They abstain from pork, in recollection of a plague.

The other customs of the Judaeans are base and abominable and owe their persistence to their depravity . . . The Judaeans are extremely loyal to one another, and always ready to show compassion, but towards every other people they feel only hate and enmity. They sit apart at meals and they sleep apart, and, although as a race they are prone to lust, they abstain from intercourse with foreign women; yet among themselves nothing is unlawful . . . The Judaeans conceive of one God only, and that with the mind alone; they regard as impious those who make from perishable materials representations of gods in man's image; that supreme and eternal being is to them incapable of representation and without end. Therefore they set up no statues in their cities, still less in their temples; this flattery is not paid to their kings, nor this honor to the Caesars . . . The ways of the Judaeans are preposterous and mean.

Despite this malicious attitude toward and perverted presentation of the Judaean religion in the writings of the great authors of this period, the Judaean religion had a great impact on the heathen world.[19]

The Judaean Sabbath was widely known, for it was unique. The idea that not only the master of the house but all, including the slaves and even the domestic animals, should work only six days a week and rest on the seventh day, astonished the pagan world. The word "sabbath" itself was a not uncommon term in informed circles. In his letter to Tiberius, Augustus writes, "Not even a Judaean, my dear Tiberius, fasts so scrupulously on his Sabbaths as I have today."[20]

Seneca, in typical misunderstanding, makes reference to Sabbath lights:[21] "Let us forbid lamps to be lighted on the Sabbath, since the gods do not need light." Juvenal, in his satires,[22] says:

Some who have had a father who reveres the Sabbath, worship nothing but the clouds, and the divinity of the heavens, and see no difference between eating swine's flesh, from which their father abstained, and that of men; and in time they take to circumcision. Having been wont to flout the laws of Rome, they learn and practice and revere the Judaean law, and all that Moses committed to his secret tome, forbidding to point out the way to any not worshipping the same rites, and conducting none but the circumcised to the desired fountain. For all this the father was to blame, who gave up every seventh day to idleness, keeping it apart from all the concerns of life.

Tacitus, with a lack of perception that has itself become classic, attributes the Sabbath to laziness:[23] "They (Judaeans) say that they first chose to rest on the seventh day because that day ended their toil; but after a time they were led by the charms of idleness to give over the seventh year as well to inactivity."

Many heathens apparently kindled lights on that day and practiced other Judaean religious observances. Josephus notes:[24]

The masses have long since shown a zeal to adopt our religious observances, and there is not one city, Hellene or barbarian, or a single nation to which our custom of abstaining from work on the seventh day had not spread, and where the fasts and the lighting of lamps and many of our prohibitions in the matter of food are not observed.

The Roman historian Dio observes:[25]

The country has been named Judaea, and the people themselves Judaeans. I do not know how this title came to be given to them, but it applies also to the rest of mankind, although of alien nationalities, who affect their laws. This class exists even among the Romans, and, though often repressed, has increased to a very great extent and has won its way to the right of freedom in its observance.

God Fearers

There were apparently many who, although Hellenes not converted to the Judaean religion, were what tannaitic authors called "God-fearing." They were in sympathy with the Judaean religion and observed various Judaean religious practices. The author of Acts relates that Paul, while in Athens, preached to the Judaeans and the God-worshippers.[26] While he was in Thessalonica, many of these devout Hellenes were converted. In Antioch of Pisidia, Paul addressed an assemblage with the words, "Men of Israel and ye that fear God."[27] Poppea, the mistress-wife of Nero Caesar, was attracted to Judaean customs; Josephus did not hesitate to call her a "religious" woman.[28] Describing the wealth of the Temple, he writes,[29] "For all the Judaeans throughout the habitable world and those who revere God, even those from Asia and Europe, have been contributing to it for a very long time." His further testimony is more explicit. During the revolt against the Romans, the pagan population of Syria rose against the Judaeans who lived in their cities and massacred them. Nonetheless, Josephus states,[30] the Syrians were still afraid,

For although believing that they had rid themselves of the Judaeans, still each city had its Judaizers who aroused suspicion, and while they shrank from killing off-hand these equivocal elements in their midst, they feared these neutrals as much as those who were of foreign religion.

In recounting the massacre of the Judaeans in Damascus, he records the pagan fear of their own wives,[31] "who, with few exceptions, adhered to the Judaean customs, and so their efforts were mainly directed to keeping the secret from them." In describing the status of the Judaeans in Antioch and the wealth of the synagogue, he adds,[32] "They were constantly attracting to their religious ceremonies multitudes of Hellenes, and these they had in some measure incorporated with themselves."

Most of those who practiced the Judaean customs and who revered the God of Israel did not become converts to the Judaean religion; but many were converted. As in every age, some did this for personal gain, as when Azizus, king of Emesa, became a convert to Judaism in order to marry Drusilla, the sister of Agrippa II.[33] Yet that was not the rule. One spectacular conversion occurred during the time of Claudius, when the royal house of Adiabene, a satellite of the Parthian Empire, was converted to the Judaean religion. Josephus[34] relates that Izates, the heir-apparent to the throne, had been convinced of the superiority of the Judaean religion by a merchant. At the same time, his mother was converted by another merchant. When Izates became king, he found that his mother was happy in her new religion, and knowing that the Judaean religion insisted on circumcision, was himself ready to undergo the operation. His mother prevented him from doing so for fear that his subjects might revolt as they might regard him as a foreigner, a Judaean. When Izates told Ananias, a Judaean stationed in Adiabene, about his mother's advice, Ananias told him to follow his mother's advice, for the worship of God was superior to circumcision. Later another Judaean, Eleazar, a Galilean, came to Adiabene and, on entering the royal palace one day, he found the king reading the Torah. He told Izates that this was not just, and that a man who was not circumcised should not read the Torah, whereupon Izates followed his counsel.[35] Both mother and son were deeply devoted to the Judaean religion and to the people. Izates sent his sons to Jerusalem for their general education and also that they might be instructed in the Judaean religion.[36] Queen Helena presented many gifts to the Temple, as did her other son Monobazus, who succeeded Izates.[37] When Izates and Helena died, King Monobazus sent their remains to Jerusalem to be buried in a magnificent tomb consisting of three pyramids, which had been built by the Queen herself.[38] During the war against the Romans, members of the royal family of Adiabene fought on the side of the Judaeans.[39]

What impelled the royal family of Adiabene to become converted to the Judaean religion is difficult to surmise. It is likely that the great number of Judaeans who dwelt in the Parthian Empire exercised a significant influence on their heathen neighbors. This enabled the missionary zeal of the Judaean merchants to have its effect. But this is only a partial answer.[40]

It is evident from the writings of the Roman historians that conversion to the Judaean religion penetrated deeply into Roman society. The testimony of Dio has been noted above. Tacitus makes no effort to conceal his venomous attitudes:[41]

For the worst rascals among other people, renouncing their ancestral religions, always kept sending tribute and contributions to Jerusalem, thereby increasing the wealth of the Judaeans . . . Those who are converted to their ways follow the same practice, and the earliest lesson they receive is to despise the gods, to disown their country, and to regard their parents, children and brothers as of little account.

Notwithstanding such slanderous accusations, many people in the Greek and Roman world became converts to the Judaean religion. How can this phenomenon be explained? The main factor was the essence of the religion propagated by the Judaeans: that God is one and universal. The God of Israel is the God of all creation; supermundane but not extramundane. He is the Creator of all mankind, loving and forbearing to all his creatures. All men are His children and all are under His providence. In His merciful yet moral judgment He has reward or punishment waiting in the future life for each man, depending on whether he has lived virtuously or wickedly. And, above all, He is too great to be represented by any image that man might fashion. The appeal of this teaching may be sensed in the sympathetic words about Moses by the geographer and historian Strabo,[42]

According to him [Moses], God is this one thing alone: that God encompasses us all and encompasses land and sea— the thing which we call heaven, or the universe, or the nature of all that exists. What man, then, if he had sense, could be bold enough to fabricate an image of God resembling any creature amongst us? Nay, people should leave off all image-craving, and, setting apart a sacred precinct and a worthy sanctuary, should worship God without an image.

By contrast, the pagan religions must have appeared decadent to any sensitive souls. Especially as the growing practice of erecting statues of their rulers, who declared themselves to be divine, must have facilitated the spread of the Judaean religion. It is true that the Stoics had an exalted philosophy of religion which taught that man is under the providence of the gods. Seneca could say[43]

The first way to worship the gods is to believe in the gods; the next to acknowledge their majesty, to acknowledge their goodness without which there is no majesty. Also, to know that they are supreme commanders in the universe, controlling all things by their power and acting as guardians of the human race, even though they are sometimes unmindful of the individual. They neither give nor have evil; but they do chasten and restrain certain persons, and impose penalties, and sometimes punish by bestowing that which seems good outwardly. Would you win over the gods? Then be good. Whoever imitates them, is worshipping them sufficiently.

There is something similar here to the personal tone and concern of the Judaean religion. That was the underlying reason why the Stoics in general were hostile to the Judaeans and their religion, regarding them as competitors for the soul of Graeco-Roman society.

In the realm of family life, however, the Judaeans had a striking claim. Its purity and fidelity were in direct contrast to the sensual and lustful life which prevailed among the Hellenes. This too attracted many to the Judaean religion.

Yet the vision of a universal God also separated the Judaean religion from the Roman ideal of religion. A Roman wanted a religion that supported and strengthened the state. From his point of view it was expedient for the state that there be gods.[44] The Judaean religion, with its God of all men, was essentially concerned with the ultimate welfare of every individual and of the people in its entirety. The state is not fundamental to its concerns and, indeed, because it has a God who sets moral standards and judges men in moral terms, because it knows the dignity of all God's children, it may even stand against the state. A universal religion is not limited to a particular state. That is its glory and was, in the Roman world, its special burden.

Conversion to Judaism

Undoubtedly the Judaeans sent special emissaries about the world to propagate the idea of the universality of God.[45] Merchants travelling from city to city also spread this gospel. But those really responsible for the conversion of the pagans to the Judaean religion were the Judaeans living in dispersion. Their refusal to worship the gods of the cities where they lived, their firm belief that the God of Israel was the one and only God of the entire universe and, finally, the nobility of the Judaean way of life, helped to make converts.

What stood in the way of their greater success was that other fundamental of the Judaean religion. It is nomistic: a religion of living by the law. For a pagan to obey all the precepts of the Torah meant a radical social readjustment. Thus, when eating, a Judaean pronounced a blessing to God; this could not be done in the home of a heathen, where images of the gods were present. When partaking of food a heathen offered libations to the gods; the heathen and the converts, therefore, could not dine together. Those who became converts consequently had as good as severed their family ties, and conversions to Judaism caused the breaking up of many families among the heathen.[46]

The uncompromising affirmation of monotheism by the Judaeans made it possible for Paul, the Judaean of the dispersion, to preach his gospel and become the apostle to the gentiles. The way had been paved for him by all those Judaeans who had worshipped the God of Israel and taught that he was universal and had no form.

Jesus and the twelve apostles were Judaeans from the land of Judaea. The Judaeans in the dispersion, however, who shed their blood preaching the universality of God, were mainly responsible for the spread of Christianity in the pagan world. It can be said that the blood of the Judaeans in the dispersion was the seed of the Church.

The original name for a convert to Judaism was *mumar,* a changer, one who had changed his religion.[47] Similarly, a Judaean who forsook his religion and accepted the Hellenistic way of life, was also called a *mumar.*[48] After the fall of the Judaean state, or perhaps shortly before, a new term, *ger,* came into use. The word *ger* occurs frequently in the Pentateuch where it has the connotation of stranger, or a newcomer to the land. The Septuagint renders it *proselytos,* with the same connotation as of one who has come to a new lànd. When the word *ger* was applied to a convert to the Judaean religion, *proselytos* underwent a similar transformation among the Greek speaking. *Mumar* remained the term for one who had forsaken the Judaean religion for the Hellenistic way of life.[49]

Originally a convert to the Judaean faith did not have to undergo any particular rites. It was sufficient that he rejected his pagan way of life and personally accepted the God of Israel as the only God.[50] Circumcision, however, became imperative, a *sine qua non* for any man who wanted to become a convert to the Judaean religion. Were he to remain uncircumcised, he would always be transgressing the pentateuchal law. Moreover, circumcision was a mark distinguishing Judaeans from other peoples. When Antiochus Epiphanes forced Hellenization upon the Judaeans, he prohibited circumcision.[51] Accordingly, the Judaeans re-emphasized the importance of circumcision.

Only after the year 65 C.E. was immersion a required rite for those converting to the Judaean religion. It was not instituted as a ritual, per se, or a dramatic ceremonial for the change of state, but as the result of a change in the laws of levitical purity. The Conclave in the year 65 decreed that all gentiles were *ipso facto* to be considered ritually unclean, in the category of *zab* (that degree of ritual disqualification associated with one who has an issue).[52] One is released from that category upon immersion. Hence, any gentile who wished to enter the Judaean community had to undergo the ritual of immersion, thus rendering himself ritually pure under the law.[53]

Converts were highly regarded by the Judaeans. The sages extolled those who had given up their idols and accepted the God of Israel. They were compared to Abraham, who had been brought up in idol worship but who in later years recognized the universality of God.[54]

The Diaspora

There were established Judaean communities throughout the Roman Empire and beyond, including many Judaean communities in Asia, Africa and Europe. According to Philo, about a million Judaeans lived in Alexandria.[55] Josephus records that 18,000 (elsewhere 10,000) Judaeans were slaughtered in Damascus, evidence that there was a large Judaean community there.[56] Antioch similarly had a large Judaean community. It would be no exaggeration to say that the Judaean population in the dispersion was not less than the population of Judaea, and perhaps exceeded it.

What was the relationship between the Judaeans living in dispersion and those who lived in the homeland? The Judaeans had emigrated from Judaea in search of greater opportunity. Nevertheless, the Judaeans in dispersion regarded Jerusalem, where the Temple stood, as their mother city.[57] They made many pilgrimages there, particularly during the holidays. Each community annually collected one-half shekel from each Judaean for the Temple, which was forwarded there by special envoy. Parthia, which had a large Judaean population, is a good example of this process. Though at that time it was considered to be distant from Jerusalem, each Judaean there paid his one-half shekel. This great sum and all the other gifts which were collected were deposited in the city of Nisibis, because of its natural fortifications and its large Judaean community. The accumulated sum was later sent to Jerusalem under a guard of over ten thousand men.[58]

Many who went on pilgrimages to Jerusalem (and those who brought the money collected for the Temple) took advantage of the opportunity to attend the house of studies, where they received instruction in the Judaean religion which they brought back to their communities. The great *Bet Din* also sent messengers to inform their coreligionists in dispersion of the dates of the festivals.[59] With this two-way flow of communication the religious life of the Judaeans in dispersion was effectively guided by the religious authorities in Jerusalem.

The Judaeans in dispersion were accorded many privileges by Rome because of the intercession of the Judaean rulers—John Hyrcanus II, Herod, and Agrippa.[60] The Judaeans living in the Roman Empire were excused from appearing in the courts on the Sabbath and after three o'clock on Fridays.[61] They were also exempt from military service because they were enjoined from working on the Sabbath and could not eat the regular fare provided in the Roman Army. The transportation of gold and silver from one country to another was strictly limited by the Roman authorities, but the Judaeans in dispersion were permitted and even protected in sending funds to the Temple.[62] On several occasions there were decrees that Judaeans living in Asia and throughout the Roman Empire should not be disturbed in the observance of their religious rites. Most important of all, the Judaean religion was formally recognized by Rome as a *religio licita*, a lawful religion.

On the other hand, the Judaeans in dispersion, living in constant contact with the Hellenes, absorbed much of their culture, especially their language. In the great cities, like Alexandria and Antioch, the vernacular of the Judaeans was Greek, and many bore Greek names. The educated class was well-versed in the culture and philosophy of the Hellenes.[63] They were more religious than their coreligionists in Judaea, but their religion was more primitive. This is understandable. The Judaeans in dispersion lived amid a foreign culture, and because of its

strong antagonism were jealous of their religious observances. But they absorbed into their religion many
ideas and customs from the surrounding cultures and
religions. For example, the heathen sacrificed and prayed
to the dead.[64] The Judaeans in dispersion were influenced
by these rites, but instead of worshipping and praying *to*
the dead, they prayed *for* the dead, a practice foreign to
Judaea.[65]

Their political attitudes, however, were far different.
The Judaeans in dispersion were rather indifferent to
Judaea as an independent state. They regarded themselves politically as citizens of their city or province—
Alexandrian Judaeans, or Antiochan Judaeans, and the
like. During the revolt against the Romans, the Judaeans
of the dispersion did not come to the aid of Judaea.[66]
They sent no volunteers to help fight the Romans, though
some who were in Judaea on pilgrimage joined the war,
as did the elite of the royal family of Adiabene. In the
Syrian cities the local Judaeans fought side by side with
their neighbors against the Judaeans of Judaea.[67] (It
can, however, be explained that this was not so much
patriotism as fear of their neighbors.) Moreover, and
of the greatest interest, there was no suppression of the
Judaeans who lived in Rome. Nero did put many Christians to death on suspicion of subversion, but the Roman
authorities apparently did not suspect them of being in
sympathy with the revolt in Judaea. In Syria, however,
they suffered greatly.

The situation may be summarized in this way: The
Judaeans in dispersion were not politically united with
the Judaeans in Judaea. They lived under different
political and social structures, and were loyal to their
respective governments, Rome or Parthia. They were
united with the Judaeans in Judaea by their religion,
which was centered in Jerusalem where the Temple was
located and where the *Bet Din haGadol* had its seat.

THE NEW RELIGIOUS GROUPINGS

Boethuseans

The Sadducees, who were dormant during Herod's reign because of suppressive measures, revived after his death. They took the name Boethuseans, after the high priestly family. The Boethuseans had the same ideology as the Sadducees. They believed that the religious life of the people should be controlled by the high priest who should be the vicar of God. They denied the validity of the Oral Law, and rejected the belief in resurrection. The Pharisees called the Boethuseans Sadducees, a term of contempt and opprobrium during that period. (An ironic reversal, since originally the word Pharisee had the negative ring, while Sadducee connoted privilege and esteem.) In the early tannaitic literature the term Sadducees is used interchangeably with Boethuseans.

The high priests and their Boethusean followers did not succeed in establishing a theocracy. They did have social status on their side, since their followers were members of the aristocratic families and of the wealthy class. Nonetheless, Josephus comments that they were boorish and arrogant,[68] and had no influence upon the people who hated most of them because of their attitudes. The life and the religion of the Judaeans were guided by the Pharisees. The Boethuseans did have one great effect. When Judaea became a province of Rome, the Boethuseans became involved in political activity. Therefore the Pharisees also had to become involved in politics, and the strife between these two factions was again both political and religious.

Essenes

The philosophy and the life of the Essenes did not change during the long period of the Commonwealth. They were exclusively interested in the purity of their members as individuals. They shunned the social, economic, and political life of the Judaeans, living apart in communities of their own. In time they became a semi-monastic order. Some of their members indulged in fore-telling what would befall individuals, but they did not claim to be prophets nor were they concerned with the future destiny of the Judaeans as a people. For them, love of God, love of virtue, and devotion to their fellow members were the aims and goals of life.

New Pharisaic Groups

Two other groups arose in Judaea in this period; both were, in reality, offshoots of the Pharisees.

The one group was termed by Josephus "the Fourth Philosophy,"[69] because he discussed it after the Sadducees, Pharisees and Essenes. This group was organized by Judas of Galilee at the time when Augustus Caesar sent Quirinius to take a census of Judaea prior to levying taxes upon the people. Judas incited the people to revolt against the Romans, and urged them not to pay taxes. He urged that Rome be not meekly accepted as their masters; for Judaeans there was but one Master, whose rule they should acknowledge.[70]

The followers of Judas from time to time committed seditious acts against the Romans. Being a small minority, they were easily suppressed by the Romans and their puppet rulers of Judaea. Not being able to engage in open battle against the Romans and their Judaean allies, Judas' followers resorted to the use of the *sica* (a short dagger) to kill those who favored the Romans, and thus gained the name Sicarii. They believed that terror must be met by terror, that anyone who submitted to the Romans was a traitor, not only to his people, but also to God.[71]

The other group, the Apocalyptists, like the Fourth Philosophy, was born of the frustration, agony, and persecution undergone by the Judaeans under the tyranny of Herod and the Roman procurators.

The Apocalyptists were in all essentials Pharisees. They shared their ideas concerning reward and punishment, Providence, resurrection, angels, and God's eventual deliverance of the Judaeans from the Romans. They did not, however, share their quietistic and passive attitudes toward the coming of the Messiah. The Apocalyptists believed that the day of deliverance was coming soon, and preached to the people to forsake evil and do good so as to hasten the establishment of the Kingdom of Heaven. They foretold the establishment of the Kingdom of Heaven only after great convulsions and sufferings.

The Pharisees also believed that God would save the Judaeans from their foreign oppressors and re-establish Judaea as a free state, but this would come through natural processes. A great general and leader would arise to avenge Israel and free the Judaeans, as David had done in his time, and Judas Makkabeus in his.

The Apocalyptists believed that Judaea would be saved by supernatural forces. They preached the gospel of no lordship of man over man—the equality of men, the only ruler over man being God. They proclaimed that God would send His Elect, or that the Anointed of Adonai would reveal himself to take revenge on the oppressors and the sinners. The aim of both the Fourth Philosophy and the Apocalyptists was the freedom of Judaea from the Roman yoke, but their means of accomplishing it differed radically. The Fourth Philosophy employed terror; the Apocalyptists opposed acts of terror and the use of violence. They preached love, leaving it to the Anointed of Adonai to smite the wicked. The Fourth Philosophy fostered political and social revolution, while the Apocalyptists propagated religious revolution as well. They were universalistic, believing that the Anointed of Adonai would rule the world.

Josephus said of the Apocalyptists that, although their hands were purer than those of the Sicarii, their intentions were impious and they ruined the peace.[72] This view seems to have been shared by the Judaeans in

general. The Sadducees opposed both groups as a menace
to their own political and economic status. The Pharisees
were also hostile to both because they did not approve
violence and terror, nor did they expect the coming of an
Anointed of God, a supernatural Messiah.

Josephus also refers to them as wicked deceivers and
sorcerers who, under pretense of divine inspiration,
fostered revolution. He singles out two whose story he
relates. One, Theudas, promised the people that he would
divide the River Jordan for them so that they could pass
through its waters. Many Judaeans followed him into the
wilderness, but before anything transpired the procurator Fadus seized a number of his followers, eventually executing Theudas. The other man is known only as
the false Egyptian prophet. He invited the people to
accompany him to the Mount of Olives, promising that
by a miracle the walls of Jerusalem would collapse, and
the people would march into Jerusalem without Roman
opposition. In a similar maneuver the procurator Felix
put many of his followers to death. Josephus obviously
considered them charlatans and their followers deluded.[73]

By and large the Apocalyptists were not deceivers but
honest, sincere people. Judaea was passing through a
time of turmoil, agony, and humiliation under the yoke
of Herod and Roman officialdom. Undoubtedly, some
cheats sought to trap the unwary and may have succeeded. So large a number devoutly awaited the day of
deliverance from Roman servitude that the Apocalyptist
movement must be considered essentially honest.

THE IDEA OF A MESSIAH

The Anointed

The word *Mashiah*, messiah, *christos* in Greek, means
"anointed." Aaron, the Tabernacle, and the vessels in it
were all daubed with oil[74] to signify that they were
consecrated, that they belonged to Adonai. So, too, when
the prophet Samuel anointed Saul, and later David, the

same nomenclature, *Mashiah*, anointed of Adonai, was used.[75] The term could even be applied to a foreign king, as in the case of Cyrus, the King of Persia.

The word *Mashiah* is used in the Pentateuch and the prophetic books only as an adjective, or in the possessive form, "My anointed," but not as a noun. The simple noun *Mashiah* appears only in the late apocalyptic literature and in the Gospels. It is also important to remember that, during the Second Commonwealth, neither kings nor high priests were anointed with oil.

There are no indications either in the Pentateuch or in the prophetic books of the coming of a personal *Mashiah* in that later, apocalyptic, sense. True, the prophets do speak of a millennium—a period of happiness and prosperity, when there will be no wars between nations,[76] but that is not the same as the expectation of a personal, apocalyptic *Mashiah*, and the difference between a millennium and a personal *Mashiah* should be kept carefully in mind. Thus Isaiah who, according to tradition, was himself of the family of David,[77] clearly longs for a period when a descendant of the family of David, imbued with the spirit of Adonai, would rule: That day would also be the time of the millennium, when the "wolf shall dwell with the lamb, and the leopard shall lie down with the kid, and the calf and the young lion and the fatling together; and a little child shall lead them."[78] There are no "messianic" expectations in this passage, only the exalted hopes of a great patriot and nationalist.

The Church Fathers and the early rabbis injected their ideas of an apocalyptic *Mashiah* into this and other biblical passages.[79] The Bible does not know of the coming of a personal messiah, natural or supernatural. Moreover, the Judaeans during the Second Commonwealth generally did not expect the coming of a personal *Mashiah*, as is evident from the literature produced during that period. The term *Mashiah* does not occur in the book of Ben Sirah, nor in the other apocryphal books—Tobit, Judith, the Wisdom of Solomon, or the Books of the Maccabees. In Maccabees II, wherein physical resurrection is stressed,[80] and the hope that all Judaeans would be gathered in Judaea is given prominence, the word *Mashiah* does not occur; the author believed these great events would be accomplished through the direct intervention of God Himself.

The belief in the coming of a supernatural messiah is first mentioned in the apocalyptic literature of the time of Herod. These Apocalyptists introduced the idea of a *Mashiah* who would reveal himself in due time, vanquish the Romans, free Judaea, sit on the throne of his father David, and usher in the millennium as predicted by the prophets of old. The author of the Psalms of Solomon wrote that the heathen nations would serve under his yoke for he would chasten all the peoples.[81] The author of the Book of Enoch[82] termed him not only anointed of Adonai, but also the Elect One, and the Man (Son of Man), and envisioned him punishing all the wicked oppressors of the Judaeans, with Sheol devouring all the sinners in the presence of the elect. One cannot help but be struck by the affinity of ideas and the similarity in the terms used in the synoptic Gospels with those found in the apocalyptic literature. The parallels make inescapable the conclusion that Jesus had either been a follower of the Apocalyptists or greatly influenced by them.

Jesus and the Pharisees

It is understandable, therefore, that Jesus had disputations with the Pharisees. The synoptic Gospels record only one controversy with the Sadducees, in reference to resurrection,[83] since the Sadducees denied this belief entirely, spiritually as well as physically. No reference to the Essenes is found in the synoptic Gospels, since they were not interested in the destiny of the people as a whole. Thus it was with the Pharisees that Jesus had his collisions, for though the fundamental principles of the Apocalyptists were Pharasaic, their extension by the Apocalyptists, and their actions and attitude towards the law, were vehemently opposed by the Pharisees. A wide gulf developed between them.

This is reflected in the controversies between Jesus and the Pharisees, as recorded in the synoptic Gospels. The Gospels record that Jesus went to the cornfields on the Sabbath, and his disciples plucked the ears of corn:[84]

The Pharisees said unto him; Behold, why do they on the Sabbath day that which is unlawful? And he said unto them, Have ye not read what David did when he was hungered, and they that were with him? How he went into the house of God, and did eat the shewbread which was not lawful for him to eat, neither for them which were with him, but only for the priests? Or have ye not read in the Torah how on the Sabbath day the priests in the Temple profaned the Sabbath and are blameless? And he said unto them, the Sabbath was made for man, and not man for the Sabbath. For the (son of) man is lord even of the Sabbath day.

According to the Pentateuch, no work can be done on the Sabbath day. Sacrifices, however, were brought to the Temple on the Sabbath, and the priests performed their duties on this day. This work was not considered a profanation of the Sabbath, in pentateuchal or Pharisaic eyes, since it was connected with the Temple. The Pharisees also allowed the profanation of the Sabbath in order to save a man's life.[85] Jesus claimed dispensation from the Sabbath law on the ground that he was the (son of) man, hence a priest, and thus "lord even of the Sabbath day." Jesus further argued his rights by stating that David, with whom he associated himself, once ate the consecrated shewbread, which was the bread of the priests, thus demonstrating man's right against the law. The Pharisees contested Jesus, saying that David ate of the shewbread properly because it was a matter of life or death; but that was not true of Jesus' disciples. Since they rejected him as (the son of) man, or the Anointed of Adonai, he was not a priest, nor was his work connected with the Temple, nor could he be called the "Lord of the Sabbath."[86]

Some of the disputations between Jesus and the

Pharisees that are given in the Gospels are anachronistic. Both Mark and Matthew record a controversy between Jesus and the Pharisees regarding the washing of hands before meals. However the institution of the washing of hands before meals took place only after the year 65 C.E. to ease the burden of the laws of purity and impurity upon the people.[87] The Pharisees could not, therefore, have complained to Jesus, at a much earlier date, that his disciples did not wash their hands before meals. Jesus countercharged that the Pharisees rejected the commandment of God in order to keep their own traditions, "For Moses said, honor thy father and thy mother, and who so curseth father or mother, let him die the death. But ye say, if a man shall say to his father or mother that by whatsoever thou mightest be profited by me is corban, [a vow], ye shall be free and ye suffer him no more to do aught for his father or his mother; making the word of God of none effect through your tradition, which ye had delivered."[88]

This dispute, like some others, shows their different attitudes toward man and society. According to the tannaitic law, based on the pentateuchal provision that a man shall not break his word, a vow has high sanctity and must be kept.[89] If, therefore, a man took a vow against a pentateuchal precept, he must still keep his vow and not observe the precept, though he makes himself liable to God's punishment for not fulfilling it. Thus the interpretation of the problem by Jesus is correct. However, to avoid a clash between two commandments in the Pentateuch—namely, "Honor thy father and thy mother," and "He shall not break his word"—the sages introduced a legal fiction to circumvent their own ruling on the stringency of vows. If a man vowed not to honor his father and his mother, he could in such a case absolve himself of his vow. This is called in tannaitic literature the "invalidation of vows."[90] The dispute reflects the differing concerns and interests of the Pharisees and Jesus. The Pharisees, as men of law and counsel, took cognizance of human weakness and knew that a person might transgress a precept. A son, on the impulse of anger, might vow not to honor his father and mother and the Pharisees, by their ruling, sought to find a way to give him the opportunity for readjustment. Jesus, as an ethical teacher, was so concerned to reach a utopian society that, disregarding man's frailty, he could not tolerate a person's ever transgressing God's laws.

This basic difference of outlook becomes evident when one contrasts the views of the Pharisees with those reflected in the Sermon on the Mount. This magnificent collection of ethical sayings which, according to tradtion, Jesus delivered somewhere in Galilee is the heart of Christianity's ethical and religious message to mankind. In scrutinizing both versions of the Sermon on the Mount,[91] one finds the utopian ethical tone reminiscent of Apocalyptist writings. To take a famous example, Jesus says:

Ye have heard that it hath been said: An eye for an eye, and a tooth for a tooth; but I say unto you that ye resist not evil; but whosoever shall smite thee on the right cheek, turn to him the other also. And if any man will sue thee at law and take away thy coat, let him have thy cloak also.

The pentateuchal law cited is called the *lex talionis,* or the law of *talio.* To understand this regulation one must bear in mind that the ancients had conceptions of the nature of crime and wrongdoing different from the moderns. Many wrongs which today are considered crimes against the state, and which the state is empowered to punish, were not so regarded in ancient times. They were held to be crimes and wrongs done by individuals against individuals, so that punishment rested in the hands of the individual wronged, or in the hands of his family or the tribe to which he belonged. The state actually had no power to interfere; it was purely a matter between the offender and the man who had suffered the loss. He could absolve the man who caused the injury from punishment entirely, or he could demand satisfaction, such as money, or even take out the eye of the man who caused the loss of his eye. The *talio* was therefore the ultimate limit the injured man could exact.[92]

The attitude of the Pharisees and of Jesus towards the law of *talio* reveals the essential difference between them in many of their controversies over Jewish laws and customs. In the early days of the Second Jewish Commonwealth, the Pharisees also felt the need of limiting the alternatives available under the *lex talionis*. This they did by a legal fiction, limiting the right of the man who suffered the loss of an eye to take out only an eye exactly like his own in size and color. Since it was impossible for two men to have organs exactly the same in every respect, the injured could not make use of the law of *talio* to effect bodily injury to his assailant. The injured man had the right only to demand monetary satisfaction for the loss of his eye, that is, for the pain, medical care, disability, and humiliation he had suffered. The law of *talio* was in reality replaced by a law of monetary compensation.[93]

Jesus, on the other hand, speaks as a utopian moralist when he says, "resist no evil." He asks them not only to refrain from demanding satisfaction by *talio*, but not to resist evil at all. Note that neither by his attitude nor by his exhortations did Jesus preach against the pentateuchal laws, for he declares:[94] "Think not that I am come to destroy the Torah or the prophets; I am not come to destroy but to fulfill." He apparently respected the law of *talio* as stated in the Pentateuch, but appealed to the conscience of the individual to rise to such a height that he would not only not exercise his rights against the evildoer, but not even resist the evil he was bent on doing.

Jesus approached the problems of his day purely as an ethical teacher. He disregarded state and society in his preaching, and addressed himself to the individual and his needs. He made ethical appeals, seeking the reconstruction of innate human nature. The Pharisees, on the other hand, sought ethical goals by means of the social controls provided by the law and its interpretation.

This difference recurs continually. In relation to divorce, Jesus says,[95] "It hath been said, Whosoever shall put away his wife, let him give her a writ of divorcement. But I say unto you, Whosoever shall put away his wife, saving for the cause of fornication, causes her to commit adultery; and whosoever shall marry her that is divorced committeth adultery." Jesus again was not opposed to the pentateuchal law of divorce, but his opinion was that Moses permitted divorce only because of the hardness of men's hearts, marriage being part of the original plan of man's creation, according to which man and wife should become one flesh, inseparable, except in the case of adultery.

On the other hand, though the Pharisees had the same view of the original intention, they maintained that "one flesh" was no longer a reality when the husband ceased caring for his wife. Under such circumstances they believed it better that husband and wife separate; and they permitted either to remarry, both steps being guided by appropriate regulation.[96] The Pharisees thus resorted to legal interpretation to reflect reality and to enhance the possibilities of marital relationships. Jesus, attributing marital discord to sin, sought rather to reconstruct sinning human nature.

Jesus further declared,[97] "Ye have heard it was said by them in old time: Thou shalt not commit adultery. But I say unto you, that whosoever looketh on a woman to lust after her hath already committed adultery with her in his heart. And if thy right eye offend thee, pluck it out and cast it from thee; for it is profitable for thee that one of thy members should perish, and not that thy whole body would be cast into Gehenna."[97a]

The Pharisees, as members of the *Bet Din*, would punish a person only when he had committed an actual act of adultery, but not for his mere intention. They did consider the coveting of a married woman a sin, but this sin could not be punished by a court, only by God. Jesus did not reject the law. He sought to surpass it by stressing the inner significance of one's motives.

The tension between law and ethics is again revealed by Jesus when he said:[98] "Again ye have heard that it was said of them of old time, ye shall not forswear thyself, but shalt perform unto the Lord thy oaths. But I say unto you swear not at all." The Pentateuch records two types of oath; in one, a man makes a solemn vow to God concerning what he will do. In the other, he makes a solemn affirmation before God that his testimony before the court is true. The Pharisees, with their interest in creating a just social order, made one's responsibility when he had sworn an oath a matter of great legal concern. Jesus, whose ethical idealism wanted man's intentions to be trustworthy beyond doubt was therefore against the taking of any oaths.

The same approach is evident in the saying:[99] "Ye have heard it was said to the ancients, thou shalt not commit murder, and whosoever shall do so shall be in danger of the judgment. But I say unto you that everyone who is angry with his brother shall be liable to the judgment, and whosoever shall say to his brother Raca, shall be liable to the Sanhedrin, but whosoever shall say thou fool, shall be liable to the Gehenna of fire." According to Pharisaic law a court could not indict a person for his intent to commit a crime or for harboring feelings of violence. Jesus once again goes beyond the pentateuchal requirement and makes motive and not action the standard of judgment.

The apogee of Jesus' ethics is reached in the statement:[100]

Ye have heard that it hath been said, thou shalt love thy neighbor and hate thine enemy. But I say unto you, love your enemies, bless them that curse you, do good to them that hate you, and pray for them which despitefully use you and persecute you.

It must be pointed out that the saying, "hate thine enemy," does not occur either in the Bible or in the tannaitic literature. Nonetheless, according to Jesus, a man is supposed to love not only his neighbor but also his enemy. The need to desist from acts of revenge can easily be understood. It is conceivable that a man who was wronged should be enjoined not to hate a culprit who was mentally unbalanced or might have committed the crime unintentionally. But if a man deliberately breaks into the home of his fellow-man and callously kills his children, as has happened repeatedly, shall he love that murderer? To ask the victim to love his torturer approaches the humanly impossible.[101]

Jesus either did not fully comprehend the nature of human beings or else wanted his teachings to be a utopian standard to which mankind should strive. His apocalyptic vision may be seen in his concern for the coming kingdom as contrasted to this world. Thus, other Apocalyptists, the authors of the Twelve Patriarchs, could say,[102] "If any man seek to do evil unto you, do him a good turn and pray for him." Judging human nature by the history of the last two millennia, it may be said that it is possible for a man to love his neighbor, that it may even be possible not to despise his enemy, but it is impossible for a man to love his enemy. Men are not only not ready for the millennium, but bitter and deep hatred still exists in the hearts of men, even among Jesus' followers. Seneca rightly said,[103] "We are mad, not only individually but nationally. We check homicide and isolate murderers; but what of war and the much vaunted crime of slaughtering whole peoples?" Utopian ethics can be practiced only in a utopian world.

The Pharisees and the Judaean Christians

The Pharisaic reaction to early Christianity was largely a response to Jesus' followers' claims that he was the long-awaited *Mashiah*. The question first must be asked, Did he himself believe that he was the Anointed of Adonai? From the synoptic Gospels at least it is certain he did not so proclaim himself, since when occasionally in response to his words or actions others said he was, he replied ambiguously.[104] According to John, the latest of the Gospels, however, Jesus several times referred to himself as the *Christos*.[105] It should also be noted that, though the Gospels state Jesus spoke with authority, they do not say that he sought to do so by some messianic right or power. There is no reliable historical evidence, therefore, that he claimed to be the Anointed of God or even King of the Judaeans, for which alleged claim he was crucified. The Pharisees, not believing that God would send a *Mashiah* to free the Judaeans from the yoke of Rome, thus opposed the disciples' teaching that Jesus was the Messiah. Nor could they condone the actions of Jesus, since his laxity toward the laws and customs of the Judaeans was in transgression of the traditions of the elders which they deeply cherished.

The disciples and followers of Jesus also claimed that he arose to life after he had been placed, dead, in his tomb. The Pharisees, who did not believe in physical resurrection, obviously denied the resurrection of Jesus. When Paul argued that Jesus then appeared to many of his followers, the Pharisees must have asked why Jesus did not appear before them as he had while he was alive.[106]

Even among the Apocalyptists, the claims for Jesus met with difficulty. Though some believed that the Anointed of Adonai would be a scion of David, others, who apparently cherished the glory of the Hasmoneans, held he would be a scion of the high priestly family, of the tribe of the levites, and they looked forward to a millennial theocracy ruled by a high priest.[107] This doctrine is echoed by Luke when he makes Jesus' mother, Mariamme, of the Davidic family, a relative of Elizabeth, the mother of John the Baptist, who was of the priestly family.[108]

Jesus had preached his gospel to the Judaeans, and admonished his disciples not to preach his gospel to the Gentiles, but "rather to the lost sheep of the house of Israel."[109] The movement founded in his name seemed destined to remain a Judaean concern. James, the brother of Jesus, and Peter followed in the footsteps of Jesus trying to make converts among the Judaeans.[110] They preached that Jesus was the Anointed of Adonai, and that the establishment of the Kingdom of God was at hand. They followed the precepts of the Torah as well as the Judaean customs, and required converts to their group to be circumcised.

James and Peter had little success in spreading the new gospel that Jesus was the son of God and had risen bodily to life from the tomb. Both the Pharisees and Sadducees opposed the view that God might manifest Himself in a bodily presence on earth. It is true that in biblical times everyone believed that angels appeared to men in human guise and that God spoke with human beings. During the Second Commonwealth, as part of the Judaean religion's revolutionary change to universalism, it was no longer believed that angels or God appeared on earth. Though the Pharisees and the Apocalyptists in particular believed in angels, they were thought of as being in heaven and fulfilling special functions. The Sadducees rejected the idea of the existence of angels entirely. The idea that God literally had a son or would come to earth as a man was an idea entirely foreign to the Pharisaic universalism which reached its climax in this period.

The followers of Jesus attracted some converts among the poor, discontented and exploited people who hoped to find social and economic equality in the new religion. Since Jesus had been crucified as King of the Judaeans, his followers were regarded as a menace to the tranquility of the country. The high priests, whose eyes were always upon their Roman masters, saw them as potential rebels and therefore persecuted the Nazarene converts. The Judaean authorities also regarded them as heretics who did not properly observe Judaean customs and the traditions of the elders.

Paul of Tarsus

The Judaean religion was based on law. Belief in God was not sufficient; one had to observe God's commands, for only by this did he express his belief. During the

Second Commonwealth, the Judaeans used the term *dat* for what moderns call "religion." This term originally had the connotation of custom or law.[111] Its adoption shows how fully nomistic the Judaean religion was. In the Gospels, by contrast, the term used is *pistis, fides,* faith. The fundamental requirement of the new religion was belief in Jesus. Paul, the chief proponent of this view, writes in his "Epistle to the Galatians:"[112]

Knowing that a man is not justified by the works of the law, but by the faith of Jesus Christ, even we have belief in Jesus Christ, that we might be justified by the faith of Jesus Christ and not by the works of the law; for by the works of the law could no flesh be justified.

And again in his "Epistle to the Romans:"[113]

Therefore we conclude that a man is justified by faith without the deeds of the law.

Here the newly born Christianity definitely breaks with the Judaean religion in which it was born. For the life of the commandments, Christianity has substituted salvation by faith alone. The two may once have been one. Now they are completely separate.

This shift in emphasis is inevitably connected with the career and character of Paul. Paul became the apostle to the gentiles; this was apparently after he had experienced continual rejection by the Judaeans to whom he preached.[114] They were particularly hostile to him, knowing that in the early days after the crucifixion of Jesus he had zealously persecuted the dead man's followers,[115] yet he now sought to persuade the Judaeans of the Diaspora not to circumcise their children and to forsake other Judaean practices.[116]

Paul made great strides among the heathen in the Graeco-Roman world. The foundation had been laid by the Judaeans of the Diaspora, who had spread the doctrine of the universality of God. Moreover, belief that a man would come from Judaea to rule over the world was widely

held, as Tacitus and Suetonius testify.[117] The tenet of a
son of God was not foreign to a pagan culture, which had
long believed that the gods had human sons: Aristaeus
was the son of Apollo, Theseus of Neptune, Heracles of
Vulcan. They also believed that the gods often manifested
themselves in bodily presence.[118] Hence, the preaching of
Paul that Jesus was the Messiah, that he arose from the
dead, and was the son of God, fell on receptive ears. But
the heathen world which had great pride in corporeal
beauty would not accept circumcision. They abhorred
it as a barbaric mutilation of the body. In order to gain
converts for his new religion, therefore, Paul had to forgo
circumcision;[119] and to make more converts, he further
compromised by abolishing other precepts of the Torah.
The break was thus complete.

5. LITERATURE AND RELIGION

EDUCATION IN JUDAEA

Since the Judaean religion was based on observance of the law, it stressed the education of the people.[1] Originally, education was the father's duty toward his son. Later, schools were established where the children were taught, and the father paid for the instruction.

During the time of strife and turmoil, when the revolt was already in progress and the various ideological groups fought one another, the sages succeeded in establishing a great institution which shaped the history of the Jews throughout the ages down to recent days. The Judaeans had always emphasized the duty of educating their children and established schools for the instruction of youth. But this was a private matter for the parents. In the year 64-65 C.E. the high priest Joshua son of Gamaliel (Gamala), introduced universal compulsory education for every child.[2] Schools were established in all communities, so that even a child of the poorest family who could not afford to pay for his education could now study. The Five Books of Moses and the prophetic books were studied and interpreted in these schools. A school was called *bet-sefer* ("house of the book," since it was the sacred books that were taught there). The

335

teachers' salaries were raised through a special school tax, which anyone who lived in the city more than twelve months, regardless of whether or not he had children, had to pay.[3]

The first chapter of the Book of Ezekiel contains a description of the *Merkabah,* the heavenly throne-chariot. This chapter was one of the favorite texts for adepts at mystic speculation. Some sages therefore sought to "store away" the Book of Ezekiel so that its description of the *Merkabah* should not be studied in the elementary schools. Joshua son of Gamaliel (Gamala), however, was able to secure a decision permitting the book to be read in the elementary schools.[4]

Education of the mature was still the primary concern. On the Sabbath day the people assembled in special houses where portions of the Torah were read, interpreted, and expounded for the people by exegetes.[5] After this reading and discussion of the Pentateuch, the assembly concluded with a reading from the Prophets, called *haftarah,* conclusion. Various exegetes are known to have attracted hosts of students to the halls of learning and to have exercised a profound influence on their hearers. The people revered and loved the exegetes especially because of their effect on the youth.

Seneca, a contemporary of Rabban Gamaliel, writes of Roman attitudes toward education:[6] "The halls of the rhetorician and the philosopher are deserted; but what a crowd there is in the kitchen," that is, in the eating places. What a vivid contrast to the situation in Judaea! Only the elite in Rome indulged in rhetoric and philosophy, and so the instructors had few disciples, as Seneca complains. In Judaea education was an indispensable part of religion, a fundamental part of life. Hence Judaeans stressed the education of their youth in the law.[7] Knowledge of the law was a religious necessity and acquiring it a religious virtue, making it understandable to the people and intelligible for their observance. Ignorance was held in contempt. Teaching the law was a great religious duty and a role commanding the highest esteem. In part this difference stems from the fact that in Rome religion was a handmaiden to the state and political duty was the prime essential of the citizen. To the Judaeans, religion was the very essence of life, and since it was a religion of law and tradition, study and teaching became intertwined with life itself. It was well said that an *am haaretz*, an ignorant man, could not be a truly pious man.[8]

PRAYER AND WORSHIP

The Significance of Prayer

In the Temple, the people worshipped God by offering daily sacrifices, as well as various sacrifices for the Sabbath, the New Moon, and the holidays as prescribed in the Pentateuch. Individuals were expected to bring special sacrifices on their own as offerings of thanks to God, or for atonement. In offering an atonement sacrifice, the worshipper made confession of his sins, and prayed to God for forgiveness. Such prayer was required of individuals only during the Second Commonwealth.[9] Otherwise there were no standard or, by Judaean practice, organized prayers; everyone prayed spontaneously to God to satisfy his needs, and there were no special buildings for prayer services as contrasted with houses of assembly for study of the Pentateuch and prophets, or of the legal traditions.

During the Second Commonwealth, the idea of God had become revolutionized. In their appeals to God, the Judaeans did not bargain nor argue with Him, as they would with a mortal king. The terms *neder* and *tefillah*, which in the Bible had the connotation of promise on condition and of argument, had now acquired new meanings. *Neder* came to be a vow, and *tefillah* or *preces*, praying, begging.[10]

Again the contrast with Rome is enlightening. Some philosophers argued that, since God exercised providence over human existence and is aware of human needs, why pray at all? Juvenal's skepticism is not untypical:[11]

Is there nothing then for which man shall pray? If you ask my counsel, you will leave it to the gods themselves to provide what is good for us, and what will be serviceable for our state; for, in place of what is pleasing, they will give us what is best. Man is dearer to them than he is to himself. Impelled by strong and blind desire, we ask for wife and off-spring; for only the gods know of what sort the sons, of what sort the wife will be. Nevertheless, that you may have something to pray for, and be able to offer to the shrines entrails and presaging sausages from a white porker, you should pray for a sound mind in a sound body.

The Judaeans, however, regarded prayer as a religious act of prime importance, though less as an expression of fear and awe than as one which emphasized the unity of man with God. To them, though God was supermundane, He was not extramundane; in prayer, man's spirit was associated with God. Moreover, though the Pharisees maintained belief in God's providence, they also taught that there is nonetheless freedom in man's action and God's response. Thus, they insisted that the sufferings of the Judaeans, as a people and as individuals, were not final punishment for past iniquities. Rather, God had chastised them with a purpose: that they should turn to Him and repent. Repentance, *teshubah*, returning to God, was the keynote of prayer. When man repented, his sin was forgiven; God, being merciful, accepted the repentants. This had its effect in this world and the next, for it was a tenet of the Pharisees that punishment for iniquities was inflicted, not so much in this world, as in the world to come, where too the righteous would receive their reward.

Style of Prayers

In this spirit the prayers of the Judaeans, using as example those recorded in apocryphal literature, may be said to have consisted of both confession and doxology.

The person who prayed, praised Him and then begged God to forgive his sin.[12] The author of the Book of the Three Children puts these words in the mouth of Azarias, when he was in the midst of the fiery furnace,

Blessed art Thou, Adonai, God of our fathers. Thy name is worthy to be praised and glorified forevermore . . . For we have sinned and committed iniquity . . . Cause not Thy mercy to depart from us, for Thy beloved Abraham's sake, for Thy servant Isaac's sake, and for the holy Israel's sake.

The author of the addition to the Book of Esther has Esther praying:[13]

Adonai, God of Israel . . . Adonai, Thou only art our King, Help me, desolate, who have no help but Thee . . . We have sinned before Thee; therefore hast Thou given us unto the hands of our enemy . . . Hear my prayer, and be merciful unto Thy inheritance; turn our sorrow into joy, that we may live.

Mordecai supplicates:

Adonai, almighty God; the whole world is in Thy power, and if Thou hast appointed me to save Israel, there is no man that can gainsay Thee . . . Adonai, Adonai, God, King, spare Thy people.

The author of the Book of Enoch, displaying the distinctive tone and concern of the Apocalyptists, has Enoch saying:[14]

Blessed be Thou, Adonai, King, great and mighty in Thy greatness, Master of the whole creation, of the heaven King of kings and God of the whole world . . . O, God and Master and great King, I implore and beseech Thee to fulfil my prayer to leave me a posterity on earth, and not to destroy all the flesh of man and make the earth without inhabitants so that there should be an eternal destruction. And now Adonai, destroy from the earth the flesh which hath aroused Thy wrath, but the flesh of the righteousness and of rightness establish as a plant of eternal seed, and hide not Thy face from the prayer of Thy servant, Adonai.

A somewhat different style of prayer is given us by Josephus, who records the prayer of Onias the "Circle Diviner" during the Hyrcanus-Aristobolus war:[15]

O, God, King of all the people, since these men standing beside me are Thy people, and those who are besieged are Thy priests, I beseech Thee not to hearken to the others against these men, nor to bring to pass what these men ask Thee to do to those others.

These prayers demonstrate that there were no standard prayers for individuals (as contrasted with the Temple rituals) during the Second Commonwealth. Each person prayed to God to help him as he saw fit. When a person felt the need for prayer, whether in difficult straits or great rejoicing, he turned to God and prayed for help or in thanksgiving. Outside the Temple, prayer was not standardized, nor were definite times and places set for it. There was even no command for the individual to pray, for the sages wanted prayer to be spontaneous, natural, the expression of the individual suppliant. This type of prayer would awaken the soul and unite the person intimately with God. It would also satisfy his inner craving that God might grant his inmost need. Only after the fall of the Judaean State was prayer standardized in a form known as *Shemoneh Esreh,* and definite times were set for prayer. Then too the houses of assembly came to be known as synagogues.[16]

When Jesus was asked by his followers how to pray, he gave them a standard prayer, now known as the Lord's Prayer.[17] It is curious that Jesus should have done so. However, this prayer is not found in the Gospel according to Mark, indicating that Mark did not know of it. Moreover, the Lord's Prayer bears great similarity to some of the prayers in the *Shemoneh Esreh.* Hence it may be postulated that the Lord's Prayer, as given in Matthew and Luke with variations, is of a later composition than the time of Jesus.

There were also no standard blessings as distinct from prayers: a person blessed God according to his capacity. The Judaeans customarily blessed God before partaking of food and after the meal (this was the institution of the *Zimmun*[18]) ; but there was no set form for this. An official formula for these blessings was instituted after the fall of the Judaean State.

Since prayers were not formally regulated in this period, women were not segregated from men when they offered prayers to God. The apocryphal literature records prayers offered by women as well as men, the prayers of Esther as well as of Mordecai.

In the pagan world sacrifices were a regular part of the act of praying. They were offered to appease the gods and to beseech their favors. The Judaean who made pilgrimages to the Temple brought the sacrifices prescribed in the Pentateuch and with his sin offering probably confessed his sins and besought God's forgiveness. Only two persons, both apparently under Roman influence, offered sacrifices when they dearly wanted their prayers to succeed: Herod when he engaged in war with the Nabataeans,[19] and Agrippa when he came to Jerusalem as King of Judaea.[20] The apocryphal literature, however, which reflects the prayers offered by the people, does not mention the offering of sacrifices in connection with prayers. It may therefore be said that by this period the Judaeans had severed the connection between individual prayer and sacrifice.

The Prayer for the Dead

The Second Book of Maccabees, which was composed in Antioch and reflects Diaspora practice, mentions prayer for the dead.[21] As already noted, such a prayer had not been in vogue in Judaea; the conception was foreign to Judaea and its religion. It represents a reaction of the Diaspora Judaeans against the heathen who prayed and sacrificed *to* the dead.[22] The dispersed Judaeans introduced prayers *for* the dead. This later became a widespread religious custom among Judaeans. The Sifre[23] states that the dead need atonement; which is to say that the living can pray for them and atone for the sins they committed while on earth. The Pesikta Rabbati says,[24] "Lest you say; When one has gone to *Gehenna* there is no coming up (resurrection) for him; if, however, the living pray for a dead person, he is taken out of *Gehenna*." (*Gehenna*, as a place of punishment, was not known during the Second Commonwealth.[25]) A late Midrash states that it was the custom to remember the dead on the Day of Atonement, and to give charity in their behalf.[26] Thus, in a development of the practice recorded in II Maccabees, there ultimately arose the religious customs of *Hashkaba*, the prayer for the dead, and the *Kaddish*. Similarly, prayer for the dead at the grave and giving charity in their behalf undoubtedly arose from the same source. The pagan idea of praying to the dead has not been entirely eradicated from Judaism and Christianity; the masses of Jews and Christians, when in great despair, often pray to their deceased next of kin, particularly if they were pious, to intercede in their behalf with God.[27]

During the Second Commonwealth prayers were rendered standing, kneeling, or prostrate: People prayed aloud, sometimes weeping.[28] It seems that prayers were rendered with uncovered heads. The priests serving in the Temple did cover their heads.[29] The author of the Epistle of Jeremiah, written by a Jew of the Diaspora, mocks the worship of idols and asks, "What kind of gods are they when the priests sit in their temples having their clothes rent, and their heads and beards shaven, and with heads uncovered?"[30] The author of this Epistle, wanting to demonstrate that these gods were obviously of no account, contrasted their worship with that in the Judaean Temple where the priests were bearded and covered their heads. In Greece and the Hellenistic world the heathen prayed with uncovered heads, while the Romans prayed with covered heads.[31] Paul, in his "Epistle to the Corinthians," calls for the removal of head-coverings:[32] "Every man praying or prophesying, having his head covered, dishonored his head." This may be because of his insistence that "The head of every man is Christ."[33] At the same time the statement records the customs of Judaea where men prayed with uncovered heads.

SCRIPTURAL AND EXTERNAL BOOKS

The Hebrew Canon

The Five Books of Moses (the Pentateuch) as well as the prophetic books were canonized well before the Herodian period.[34] The Hebrew canon during the Second Commonwealth therefore consisted of thirteen books: the Five Books of Moses and eight books of the prophets—Joshua, Judges, Samuel, Kings, Isaiah, Jeremiah, Ezekiel and The Twelve (minor prophets).[35] The Books of Psalms, Proverbs, Job, Daniel, Ezra, Nehemiah, Lamentations, Ruth, and Song of Songs—which are known as Hagiographa (*Ketubim*)—were canonized at the conclave in the year 65 C.E., which took place after the victory of the Judaeans over the Roman general Cestius. Though this conclave will be discussed below, it must be said here that the canonization proceedings were stormy. Song of Songs was included only after a violent debate between the Shammaites, who opposed it, and the Hillelites, who favored it.[36] The Book of Psalms was recognized to include the hymns recited in the Temple, like the *hallel* and the hymn sung when Judas Makkabeus dedicated the Temple, as well as the fifteen hymns which the Levites sang while ascending the fifteen steps from the Court of Women to the Court of Men.[37] Kohelet was rejected after heated argument.[38] The Books of Chronicles, however, were included among Holy Scriptures. The narratives of Chronicles vary from those of the Books of Samuel and Kings and the author even doctored historical facts in order to glorify the Davidic family. According to the Book of Kings, King Manasseh was very wicked. Despite the warnings of the prophets, Manasseh continued his abominations and died as a wicked king.

Chronicles however states that the Assyrian Army captured Manasseh and carried him to Babylon. There he repented and God returned him to his kingdom in Jerusalem.[39] The motive behind this canonization seems clear. At the time of the conclave, the family of David was held in great esteem, for many Judaeans looked to the day when a scion of David would rule in all his glory over Judaea. The sages probably canonized the Books of Chronicles to counterbalance the Books of Samuel and Kings. Since the prophetic books had been canonized long before, the Books of Chronicles were placed among the Hagiographa.[40]

It should be noted that at this time the texts of the canonized books did not have the final letters (*kaph, mem, nun, peh, sade*), nor did they have *matres lectionis* (i.e., *aleph, he, waw, yod*) as vowels.[41] The books not included in the Hebrew canon were considered "outside books," heretical books, the reading of which was prohibited.[42]

The Literature of the Pharisees

Of the various groups, or schools, flourishing in Judaea during the Herodian and post-Herodian periods, there is substantial literature from the Pharisees and the Apocalyptists; but there is no literature extant from the Sadducees, the Essenes, or the Sicarii (Fourth Philosophy). The reasons are plain. The tannaim, the sages, were the heirs of the Pharisees and perpetuated their spirit and their literature. The Apocalyptists were the forerunners of Christianity, and their literature was preserved by the Church. The Sadducees disappeared after the destruction of the Temple; they probably wrote books, but they had no spiritual heirs to preserve them. The Pharisees, who opposed their views, preserved traces of their position only so as to record their own in opposition.

The Essenes were individualists who did not seek converts to their group. Pliny the Elder, who met them on the west side of the Dead Sea after the destruction of

the Temple, described them as a people living in isolation, tired of life, with only palm trees for company.[43]
They may have written some books, on angelology, immortality of the soul, or the laws of impurity. But they
ultimately disappeared through their isolation and self-
destructive regimen. Since neither Jews nor Christians
had any interest in them, their literature vanished with
them. (It is a cause for much speculation that the New
Testament, which makes reference to all other groups,
does not mention the Essenes.)

The Sicarii probably wrote books, but they also left
no followers after the Bar Kokhba period. The Christians were hostile toward them for envisaging a military
Messiah. The Judaeans held them greatly responsible for
the misfortunes which befell them—the burning of the
Temple and the destruction of the State. Thus any literature they produced was quickly lost.

Halakic Literature

During the Herodian period, the Pharisaic literary
tradition was concentrated on the *halakah*, the Judaean
way of life as prescribed by law and tradition. When
Rabbi Judah the Prince codified the Mishne about the
year 200 C.E., he collated various *halakic* texts, many
going back several generations. Many citations in the
Mishne are Pharisaic formulations from the period of
the Second Commonwealth. This is evident not only in
their content, but also in their wording and style. For
example, the first part of the first Mishne of Kiddushin
states that a woman may be acquired in one of three
ways: with silver (money) paid by the groom to the
father of the girl; by *shetar*, a deed, written by the father
of the girl transferring his daughter to the groom; by
usus; the Mishne which states that a heathen slave may
be acquired either by silver (money), *shetar*, or possession; the first part of the Mishne Shabbat, and the first
part of the first Mishne of Baba Kama—these are examples of *halakot* enacted during the Second Common-

wealth. It is not surprising, therefore, that some of the words and expressions in the Mishne were no longer known to the first generation of the amoraim. A collection of all the various sections of the Mishne and the Tosefta composed by the sages during the Second Commonwealth, including all the dialogues between the Sadducees and the Pharisees, would comprise a considerable literature. It would be, moreover, the only Hebrew literature extant from that great period.

Apocalyptic Literature: The Psalms of Solomon

The Apocalyptists were visionaries. They followed the manner and the ways of the prophets, occupying themselves with revelation. Three apocalyptic books from the period of the Second Commonwealth survived: the Psalms of Solomon, the Book of Enoch, and the Testament of the Twelve Patriarchs. These were originally written in Hebrew, but only Greek translations are now known.

The Psalms of Solomon were not written by one man or during one period. The book is the work of several authors, from 100 B.C.E. to 50 C.E.[44] Its final redaction may be of an even later period.

The authors, while propagating the view that man has freedom of choice, recognized the operation of a universal Providence in all human affairs, a characteristic Pharisaic doctrine. The Pharisaic doctrine of retribution is also asserted, with emphasis on a day of judgment when the righteous, who feared Adonai, shall rise again into life eternal. (From the wording employed, it is not clear whether bodily or spiritual resurrection is meant.) On the other hand, the inheritance of sinners was to be destruction and darkness.[45] The use of the word *Sheol* in this context, and not *Gehenna*, indicates that this chapter was written before the destruction of the Temple.

The authors painted a dark picture of the religious and social life of the people. One might therefore conclude that Judaea was full of wicked men and sinners, while the righteous, the saints of God, were a minority devoured by the rapacity of the trangressors. However, the authors were Apocalyptic idealists, and thus prone to exaggerate the transgressions and wickedness of the people. Their words cannot be taken as a reasonable evaluation of the moral, religious, and social conditions of the people. Like the prophets whose spirit they emulated, and whose phraseology they borrowed, they chided the people with passion and indignation. Like many of the prophets, the author of chapter 11 of the Psalms of Solomon loved Jerusalem and visualized her future glory.

Chapters 12 and 13 contain a detailed description of the messiah and his kingdom. The time of the messiah's coming is known to God only, but the author prays that it be early.[46] He will be a descendant of David. He will be King over Israel, gather the scattered tribes and establish a holy Jerusalem as in the days of old. He will conquer the heathen, not by force of arms, but with the words of his mouth. They will be subject to him, and bring him tribute. The phrase *Meshiach Adonai*, the Anointed of Adonai, occurs for the first time in Judaean literature in these Psalms.[47] Still there is no allusion that the messiah will be a supernatural being endowed with divine power. He will be a man, a human being, the servant, the vice-regent of God, and Adonai Himself is his King.[48] But he will be free from sin "so that he may rule a mighty people, and rebuke princes and overthrow sinners by the might of his words." These chapters are of great significance for the history of the origin of Christianity.

The Book of Enoch

The Book of Enoch cannot be described in brief scope. Originally it was written partly in Hebrew and partly in Aramaic, and it may be said that the book relates the visions Enoch had while in heaven. It is the composition of many writers of various periods, with no unity of authorship, time or ideas.[49] In some chapters the doctrine of the life to come assumes a resurrection in a physical body, whereas in other sections it is entirely spiritual.[50] The messiah in one section is referred to as temporary, while in other sections the messianic kingdom is referred to as eternal.[51] Angelology as well as eschatology varies in different sections of the book. Some parts were composed during the reign of Herod and perhaps even earlier, whereas other parts were written during the time of the procurators. The final compilation of the book may have taken place after the destruction of the State of Judaea. It is generally and correctly divided into six sections.

The second section contains a description of the after life. When God shall sit upon His throne of glory, all books of the living shall be open for Him. The sinners, in anguish and affliction, will not be able to save themselves. They will be consumed as straw in the fire, and sink as lead in water. And there shall be no one to save them. They shall not rise again, "For they have denied the Lord of spirits and His Anointed." The holy ones will dwell in the heavens; they will praise and thank the Lord of spirits. Then too the son of man (human) shall be named, "In the presence of the Lord of spirits, and his name before the Head of days." In these chapters the Messiah is called variously the Elect One, His Anointed, and the Son of Man (man). His mission is to establish his kingdom and to judge the world.

In the section which follows, Enoch describes the physical phenomena of the heavenly system and gives a scientific analysis of the calendar. In the remaining two sections Enoch tells Methuselah, his son, about the coming Deluge, and the terrors of the Day of Judgment.

The book was based on a description of Enoch in the earlier Book of Jubilees which says in part:[52] "And he (Enoch) was the first among men that are born on earth . . . And what was and what will be he saw in a vision of his sleep, as it will happen to the children of men throughout the generations until the Day of Judgment. He saw and understood everything, and wrote his testimony." This description, in its full length, undoubtedly served for the authors of the Book of Enoch as a prototype and made it easy to ascribe their visions to Enoch.[53]

The book was considered semi-canonical by the early Christians and was of great help to the early Church Fathers in propagating the doctrine that Jesus was translated into heaven. They could point out that Enoch was already taken up into heaven, and that his writings foretold that the Lord would come to judge the people of the world.[54] The Jews, to counteract such propaganda, ignored or deprecated Enoch.[55] Onkelos renders the phrase in the Pentateuch "for God took him" as "he died." A Midrash states that he was a hypocrite, at times righteous, at other times wicked. A sage of the second century C.E. comments that the *Schechinah,* God, never descended to earth and no human being ever ascended to heaven.[55a]

When Christianity had become a separate religion, fully apart from Judaism, Enoch and the tradition of his writings were reclaimed by the Jewish mystical tradition. The Targum according to Jonathan renders the pentateuchal phrase "for God took him" as "Enoch ascended into heaven and he was called Mettatron the great scribe." The *Zohar* makes frequent references to Enoch and his writings; for example, "It is said in the Book of Enoch," "I found it in the Book of Enoch," "In the book of the mysteries of Enoch."

The Testament of the Twelve Patriarchs

The Testament of the Twelve Patriarchs is also the work of more than one author and one period.[56] The bulk of the book was composed during the post-Herodian period. Many sections in it were added shortly before the destruction of the State of Judaea. The book as it now stands was compiled after the destruction of the Temple, and has additions by Jews and Christians. The Hebrew text of the Testament of the Twelve Patriarchs was still extant in the Middle Ages and there are midrashim based on it. Only the Greek translation is available today.

The Testament of the Twelve Patriarchs gives the final wisdom of each of the twelve sons of Jacob. Its concern is largely ethical. Each patriarch relates the history of his own life, confessing the sins he has committed, and telling of his repentance for them. He admonishes his descendants to avoid them and to live righteously. Some of the patriarchs prophesy what will happen to their descendants.

Reuben confesses his fornication with Bilhah. He admonishes his descendants to pay no heed to women and to avoid them. He warns that women use their wiles to ensnare men, even enticing the Watchers (angels).

Simeon admits his jealousy of Joseph and his desire to slay him. He repents, and admonishes his descendants not to harbor jealousy towards their fellow men.

Levi tells his descendants that he had been destined to be high priest. He confesses that he and his brother Simeon were too zealous in the slaying of Shechem and Hamor to avenge his defiling Dinah. He says that he had become haughty and advises his descendants to avoid pride.

Judah appeals to his descendants to remove from their hearts any thought of haughtiness, not to glory in their strength and to avoid drunkenness. He attributes his affair with Tamar to having been drunk. "For if a man drink wine to drunkenness, it disturbeth his mind with filthy thoughts, and heateth the body to carnal union; if the occasion of the lust be present, he worketh the sin, and is not ashamed."[57]

Issachar stresses uprightness of heart. He tells his descendants not to bear envy or malice toward anyone.

Zebulun emphasizes mercy and compassion. He says that when his brethren threw Joseph into the well, he felt great pity. He commands his descendants to show mercy towards their neighbors and have compassion for all, beasts as well as men.

Dan speaks of truth and justice, and the evil of

jealousy. He confesses that when his brothers sold Joseph into slavery, he was glad. He urges his descendants to depart from wrath, hate, and lying; to love truth and beware of jealousy.

Naphtali recommends goodness of heart. He adjures his descendants neither to covet nor use vain words to beguile their souls.

Gad lays stress on the sin of hate. He commands his descendants not to go astray through the spirit of hatred. Hatred, he says, is evil, and is constantly met with lying.

Asher declares that there are two ways given by God to man : the good and the evil. He commands his descendants to hold to the good and avoid the evil, to follow the commandments of God, and to seek the truth.

Joseph stresses humility and long suffering. He tells his descendants that he saw in his life both envy and death, but they did not lead him astray. He tells how his brothers disliked him and contemplated slaying him, eventually selling him as a slave. In spite of all they did, he never lost his love for them. He says to them, "If anyone seeketh to do evil unto you, do well unto him and pray for him."[58]

Benjamin emphasizes the fear of God and the love of fellow men. If one possesses these virtues, and is a good man, "he is not in the power of the deceit of the spirit of Beliar, for the angel of peace guideth his soul."[59]

The Testament of the Twelve Patriarchs emphasizes the evils of hatred, lying, envy, lust, covetousness, jealousy, and haughtiness, and the virtues of fear of God, love of neighbor, truthfulness, purity, generosity, long suffering, and observance of the law. Angels and demons are referred to in the book, but unlike the Book of Enoch wherein angels are given proper names—Michael, Gabriel, Uriel, etc.—no names are applied to the angels in this work. Demons are mentioned by name, viz., Satan, Beliar, and *Diabolos* (devil). The doctrine of physical resurrection is emphasized. The righteous will be resurrected and will live in paradise, and they will eat of the tree of life.[60] The wicked will receive strict retaliation and be punished in the same manner as that in which he sinned.[61]

The term *Mashiach* occurs once in this book, but as an adjective in "the anointed high priest."[62] The authors do, however, speak of a redeemer who will save the Judaeans.[63] The testament of Levi predicts that the future king will be of the tribe of Judah, as does the testament of Judah. In the testament of Dan, the future savior is expected of the tribes of Judah and Levi. Similarly, in his testament, Joseph says to his children, "Do ye therefore, my children, observe the commandments of the Lord, and honor Levi and Judah; for from them shall arise (unto you) one who saved Israel."

During the Second Commonwealth there was continuous dissension between two groups: one propagating the idea of a theocracy, maintaining that the head of the Judaean community should be a scion of the family of the high priest; the other group maintaining that the leadership of the Judaean community should be in the hands of a scion of the family of David. Both views are presented in this book. The prophecy that the future ruler should be of the tribe of Levi was probably interpolated after the destruction of the Judaean State. After the war, when the Judaeans lost their state and began to reorganize their community, the clash between the two factions was revived: whether leadership was to come from the tribe of Levi, a priest, or from the tribe of Judah, of the family of David, that is, a descendant of Hillel. The group who stood for the priestly family won: Rabban Jochanan ben Zakkai, a priest, assumed the leadership of the new Judaean community.[64] The doctrine that the future savior should be of the tribe of Levi as well as of Judah is reflected in the Gospel according to Luke, wherein Mary is said to have been related to the priestly family.[65]

A significant characteristic of the Testament of the Twelve Patriarchs is the universalism of the authors. True followers of the Pharisees, they believed in the universality of God; that the God of Israel is the God of all mankind, and that when the new Temple is built, the spirit of God will pass on to the gentiles.[66]

Levi, in his testament, admonishes his descendants against their unlawfully taking to wife the daughters of the gentiles. The admonition is not found in the testaments of the other patriarchs. This can be explained by the fact that there was no general prohibition against marrying a gentile woman if she had become converted to the Judaean religion; but the priests, descendants of Levi, were prohibited from taking a gentile woman in marriage even if she had converted to the Judaean religion.[67]

To say that the books of the Apocalyptists influenced the rise of Christianity would not convey the full influence of this literature. Pharisaic Apocalyptism, as revealed in these books, was the forerunner of Christianity. The ideas of the *Mashiach,* original sin, atonement, martyrdom, physical resurrection, even the conception of non-resistance, all have their origin in this literature. It would not be an exaggeration to say that the books of the Apocalyptists had more direct effect on the origin of Christianity than the canonical books of the Hebrew Bíble. It is true that the early Church Fathers, in proving the truth of Christianity, always referred to the Hebrew Bible. This is not because the Apocalyptic literature was not considered the main source of Christianity, but because, in order to combat the Judaeans, they had to prove that Jesus was the true messiah from the books sacred to the Judàeans. The Apocalyptic books, rejected by the Judaeans, were revered by the Christians, and the Church preserved them down to the present day. The Apocalyptic literature, however, had an impact on one segment of the Jewish people, the cabalists. Jewish mysticism is a part of the chain of development of the Apocalyptic literature.

Megillat Ta'anit

The scroll known as Megillat Ta'anit has no parallel in the Hebrew literature of the Second Commonwealth. It is not written as a historical narrative, or as wisdom literature, or as apocalyptic vision. It offers a list of days on which, by reason of the events associated with them, the Judaeans were not to fast. The events are arranged according to the Hebrew dates, and divided according to the calendar into twelve chapters corresponding to the twelve months from Nisan to Adar.[68] The name Megillat Ta'anit, the Scroll of Fasts, is a misnomer since it does not give the days of fasts; on the contrary, it lists days of such national joy that no fast, public or private, might be permitted. It is safe to assume that the name was originally Megillah, Scroll, and later the word Ta'anit, fasts, was added.[69] This scroll may properly be called the Judaean *monumentum aere perennius.*

The earliest date cited is the consecration of the House of Yahweh, in the days of Zerubbabel, on the first day of Nisan, 515 B.C.E.[70] From the first day of Nisan until the fourteenth day of that month were declared semi-holidays. The latest joyful days recorded are the seventh day of Kislev, November 25, 65 C.E., in commemoration of the great victory over Cestius, [71] and the second day of Shebat, January 19, 66 C.E., when the provisional government was established and its officers were inaugurated.

The Megillah, which is written in Aramaic, was almost certainly completed after this last date. Eleazer, son of Hanina, one of the leaders of the revolt against the Romans (Josephus considered him a prime instigator) was responsible for its composition.[72]

Megillat Ta'anit carried legal authority; it is cited in the Mishne with the expression used for the Bible itself— "It is written."[73] Thus it is the earliest source for the required observance of the semi-festivals of Hanukkah and Purim. With the exception of these two semi-festivals, all the others mentioned have sunk into oblivion. This was natural. They had become celebrations largely because of their connection with the victories of the Judaeans over the Syrians or the Romans. When Judaea lost her independence and the Temple was burned, the *raison d'être* for the semi-holidays was gone. The people no longer commemorated national victories over their oppressors. Their observance was not formally abrogated by the sages; they just gradually disappeared from the practice of the people, while Hanukkah and Purim, which had enduring religious significance, continued.[74] His purpose in compiling this list was to demonstrate that the Judaeans had been victorious over their Syrian oppressors and, in recent times, over the Romans as well. If the Syrians, a great power in their time, were conquerable, the Romans also were conquerable. Thus he hoped to inspire his fellow Judaeans with courage and arouse them to continue their war against the Romans with determination.

LANGUAGES AND SOCIAL CONTACTS

Before the revolt against the Romans, Judaea was a trilingual country, with Hebrew, Aramaic and Greek spoken. Hebrew was used in the academies of learning and in the schools. The *halakot* (laws) were written in Hebrew. Among the Judaean elite, conversation was in Hebrew. Aramaic, however, was the vernacular, the language of the masses, and in Galilee it was spoken by every class. Judaean deeds were written in Aramaic,[75] as were marriage contracts proper and the *ketubah*. This made it possible to have easy commercial transactions with the neighboring countries since they, too, spoke Aramaic. In fact, its use extended to peoples living beyond the Euphrates, though the Aramaic spoken in Judaea was the western dialect, while that used beyond the Euphrates was the eastern. Books for the people at large were written in Aramaic, the Megillat Ta'anit being the prime example. So too the sayings of Jesus as recorded in the Gospels were in Judaean Aramaic.[76]

The third language spoken in Judaea was Greek. It possessed great magic for all the peoples of Asia Minor, and even penetrated into Italy. The language of the vanquished became the fashion of its conqueror. Juvenal in his satires mocked the people of Italy who spoke Greek:[77]

> They talk nothing but Greek, though it is a greater shame for our people to be ignorant of Latin . . . All this may be pardoned in a girl; but will you, who are hard on your eighty-sixth year, still talk in Greek? That tongue is not decent in an old woman's mouth.

It is logical that the Judaeans, ruled by Rome and surrounded by Hellenist populations, would for political, social, and economic reasons speak Greek. This was particularly true of those who were associated with the government, the high priestly families and the aristocracy, and those who transacted business with the outside world.[78] The process was accelerated by the special fate of certain cities. Some, like Ashdod, were originally part of Judaea, but later became independent and had a mixed population. Jabneh is another example, and one could cite a number of other cities on the borders of Judaea with mixed populations. Caesarea must, of course, receive special mention, for it became the second most important port in the eastern Mediterranean. Its mixed population is well attested.

As commerce grew, so did the use of Greek words and terms. Many Hellenists who lived in the cities of mixed population were employed in various trades and professions, and technical terms became an accepted part of Hebrew usage. Hebrew simply did not have the vocabulary for the highly developed industrial and commercial transactions, or for institutional forms that had come into being. The Judaeans therefore borrowed from the vast treasure of the Greek language, thus creating the abundance of Greek words and terms employed in the Hebrew literature of this period.

Despite the great popularity and widespread usage of Greek in Judaea, no literature was composed there in Greek, but only in Hebrew or Aramaic; the Judaeo-Greek literature was composed only in the Diaspora. Nor did the glory of Hellenism have much effect on the

Judaean religion. It remained true to the form shaped by the sages. Neither glory nor persecution could change it.[79]

Gnosticism (from the word *gnosis*), the seeking of knowledge and revelation from God, was widespread among the peoples bordering the Judaean State. It became a highly ramified school of thought in the Hellenistic world, but did not take root in Judaea. The gnostic was considered a diviner, employing magic, theurgy, sorcery. Some of these men were sincere, but someone who was psychically abnormal, his head full of mystical doctrines, could easily believe himself to have visions of the other world and to possess divine power.[80] Simon Magus of Samaria may have been of this category.[80a]

Through the time of the Revolt, the Judaeans were divided into three groups: Sadducees, Pharisees, and Essenes. The Sadducees were regarded by the Pharisees with contempt as not conforming to the mainstream of the Judaean religion. Undoubtedly there were many who denied Revelation and the belief that the Five Books of Moses were given by God on Mount Sinai. Many did not believe in a future world,[81] but they were individuals; there was no organized group with a definite ideology and philosophy.[82]

Notwithstanding the oft-mentioned distance and even the antagonism between the heathen, who were polytheists, and the Judaeans, who believed in one God of the entire universe, there was, in general, a relationship of decency and civility between them. Commerce proceeded without interruption; even social intercourse was part of the regular way of life. The Judaeans would not partake of food in the homes of the heathen, where there were images of gods, but many who were not stringent in matters of levitical purity purchased bread and oil and wine from them.[83] When a heathen affixed his signature as a witness to a deed, it was valid; his testimony in court was accepted.[84] Heathens were regularly employed by Judaeans in housework. That minority of the wealthy who practiced polygamy must have employed heathen eunuchs, for according to pentateuchal law, no Judaean could be made a eunuch.[85] Heathen women were employed as maids, and the Judaeans probably had heathen women as concubines.

The Conclave of 65-66

This relationship ceased when the Judaeans launched their war against the Romans. Every war arouses extreme nationalism among those waging it, and this war was no exception. The Judaean leaders employed every means to foment hatred against the Romans and segregate the Judaeans from them and their allies. Xenophobia became the prevailing attitude in Judaea, and this explains many of the rulings of the Conclave convened after the victory over Cestius. One ruling prohibited Judaeans from speaking the Greek language.[86] The Conclave further decreed that heathen food products were ritually unclean. The acceptance of gifts for the Temple was prohibited.[87] The signature of a heathen on a deed, as well as his testimony, were now unacceptable.[88] The employment of a heathen in the home and sexual relations with heathen women were prohibited.[89] As a Mishne puts it, "If one has sexual intercourse with a heathen woman, zealots may lynch him."

To strengthen the segregation of the Judaeans from the heathen, the latter were declared, *ipso facto*, ritually unclean, in the degree of a *zab*.[90] According to the pentateuchal law, a *zab*, after having undergone the ceremony of immersion, had to bring a sacrifice of two doves. Thus a heathen, to become a convert to the Judaean religion, not only had to immerse himself but bring a sacrifice of two doves.[91] Some later sages endeavored to revoke some of the decrees against the heathen, but in general the law remained as it had been fixed at the Conclave.[92] What had been motivated by a given political situation acquired religious permanence.

Some of the decrees adopted at this Conclave were

directed against the Sadducees, particularly against the high priests who at that time were Sadducean. It was decreed that everything defiled the priest, and that in order to eat the sacred food, *terumah,* not only did he have to undergo immersion, but he had to wait until sunset.[93] It was further decreed that anything defiles the *terumah,* and that *terumah* which has been defiled cannot be used and must be burned.[94] The same Conclave decreed that the Holy Scriptures defiled the hands.[95] This decree was aimed against the Sadducees who accepted only the written law and rejected the oral law. This is evident from the complaint of the Sadducees, "The Sadducees say we complain against you Pharisees, for you say 'The Holy Scriptures defile the hands, the writings of Homer do not defile the hands.' "[96]

This Conclave again brought up the principle of intention introduced by Hillel; that an act without intention, although willed, was not considered a legal act. Shammai had strongly opposed this innovation, and the Shammaites again opposed this principle.[97]

At the Conclave three different units of eighteen measures were discussed. Eighteen were unanimously adopted; eighteen were adopted by a majority; the other eighteen remained undecided. The religious leadership of the country was obviously not united, particularly because its Hillelites were not zealous about the war. The coalition government, which consisted of Sadducees and Pharisees, was even more divided. Many of its members were for peace, and looked for an opportunity to make peace with the Romans. Nor was the people as a whole of a single determination as they launched a war against the Roman Empire. The Conclave of the year 65-66 sealed a fateful chapter in the history of the Judaean people.

Appendices

APPENDIX I

MEGILLAT TA'ANIT

These following are the days on which fasting is forbidden, and on some of which it is also forbidden to mourn.[1]

I. (a) From [the 1st until the 8th] of Nisan, the daily offering was instituted—mourning is forbidden.[2]

 (b) From the 8th thereof until the close of the festival (of Passover) a holiday of a week was declared, during which mourning is forbidden.[3]

II. (a) On the 7th of Iyyar, the dedication of the wall of Jerusalem took place, and it is forbidden to mourn thereon.[4]

 (b) On the 14th thereof the Minor Passover [was slaughtered] and mourning is forbidden.[5]

 (c) On the 23rd thereof the garrison departed from Jerusalem.[6]

 (d) On the 27th thereof payment of the tribute from [Judah and] Jerusalem was discontinued.[7]

III. (a) On the 14th of Sivan the tower of the Fort was captured.[8]

 (b) On the 15th and 16th thereof the people of Bethshan and the valley were exiled.[9]

 (c) On the 25th thereof the publicans were removed from Judah and Jerusalem.[10]

IV. On the 4th (10th) of Tammuz the book of the decrees was removed [mourning is not allowed].[11]

V. (a) On the 15th of Ab, the day of Xylophoria, mourning is forbidden.[12]

 (b) On the 24th thereof we return to our Law.[13]

VI. (a) On the 7th of Elul fell the dedication of the wall of Jerusalem; mourning is forbidden.[14]

363

    (b) On the 17th thereof the Romans departed from Judah and Jerusalem.[15]

    (c) On the 22nd thereof we began to slay the wicked.[16]

VII.   On the 3rd of Tishri the "mention" (of the reigning rulers) on documents was discontinued.[17]

VIII. (a) On the 23rd of Heshvan the Sorega was removed from the Azarah.[18]

    (b) On the 25th thereof the wall of Samaria was taken.[19]

    (c) On the 27th thereof the offerings of fine flour were again begun to be brought on the altar.[20]

IX.   (a) On the 3rd of Kislev the ensigns were removed from the Court.[21]

    (b) On the 7th thereof is [a holiday].[22]

    (c) On the 21st thereof was the day of Mount Gerizim [on which mourning is not allowed].[23]

    (d) On the 25th thereof is the day of Hanukkah: for eight days mourning is forbidden.[24]

X.   On the 28th of Tebeth the Assembly sat in judgment.[25]

XI.   (a) On the 7th of Shebat is a holiday, whereon mourning is not allowed.[26]

    (b) On the 22nd thereof the work that the enemy commanded to bring into the Temple was stopped; mourning is not allowed.[27]

    (c) On the 28th thereof [king Antiochus] departed from Jerusalem.[28]

XII. (a) On the 8th and the 9th of Adar supplications were offered and the *shofar* was sounded for rain.[29]

    (b) On the 12th thereof is the day of Tyrian.[30]

    (c) On the 13th thereof is the day of Nicanor.[31]

    (d) On the 14th and the 15th thereof [are the days of] Purim, on which mourning is not allowed.[32]

    (e) On the 16th thereof the building of the wall of Jerusalem was begun; mourning is forbidden thereon.[33]

(f) On the 17th thereof the Gentiles arose against the refugees of Sepphoris in the province of Chalcis and in Bet Zabdain; but salvation came.[34]

(g) On the 20th thereof the people fasted for rain.[35]

(h) On the 28th thereof glad tidings came to the Judaeans that they were not to be prevented from studying the Torah. Mourning is not permitted thereon.[36]

DIALOGUES BETWEEN THE SADDUCEES AND THE PHARISEES

The Sadducees say: We protest against you, Pharisees, because you declare that an object (that is, detached seed) upon which water has been poured is clean. The Pharisees say: We protest against you, Sadducees, that you declare clean a stream of water which comes from a cemetery.[1]

The Sadducees say: We protest against you, Pharisees, because you say, "If my ox or my ass, who are not obliged to observe commandments, cause injuries, I am responsible; but, then, if my bondman or my bondwoman, who are obliged to fulfill certain commandments, cause injuries, I should certainly be responsible." They [the Pharisees] said to them [the Sadducees]: No! As you argue concerning my ox or my ass, which have no understanding, would you likewise argue concerning my bondman or my bondwoman who do have understanding?[2]

Said the Boethuseans [Sadducees]: We protest against you, Pharisees: the daughter of my son who derives her claim from my son, who in turn derives his claims from me, is entitled to inherit me, surely my daughter, who derives her claim directly from me, should certainly have the right to inherit me. Said the Pharisees: No! If you speak about the daughter of my son, she has the right to share the inheritance with her brothers; but my own daughter does not share the inheritance with her brothers.[3]

Said the Sadducees: We protest against you Pharisees because you say the Holy Scripture defiles the hands, [but] the writings of Homer do not defile the hands.[4]

Said the Galilean [Judah]: I protest against you Pharisees because you write into the documents the name of the ruler together with the Name [divine]. [Said the Pharisees:] We protest against you, Galilean, for you write the name of the ruler on the same page with the Name [divine], i.e., in the Torah you write Pharaoh, king of Egypt, by the side of the Name [divine].[5]

THE SADDUCEES AND THE PHARISEES IN THE
WRITINGS OF JOSEPHUS

The Pharisees are those who are considered most skillful in the exact interpretation of the laws, and who hold the position of the leading sect. They attribute everything to fate and to God; they hold that no act, right or otherwise, rests, indeed, for the most part with men, but that in each action fate plays a part. Every soul, they maintain, is imperishable, but the soul of the good alone passes into another body, while the souls of the wicked suffer eternal punishment.

The Sadducees, the second in order, do away with fate entirely, and maintain that God is not concerned in our doing or not doing what is evil. They say that man has the free choice of good and evil and that it rests with each man's will whether he follows the one or the other. As for the immortality of the soul after death, penalties in the underworld or rewards, they will have none of these.

The Pharisees are friendly to one another and cultivate harmonious relations with the community. The Sadducees, on the other hand, are, even among themselves, rather boorish in their behavior, and in their intercourse with those of their own party are as rude as they are to strangers. *War* 2. 8. 14 (162-166).

At this time there were three schools of thought among the Judaeans who had different opinions concerning human affairs: one called the Pharisees, the second the Sadducees, and the third the Essenes. As for the Pharisees, they say that some actions, but not all, are the work of Fate; some of the events depend upon ourselves whether they shall take place or not. The sect of the Essenes, however, declared that Fate governs all things and that nothing befalls man unless it be in accordance with her decree. The Sadducees do away with Fate, holding that there is no such thing and that the human actions are not achieved in accordance with her decree; but they suppose that all our actions are in our own power, so that we are ourselves the cause of what is good, and we suffer misfortune through our own thoughtlessness. *Ant.* 13. 5. 9 (171-173).

As for Hyrcanus, the envy of the Judaeans was aroused against him by his own successes and those of his sons; particularly hostile to him were the Pharisees, who are one of the Judaean schools [of thought], as we have already related. These have such great influence over the multitude that even when they speak against a king or high priest they are immediately believed. Hyrcanus was a disciple of theirs and was greatly loved by them. Once he invited them to a feast and entertained them very kindly and, when he saw them in good spirits, he began by saying that they knew of his wish to be righteous and that he tried to please God and them in everything he did—for the Pharisees profess such beliefs. At the same time he asked them, if they observed him doing anything wrong or straying from the right path, to lead him back to it and correct him. But they testified to his being altogether virtuous, and he was delighted with their praise. But one of the guests, named Eleazar, a man of ill temper and delighting in seditious practices, said, "Since you have asked to be told the truth, if you wish to be righteous, give up the high priesthood and be content with the leadership over the people." And when Hyrcanus asked him for what reason he should give up the high priesthood, he replied, "Because we have heard from our elders that your mother was a captive in the reign of Antiochus Epiphanes." The story was false, and Hyrcanus was furious with the man, and all the Pharisees were very indignant.

Now there was one Jonathan, a great friend of Hyrcanus, belonging to the school of the Sadducees whose opinions are contrary to those of the Pharisees. He told Hyrcanus that Eleazar's slanderous statement had the approval and was in accord with the sentiments of the Pharisees. This, he added, would be clear to Hyrcanus if he inquired of them what punishment Eleazar deserved for what he had said. And so Hyrcanus asked the Pharisees what penalty they thought he deserved—for, he said, he would test whether the slanderous statement had not been made with their approval if they fixed a penalty commensurate with the crime. They replied that Eleazar deserved stripes and chains; for they did not think it right to sentence a man to death for slander, and anyway the Pharisees were lenient in the matter of punishment. At this Hyrcanus became very angry and began to believe that the man had slandered him with their approval. And Jonathan, in particular, inflamed his anger and so worked upon him that he brought him to join the Sadduceans, and desert the Pharisees, and abrogate the regulations which they had established for the people, and punish those who observed them. Out of this grew the hatred of the masses for him and his sons. But of this we shall speak hereafter; for the present I wish merely to explain that the Pharisees had passed on to the people certain regulations handed down by former generations and not recorded in the Laws of Moses, for which reason they are rejected by the Sadducean group, who hold that only those regulations should be considered valid which were written down, and that those which had been handed down by former generations need not be followed. And concerning these matters the two parties came to have controversies and serious differences, the Sadducees having the confidence of the wealthy alone but no following among the populace, while the Pharisees had the support of the multitude. *Ant.* 13. 10. 5-6 (288-298).

There was also a group of Judaeans priding itself on its adherence to ancestral custom and claiming to observe the laws which God approves; and by these men, called Pharisees, the women were guided. These men were able to help the king greatly because of their foresight, and yet they were obviously intent upon combating and injuring him. At least, when the Judaeans affirmed by an oath that they would be loyal to Caesar and to the king's government, these men, over six thousand in number, refused to take this oath; and when the king punished them with a fine, Pheroras' wife paid the fine for them. In return for her friendliness they foretold—

for they were believed to have foreknowledge of things through God's appearing to them—that by God's decree Herod's throne would be taken from him, both from himself and his descendants, and the royal power would fall to her and Pheroras and to any children that they might have. These things, which did not remain unknown to Salome, were reported to the king, and also how they had perverted some persons at the court. And the king put to death those of the Pharisees who were most to blame and the eunuch Bagoas and a certain Karos, who was outstanding among his contemporaries for his surpassing beauty and was loved by the king. He also killed all those of his household who approved of what the Pharisees said. *Ant.* 17. 2. 4 (41-44).

The Judaeans, from ancient times, had three philosophies concerning their traditions: the Essenes, the Sadducees, and thirdly the group who were called the Pharisees. . . .

The Pharisees simplified their standards of living and despised luxuries. They followed the guidance of that which their doctrine had selected and transmitted as good, attaching the chief importance to the observance of those commandments which their doctrine seemed to dictate to them. They show respect and deference to their elders; nor do they rashly presume to contradict them in anything which they have introduced. Though they postulate that everything is brought about by fate, still they do not deprive the human will of the pursuit of what is in man's power, since it was God's good pleasure that there should be a coalition between fate's council-chamber and such men as choose to associate themselves with it, with virtuous or vicious intent. They believe that souls have power to survive death and that there are rewards and punishments under the earth for those who have led lives of virtue or of vice; eternal imprisonment is the lot of evil souls, while the good souls shall revive and live again. Because of these views, they are extremely influential among the people; and all vows and rites of divine worship are performed according to their direction. This is the great tribute that the people of the cities paid to them by practicing the highest ideals both in their way of living and in their discourse.

The Sadducees hold that the soul dies with the body. They do not accept the observance of anything besides what the Law enjoins upon them; in fact, they consider it a virtue to dispute with the teachers about the part of wisdom which they pursue. There are but few men to whom this doctrine has been made known, although they are men of the highest standing. They accomplish almost nothing. For, whenever they assume some office, though they submit unwillingly and perforce, yet they do submit to the formulas of the Pharisees because the multitude would not otherwise tolerate them. *Ant.* 18. 1. 2 (11-17).

He (the high priest Ananus) followed the school of the Sadducees, who are very rigid in judging offenders above all the rest of the Judaeans. *Ant.* 20. 9. 1 (199).

I (Josephus) began to govern my life by the doctrines of the Pharisees, a sect having points of resemblance with that which the Hellenes call the Stoic School. *Vita* 12.

This Simon (the son of Gamaliel) was a native of Jerusalem, of a very illustrious family, and of the School of the Pharisees who have the reputation of being unrivaled experts in the rules of their fathers. *Vita* 191.

THE CHRIST PASSAGE IN JOSEPHUS

In all editions and extant manuscripts of Josephus' book of *Antiquities,* there is a well known Christ passage wherein he refers to Jesus as the Christ, who was condemned by Pilate to the cross at the suggestion of the principal men of Judaea.

3. [Γίνεται δὲ κατὰ τοῦτον τὸν χρόνον Ἰησοῦς σοφὸς ἀνήρ, εἴγε ἄνδρα αὐτὸν λέγειν χρή· ἦν γὰρ παραδόξων ἔργων ποιητής, διδάσκαλος ἀνθρώπων τῶν ἡδονῇ τἀληθῆ δεχομένων, καὶ πολλοὺς μὲν Ἰουδαίους, πολλοὺς δὲ καὶ τοῦ Ἑλληνικοῦ ἐπηγάγετο· ὁ χριστὸς οὗτος ἦν. καὶ αὐτὸν ἐνδείξει τῶν πρώτων ἀνδρῶν παρ' ἡμῖν σταυρῷ ἐπιτετιμηκότος Πιλάτου οὐκ ἐπαύσαντο οἱ τὸ πρῶτον ἀγαπήσαντες· ἐφάνη γὰρ αὐτοῖς τρίτην ἔχων ἡμέραν πάλιν ζῶν τῶν θείων προφητῶν ταῦτά τε καὶ ἄλλα μυρία περὶ αὐτοῦ θαυμάσια εἰρηκότων. εἰς ἔτι τε νῦν τῶν Χριστιανῶν ἀπὸ τοῦδε ὠνομασμέ-νον οὐκ ἐπέλιπε τὸ φῦλον.][1]

Ever since the sixteenth century, the authenticity of this passage has been suspected. From the time of Reformation down to our own day, many scholars have argued against the genuineness of the passage. Schürer,[2] Niese,[3] and Norden[4] reject this passage as a genuine statement by Josephus and claim that, if not all, at least a great part of it is a Christian interpolation. Their principal argument against the genuineness is that Josephus, a loyal Jew, could not have written that Jesus was Christ and that "on the third day [he] appeared to them restored to life." On the other hand, scholars like Burkitt,[5] and Harnack[6] maintain the authenticity of this passage. Some scholars maintain that the phrases, "Jesus was the Christ" and "he arose from the dead," are indeed Christian interpolations, while the entire passage is genuine.[7] The Greek style of this passage is the style of Josephus, Thackeray wrote, "If these words are a Christian interpolation, they are an artistic forgery."[8] No doubt, they are an artistic forgery.

None of the Church Fathers of the ante-Nicene period quotes this Christ passage. Origen on three occasions quotes the James passage with some variations.[9] He says that according to Josephus the execution of James, the brother of Jesus who was called Christ, caused the destruction of the Temple. This statement is not found in *Antiquities*. The author of *Chronicom Paschale*[10] quotes the same James passage, not from *Antiquities*, but from *War*. Eusebius, in the name of Hegesippus, states that James was thrown from the roof of the Temple, stoned, killed and that immediately thereafter Vespasian laid siege to Jerusalem.[11] None of these Church Fathers refers to the Christ passage. According to Origen, the James passage was given by Josephus in *Antiquities*, while according to the *Paschale* this passage is recorded in *War*. There is no such passage in our edition of *War* by Josephus. Both Origen and Hegesippus, according to Eusebius, connect the killing of James with the burning of the Temple.

Origen not only does not refer to the Christ passage but, from his language, it is impossible to assume that he knew of this passage. He wrote, "Now this writer (Josephus), although not believing in Jesus as the Christ, in seeking after the cause of the fall of Jerusalem and the destruction of the Temple, whereas he ought to have said that the conspiracy against Jesus was the cause of these calamities befalling the people, since they put to death Christ, who was a prophet, says nevertheless—being, although against his will, not far from the truth—that these distresses happened to the Jews as a punishment of James the Just."[12] If the Christ passage indeed appeared and had the phrase "He was the Christ," it seems impossible to assume that Origen, who quotes the James passage, would ignore the Christ passage. Furthermore, he would not have said that Josephus did not believe that Jesus was the Christ, for the Christ passage contained the phrase "He was the Christ." The first of the Church Fathers to quote the Christ passage from Josephus is Eusebius. Therefore it is logical to assume that the phrase, "He was the Christ," was interpolated some time in the early fourth century, since none of the ante-Nicene fathers ever refers to it.

The scholars who uphold the authenticity of the passage claim that no Christian would have described Christians as a "tribe," and that therefore the word "tribe" shows this passage to have been written by Josephus. It is true, throughout the entire literature of the ante-Nicene Fathers the word "tribe" "race" as referring to Christians is never used either by the Fathers themselves or by quoting pagan writers. The first to use this word "tribe" with reference to Christians was Eusebius when quoting Pliny the Younger and the Emperor Trajan. Eusebius tells us, in the name of Tertullian, that when Pliny the Younger, governor of Bithynia, wrote to Trajan asking for instructions about the Christian tribe, Trajan in reply wrote that, "The tribe of Christians should not be sought after, but when found should be punished."[13] Tertullian, in telling about the persecutions,[14] used the word "Christians" and *hoc genus*, "this people," but not the word *tribus*. Rufinus, who lived at the end of the fourth and the beginning of the fifth centuries, translated Eusebius' *Ecclesiastical History* into Latin. In translating this passage by Eusebius, he does not use the word *tribus*, as we should expect from the word *phulon*, but the word *Christiani* alone,[15] since Rufinus, who was acquainted with the work of Tertullian in the original Latin, did not find the word *tribus* and hence ignored the word. In this instance he departs from his usual literal translation in favor of Tertullian's own phrase.

Pliny's letter to the Emperor Trajan reads in part as follows:

It is a rule, lord, which I inviolably observe, to refer myself to you in all my doubts; for who is more capable of guiding my uncertainty or informing my ignorance? Having never been present at any trials of the Christians, I am unacquainted with the method and limits to be observed either in examining or punishing them. Whether any difference is to be made on account of age, or no distinction allowed between the youngest and the adult; whether repentance admits to a pardon, or if a man has been once a Christian it avails him nothing to repent; whether the mere profession of Christianity, albeit without crimes, or only the crimes associated therewith are punishable—in all these points I am greatly doubtful. . . . Those who deny they were, or had ever been, Christians, who repeated after me an invocation to the gods and offered adoration, with wine and frankincense, to your image which I had ordered to be brought for that purpose together with those of the gods, and who finally cursed Christ—none of which acts, it is said, those who are really Christians can be forced into performing—these I thought it proper to discharge. Others who were named by the informer at first confessed themselves Christians and then denied it—true, they had been of that persuasion but they had quitted it, some three years, others many years, and a few as much as twenty-five years ago. They all worshiped your statue and the images of the gods and cursed Christ.[16]

The letter of Trajan to Pliny reads in part as follows:

The method you have pursued, my dear, in sifting the cases of those denounced to you as Christians, is extremely proper. . . . Information without the accuser's name subscribed must not be admitted in evidence against anyone as it is introducing a very dangerous precedent, and by no means agreeable to the spirit of the age.[17]

It is certainly strange that in the letter of Pliny to Trajan and the reply of the emperor, the phrase "tribe of Christians" is not used, but only Christians, and the source (Tertullian), from which Eusebius draws the term "tribe," is not prefixed to the word Christians. Eusebius in quoting these passages prefixed the word *tribe* in speaking of Christians.

In sum: The non-Christian writers in speaking of Christians did not prefix the word "tribe," nor did the early Church Fathers in quoting the non-Christian writers about Christians ever prefix the word "tribe." Eusebius was the first to do so. It was previously stated that those who maintained the authenticity of the Christ passage argued that no Christian would use the phrase "tribe of Christians," hence it came from the hand of Josephus. But, as was demonstrated above, neither non-Christians nor the Church Fathers before the time of Eusebius employed the term "tribe of Christians" when quoting non-Christian writers. My conclusion was that the phrase "tribe of Christians" which is found in the Christ passage of Josephus came from the same author who used it in quoting pagan writers. Eusebius interpolated this passage in Josephus.

The theory that Eusebius interpolated the Christ passage in Josephus may be questioned on the ground that Eusebius was not a forger, and that this supposition is not in accord with what was known of his character.

Every student of the history of religion knows that interpolation was not considered forgery. The early Christians interpolated many passages of a Christian nature in the Septuagint version of the Bible. Justin Martyr was so convinced of the genuineness of these passages that he accused the Jews of removing them from the Hebrew text. To cite two instances: Justin Martyr, in his *Dialogue with Trypho,* accused the Jews of removing the following passages from the Hebrew Bible:

And Esdras said to the people, this passover is our Savior and our refuge.

Likewise he quotes the following passage from Jeremiah:

The Lord God remembered His dead people of Israel who lay in the graves; and He descended to preach to them His own salvation.[18]

Needless to say these passages were not in the Hebrew Bible, but were interpolated in the Septuagint by Christians.

Eusebius was a theologian interested in showing that Jesus was the Christ whom the prophets had foretold and that he suffered as had been prophesied. He was also a historian, a student and admirer of the works of Josephus. He wrote the history of the Church and was interested in giving an account of the earthly life of Jesus. In reading Josephus' history of the Jews, he was doubtless surprised to find no mention of Jesus. Feeling certain about Jesus' earthly life and his crucifixion under Pontius Pilate, he certainly thought that the complete omission of the story from Josephus was due either to the author's malice or to the deletion of this passage by the Jews, as Justin Martyr thought that the Jews had removed certain Christian passages from the Hebrew Bible. Eusebius therefore took it upon himself to restore the passage which he thought had been deleted.

He had to restore the passage not only in the language of Josephus, with which he was thoroughly familiar, but also in words which Josephus might have used as a non-Christian, and which nevertheless would not be offensive to the Christian point of view, that is, his own. Eusebius was careful to make Josephus retain his Jewish character. It is therefore easy to understand such phrases as "he was a wise man" and "even now the tribe of Christians, so named from him, is not extinct." He thought that these phrases were in consonance with the spirit of Josephus' work as of a non-Christian. The phrases "He was the Christ" and "as the divine prophets had foretold these and ten thousand other wonderful things concerning him" are in accord with the Christian view, that is, his own view.[19]

APPENDIX V

CHRONOLOGICAL TABLE OF THE HIGH PRIESTS

Ananel (Hananel)
Aristobolus
Ananel
Joshua, son of Phabes (Phabi)
Simon, son of Boethus (or rather Boethus himself was appointed high priest by Herod)
Matthias, son of Theophilus
Joazar, son of Simon (grandson of Boethus)
Eleazar, brother of Joazar
Joshua, son of See
Joazar, grandson of Boethus (for the second time)
Ananus, son of Seth
Ishmael, son of Phabi
Eleazar, son of Ananus
Simon, son of Camith
Joseph Caiaphas, son-in-law of Ananus
Jonathan, son of Ananus
Theophilus, brother of Jonathan
Simon, son of Boethus
Matthias, son of Ananus
Elionaeus, son of Contheros
Joseph, son of Cami
Ananias, son of Nedebaeus
Ishmael, son of Phabi
Joseph Cabi, son of Simon
Ananus, son of Ananus
Joshua, son of Damnaeus
Joshua, son of Gamala (Gamaliel)
Matthias, son of Theophilus

APPENDIX VI

THE PROCURATORS

Coponius   6-9
Marcus Ambivius   9-11
Annius Rufus   11-14
Valerus Gratus   14-26
Pontius Pilate   26-36
Marcellus   36-37
Marullus   37-41
Fadus   45-46
Tiberus Julius Alexander   46-48
Ventidius Cumanus   48-52
Marcus Antoninus Felix   52-59/60
Porcius Festus   59-60/62
Albinus   62-64
Gessius Florus   64 until the end of 65

APPENDIX VII

KEY FIGURES AND EVENTS IN JUDAEA

Herod became king tenth of Tebet January 13/14, 37 B.C.E.
Aristobulus was appointed high priest   36
Aristobolus was drowned in the Autumn   36
A severe earthquake occurred in Judaea in
   which thirty thousand people perished Spring 31
Octavian Caesar defeated Antony at Actium
                   September 2. 31
Hillel was appointed Nasi of the Great *Bet Din*   31
Hyrcanus the grandfather of Mariamme was
                     executed 30
Queen Mariamme was executed   29/28
Alexandra, mother of Mariamme, was executed   28/27
Building of the Temple   20
The city of Caesarea was completed   10
Agrippa, son of Aristobolus, was born   10
Alexander and Aristobolus were executed   7
Antipater, son of Herod, was executed   4
The two sophists were executed   March 13, 4
On that very night there was an eclipse of the
   moon
Herod died   Adar 28, 4
Archelaus was appointed ethnarch   4
Archelaus was banished to Vienne   6 C.E.
Judaea was made a province of Rome   6
Augustus Caesar died   14
John the Baptist was slain   33/34
Jesus of Nazareth was crucified in the Spring   34
Tiberius Caesar died   37
Agrippa was appointed king over the tetrarchy
   of his uncle Philip   37
Gaius Caligula ordered to erect a statue of
   himself in the Temple   39/40
Gaius Caligula was assassinated   January 24, 41
Claudius Caesar appointed Agrippa king of
   Judaea   41

King Agrippa died   44
Judaea again became a province of Rome   44
Nero became emperor of Rome   October 13, 54
Paul (Saul) came to Jerusalem for the second
    time and was arrested during the procurator-
    ship of Felix   58/59
The revolt against Rome broke out   June 4, 65
The Romans were forced to leave Jerusa-
    lem Tishri 3   September 24, 65
Menachem, the leader of the Sicarii, was assassi-
    nated   Autumn 65
The Judaeans defeated the army of Cestius
    Kislev 7   November 25, 65
Massacre of the Judaeans in Syria   December 65
A provisional government was established to per-
    secute the war against the Romans   January 66
A conclave of spiritual leaders assembled. The
    Scriptures were canonized and became the
    third part of the Hebrew Canon   End of 65
                                        beginning of 66
Megillat Ta'anit was compiled   beginning of 66

APPENDIX VIII

SABBATICAL CYCLES

38-37.[1] 31-30, 24-23, 17-16, 10-9, 3-2, 5-6 (C.E.) 12-13,
19-20, 26-27, 33-34, 40-41,[2] 47-48, 54-55, 61-62.

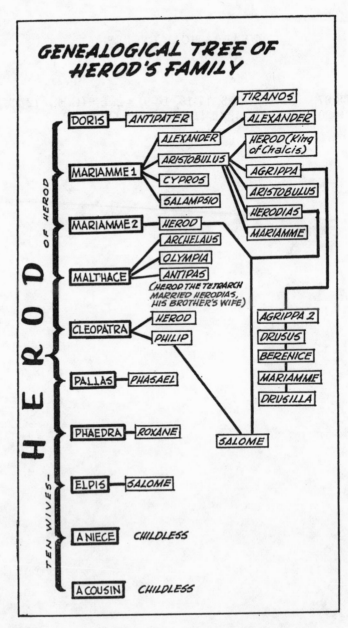

GENEALOGICAL TREE OF
HEROD'S FAMILY

THE TERMS SYNEDRION, SANHEDRIN
(BET DIN)

It is well known that the word Sanhedrin is of Greek origin: *synedrion*. The word *synedrion* has the connotation of assembly, a gathering of people. From Greek literature it is evident that the *synedrion* was not a permanent institution. It was invoked by the rulers of the state for advice and consultation whenever the need arose.

Herodotus (484-425 BCE) used the term *synedrion* in a number of places in the sense of an assembly convened for a certain purpose. In his narrative of the capture and burning of the hall of the Acropolis, when the Greeks of Salamis were divided in their opinion as to the continuation of the war, he states that those who were for the continuation of the struggle left the *synedrion*, assembly, and embarked on their vessels to fight further.[1] In another passage he relates that on the one occasion when Themistocles found the Peloponnesians were outvoting him he left the *synedrion*, conference.[2] Herodotus further relates that Aeginna Aristides, an Athenian, once came to the place of the *synedrion*, council, and called Themistocles out.[3]

Xenophon (434-355) also employed the word *synedrion* in the sense of council. In his *Hellenica*, Xenophon says that Hermocrates enjoyed the greatest reputation in the *synedrion*, council.[4] In his book *Memorabilia*, he says that Euthydemus was reluctant to join the *synedrion*, council.[5]

Isocrates (436-388), in his oration to Nicocles, contrasts the inefficiency of a democracy to the advantage of a monarchy, and says: "When they assemble in *synedria* you will find them more often quarreling with each other than deliberating together, while the latter [the monarchy], for whom no *synedrion* or times of meetings are prescribed but who apply themselves to the state's business both day and night, do not let opportunities pass them by but act in each case at the right moment."[6]

The historians Thucydides (460-395) and Polybius (205-123) used the term *synedrion* in the meaning of assembly.[7] Polybius states that during the wars in which the Romans were engaged against Hannibal, Tiberius [consul] had many *synedreue*, conferences, with Publius Scipio.[8] In another passage Polybius used the term *synedrion* in the sense of a meeting or conference. He says that "the leaders of the Gauls, on seeing the campfires at night, surmised that the enemy had arrived and held a *synedros*, a council."[9] In the same vein the word *synedrion* was used by Demosthenes (384-322).[10] Strabo (63 BCE-23 CE) used the term *synedrion* in the sense of a conference. Of the members of the Lycian League who had the right to vote, he says: "They come together from each city to a general conference, *synedrion*. . . . At the conference, *synedrion*, they first choose a Lyciarch, and then other officials of the league and courts of justice, *dikasteria*, are designated." (*Geography*, 14.3)

The author of II Maccabees relates that when Demetrius ascended the throne Alcimus went to see him and complained about Judah Maccabee. Demetrius called Alcimus into a *synedrion*, a conference.[11] It is well known that II Maccabees is an epitome of a larger work by Jason of Cyrene. This work was written in Greek and made use of Greek sources. Thus the word *synedrion* was used in Greek literature in the sense of conference or council, military or civil.

The Septuagint version of the Pentateuch does not employ the word *synedrion*. In the Septuagint version of Jeremiah the word *synedrion* occurs once.[12] Likewise in the Book of Psalms the term *synedrion* is also found only once.[13] In the Book of Proverbs the term *synedrion* occurs eight times in the sense of council.[14] However, the exact date of the Greek translation of these biblical books cannot be ascertained.

The term *synedrion* occurs frequently in Judeo-Hellenistic literature in the sense of assembly or council. In the book of Ben Sira the word *synedros* has the meaning of to sit together: "Sit not, *synedreue*, in judgment with sinners."[15] "Remember your father and your mother when thou sittest, *synedreuis*, among great men."[16] In the book of Judith the term *synedrion* was used in the sense of council of Holofornes.[17]

In the Songs of Solomon, which have come down to us in Greek, though the original was in Hebrew, the word *synedrion* was used in the sense of a council.[18] Similarly, the word *synedrion* was used in IV Makkabees in the sense of a council.[19]

Philo in his writings mentions the word *synedrion* quite frequently in the sense of an assembly or council.[20] He also refers metaphorically to the soul as the *synedrion*, the assembly of the body.[21]

Josephus uses the word *synedrion* quite often in his works. In his book *Jewish War*, the term *synedrion* is always used in the sense of council or conference. Josephus tells us that when Herod presented the case against his sons to Augustus Caesar, Augustus granted him complete freedom of action. However, he advised Herod "to hold an inquiry into the plot before a joint *synedrion*, council, of his own relative and provincial government."[22] In another passage Josephus says that when Herod became indignant at the wife of his brother Pheroras, he "assembled a *synedrion*, council, of his friends and relations and accused this wretched woman of numerous misdeeds."[23] Josephus further relates that when Herod became aware of the plots of his son Antipater he "assembled a *synedrion*, council, of his relatives and friends."[24] In another passage the historian says that after the death of Herod, when the rivals for the kingdom of Judaea presented their cases for Augustus to decide, the emperor "summoned a *synedrion*, council, of the leading Romans."[25] Augustus, after hearing the case, dismissed the *synedrion*, council.[26] Josephus further says that when a Jewish embassy came to Rome to present their case against the Herodian family, "Caesar assembled a *synedrion*, council, composed of the Roman magistrates and his friends in the temple Palatine Apollo."[27] After hearing the case presented by the embassy, Augustus dismissed the *synedrion*.[28]

In *Antiquities*, which was composed in the year 93 C.E., the term *synedrion* appears many times. Josephus says that Gabinius divided the country of Judaea into five *synedria*, councils.[29] The historian relates that when Herod was accused of killing innocent men while he was governor of Galilee, he was summoned to appear before a *synedrion*.[30] Here for the first and only time Josephus uses the term *synedrion* in the sense of a court. In all other cases he does not use the term *synedrion* in the sense of a court but of a council, called by the ruler for a particular purpose. He tells us that Herod, in order to find a reason for executing the deposed king Hyrkanus, produced a letter before the *synedrion* which Hyrkanus had supposedly written to Malchus.[31] Josephus further relates that when the Levites insisted that King Agrippa allow them to wear linen garments such as were worn by the priests, Agrippa called a *synedrion* to give them permission to do so.[32] Josephus states that the high priest appointed a *synedrion*, council, of judges and charged James with transgression.[33]

Josephus, in his *Vita*,[34] says that after his arrival in Galilee he wrote a full report to the *synedrion*, council, of Jerusalem concerning the conditions in the country.[35] Thus we see that the term *synedrion* in the sense of a court was used for the first and only time in his book *Antiquities*, composed in the year 93 C. E.

In the Talmud the term Sanhedrin has the meaning of court. The problem now confronts us as to how the word *synedrion*, which was used in the entire Greek literature as well as in Judeo-Hellenistic literature in the sense of council, came to be termed in the Talmud a court. Further, how is it that Josephus in his first book, *Jewish War*, does not use the term *synedrion* in the sense of a court, while in his book *Antiquities*, which was composed two decades later, he uses the term *synedrion*, although only once, in the sense of a court? To answer this question we must give a short survey of the development of the judiciary system among the Judaeans.

DEVELOPMENT OF THE JEWISH JUDICIAL SYSTEM

In the early period of Jewish history there was no organized court as such. In the book of Exodus we read, "But if a servant shall plainly say, 'I love my master, my wife, my children, I will not go out free,' then his master shall bring him unto *Elohim*."[36] In the Talmud the word *Elohim* was interpreted to mean judges.[37] The Septuagint renders the word *Elohim* the court of God. In the same book it is further stated, "For every matter of trespass, whether it be for an ox . . . both parties shall come before *Elohim*; he whom *Elohim* shall condemn shall pay double unto his neighbor."[38] Again the Talmud interprets the word *Elohim* as judges.[39]

The book of Exodus tells us that Moses judged the people. However, his father-in-law, Jethro, advised him to appoint others who would judge the people. Only a matter of great importance, he told Moses, should be brought before him, while small matters should be judged by the appointees.[40] In the book of Deuteronomy it is stated that the Jews were directed to appoint judges and officers in the cities who were to judge the people with righteous judgment.[41] In the same book we read, "If there arise a matter too hard for thee in judgment . . . and thou shalt come unto the priests, the Levites, and unto the judge that shall be in those days; thou shalt inquire, and they shall declare unto thee the sentence of judgment."[42]

Was there thus instituted a court of justice in the early days of the Hebrews? There is no historical evidence of such an institution. According to the Bible, Moses was the chief justice. After his death Joshua became the supreme judge. After the death of Joshua those who saved the Israelites from their oppressors by military exploits became judges. The Book of Judges says, "When God raised them up judges, then God was with the judge and saved them out of the hands of their enemies all the days of the judge."[43] Othniel, the son of Kenaz, judged Israel because he had defeated the king of Aram. In fact, all the men who helped the Israelites defeat their enemies became their leaders and their judges. Among them was a woman named Deborah, who also judged the children of Israel; she had participated in the defeat of Sisera, the captain of the king of Canaan.[44]

The prophet Samuel was also the chief judge of Israel. When he became old he appointed his sons judges of Israel. However, his sons were not righteous, took bribes and perverted justice. Then, according to the Book of Samuel, the elders assembled and came to Samuel and said to him, "Behold, thou art old and thy sons walk not in thy ways; now make us a king to judge us like all the nations."[45]

The duty of the king was not only to rule the people and defend them against their enemies in war but also to judge them in their personal quarrels. The author of II Samuel relates that when Absalom plotted for the throne of his father, David, he used to rise early to meet the man who "had a suit which should come to the king for judgment," and he used to tell the people, "Oh that I were made judge in the land that every man who hath any suit or cause might come unto me and I would do him justice."[46] Solomon, after ascending the throne of his father, prayed to God that among other things God should grant him "an understanding heart to judge."[47] Indeed, to show that God had granted him "an understanding heart to judge," the Bible relates the well-known story of the quarrel between the two harlots who claimed the same child.[48] The kings who ruled after Solomon were also judges.

During the period of the first Temple the kings themselves were judges. In order to arbitrate the disputes between fellow men throughout the country and to exact judgment on those who transgressed the laws, the kings appointed judges in different cities who were subordinate to themselves. The author of the Book of Chronicles states that King Jehoshaphat appointed judges in every city for controversies and for transgressions of the laws of God.[49] According to Aristotle, it was the custom of all the states where lawful monarchy ruled that the kings were judges. Aristotle further tells us that they had supreme command in war and control over all sacrifices that were not in the hands of the priestly class. In addition to these functions they were judges. Some gave judgment on oath and some did not. The oath was taken by holding up the scepter.[50]

After the Restoration supreme authority over the Judaeans was vested in the high priests. This authority was confirmed by the kings of Persia, and later by the Ptolemaic and Salucidean rulers. In the year 444 B. C. E. the Pentateuch was canonized. According to Deuteronomy, the right to judge and instruct the people was given to the priests.[51] Thus the new Judaean settlement was established as a theocracy since jurisdiction over the Judaeans was vested wholly in the high priest-pontiff, who had sole authority over the Judaean people. The authority to judge the people was transferred from the kings to the priests.[52]

In the decree which the Persian kings gave to Ezra, authorizing him to appoint judges, the term *dayyonim* was used.[53] The term *dayyon* became the accepted term for a judge, and the term for court was *Bet Din*. That the court was called *Bet Din* is evident from the early tannaitic literature and from the early Judeo-Hellenistic literature. The author of the Book of Susanna relates that two elders accused Susanna of adultery and she was

condemned to death. However, a young man named
Daniel protested against the verdict and told the people
that the elders had testified falsely. She was brought
back to the *kriterion*,[54] courthouse, *Bet Din*. The men
who tried her were called *kritais*,[55] judges, *dayyonin*.
During the period of the theocracy, the high priest
presided over the *Bet Din;* he was called *Nasi*.[56] The high
priest had a council of elders called the *gerousia*,[57] which
aided him in rendering judgment and administering the
country.

With the establishment of the commonwealth, the
high priest was shorn of his authority as the head of all
the Judaeans. He no longer had the right to appoint religious judges.[58] Neither did the civil rulers, the Hasmoneans, and the Herodians have the right to interpret
religious laws. The judiciary system went through a
radical transformation. A court, a *Bet Din*, was instituted, independent of the high priests and the civil
authorities, to try religious offenders. It consisted of
twenty-three members and had a seat in every important
city. To interpret the laws, a new institution was established as a legislative body. It was called *Bet Din Ha-
Gadol*, the Great Court, and consisted of seventy-one
members. At the head of the Great Court were two men,
the *Nasi*, president, and the *Ab Bet Din*, father of the
court, second to the *Nasi*. Thus the judiciary system in
Judaea during the Second Commonwealth consisted of
two branches: the trial court, consisting of twenty-three
members, which tried religious offenders, and the legislative court, consisting of seventy-one members, which
interpreted the laws.[59] Each court had a *mufla*, a prosecutor, one who presented the case before the court.[60]

The religious court was called in Hebrew *Bet Din*,
and in Greek *kriterion*, or *dikasterion*, while the court
which decided on state matters or on matters relating to
the king was called in Greek *synedrion*.

When Judaea became a Roman province a procurator
was appointed. The internal civil matters of Judaea
were in the hands of the high priest. He was responsible

for the tranquility of the country. The high priest had the same right as the king to call a *synedrion* and to examine any suspect who stirred up trouble against the Romans; but there was a difference in their powers. The king called a *synedrion* and had the power to put the defendant to death or to inflict any other punishment upon him, while the high priest had only the duty of summoning a *synedrion*, examining the case, and then presenting the case before the procurator.[61]

In the year 70 C. E. the Romans conquered Jerusalem and the Judaeans were deprived of their political independence. As a result of the destruction of the Temple, the position of high priest disappeared. The only remaining authority was the religious court. In Judaea the religious court assumed the responsibility of supervising the people and representing the Judaeans before the Roman authorities.[62] This responsibility, which had been held before by the high priests, was thus transferred to the religious court. The religious court, which prior to the destruction of the Temple had no civil responsibility, dealt with civil matters after the destruction. The term *synedrion*, which before the destruction of the Temple had been used in connection with councils which were summoned first by the kings and later by the high priests for civil matters, was now used to designate the religious court, since it also took up civil matters. After the destruction of the Temple the court was called by its old name, *Bet Din*, and also by the Hebraic form of the Greek *synedrion*, Sanhedrin.[63] The name Sanhedrin, as applied to the religious court of Judaea, was even Latinized. Theodosius, in his laws against the Jews, uses the phrase *Palaestinae Synedriis*.[64]

The term Sanhedrin never occurs in tannaitic literature prior to the destruction of the Temple. Only in the tannaitic literature of the period after the destruction of the Temple does the term Sanhedrin occur. The *Targum Onkelos* to the Pentateuch, which was composed after the destruction of the Temple, does not use the term Sanhedrin but *Bet Din*,[65] while the *Targum Jonathan* to the

Pentateuch, which is the product of a later period, does use the term Sanhedrin.[66] Neither does the term Sanhedrin occur in the Septuagint version of the Pentateuch. Although the term Sanhedrin became synonymous with *Bet Din,* the old term for the head of the court, *Ab Bet Din,* remained. The individual member of the court was still called *dayyon.* The Talmud never uses the singular form of the collective term Sanhedrin.

Josephus, in his book *Jewish War,* published in 73 C. E. shortly after the destruction of the Temple, uses the term *synedrion* in the sense used by the Greek writers, namely, an assembly called by the rulers to deal with emergencies. On the other hand, when Josephus relates the trials of Herod and Zacharias, he does not use the term *synedrion* but the Greek term *dikasterion,* court.[67]

Josephus, in his book *Antiquities,* published *circa* 93 C. E. uses the term *synedrion* for court.[68] The reason Josephus applies the term *synedrion* to court is due to the fact that his book was published more than two decades after the destruction of the Temple when the term *synedrion,* Sanhedrin, was already applied to the Judaean courts.

Thus we believe we have established the following facts. During the Second Commonwealth the *Bet Din* tried religious offenders, while the Judaean kings and later the high priests from time to time summoned the *synedrion,* council, to deal with civil and political matters. The nomenclature *synedrion,* Sanhedrin, for the Judaean court came into vogue after the destruction of the Temple.[69]

Notes

NOTES

PART ONE

Chapter 1

1. Cf. I, pp. 410-411, nn. 70-71; *Ant.*, 14.16.4 (487), "On the solemnity of the fast:" *jejunii solemnitate.* Cf. also *Josippon, ad. loc.*
2. Cf. I, p. 400.
3. *Ibid.*, 400-409, 411.
4. Herod was born in the year 73 B.C.E.
5. Cf. I, pp. 400-401.
6. *Ibid.*, 83, 409.
7. *Ibid.*, 400.
8. See below, p. 28.
9. See below, p. 333.
10. Cf. S. Zeitlin, "Herod," in *JQR*, LIV (July 1963), pp. 1-27. See below, pp. 38.
11. See below, p. 127.
12. *Ant.*, 15.1.2 (6).
13. *Ibid.*, 15.7.10 (260-264); Cf. W. Otto, "Herodias," Paulys *Real-Encyclopadie;* Shalit, *Herod* (in Hebrew), pp. 82-83.
14. *Ant.*, 15.7.10 (264). About the Sons of Baba, see Talmud B.B.3.
15. *Ant.*, 14.10.2 (476); 15.1.2 (7); S. Zeitlin, *Megillat Taanit as a Source for Jewish Chronology and History in the Hellenistic and Roman Periods* (1922), ch. 3.
16. Cf. *Ant.*, 15.1.1 (4); J. Derenbourg, *Essai sur L'Histoire et la Géographie de la Palestine*, pp. 148-150; Lehman, "Le Procès d'Herod," *REJ*, XXIV, 68-81; S. Zeitlin, "Sameas and Pollion," *Journal of Jewish Lore and Philosophy* (1919), pp. 61-67.
17. Cf. S. Zeitlin, "Hillel," *JQR*, LIV (October 1963), pp. 161-173; *Ant.*, 17.2.1 (26).
18. *Ant.*, 14.1.3 (9).

19. *Ibid.*, 15.2.4 (22); but cf. Mishne Parah, 3.5; Hanamel the Egyptian."
20. *Ant.*, 15.2.5 (23-24); cf. also vol. I, 383.
21. *Ant.*, 15.2.6 (25-30).
22. *Ibid.* (30).
23. *War*, I.13.3 (439).
24. *Ant.*, 15.2.7 (31).
25. II Mac. 4.34.
26. *Ant.*, 15.2.7 (31).
27. *Ibid.*, 3.1 (39-41).
28. Cf. I, pp. 61 ff.
29. *Ibid.*, 124-125.
30. I. Mac. 14.35-45; vol. I, pp. 147-149, 344-346.
31. Herod's position must be kept in mind. To appoint Aristobolus to the office of high priest would have been suicidal, since his own position was still precarious. He had enemies within and outside the country. Cleopatra, as previously noted, carried deep animosity toward him and she exerted great influence over Antony. Aristobolus, the grandson of Hyrcanus II, who was now in captivity in Parthia, could, with her aid and that of the adherents of the Hasmonean family, ultimately succeed in removing Herod from the kingdom and proclaiming himself king.
32. *Ant.*, 15.3.2 (42-48).
33. Aesop had been suspected of complicity in the death of Antipater, Herod's father. He now sought to ingratiate himself with Herod.
34. Plutarch, *Antony*, 54 (Dio, 49.41; *CAH*, 10, ch. 3). After the victory of Octavian and Antony over Brutus and Cassius at Philippi, in October 42, Antony cherished an ambition to carry out Julius Caesar's dream to subdue the Parthians. In the meantime, ensnared by the charms of "the serpent of the Nile," he indulged in boisterous and sensual pleasures and neglected to organize the campaign against Parthia.
35. Plutarch, ibid., 36.
36. Dio, 49.32; *Ant.*, 15.4.1 (92).
37. Dio, 49.41.
38. Plutarch, *Antony*, 49.
39. *Ant.*, 15.4.1 (92).
40. Velleius Paterculus, *Compendium of Roman History*, 2.82. *Hanc tamen Antoninus fugam suam, quia vivus exierat, victoriam vocabat.*
41. *Ant.*, 15.4.1 (14-16).
42. Cf. I, p. 396.
43. Ant., *ibid.* (21).
44. Cf. also Schürer, *Geschichte*, I, 362; Otto, *op. cit.*, p. 42; A.H.M. Jones, *The Herods of Judaea* (Oxford, 1938) p. 54.
45. *Ant.*, 15.3.3 (50-56); 4 (57-61).
46. *Ibid.*, 5 (62-64).
47. Cf. *War*, 1.22.4 (441-443). According to *Ant.*, 15 (65),

Joseph was the uncle of Herod; cf., however, *ibid.* (169). See
also S. Zeitlin, "Herod," *JQR*, LIV (July 1963), pp. 10-11.

48. *Ant., ibid.* (68-69).
49. *Ibid.* (71).
50. *Ibid.* (72).
51. Cleopatra had killed her brother and caused the death of her
sister as threats to her ambition. Antony, after his victory
over Brutus and Cassius, killed his political opponents,
Cicero among them. Even his uncle, the brother of his
mother, was among those proscribed by him.
52. *Ant.*, 15.3.8 (78-79); *War*, 1.18.5 (361-362). According to
Plutarch, *Antony*, 36, Antony in the year 36 gave to Cleopatra as a present Phoenicia, Coele-Syria, Cyprus and a
large part of Cilicia; and still further the balsam-produc-
ing part of Judaea, and all that part of Arabia Nabataea
which slopes toward the outer sea. Cf. also Dio, 49.32.
53. Cf. I, pp. 306-307.
54. *Ant.*, 15.3.9 (81); cf. A.H.M. Jones, *The Herods of Judaea.*
55. *War*, 1.22.3 (439).
56. On these incidents see *Ant.*, 15.3.9 (84-85, 87).
57. *Ibid.*, 15.7.9 (253-258); cf. *War*, 1.24.6 (486).
58. *War*, 1.24.6 (486).
59. *Ant.*, 15.4.2 (96).
60. She seduced Julius Caesar and Antony in order to secure
her rule over Egypt, as she did not want to be a client-
queen but a factor in the affairs of Rome. Even her affair
with the young Pompey was for the sake of power. She was
tireless and fearless in seeking to achieve her goal. Her
voice had the seductive quality which attracted men. Highly
educated, she conversed in many languages including
Aramaic and Hebrew. Cf. I, p. 386, n. 100.
61. On the chronicles of Herod, see *Ant.*, 15.6.3 (174).
62. *War*, 1.19.1 (364).
63. *Ant.*, 15.10.4 (366).
64. *War*, 1.13.8 (265).
65. *Ibid.* (419).
66. *Ibid.*, 7.6.2 (171-172). Queen Salome had considered it a
strong fort and had deposited the state treasury there. It
was taken by Gabinius who destroyed it. Herod now rebuilt it.
67. *War*, 7.8.3 (280-293). It had been built by Jonathan, the
brother of Judah the Makkabee.
68. The eastern road is called The Snake, because of its resemblance to that reptile in its narrowness and continual
winding; for its course is broken by skirting the jutting
crags and, returning frequently upon itself and gradually
lengthening out again, it makes for painful headway. One
traversing this route must firmly plant each foot alternately;
he is constantly faced with destruction, for on either side
yawn chasms so terrifying as to daunt the hardiest.
69. *War*, 7.8.4 (299-300). Cf. Y. Yadin, *Masada* (New York,
1966).

70. See S. Zeitlin, "Masada and the Sicarii," *JQR*, LVI (1965), pp. 299-317.
71. Plutarch, *Antony*, 58.
72. Dio, 50.3. See I, pp. 391-392.
73. Plutarch, *Antony*, 61.
74. *Ant.*, 15.5.1 (109-110).
75. Later Herod boasted to Octavian that he had advised Antony to kill Cleopatra. If this were true, he must have done so when Herod was with Antony in Ephesus. Besides, if Herod gave this advice to Antony, he did not fully grasp the underlying forces which brought about the conflict and ultimately the war between Octavian and Antony. Octavian did use the name Cleopatra, Queen of Egypt, for propaganda purposes, to rally the Roman against Antony. After his victory over Sextus, Octavian had said there would be civil wars no longer. He made the war against Antony not a civil war but a war against Cleopatra. Historically she was used only as a screen, for ultimately Antony or Octavian had to be eliminated. There could be only one dictator over the Roman Empire. Each one had long nurtured the ambition to be the dictator of Rome, and this had to be settled on the battlefield, as had been the case between Caesar and Pompey.
76. *Ant.*, *ibid.* (111-120).
77. The earthquake occurred in the early spring of 31 B.C.E. Cf. *War*, 1.19.3 (370); S. Zeitlin, *Megillat Taanit*, 33. 25-26.
78. *Ant.*, 15.5.2 (123-124).
79. *Ibid.* (127-147).
80. *Ibid.* (147-160); *War*, 1.19.4 (375-385).
81. Plutarch, *Antony*, 71-72; Dio, 50.33.
82. Plutarch, *ibid.*, 71-72.
83. Dio, 51.7; *Ant.*, 15.6.7 (195-196).
84. Dio, 51.1-4; Plutarch, *Antony*, 74.
85. *Ant.*, 15.6.2 (165-173).
86. *Ibid.*, (174-175).
87. Cf. I, pp. 383-384.
88. *Ant.*, 15.6.5 (184).
89. The fortress Alexandrion was about three miles southwest of the confluence of the Jabbok and Jordan Rivers. (Cf. Abel, *Géographie de la Palestine*, pp. 241-242; *BASOR*, April 1936).
90. *Ant.*, 15.6.5 (185).
91. *War*, I.20.1 (388-390).
92. *Ant.*, 15.6.6 (191).
93. *War*, 1.20.1 (392); *Ant.*, 15.6.5 (195). Cf. also Plutarch, *Antony*, 71, "He (Antony) heard that Herod the Judaean, with sundry legions and cohorts, had gone over to Caesar." Cf. also above. pp. 21-22.
94. Cf. Dio, 53.25; 54.9.
95. *Ant.*, 15.6.7 (200-201).
96. Dio, 51.6.
97. Plutarch, *Antony*, 74.

98. To cite only one example from the history of that age, Antiochus IV, Epiphanes, gave orders to Andronicus to kill his own nephew, the boy Antiochus, the son of King Seleuces IV, in order to get rid of a pretender to the throne. Later Antiochus IV put Andronicus to death to show that he himself had taken no part in the murder of his nephew. Cf. Diodorus, 30.7; I, p. 80.
99. Plutarch, *Antony*, 76-77.
100. *Ibid.*, 78.
101. Suetonius, *Augustus*, 17; Dio, 51.11.
102. Cf. Dio, 51.13; Plutarch, *Antony*, 86.
103. Suetonius, *ibid.*; cf. also Dio, 14.
104. Strabo, 17.10.
105. Dio, 51.15.
106. Dio, 51.17.
107. Cf. *CAH*, 10, ch. 3.
108. *Ant.*, 15.7.3 (217); *War*, 1.20.3 (396).
109. *Ant.*, 7.1 (202-205).
110. Cleopatra committed suicide in the year 30; Mariamme was executed in 29-28.
111. *Ant., ibid.* (222-226).
112. *Ant., ibid.* (224-230); cf. *War*, 1.22.4-5 (441-443).
113. Cf. S. Zeitlin, "Herod," *JQR*, LIV (July 1963), 17-19.
114. See I, p. 383.
115. *Ant., ibid.*, 6 (237-239).
116. *Ant.*, 15.7.5 (236); *War*, 1.22.2 (435).
117. She was born 55-54 B.C.E.
118. *War*, 1.28.4 (563).
119. *Ant., ibid.* (232-233).
120. S. Zeitlin, "Herod," *JQR*, LIV (1963), 19-20.
121. *Ant., ibid.* (241-242). Herod's agony supposedly was immortalized by Byron in the opening lines of "Herod's Lament for Mariamme," in *Hebrew Melodies*:
    Oh Mariamme! now for thee
    The heart for which thou bled'st is bleeding.
    Revenge is lost in agony,
    And wild remorse to rage succeeding.
    Oh Mariamme! where art thou?
122. Talmud, B. B. 3.
123. *Ant.*, 15.7.4 (222). "One noon the king lay down to rest and, out of the great fondness which he always had for her, called for Mariamme. And so she came, but did not lie down in spite of his urging."
124. *Ibid.*, 7-8 (343-351).
125. About the Sons of Baba see above p. 6; *Ant.*, 15.7.10 (262-263); cf. ed. Niese, where he has the reading, "ten" for "twelve." Cf. also Otto, *op. cit.*
126. *Ant., ibid.* (260).
127. *Ibid.* (259).
128. *Ibid.*, 8 (267-276). *Thymelikoi*, association of entertainers: cf. Plutarch, *Sulla*, 36.
129. *Ibid.* (277-279; 282-289).

130. *Ibid.* (290).
131. Satire 3. 272-275; Suetonius, *Augustus*, 43.
132. Ex. 21.27.
133. *Ibid.*, 21.2; 22.2. See *Ant.*, 4.8.27 (242) ; S. Zeitlin, "Slavery," in *JQR*, LIV (Jan. 1963), pp. 186-187. See below pp. 271-277.
134. *Ant.*, 16.1.1 (1-15) ; cf. S. Zeitlin, *ibid.*
135. M. Git., 4.6; Tos. Git., 4.2. Cf. below, p. 273.
136. *Ant.*, 15.9.5 (330).
137. On the Apocalyptists, see below pp. 320-321. Herod cannot be compared to Jannaeus Alexander, whom the Pharisees fought in open battles. That civil war was not only motivated by religion but also by politics. Since Jannaeus Alexander was a Sadducee, he and his partisans wanted to enforce their views againt the Pharisees. Not only were the two parties divided religiously, but they had diametrically opposite views as to how the state should be governed, and this brought about the civil war. When Herod became king he endeavored to annihilate the Sadducees. The Pharisees, for their part, remembered that the wars against Jannaeus Alexander and later against Aristobolus led to the capture of the Temple by Pompey and brought about the destruction of Judaea as an independent state.
138. *Ant.*, 15.10.4 (366-368).
139. *Ibid.*, 8.5 (292-298) ; *War*, 1.21.2 (403).
140. Dio, 53.16; cf. *The Acts of Augustus*, 6.34.
141. C. Petronius was governor of Egypt in the years 24-21.
142. *Ant.*, 15.9.1-2 (299-316) ; cf. Otto, *op. cit.*
143. *Ant.*, 15.9.3 (317); Strabo, 16.22-24; Dio, 54.5; Pliny *Natural History*, 6. 181; *CAH*, 10, ch. 9.
144. *Ant.*, 15.9.3 (319-322).
145. *Ibid.*, 17.11.2 (308).
146. *War*, 1.28.4 (562-563) ; *Ant.*, 17.1.3 (19-21).
147. *Ibid.*, 16.8.1 (230). "The king had some eunuchs of whom he was immoderately fond because of their beauty."
148. *Ibid.; War*, 1.24.7 (488). "There were three eunuchs who held a special place in the king's esteem, as is indicated by the services with which they were charged: one poured out his wine, another served him his supper, and the third put him to bed and slept in his chamber."
149. *Ant., ibid.; War, ibid.*
150. *Ant.*, 17.2.4 (44). "A certain Karos who was outstanding among his contemporaries for his surpassing beauty and was loved by the king."
151. *Ibid.*, 15.9.3 (318).
152. Mark Agrippa married Julia, the daughter of Augustus: Suetonius, 63.
153. *War*, 1.21.9 (417) ; *Ant.*, 16.5.2 (142).
154. *War, ibid.*
155. *Ibid.* (418) ; *Ant.*, 16.5.2 (145).
156. *War, ibid.* (416).
157. *Ibid.*, 10 (419) ; *Ant.*, 15.9.4 (323).
158. *Ant.*, 14.15.4 (419).

159. *War*, 1.21.11 (422); *Ant.*, 16.5.3 (146-149).
160. Cf. *Ant.*, 15.9.6 (331-338); *War*, 1.21.5 (408-415).
161. *Ibid.*
162. The port was named Sebastos, that is, Augustus. *Ant.*, 15.9.6 (341); 16.5.1 (136); 17.5.1 (87). Cf. Otto, *op. cit.*; Schürer, *op. cit.*, 1.
163. N.E. of the Sea of Galilee. Aurantis is south of Trachonitis.
164. *Ant.*, 15.10.1 (344-345).
165. Cf. Dio, 54.9.
166. *Ant.*, *ibid.* (345-348).
167. Cf. Dio, 53.32; *Ant.*, 15.10.2 (250).
168. *Ibid.* (351-353).
169. Dio, 54.7.
170. *Ant.*, *ibid.* (355-358).
171. *Ibid.* (359-360).
172. *Ibid.* (362).
173. See below p. 63.
174. *Ibid.* (363-365).
175. *Ibid.*, 4 (369); cf. also 17.2.4 (42).
176. Cf. *Against Apion*, 2.70; S. Zeitlin, "The Tefillah, Shemoneh Esreh," *JQR*, LV (Jan. 1964), 225-226.
177. *Ant.*, 15.10.4 (370); cf. above, p. 6, n. 19.
178. *Ant.*, *ibid.* (371).
179. *Ibid.*, 5 (373-378). On Menaemus (Heb. Menachem), see L. Ginzberg, *On Jewish Law and Lore* (Philadelphia, 1955), p. 101; S. Hoenig, *Tarbitz* (1965); I. Rosenthal, *ibid.*
180. Cf. I, pp. 194, 319.
181. *War*, 2.8.12 (140).
182. Cf. below pp. 101-102.
183. *Ant.*, 17.2.4 (41-44).
184. *Ibid.* (44-45).
185. *Ibid.*, 14 (365).
186. Cf. I, 8-9.
187. *Ibid.*, 353-354, n. 41; 410.
188. *Ant.*, 15.11.1 (380-387).
189. *Ibid.* (388-390).
190. *Ibid.* (395-400).
191. *War*, 5.5.1 (184-189).
192. Cf. M. Mid. 2.1.
193. *Ant.*, *ibid.* (398-400); cf. F. J. Hollis, *The Archaeology of Herod's Temple* (London, 1934); André Parrot, *Le Temple de Jérusalem*, ch. 4.
194. *Ant.*, *ibid.* (413-414).
195. Cf. M. Mid., 1.3; *ibid.* (415-416); Parrot, *op. cit.*, fig. 20; Acts 3.11.
196. M. Mid., 1.3.
197. Cf. M. Mid., *ibid.*; Tamid 27.
198. There was no special "Court of Gentiles" in the Temple; it was open to all. Cf. M. Kelim 1.8.
199. M. Mid., 2.3; *War*, 5.5.2 (193).
200. One of these slabs was discovered in 1871 by Clermont-

Ganneau; it is now in the museum in Istanbul. Cf. *JQR* (1946), 387-405; *ibid.* (1947), 111-118.

201. Cf. M. Kelim 1.8; M. Mid., 2.3; *War,* 5.5.2 (194).
202. Cf. M. Kelim 1.8; M. Mid., 2.5
203. *War, ibid.;* M. Mid., *ibid.*
204. *War, ibid.,* 3 (201-202); M. Mid., 2.3.
205. M. Mid., 2.5; *War, ibid.* (201-205). The *Azarah* of the men was considered more sacred than that of the women. No women were allowed to enter the *Azarah* of the men, but the men were not excluded from the *Azarah* of the women. Cf. I, pp. 256-259.
206. M. Mid., 2.6.
207. *Ibid.; War,* 6 (225). "In front of it stood the altar, fifteen cubits high, and with a breadth and length extending alike to fifty cubits, in shape a square with horn-like projections at the corners, and approached from the south by a gently sloping acclivity."
208. *Propylaeum, ibid.;* cf. I, p. 258.
209. *War, ibid.,* 4 (217); cf. also M. Mid., *ibid.*
210. *War, ibid.,* 4-5 (207-219); cf. I, pp. 256-258.
211. *Ant.,* 15.11.5 (421); *War,* 1.21.1 (401).
212. See below, p. 228.
213. *War,* 5.5.6 (222-223). B.B. 4. Tacitus, *History,* 5.11.
214. *Ant.,* 15.11.7 (425); Tan. 23.
215. *Ant., ibid.* (423). *Josippon, ad. loc.; The Wars of the Jews,* 1688, p. 62.
216. *Ibid.* (421-423).
217. II Chron. 28.3.
218. B.B. 4; Suk. 51; cf. the readings recorded by Rabinovicz in his *variae lectiones.*
219. *Ant., ibid.* (409).
220. *Ibid.,* 4 (424); (403-408).
221. See below, p. 140.
222. Dio, 54.24. See Reinhold, *Marcus Agrippa* (1933).
223. *Ant.,* 16.2.1 (12-24).
224. *Ibid.,* 3 (27-30); 4 (31-57).
225. Cf. *Ant.,* 1.3.6 (94-95); 12.3.2 (127-128); B. Z. Wacholder, *Nicholas of Damascus* (1962), ch. 1.
226. Cf. *Ant.,* 17.5.4 (99); *War,* 2.2.3 (21).
227. Cf. A. Büchler, "The Sources of Josephus for the History of Syrian Antiquities XII, 3-XIII, 14," *JQR,* O.S. (1896); H. St. Thackeray, *Josephus the Man and the Historian* (New York, 1929), pp. 62-64; Otto, *op. cit.;* R. Laquer, *Der Jüdische Historiker Flavius Josephus* (Giessen, 1920). The question of the sources used by Josephus will be dealt with in a forthcoming volume.
228. *Ant.,* 16.2.5 (58-60).
229. *Ibid.,* 12.3.2 (125-126); 16.6.4-5 (167-170).
230. *Ibid.,* 16.6.1-3 (160-166).
231. *Ibid.,* 2 (160-165); 6 (171). These decrees were issued *c.* 14-13 B.C.E.
232. *Ibid.,* 2.5 (63-65).

233. See below, p. 60.
234. *Ibid.*, 9.1 (271-274; 276-277).
235. *Ibid.*, 5.1 (136-141).
236. Caesarea was declared to be *hutz la'aretz*, outside the land of Israel, i.e., a part of the land of the gentiles. Cf. Tos. Sheb. 8. The Talmud states (Shab. 15) that the sages of the "eighty years" before the destruction of the Temple, i.e., 10 B.C.E., declared that the land of the gentiles is ritually unclean. Cf. S. Zeitlin, *Yagdil Torah* (1920).
237. Cf. *Ant.*, 17.6.2 (151); *War*, 1.33.2 (649-650).
238. *Ant.*, 16.7.1 (179-183). Cf. *ibid.*, 7.15.3 (393); *War*, 1.2.5 (61). See I, p. 157.
239. Cf. I, p. 157.

Chapter 2

1. *Ant.*, 15.10.1 (342-343).
2. *Ibid.*, 16.1.2 (6-10).
3. *Ibid.* (11).
4. *Ibid.*, 16.3.1 (66).
5. *Ibid.* (67).
6. *Ibid.*, 3 (73).
7. *Ibid.*, 3 (78-80).
8. *Ibid.* (81-84); *War*, 1.23.1 (445-448).
9. *Ant.* (85-86).
10. According to *Ant.*, 6 (106), *War*, 1.23.3 (452), Herod took his sons to Rome, while according to *Ant.*, *ibid.* (91) the meeting with Augustus took place in Aquileia, a port at the north end of the Adriatic. See also *War*, *ibid.* (454).
11. *Ant.*, *ibid.* (92-120).
12. *Ibid.*, 4 (121-126).
13. *Ibid.*, 5 (127-128); *War*, 4 (455).
14. *Ibid.*, 6 (130-131); *War*, *ibid.* (455).
15. *Ant.*, *ibid.* (133); *War*, 5 (157).
16. *Ant.*, 17.5.1 (92).
17. *Ibid.* 16.4.6 (134-135).
18. *Ant.*, *ibid.*, 16.7.2 (188).
19. *Ibid.*, (193); *War*, 1.24.2 (475-476).
20. *War*, *ibid.* (478); *Ant.*, *ibid.*, 3 (200-201).
21. *War*, *ibid.* (479); *Ant.*, *ibid.* (203-204).
22. *Ant.*, *ibid.*, 3 (194-196).
23. *Ant. ibid.*, 4-5 (206-219).
24. *Ant.*, 16.8.1 (229-232).
25. Lev. 20.13.
26. *Ant.*, *ibid.*
27. *Ibid.*, 4 (244-251); *War*, 1.24.7 (488-497).
28. *Ant.*, *ibid.* (253).
29. Cf. Velleius Paterculus, *History of Rome*, 40; Dio, 44, 24; *Ant.*, 18.2.4 (39-52). Cf. E. Täubler, *Die Parthernachrichten*

bei Josephus (1904); N. Debevoise, *A Political History of Parthia* (1938).

30. *Ant.*, 16.8.5 (255-257).
31. Lev. 20.19-20.
32. *War*, 1.24.8 (493).
33. *War*, 16.8.1-5 (230-260).
34. *Ibid.*, 6 (261-268); *War*, 1.25.1-5 (498-510).
35. With regard to Herod's procedure towards his sons, he acted under the rights invested in him as father. Under the Roman law of *patria protestas*, the father had the rights of life and death, *jus vitae et necis*, over his sons. Indeed, when Alexander defended himself before Augustus Caesar he said, "For if you (Father) had intended to take severe actions against us, you would not have brought us before the savior of all mankind. For having both the authority of a king and the authority of a father, you might have punished the guilty. But your bringing us to Rome and making Caesar a witness was the act of one who meant to save us, since no one who intends to kill another brings him to a sanctuary or a temple." When Herod brought the case of Alexander and Aristobolus, and later Antipater, before Caesar it was not because he had not the right to put them to death, but because he wanted the approval and good will of the Emperor, who was his patron. There may have been still another reason why Herod wanted Caesar's sanction: both Alexander and Aristobolus, as well as Antipater, had been designated by him as the heirs to the throne and had been confirmed by Caesar. Therefore, Herod sought the Emperor's approval when he wanted to put the heirs to death.
36. *Ant., ibid.* (270); *War, ibid.*, 6 (511-512).
37. *Ibid.*, 16.10.1 (300-310).
38. *Ibid.*, 2 (212).
39. *Ibid.*, 3 (314).
40. *Ibid.*, 4 (317-318).
41. *Ibid.* (319); *War*, 1.26.3 (529).
42. *Ant., ibid.*, 5 (320-321).
43. *Ibid.*, 6 (325-327).
44. *Ibid.*, 7 (328-332).
45. *Ibid.* (332).
46. *Ibid.* (334).
47. *Ibid.* (334).
48. *War*, 1.24.6 (487).
49. *Ant.*, 16.7.6 (220-225).
50. *Ibid.*, 17.9.4 (296).
51. *Ibid.* 16.7.6 (224-225).
52. Cf. Nelson Glueck, *BASOR* (1953).
53. *Ant., ibid.*, 9.1 (273-280).
54. *Ibid.* (281-285).
55. *Ibid.*, 16.9.8 (286-294).
56. *Ibid.*, 10.8 (335).

57. *Ibid.*, 9.4 (294-295); cf. N. Glueck, *On the Other Side of the Jordan* (New Haven, 1940).

58. *Ant., ibid.*, 9 (336-355).

59. *Ibid.* (354-355).

60. *Ibid.*, 17.2.1 (23).

61. Cf. Carl Kraeling, *JBL* (1932), pp. 333-335.

62. There was great hostility between the Romans and the Parthians. The cold war which prevailed bordered on the brink of actual war. In the year 1 B.C.E., Augustus Caesar, writing to the King of Parthia, addressed him as Phrataces, omitting the appellation of "king." In reply, Phrataces, calling himself "king of kings," addressed Augustus simply as "Caesar," without the appellation of Augustus and Imperator. Cf. Dio, 55.20.

63. *Ant.*, 17.2.1-2 (25-26).

64. Cf. *Vita* 54, "The Babylonian Judaeans, as they are called in Ecbatana."

65. *Ant.*, 17.2.2-3 (27-31).

66. *Ant.*, 11.1 (356-357).

67. *Ibid.* (358-360).

68. *Ibid.*, 2 (361-367).

69. Deut. 21.18-21; cf. *Ant.*, 4.8.24 (280-281).

70. Cf. M. Sanh. 8; Talmud, *ibid.*, 71.

71. Deut. 21.20-21.

72. *Ant.*, 16.11.3 (367-369).

73. *Ibid.* (370-372).

74. *Ibid.*, 4-5 (375-383).

75. *Ibid.* (386).

76. *Ibid.*, 6 (387-390).

77. *Ibid.*, 7 (393).

78. *Ibid.* (394); *War*, 1.27.6 (550-551).

79. Cf. I, 409.

80. *War*, 1.28.1 (552).

81. *Ibid.*, 4 (562-563); *Ant.*, 17.1.3 (19-20).

82. *Ant.*, 17.1.1 (10).

83. See above p. 45.

84. *War*, 1.29.4 (578-579); *Ant.*, 17.3.3 (58).

85. Cf. *Ant.*, 7.5.2 (92).

86. Cf. I, 409-411.

87. Cf. *Ant.*, 17.4.2 (78).

88. *Ant., ibid.*, "For he (Herod, the son of Mariamme) had been named to the throne."

89. *War*, 1.28.2 (556-558); *Ant.*, 17.1.2 (12-14).

90. *Ant., ibid.* (16-17).

91. *Ibid.* (42-43). See above p. 45.

92. *Ant., ibid.*, 3 (46-50); *War*, 1.29.2 (571-572).

93. *Ant., ibid.* (50-51).

94. *Ibid.* (52-53).

95. *War*, 1.28.1 (554-555); *Ant.*, 7.1.1 (6-7).

96. *War, ibid.*, 2 (573).

97. *War, ibid.*, 30 (587-589).

98. *War, ibid.*, 29.2 (573).

99. *War, ibid.; Ant., ibid.* (53).
100. *War, ibid.* (577); *Ant., ibid.* (55-57).
101. *Ant., ibid.,* 4.3 (80).
102. *Ant., ibid.,* 4.1 (61-65).
103. *Ant., ibid.,* (70-77); *War, ibid.* (590-599).
104. *Ant., ibid.* (78); *War, ibid.* (599-600).
105. *War, ibid.* (593).
106. *Ant., ibid.* (73-75).
107. *Ibid.,* 3 (79-80); *War, ibid.,* 31.1 (601-603).
108. *Ant., ibid.,* 5 (83-84).
109. *Ant., ibid.* (83-88); *War, ibid.,* 3-4 (609-616).
110. P. Quintilius Varus succeeded Saturninus as legate of Syria c. 6 B.C.E.; cf. *War,* 1.31.5 (617); *Ant.,* 17.5.2 (89), 9.3 (221).
111. *War, ibid.,* 5.5 (617-619); *Ant., ibid.,* 2 (90-91).
112. *War, ibid.* (618); *Ant., ibid.* (92).
113. *War, ibid.,* 32.1.3 (620-636); *Ant., ibid.* (93-98).
114. *Ant., ibid.,* 4 (100-105); *War, ibid.,* 3 (629-636).
115. *Ant., ibid.,* 5 (106-111, 120).
116. *Ibid.,* 7 (130-132).
117. *Ibid.* (134-139); *War, ibid.,* 6 (641-643).
118. *Ant., ibid.,* 8 (142-145); *War, ibid.,* 7 (644-645).
119. *Ant., ibid.,* 6.1 (145-147); *War, ibid.,* (644-646).
120. *War, ibid.,* 32.2 (648). The term sophists had also the connotation of a scholar who lectured for money. In *Ant., ibid.* (150) and (152), both terms, *sophistai* and *exegetai,* interpreters, are used.
121. Cf. *War, ibid.* (650). "It was, in fact, unlawful to place in the Temple either images or busts or any representation whatever of a living creature."
122. Josephus, who was a follower of the Pharisees, believed in the immortality of the soul, but not in bodily resurrection.
123. *Ant., ibid.,* 3 (155-159); *War, ibid.,* 2 (648-650).
124. *Ant., ibid.* (161-163); *War, ibid.,* 3 (656).
125. *Ant., ibid.,* 4 (164).
126. *Ibid.* (166-167).
127. *Ibid.;* cf. F. K. Ginzel, *Specieller Kanon der Sonnen und Mond Finsternesse (900) B.C.-A.D. 600* (Berlin, 1899). Cf. Suk. 29.
128. Cf. Pliny, *Natural History* 5.15: "*eodem latere est calidus fons medicae salubritatis Callirroe aquarum gloriam ipso nomine praeferens.*" On the same side there is a hot spring possessing medical value, the name of which, Callirrhoe, itself proclaimed the celebrity of its waters. The word *c(k)allirrhoe* in Greek has the meaning of beautiful flowing. Cf. also Midrash R., Gen. 33, 37.
129. *Ant., ibid.* (170-171); *War, ibid.,* 5 (656-658).
130. *Ant., ibid.* (174-175); *War, ibid.,* 6 (659-660).
131. *Ant., ibid.,* 6 (181).
132. Cf. *Ant., ibid.,* 9.5 (233); see below, p. 125.
133. Matt. 2.16.

134. Cf. S. Zeitlin, "The Dates of the Birth and the Crucifixion of Jesus," *JQR*, LV (1965), 1-8.
135. *Ant., ibid.* (82-187); *War, ibid.* (661-664).
136. *Ant., ibid.*, 8.1 (188-190); *War, ibid.* (664).
137. *War, ibid.*, 8 (665-669); *Ant., ibid.* (190-195).
138. Probably the will was composed by Nicholas and Ptolemy, friends of Archelaus, when Herod was not of sound mind.
139. *Ant., ibid.*, 3 (196-199); *War, ibid.*, 9 (670-673).
140. Herod died at the end of the Month Adar in the year 750 A.U.C., 4 B.C.E.
141. See below, p. 260.
142. I, 312-313. Cf. A.H.M. Jones, *The Herods of Judaea*, p. 169; A. Shalit, *King Herod* (Hebrew), pp. 442-443.
143. See below, p. 138.
144. Cf. *Ant.*, 19.6.3 (299).
145. See below, p. 122; cf. also Tacitus, *Ann.*, 1.78; Dio, 52.6.28; J. Marquardt, *Römishe Staatsverwaltung*, ch. "Die Agaben der Provinzen"; W. T. Arnold, *The Roman System of Provincial Administration*, ch. 5, "The System of Taxation."
146. Cf. *War.*, 2.14.4 (287); Luke 19.1-2.
147. Cf. *Ant.*, 17.2.1 (25), 2 (27).
148. *War*, 1.21.2 (403).
149. Cf. below, p. 137.
150. Cf. Talmud Sanh. 48.
151. I, 306-307.
152. Cf. M. Ab. Zara 1.5; M. Sheni 4.1; P. Talmud Shab. 14.4; Pliny *N.H.*, 13.9.45; *Sicciores ex hoc genere nicolai.*
153. Cf. Hulin 139; Bezah 24.
154. Cf. above p. 61.
155. Cf. I, 373-392.
156. See *Ant.*, 18.5.4 (130, 133).
157. Cf. below, p. 230.

Chapter 3

1. Simon the Hasmonean and his son John Hyrcanus, being Pharisees, enforced the pharisaic laws. John Hyrcanus, who became a Sadducee, abrogated the laws which were enacted by the Pharisees. His son Jannaeus Alexander enforced the laws of the Sadducees. His wife, Queen Alexandra, on the other hand, being in sympathy with the Pharisees, restored their power. Antigonus, the last of the Hasmonean kings, was a Sadducee and enforced Sadducean practices. The struggle for power in the Hasmonean family was really to some extent a civil war between the Sadducees and the Pharisees.
2. I, p. 12.
3. Cf. I, pp. 443 f.
4. Cf. below, p. 302.
5. Cf. above, p. 37.
6. Cf. above, p. 44.
7. Cf. Psalms of Solomon, 17.5-9, 25-51; 18.1-10.

8. Cf. above, p. 45. This group persuaded Phehohas, Herod's brother, and Bagoas, the beloved eunuch of the king, to poison Herod. They promised Pheroras that his children would inherit the kingship over Judaea. They foretold Bagoas that he would marry and have children.

9. See below, p. 140.

10. *Ca.* 34-62 C.E. *At cum Herodis venere dies unctaque fenestra dispositae pinguem nebulam vomuere lucernae portantes violas rubrumque amplexa catinum cauda natat thynni, tumet alba fidelia vino, labra moves tacitus recutitaque sabbata palles* . . . (Satire 5.180-184).

11. Matt. 22.16; in Luke 20.19-25 the Herodians are not mentioned.

12. Cf. I, pp. 202-212.

13. Cf. above, p. 7.

14. See S. Zeitlin, "Hillel," in *JQR*, LIV (Oct. 1963), 173.

15. The word *polio* in the Greek literature was used metaphorically, "hoary," "venerable." In the Talmud, Hillel was called *zaken*, "the elder."

16. Cf. Sota 21. Some late authorities in the Talmud stated that Hillel was a descendant of the Davidic family.

17. Cf. Ex. 12.15, and Deut. 16.8.

18. Ex. 12.2, and 12.5.

19. Lev. 13.13, and 13.17.

20. *Ibid.*, 23.10-14; M. Men 10.5.

21. *Yer.* Pes. 6.1; Cf. S. Zeitlin, "The Halaka," *JQR* (1948), pp. 17-20; *idem*, "Un temoignage pour eux," *REJ*, LXXXVII, (1929), 79-82.

22. I, 425.

23. Cf. Yoma 35.

24. Cf. S. Zeitlin, "Hillel," *JQR*, LIV (1963), 172.

25. *Ibid.*

26. Cf. Num. 28.2; 9.13.

27. Cf. *Yer.* Pes. 6.1; *Bab.*, *ibid.*, 66; Tos., *ibid.*, 4.1-3.

28. Gen. 44.8; "Behold, the money, which we found in our sacks' mouths we brought back unto thee out of the land of Canaan; how then should we steal out of your Lord's house silver or gold?" Cf. also Ex. 6.12; "Behold the children of Israel have not hearkened unto me; how then shall Pharoah hear me?" To cite another example, in the Book of Jeremiah (12.5) the prophet said, "If thou hast run with the footmen and they have wearied thee, then how canst thou contend with horses?"

29. Cf. *Yer.* Pes. 6.1; *Bab.*, *idem*, 66.

30. Cf. above, p. 44; S. Hoenig, in *Bitzaron* (1965), 87 ff.; Rosenthal, *ibid.*

31. Cf. S. Zeitlin, "The Semikah· Controversy between the Zugoth," in *JQR*, VII (1917), 449-517.

32. I, pp. 207-208.

33. Cf. S. Zeitlin, "The Halaka," *JQR* (1948).

34. The founders were two jurists, Ateius Capito, a conservative, who adhered to the law as he himself had received it, and Antisthius Labeo, who had an independent spirit. Antisthius

Labeo was inclined to break with the established laws if such were life's demands. The schools, however, were named after later jurists, their disciples. The followers of Capito were called Sabinians, after Capito's pupil, Masius Sabinus. Those who followed Labeo's views were called Proculians, after Julius Proculius, a pupil of Labeo's disciple, Nerva (the grandfather of the Emperor Nerva). From the days of Augustus Caesar to the days of the Emperor Antoninus, every jurist enrolled himself in one school or the other and was known either as a Sabinian or a Proculian. Cf. *Gaii Institutionum Iuris Civilis Commentarii Quatuor.*

35. Cf. S. Zeitlin, "Talmud," in *Encyclopædia Britannica* (1963).

36. *Idem,* "Studies in Tannaitic Jurisprudence: Intention as a Legal Principle," in *Journal of Jewish Law and Philosophy* (1919), pp. 219-311.

37. Three controversies are recorded in M. Ed. 1:1-3; and one is given in Talmud Shab. 17. See also Tosefta Toh. 10.2.

38. E.g., Eliezer's name is given before the name of Rabbi Joshua.

39. Cf. M. Ed. *ad. loc.;* M. Hag. 2.2; S. Zeitlin, "The Semikah Controversy," in *JQR,* VII (1917), 500-514.

40. Lev. 11.35.

41. Talmud Shab. 17.

42. Cf. Ex. 16.5; Talmud Bezah 2-8; M. Shab. 24.4.

43. M. Bezah 1.1.

44. Cf. S. Zeitlin, "Studies in Tannaitic Jurisprudence," *loc. cit.,* p. 307.

45. Cf. M. Kid. 1.

46. Cf. Tos. Kid. 1.3.

47. Cf. Tos. Yeb. 11.10; *Bab., idem,* 96.

48. Cf. Lev. 1.4, 3; 2.8.

49. Cf. S. Zeitlin, *Religious and Secular Leadership,* I (Dropsie College, 1943), 67-71.

50. Cf. M. Hag. 2.3. The view of the Shammaites prevailed at first. Once on a festival Hillel brought an animal to be slaughtered as a burnt-offering. The Shammaites protested against it, and Hillel had to change his mind; he told them he would sacrifice the animal as a peace-offering. Cf. *Yer.* Hag. 2. Cf. Tos. *ibid.;* S. Zeitlin, "The Semikah Controversy between the School of Shammai and Hillel," *JQR,* LVI (1966), 240-244.

51. Shab. 31.

52. Cf. Tobit 4.15; The Testament of the Twelve Patriarchs; The Testament of Joseph, 18.2 (ed. Charles).

53. Lev. 19.18, 34.

54. Matt. 5.44; cf. below, p. 236.

55. Cf. S. Zeitlin, *Who Crucified Jesus?* (Harper Bros., 1942), p. 126.

56. Ab. d'R Nathan 15, Ed. Schechter; cf. Shab, 31. "A certain man came to Shammai and said to him: 'How many Torahs have you?' 'Two,' Shammai replied, 'one written and one oral.' The man said to Shammai, 'In the written law I trust you, while

the oral law I do not trust' (I am not prepared to accept). Shammai rebuked him and dismissed him in a huff. Then the man went to Hillel and asked him the same question, 'How many Torahs have you?' 'Two,' Hillel replied, 'one written and one oral.' The man said to him, 'In the written law I have confidence. In the oral law I have no confidence, and I am not prepared to accept it.' 'My son,' Hillel said to him, 'sit down.' Hillel wrote out the alphabet and asked the man, 'What is this?' The man replied, 'This is an *aleph*.' Then Hillel asked, 'What is this?' The man answered, 'This is a *bet*.' Hillel then said to the man, 'How do you know this is an *aleph* and this is a *bet*?' The man answered, 'Because that was handed down to us.' Hillel then said to him, 'If you accept the names of the letters because they came to us by tradition, so you must take the oral law also in good faith.' "

Another anecdote involves a test of Hillel's love for his fellow-man. Once two men made a wager of four-hundred *zuz* to be given to the one who could put Hillel in a rage. One of them went to Hillel on the eve of Sabbath. Hillel was washing his head. The man knocked at the door. "Where is Hillel? Where is Hillel?" he called. Hillel put on his cloak and came out to him. "My son, what is it?" The man replied, "I have a question to ask." "Ask," said Hillel. The man asked, "Why are the heads of the Babylonians long?" "My son," Hillel said, "Indeed you ask a great question. Since there are no skillful midwives there, when the infant is born slaves and maid servants tend it on their laps. That is the reason why the heads of the Babylonian are long. Here, however, there are skillful midwives and when an infant is born it is taken care of in a cradle." The man went away, waited for a while, came back and knocked again on Hillel's door. "Where is Hillel? Where is Hillel?" he called. Hillel put on his cloak and came out to him. "My son, what is it," he said. The man replied, "I have to ask you a certain question." "Ask," said Hillel. The man asked, "Why are the eyes of the Tadmorites bleary?" Hillel replied, "Because they live in the desert and the winds blow the sand in their eyes." The man departed, waited for a while, and knocked again on Hillel's door calling, "Where is Hillel? Where is Hillel?" Hillel put on his cloak and came out, saying, "What is it that you wish to ask?" The man said, "I have a certain question. Why are the African's feet flat?" Hillel replied, "Because they dwell in watery marshes and all the time they walk in water. That is why their feet are flat." The man then said, "I have many questions to ask but I am apprehensive that you may become angry." Hillel said, "Ask as many as you have." The man asked, "Are you the Hillel, the *Nasi*?" Hillel answered, "Yes." The man said, "May there be no more like you in Israel!" Hillel asked, "Why?" The man answered, "Because of you I lost four-hundred *zuz*." Hillel said to the man, "Be tame in your spirit. Better that you have lost four-hundred *zuz* on account of Hillel than Hillel should become irritable."

57. A *takkana* is an amendment of early law, either pentateuchal or old halakic. It was introduced by the sages generally for the purpose of harmonizing religion and life. Hence a *takkana* tends to leniency.
58. Deut. 15.1-3.
59. M. Sheb. 10.1; cf. also I, pp. 311-312.
60. M. Sheb. 10.2-4; Git. 4; cf. S. Zeitlin, "Prosbol: A Study in Tannaitic Jurisprudence," *JQR*, XXXVII (1947), 341-362. The fact that Hillel's *takkana* was called in the Talmud by the Greek term *pros boulé* does not necessarily prove that Hillel adopted this *takkana* from the Hellenes. When Hillel introduced the *takkana*, the people referred to it in this fashion. The term *prosbol* is a loan-word; the principle of it is Hillelite. Further, there is no evidence in the tannaitic literature that Hillel himself employed the term *prosbol*.
61. Cf. S. Zeitlin, *op. cit.*, pp. 355-356.
62. Cf. Lev. 25-29.
63. I, pp. 216-218.
64. Talmud, Ar. 9.5.
65. Cf. Talmud B.M. 104; *Yer*. Ket. 4.8.
66. Tos. Ket. 4; *Yer. ibid.*, 4.8.
67. M. Abot. 1.14.
68. *Ibid.*, 1.13.
69. Talmud, Suk. 53; cf. I, p. 249.
70. M. Abot. 2.4.
71. *Ibid.*, 2.6; Suk. 53.
72. M. Abot, 1.15.
73. Ex. 20.8.
74. Talmud Bezah 16.
75. Talmud Suk. 20.

PART TWO

Chapter 1

1. *Ant.*, 17.8.4 (200); *War*, 2.1.1 (1-2).
2. *Ant., ibid.* (201-204).
3. *Ibid.*, 205.
4. *Ibid.*, 9.1 (206).
5. *Ibid.* (206-208).
6. *Ibid.* (209).
7. *Ibid.*, 9.3 (213-218); *War*, 2.1.3 (10-12).
8. Called Poplas in *War, ibid.*, 2.1 (14).
9. *Ant., ibid.* (219-220); *War, ibid.*, 2 (14-15).
10. *Ant., ibid.* (221-223).
11. Antipas claimed that the last will should not be validated since it was only a *epidiathke*, a codicil.
12. Cf. *Ant., ibid.*, 4-5 (225-228); *War, ibid.*, 3-4 (20-22).
13. *Ant., ibid.* (229-232); *War, ibid.* (25).
14. Gaius died in 4 C.E.
15. *Ant., ibid.* (230-232); *War, ibid*, 5-6 (26-32).
16. *Ant., ibid.* (243).

17. *Ant., ibid.,* 6(240-247) ; *War, ibid.,* 6(33-36).
18. *Ant., ibid.,* 7(248-249) ; *War, ibid.,* 7(37-38).
19. *Ant., ibid.,* 10.1(250).
20. *Ibid.,* 11.1(330) ; *War,* 2.6.1(80-81).
21. *Ant., ibid.; War, ibid.*
22. *Ibid.*
23. See I, pp. 351-352. The Judaeans were naive in not realizing that the rule of Rome was not of the same order as the rule of the Persians, the Ptolemies, or the Seleucids. Rome was a ruthless, centralized, bureaucratic system, different from that of the governments under which Judaeans had previously lived. The provincial system was also strongly centralized and was under the rule of the legates and procurators. During the Ptolemic and Seleucid periods the high priest was the ruler over the religious and social life of the people. The government did not disturb their life. While Rome did not interfere in the religious life of the people, the legate and the procurator ruled with an iron hand and suppressed any movement aiming at freedom.

On the other hand, the Judaeans became politically conscious during the time of the Ptolemies and the Seleucids. They had become deeply attached to their national life since the victory of the Hasmoneans. It had sparked in them great national pride for which they were ready to sacrifice their lives.
24. Cf. *Ant., ibid.* (300); *War, ibid.* (80).
25. Velleius Paterculus, *History of Rome,* 2.117, *"Quam pauper divitem ingressus dives pauperem reliquit."*
26. Cf. Philo, *Embassy to Gaius,* 23(155-157).
27. See above, p. 76, n. 62.
28. *Ant., ibid.,* 11.3(315-316). The argument of Nicolas was Ciceronian. *Suppressio veri,* suppression of the truth. Nicolas knew well that Herod had made Judaea a police state. Everyone there had been spied upon, both in the city and on the highway; and an assembly even of two or three persons was prosecuted. There was no possibility of any complaint. If one was suspected of having complained, he was tortured and put to death. When Augustus Caesar was in Syria, the Gadarenes complained against Herod. When they sensed that Caesar would turn them over to Herod, they committed suicide. They feared that Herod would torture them. Hence there was no way of complaining to Caesar while the tyrant was still alive.
29. *Ant., ibid.,* 4(17) ; *War, ibid.,* 6.3(93).
30. *Ant.,* 17.10.1(250-253) ; *War,* 2.2.2(18).
31. *Ant., ibid.,* 2(254).
32. *Ibid.* (257).
33. *Ibid.* (259-264).
34. *Ibid.,* 3(265).
35. *Ibid.* (262-268).
36. *Ibid.,* 4(269-270).
37. Cf. I, p. 372.

38. *Ant., ibid.,* 5 (271-272).
39. Cf. below, p. 216.
40. *Ant., ibid.,* 6 (273-277); *War,* 2.4.2 (57-59); Tacitus, *Hist.,* 5.9: "After Herod's death, a certain Simon assumed the name of king without waiting for Caesar's decision. He, however, was put to death by Quintilius Varus, the legate of Syria; the Judaeans were repressed and the kingdom was divided into three parts and given to Herod's sons." *Post mortem Herodis, nihil expectato Caesare, Simo quidam regium nomen invaserat.* . . .
41. *Ant., ibid.,* 7 (278-285).
42. Cf. Abel, G.P. 2.251; Albright, *BASOR* (1923).
43. Seven miles northeast of Emmaus. Cf. Abel, *op. cit.,* 2.448.
44. *Ant., ibid.,* 9 (286-294); *War,* 2.5.1 (66-71).
45. *Ant., ibid.,* 10 (295-297).
46. *Ibid.* (297-298); *War, ibid.,* 2-3 (72-79).
47. Cicero, *in Verrem* 5.66.
48. Varus looked upon the inhabitants of Germany as having only limbs and voices. His attitude provoked a revolt in the year 9 C.E., which resulted in the crushing of the entire Roman army. It was the greatest defeat that Rome suffered since Crassus. In the words of the Roman historian Velleius Paterculus (*History of Rome,* 2.9; Tacitus, *Ann.,* 1.60), the only ` courage he had was to commit suicide. Augustus, upon learning of the disaster, rent his garments (Dio, 56) and was so greatly affected that for several days in succession he did not cut his beard or hair. His state of mind was such that from time to time he cried, "Quintilius Varus, give me back my legions!" *Quintili Vare, legiones redde!* He observed the day of the disaster each year as one of sorrow and mourning. (Suetonius, *Augustus,* 23). The Judaeans likewise observed a day of mourning which was called *Polemos of Varus,* the War of Varus, in commemoration of his suppression of the uprising in Judaea. Cf. *Seder Olam,* 30; S. Zeitlin, *Megillat Taanit,* p. 62, n. 140.
49. *Ant.,* 17.11.4-5 (317-323); *War,* 2.6.3 (93-100).
50. *Vita Augustae.* Cf. R. Laqueur, "Nikoloas," Paulys R.E. 17; B.Z. Wacholder, *Nicholaus of Damascus* (1961). Cf. also Plutarch, *Brutus* 53 (3-5).
51. *Ant.,* 17.7.1 (324-331); *War,* 2.7.1 (101-105).
52. *Ant., ibid.* (332-338); *War, ibid.,* 2 (106-110).
53. *Ant., ibid.,* 13 (339).
54. *Ant., ibid.,* 10.7 (284).
55. *Ant., ibid.,* 13.1 (340); see *Ant.,* 18.2.2 (31); Pliny *N.H.,* 13.9.44.
56. *Ant., ibid.* (340).
57. *Ibid.* (341); cf. Lev. 18.16.
58. Cf. Dio, 55.18-21.
59. Suetonius, *Augustus,* 93.
60. *Ant.,* 17.13.2 (342); *War,* 2.7.3 (111). According to the Roman historian, Dio (55.27), his brothers accused Arche-

laus of some wrongdoing. Cf. also Strabo, 16.2.46. The accusation must have been serious, for both the Judaeans and the Samaritans, in spite of the deep animosity existing between them, to send their leading men to Caesar to complain against Archelaus.

61. *Ant., ibid.* (344) ; *War, ibid.;* Strabo, *ibid.*
62. According to Jerome, Archelaus was buried in Bethlehem. However, cf. Josephus, *loc. cit.;* Dio, *loc. cit.*
63. *Ant., ibid.* (341).
64. Cf. *Ant.,* 17.13.5 (355) ; 18.2.1 (26-27). See Tacitus, *Ann.,* 6.41.
65. *War,* 2.8.1 (117).
66. W. T. Arnold, *The Roman System of Provincial Administration* (London, 1879), pp. 110-121.
67. *War,* 2.8.1 (117).
68. Strabo gives a full description of provincial government at the time of Augustus. "The provinces have been divided in different ways at different times, though at the present time they are as Augustus Caesar arranged them; for when the native land committed to him the foremost place of authority and he became established as lord for life of war and peace, he divided the whole of his empire into two parts and assigned one portion to himself and the other to the Roman people; to himself, all parts that had a military guard (that is, the part that was barbaric and in the neighborhood of tribes not yet subdued, or lands that were sterile and difficult to bring under cultivation, so that, being unprovided with everything else but well provided with strongholds, they would try to throw off the bridle or refuse obedience), and to the Roman people all the rest, in so far as it was peaceable to rule without arms; and he divided each of the two portions into several provinces, of which some are called "Provinces of Caesar" and the others "Provinces of the people." And to the "Provinces of Caesar" Caesar sent legates and procurators, dividing the country in different ways at different times and administering them as the occasions required:" 17.3.25. Egypt, Syria and Judaea were imperial provinces.
69. Cf. Cicero *in Verrem* 2.3.42; cf. also J. Marquand, *op. cit.,* pp. 197-198.
70. Cf. Cicero, *ibid.,* 2.2.70.
71. Cf. Cicero, *To Atticus,* 11.10, "*P. Terentius, meus necessarius, operas in portu et scriptura Asiae pro magistro dedit.*" Cf. Arnold, *op. cit.* These taxes were levied at the time of the Republic. Cf. Cicero, *in Verrum* 2.3.6.
72. I, pp. 369-370.
73. Cf. *Ant.,* 18.3.1 (55) ; 5.3 (120-122) ; *War,* 2.9.2 (169-170) ; cf. also Tacitus, *Hist.,* 2.79.
74. Cf. *War,* 2.8.15 (201-302).
75. Cf. Arnold, *op. cit.,* p. 202.
76. The Hebrew word *parhedrion* is of Greek derivation,

paredros, "coadjutor." Cf. S. Zeitlin, "Bouleuterion and Parhedrion," *JQR*, LIII (Oct. 1962), 169-170.

77. *Ant.*, 20.10.5(251).
78. Cf. *ibid.*, 18.1.1(3).
79. *Ibid.* (4-5); *War*, 2.8.1(118).
80. *Ant.*, *ibid.*, 2.1(26).
81. *Ant.*, *ibid.*, 2(29). The Samaritans in the early period abhorred the Temple of Jerusalem because they believed it vied with their temple on Mount Gerizim. They maintained that Moses had ordered that a sanctuary be built on Mount Gerizim. (See I, pp. 26-29). As a matter of fact, a few years later a man who declared himself a prophet led a multitude of Samaritans to Mount Gerizim and promised to reveal to them sacred vessels which, he said, had been buried there by Moses. (See further below, p. 143.) In throwing human bones into the Temple area, the Samaritans meant to show not only their contempt for the Temple, but also their intention of defiling it.
82. Cf. above, p. 52.
83. *Ant.*, *ibid.* (27).
84. *Ibid.* (31).
85. *Ibid.* (32).
86. Suetonius, *Tiberius*, 1-24.
87. *Ant.*, *ibid.* (33-35).
88. *Ibid.* (35).
89. Philo, *Embassy to Gaius* (38); *War*, 2.9.2-3(169-174).
90. *War*, *ibid.*; *Ant.*, 18.3.1 (55-59).
91. *War*, *ibid.*, 4(175); *Ant.*, *ibid.*, 2(60).
92. Dio, 58.26; Suetonius, *Tiberius*, 66; Tacitus, *Ann.*, 2.4.58; 6.31-32; *Ant.*, 18.2.4(39-52). Cf. E. Täubler, *Die Parthernachrichten bei Josephus* (Berlin, 1904).
93. *Ant.*, 18.6.1(85-87).
94. *Ibid.* (89).
95. *Ibid.*, 3(90).
96. *Ann.*, 2.42: *et provinciae Suria atque Iudaea, fessae oneribus deminutionem tributi orabant.*
97. *Ant.*, 18.4.3(90-91).
98. Suetonius, *Tiberius*, 73.
99. Tacitus, *Ann.*, 1.80.
100. *Ant.*, 18.6.5(173-176).
101. *Ant.*, 18.2.1(28); *War*, 2.9.1(168). Cf. Mark 8.27; Matt. 16.13.
102. *Ant.*, *ibid.*
103. *Ant.*, *ibid.*, 4.6(106-107).
104. Cf. *ibid.*, 5.4(136).
105. *Ibid.*, 4.6(106-108).
106. *Ibid.*, 2.1(27).
107. *Ibid.*, 2.3(38).
108. *Ibid.* (37-38).
109. *Ibid.* 5.1(109).
109a. According to Mark 6.17, Herodias was the wife of Philip.
110. *Ibid.* (110-111). See N. Glueck, "Exploration in the Land of

Ammon," *Bulletin of the American School of Oriental Research* (Dec. 1937).

111. *Ant., ibid.* (112-115); cf. Schürer, *Geschichte,* 1.
112. *Ibid.* (136).
113. Lev. 18.16.
114. *Ant.,* 18.5.2 (116-119).
115. The word "others" is puzzling. Who were the "others"? Eusebius, *Ecclesiastical History,* 1.11, has "And when the rest collected, for they were greatly excited at hearing his words, Herod feared his great persuasiveness with men lest it should lead to some rising, for they appeared ready to do everything under his advice. He therefore considered it much better, before a revolt should spring from John, to put him to death."
116. We do not find an expression *ha'mathbil,* "the baptizer," in the Hebrew literature of that period.
117. Cf. Mark 6.17-29; Matt. 14.3-11; Luke 3.19; 9.9.
118. Mark 6.21-29. Luke gives the genealogy of John saying that he was the son of Zachariah and Elizabeth, who were of the priestly clan. Elizabeth was related to Miriam, mother of Jesus.
119. Cf. Mark 6.17; Matt. 14.4.
120. Mark 6.22; Matt. 14.11. Cf. *Ant.,* 18.5.4 (137).
121. Mark 1.4. "John did baptize in the wilderness and preached the baptism of repentance for the forgiveness of sins." Cf. also Luke 3.3; Matt. 3.4-12. See F. Jackson and K. Lake, *The Beginnings of Christianity,* I (1920), pp. 101-110.
122. Suetonius, *Vitellius,* 2; *Ant.,* 18.4.5 (101-105).
123. *Ibid.,* 5.3 (120).
124. *Ibid.* (120-124).

Chapter 2

1. See M.S. Enslin, *The Prophet from Nazareth* (1951); cf. also C.H. Guignebert, *Jesus,* p. 230: "Of facts which can be utilized by the historians, which really bring us near the true Jesus, there are none, or very few, even for those who are not hampered by critical scruples."
2. Cf. S. Zeitlin, "The Christ Passage in Josephus," *JQR,* XVIII (1928), 230-255; *idem, Josephus on Jesus* (1931), pp. 61-70. See Appendix IV.
3. *Ant.,* 20.9.1 (200). Cf. S. Zeitlin, *op. cit.*
4. *Ann.,* 15.44. *Ergo abolendo rumori Nero subdidit reos et quaesitissimis poenis adfecit, quos per flagitia invisos vulgus Christianos appellabat. Auctor nominis eius Christus Tiberio imperitante per procuratorem Pontium Pilatum supplicio adfectus erat; repressaque in praesens exitiabilis superstitio rursum erumpebat, non modo per Iudaeam, originem eius mali, sed per urbem etiam quo cuncta undique atrocia aut pudenda confluunt celebranturque.* "In order to destroy the rumor (Nero was accused of having set fire to

Rome), Nero invented a charge of guilt and punished with the utmost cruelty a class of men hated for their vices whom the crowd called Christians. Christus, the founder of the name, had undergone the death penalty in the reign of Tiberius, by sentence of the procurator Pontius Pilatus; but the pernicious superstition was checked only for a moment, only to break out once more, not only in Judaea, the home of the disease, but in the capital itself, where all things horrible or shameful in the world collect and find a vogue."

5. Cf. S. Zeitlin, "Jesus in the Early Tannaitic Literature," *Abhandlungen zur Erinnerung an Hirsch Perez Chajes* (Vienna, 1933), pp. 295-308; *idem*, "Talmud," *Encyclopædia Britannica* (1963).

6. Cf. Eusebius, *Ecclesiastical History*, 2.15; 3.39.

7. Cf. S. Zeitlin, "The Crucifixion of Jesus Re-examined," *JQR*, XXXI (1941), 47-48; M.S. Enslin, *Christian Beginnings* (1938), pp. 386-387; E. Gould, *The Gospel According to St. Mark*.

8. Cf. Enslin, *op. cit.*; Guignebert, *op. cit.*, pp. 35-42, 50-57.

9. Eusebius, *op. cit.*, 3.4. See A. Harnack, *The Date of the Acts and the Synoptic Gospels* (1911); H.J. Cadbury, *The Making of Luke-Acts* (London, 1927).

10. Cf. S. Zeitlin, *Who Crucified Jesus?*, pp. 110-113; A. Loisy, *Le Quatrième Evangile* (Paris, 1921); S.W. Bacon, *The Fourth Gospel in Research and Debate* (1918); H.L. Jackson, *The Problem of the Fourth Gospel* (Cambridge, 1918).

11. Cf. Matt. 2.1.

12. See above, pp. 92-95.

13. Luke 2.1-5. See above, p. 137. Cf. also H.F. Clinton, *Fasti Hellenice* (Oxford, 1830), p. 256; E. Schürer, *Geschichte*, I, 524-527.

14. Tertullian, in his treatise *Against Marcion* (4.19) states that in the time of Jesus a census was taken in Judaea by Sentius Saturninus: *Sed et cenus constat actos sub augusto nunc in Iudaea per Sentium Saturninum aput quos genus eius inquirere potuissent.* Saturninus was the legate of Syria during the years 9-6 B.C.E. It can be seen from another treatise by Tertullian that he erred in his statement. In his treatise *Adversus Iudaeos* 8: *Videamus autem quoniam quadragesimo et primo anno imperii Augusti, quo post mortem Cleopatrae XX et VIII annos imperavit nascitur Christus.* "Let us see, moreover, how in the forty-first year of the Empire of Augustus, when he had been reigning XX and VIII years after the death of Cleopatra, Christ was born." Thus Tertullian placed the date of the birth of Jesus in the twenty-eighth year after Cleopatra's death. She died in the first day of the seventh month, later renamed Augustus, in the year 30 B.C.E. Twenty-eight years after the death of Cleopatra would be the year 2 B.C.E. Thus Jesus could not have been living during the time of Saturninus, who was a legate in Syria between the years 745-748

A.U.C., 9-6 B.C.E. Cf. also *The Stromata* of Clement of Alexandria (d.c. 217 C.E.). "From the time of the birth of the Lord to the death of Commodus are, in all C and XCIV years, one month thirteen days." Emperor Commodus was slain on the thirty-first of December 192 C.E., which would make the date of the birth of Jesus 2 B.C.E. Cf. also Eusebius, *Ecclesiastical History* 1.5.1-3. Cf. further Clinton, *op. cit.*; Zeitlin, "The Dates of the Birth and the Crucifixion of Jesus," in *JQR*, LV (July 1964), 1-6.

15. Cf. *Stromata*, 1.21. "Others say that he (Jesus) was born on the twenty-fourth or twenty-fifth of Pharmuthe." According to Josephus the Egyptian month Pharmuthe corresponds to the Hebrew month Nisan. Cf. further, S. Zeitlin, *op. cit.*

16. Cf. Matt. 2.5, 22; Luke 2.4.7, 39.

17. Mark 1.9, 24; 10.47.

18. John 7.41.

19. Luke 2.1-20.

20. Matt. 2.9-16; 18-23.

21. Luke 13.32. The fox was regarded as the sliest among the beasts. See Talmud Ber. 61.

22. Matt. 2.6. In giving the genealogy of Jesus as the son of David, the Gospels record two lists. Matthew traces the descent of Jesus from David through his son Solomon. Luke, however, traces Jesus as a descendant of David's other son, Nathan. This is an impressive discrepancy between the synoptics.

    One reason advanced for these two different genealogies of Matthew and Luke is that each had a different record. Even if this were so, the question still remains why did Luke ignore Solomon and his descendants, the kings of Judaea, whose names are recorded in the Bible? Why should Luke record the names of the descendants of Nathan, names which are not recorded in the Bible?

    Is not the true reason for these variations in the genealogy of Jesus to be found in this: that Luke had a theological reason for not giving Jesus' genealogical tree through Solomon. Solomon was the son of Bathsheba, who had committed an adulterous act. The Gospel of Luke, therefore, chose rather Nathan, another son of David, as the line of descent through which Jesus' ancestry was to be traced.

23. The modern city of Nazareth is situated S.E. of Sepphoris and S.W. of Tiberias. The name of the city of Nazareth is not found either in the Bible or in the Talmud, nor in the writings of Josephus. Neither the names Nazareth nor Nazarene are mentioned in the Epistles or in the Apostolic Fathers. Therefore some scholars are of the opinion that Nazareth does not designate a city, that Jesus was not born in Nazareth. An attempt was made to explain that the surname of Jesus was derived from the word *netzer*, meaning branch, and that it signifies that Jesus was the offshoot of the stem of Jesse, the father of David. (Cf. Isa. 11.1.) Some suggested that the surname of Jesus was derived from

the word *nazir*, which may be translated as "holy," "consecrated." Cf. Matt. 2.23, "And he came and dwelt in a city
called Nazareth, that it might be fulfilled, which was spoken
by the prophets, he shall be called a Nazarene." See further
Ch. Guignebert, *Jesus*, pp. 78-89.

24. Luke 2.21.
25. *Ibid.*, 24. Cf. Lev. 12.6-8.
26. Matt. 13.55.
27. *Ibid.*
28. Luke 2.41-42.
29. Mark 6.3. "Is this the carpenter, the son of Mary, the brother
    of James and Joses, and of Judah and Simon?"
30. See A. Loisy, *L'Evangile selon Mark* (Paris, 1912); Ch.
    Guignebert, *La Vie Cachée de Jésus* (Paris, 1924).
31. Luke 3.23.
32. *Ibid.*, 3.1-3. Tiberius became Emperor in the year 14 C.E.
    Cf. Suetonius, *Tiberius;* Dio, 57.
33. Matt. 3.4, 6; Mark 1.4, 6; Luke 3.3.
34. Mark 9.11-13; Matt. 17.11-13; John 1.20-28.
35. Cf. Mark 1.21, 6.2; Matt. 12.9; Luke 4.15-16.
36. John 4.2.
37. Cf. Matt. 28.19.
38. Acts 2.38; 8.12-13.
39. Cf. S. Zeitlin, "L'Origine de L'Institution du Baptême pour
    les Proselytes," *REJ* (1934), pp. 61-68.
40. Cf. M.S. Enslin, *Christian Beginnings*, ch. 10, pp. 149-153;
    S. Zeitlin, "The Duration of Jesus' Ministry," *JQR*, LV
    (1965), pp. 187-191.
41. Cf. John 3.25-26; Matt. 9.14; Mark 2.18; Luke 7.19-20.
42. Cf. M.S. Enslin, *op. cit.;* S. Zeitlin, *op. cit.;* M. Goguel, *The
    Life of Jesus.*
43. 1.14. "Now after that John was put in prison, Jesus came
    into Galilee preaching the gospel of the Kingdom of God."
    According to John, Jesus went to Judaea with his disciples
    at the same time that John was baptizing in Enon near
    Salim. The evangelist added, "for John was not yet cast into
    prison." (3.20-24.)
44. Ch. Guignebert, *op. cit.*, ch. 9.
45. John 2.13, 23; 5.1; 6.3-4; 7.1-2; 10.22-23.
46. Cf. Clement of Alexandria, *Stromata*, 1.21; Tertullian also
    states that Jesus' ministry lasted one year, and that he was
    crucified in the consulate of Rubellius Geminus and Fufius
    Geminus. *Quae passio huius exterminii intra tempora LXX
    hebdomadarum perfecta est sub Tiberio Caesare, consulibus
    Rubellio Gemino et Fufio Gemino. Adversus Iudaeos, 8.*
47. Irenaeus, who lived in the second half of the second century,
    opposed the view of those who maintained that Jesus'
    ministry lasted only one year. He asserted that it lasted
    much longer ... *affirment, dicunt uno anno eum praedicasse,
    et duodecimo mense passum. Contra Haereses, 2.22.5.* The
    Church historian Eusebius also maintained that Jesus'

ministry lasted not a full four years. *Ecclesiastical History*, 1.10.

48. 1.15. The word gospel has the connotation "good news," a translation of the Greek word *euangelion*. With this word Mark opened his narration bringing good tidings that Jesus, the Messiah, the Son of God, had come.

49. Matt. 13.52-56; Mark 6.4; Luke 4.24.

50. Matt. 9.12.

51. Cf. Mark 9.17; 10.17, 20; 12.14; Matt. 8.19; 19.16; Luke 8.49; 9.38; 10.25; Luke 10.39; 11.1.

52. John 3.2; 1.38, "Rabbi (which is to say teacher)." It is possible that John, writing for the pagans, who were unacquainted with the term rabbi, interpreted it as meaning teacher. The connotation of the term rabbi as teacher came into vogue after the destruction of the Second Temple. John, in describing the controversies between Jesus and the Judaeans and the Pharisees, put into the mouth of Jesus the expression, "your Torah, your law." Cf. John 8.17, "It is written in your law that the testimony of two men is true." Cf. also 10.34; 15.25. The Gospel according to John, by its use of "your" in connection with the Torah, reveals that its message was directed to gentile Christians.

Another example that might well demonstrate the nature of the people to whom the Gospel according to John was written can be found in such phrases "Judaean Passover" and the "Judaean Feast of Tabernacles." This implies that this gospel was intended for gentile Christians to whom such a descriptive adjective as "Judaean" might be necessary. The names "Passover" and "The Feast of Unleavened Bread" are mentioned in the synoptic Gospels but never with the word "Judaean." Since they were written for Judaean Christians, the term "Judaean" would have been superfluous. Cf. S. Zeitlin, *JQR*, XXVIII (1937), 392-394; *idem, JQR*, LIII (1963), 345-349. *Idem, Who Crucified Jesus?*, pp. 110-112.

53. Cf. Mark 3.11; cf. also Matt. 16.16; Luke 4.3.

54. Mark 2.10, 27; Matt. 16.13. Cf. M.S. Enslin, *op. cit.*, pp. 162 f.

55. Mark 3.14-18; Matt. 10.1-4; Luke 6.13-16. The disciples were Simon (called Peter, meaning rock in Greek), his brother Andrew, both fishermen; James, the son of Zebedee; John and his brother James, whom Jesus surnamed Boanerges (meaning the sons of thunder—they were impulsive and quick to anger); Philip; Bartholomew; Thomas Mark, the publican; James, son of Alphaeus; Thaddaeus; Simon, the Canaanite (the zealot); and Judas Iscariot.

56. Matt. 10.5. According to Luke 10.1, Jesus appointed seventy (two) and sent them out to preach his gospel. Cf. Ex. 24.1; Num. 11.16.

57. Cf. Luke 17.11-16; John 4.40; Mark 7.24.

58. Matt. 5.39-44.

59. Matt. 11.23-24.

60. Matt. 12.30; Luke 11.23. Cf. also Mark 9.40, "For he that is not against us is on our part."
61. Matt. 5.12.
62. Some manuscripts have "a Greek woman."
63. Mark 7.27; Matt. 15.22-26.
64. Cf. Matt. 9.23; Luke 5.29.
65. Luke 7.36.
66. Cf. Mark 3.31-33; Matt. 12.46-47; Luke 8.19-21.
67. Ex. 20.12.
68. Mark 8.29-30; Matt. 16.16.
69. Mark 8.33.
70. Matt. 16.15-20.
71. Cf. M.S. Enslin, *The Prophet of Nazareth* (New York, 1961); M. Goguel, *The Life of Jesus* (New York, 1933); Ch. Guignebert, *Jesus* (New York, 1956).
72. Matt. 17.24-27. Josephus states in *War*, 7.6.6 (218), "On all Judaeans, wheresoever resident, he (Vespasian) imposed a poll-tax of two drachmas, to be paid annually into the capitol as formerly contributed by them to the Temple at Jerusalem." This tax was called *fiscus Judaicus*. It was not levied on the Judaeans as an ethnic group, but was rather a religious tax upon those who professed the Judaean faith. According to the Roman historians, Suetonius (*Domitian* 12) wrote, "Besides other taxes, that on the Judaeans was levied with utmost rigor, and those were prosecuted who, without publicly acknowledging that faith, yet lived as Judaeans." *Praeter ceteros Iudaicus fiscus acerbissime actus est ad quem deferebantur, qui vel improfessi.* . . . Dio also wrote that the tax had to be paid by "all who observed their ancestral customs." It seems that the story recorded in Matthew connecting the payment of the tribute to the Temple with temporal power is an anachronism.
73. Mark 12.13-17; Matt. 22.17-21; Luke 20.22-25.
74. Cf. John 10.40; 11.7.
75. Mark 10.32-33; John 11.8.
76. That Jesus took this road instead of the usual way through Samaria and Judaea may indicate that Jesus and his disciples wanted to avoid the populated country where most of the inhabitants were hostile and the Roman authorities had many spies to keep surveillance over any manifestation that might lead to a disturbance.

There has been considerable debate as to the historical value of the Gospel according to John. Many scholars maintain that this gospel is a work of theology devoid of historical value. On the other hand, New Testament scholars are of the opinion that the Gospel according to John presents reliable historical information about Jesus, Cf. A.J.B. Higgens, *The Historicity of the Four Gospels* (London, 1960); R. E. Brown, *The Gospel According to John*, The Anchor Bible (New York, 1966).

The synoptic Gospels, as well as the Gospel according to

John, are based on tradition which the authors had either
in writing, or, most probably, by oral transmission. To
present the life of Jesus, a historian must carefully examine
all the sources available. It seems that the duration of Jesus'
ministry as well as his visits to Jerusalem as given by John
offer the correct historical information and are supported
by some of the early Church Fathers.

77. Mark 11.1; Matt. 21.1-2; Luke 19.29-30.
78. Mark 11.8-9; Matt. 21.9.
79. John 12.13.
80. Mark 14.3.
81. Mark 11.15; Matt. 21.12.
82. Luke 19.45; cf. also John 2.13-16.
83. John 11.47-50.
84. Mark 14.1.
85. Matt. 26.3.
86. Luke 22.1.
87. Mark 14.10-11; Matt. 26.14-16; Luke 22.3-6.
88. John 13.27-30.
89. Mark 14.12-26; Matt. 26.19-29; Luke 22.7-20.
90. Cf. John 13.21-30.
91. Mark 14.43-65; 15.1; Matt. 26.47-75; 27.1; Luke 22.47-71.
92. John 18.26.
93. On the schism, cf. Eusebius, *The Ecclesiastical History*,
     5.23-24; Ch. Guignebert, *Jesus*, p. 426, and the literature
     there quoted.
94. Many New Testament scholars have tried in various ways
     to reconcile this contradiction. All critical, objective scholars
     of the New Testament have held that this contradiction is
     irreconcilable. See C.S. Davidson, *An Introduction to the
     Story of the New Testament*, vol. II; C. Torrey, "The Date
     of the Crucifixion According to the Fourth Gospel," *JBL*
     (1931), pp. 227-241; S. Zeitlin, "The Date of the Cruci-
     fixion According to the Fourth Gospel," *ibid.* (1932), pp. 263-
     271; Guignebert, *op. cit.*, pp. 429-431.
95. Cf. Mark 14.43-72; 15.1.
96. Cf. Matt. 26.47-75; 27.1-26.
97. Cf. Luke 22.66, 67; 23.2.
98. Mark 14.53, 65; Matt. 26.57-68.
99. Talmud Kerit. 7.
100. M. Sanh. 7.5.
101. The term "Power" was one of the circumlocutions for God.
102. Luke 23.2.
103. Mark 15.2; Matt. 27.11; Luke 23.3; John 18.33.
104. This custom is recorded only in the Gospels. There is no
     mention of it in rabbinic literature.
105. Mark 15.9-15.
106. Matt. 27.11-26.
107. Luke 23.13-25.
108. John 18.2-5, 12-14.
109. *Ibid.*, 18-28.
110. Cf. Justin Martyr, *Dialogue with Trypho*, 72, "This Pass-

over is our Saviour and our refuge." Cf. also *ibid.*, 111, "And as the blood of the Passover saved those who were in Egypt, so also the blood of Christ will deliver from death those who have belief."

111. John 1.29.
112. *Ibid.*, 19.33.
113. Num. 9.12.
114. Cf. II Baruch 23.4-7.
115. Cf. Irenaeus, *Contra Haereses* 5.23. *Manifestum est itaque, quoniam in illa die mortem sustinuit Dominus, obediens Patri, in qua mortuus est Adam inobediens Deo. In qua autem mortuus est, in ipsa et manducavit. Dixit enim Deus: "In qua die manducabitis ex eo, morte moriemini. Hunc itaque diem recapitulans in semetipsum Dominus, venit ad passionem pridie ante sabbatum, quae est sexta conditionis dies, in qua homo plasmatus est.* "It is clear that the Lord suffered death, in obedience to His Father, upon that day on which Adam died while he disobeyed God. Now he died on the same day in which he did eat. For God said, 'On that day on which ye shall eat of it, ye shall die by death.' The Lord, therefore, capitulating in Himself this day, underwent his suffering upon the day proceeding the Sabbath, that is the sixth day of the creation, on which day man was created; thus granting him a second creation by means of his passing, which is that [creation] out of death."
116. John 18.33-37.
117. *Ibid.*, 19.6.
118. There is no Jewish law, either in the Bible or in the Talmud, to the effect that a person who claimed to be the "Son of God" is liable to capital punishment. The use of the expression "Son of God" was common among the Apocalyptists. In the book of Enoch 105.2, the expression is found "And I and My Son."
119. John 19.12-15.
120. Cf. Mark 15.24.
121. John 19.19. Cf. Suetonius, *Caligula*, 32.
122. John 19.22-23. According to the Roman law, at the time of Jesus, the executioners took the minor spoils of those whom they crucified. This confirms the opinion that Jesus was put to death as a political offender, for in the case of anyone put to death by the religious Sanhedrin, his property belongs to his heirs; but the property of anyone put to death for political reasons belongs to the state. Cf. Sanh. Tosefta, *ibid.*, 4.
123. John 6.15.
124. Cf. S. Zeitlin, "The Duration of Jesus' Ministry," *JQR*, LV (1965), 200.
125. Cf. Ch. Guignebert, *Jesus*, p. 432. "It is possible that the tradition knew that Jesus died about the time of Passover. This fact, together with the desire to connect the institution of the Eucharist with the Last Supper, brought about

. the transformation of the Supper into the paschal meal."
126. In the opinion of Cicero, crucifixion is *crudelissimum teter-rimumque supplicium.*
127. Cf. note 122.
128. Cf. Luke 23.27.
129. See further below, pp. 323-331.

Chapter 3

1. Gaius was surnamed Caligula, "Little Boots," because he was brought up among the soldiers and wore military boots, *caligae.* Suetonius, *Gaius Caligula,* 9; Dio, 57.5.
2. Cf. Suetonius, *ibid.,* 13. Cf. also Philo, *Embassy to Gaius,* 2.
3. Cf. above, p. 151.
4. *Ant.,* 18.6.10(437) ; *War,* 2.9.6(181).
5. Philo, *op. cit.*
6. *Ant.,* 18.7.2(256) ; Dio, 59.6. Cf. also Suetonius, *Gaius Caligula,* 37.
7. *Ibid.,* 22.
8. *Ibid.,* 26; Dio, 59.10.
9. Suetonius, *ibid.*
10. Suetonius, *ibid.,* 23; Dio, 59.3.
11. Suetonius, *ibid.,* 21.
12. Suetonius, *Vitellius,* 2; cf. also Dio, 59.27.
13. Dio, *ibid.*
14. Suetonius, *ibid.;* Dio, 59.17; Tacitus, *Ann.,* 43-46; Josephus, *Ant.,* 18.4.5(101-105). Cf. Täubler, *Die Parthernachrichten bei Josephus* (1904).
15. Suetonius, *Gaius Caligula,* 22.
16. Dio, 59.28. Cf. also *Ant.,* 19.1.2(11).
17. Suetonius, *ibid.,* 24.
18. Philo, *Flaccus,* 6.8.
19. Cf. *ibid.,* 6-8.
20. The history of this event will be related in the volume dealing with the history of the Judaeans in the Diaspora.
21. Philo, *Embassy to Gaius,* 30.
22. *Ibid.;* cf. also Jackson and Lake, *Beginnings of Christianity,* I, ch. 3, p. 265.
23. *Ant.,* 18.8.2(261-262) ; *War,* 2.10.1(184-187) ; Tacitus, *Hist.,* 5.9. *Dein iussi a C. Caesare effigiem eius in templo locare arma potius sumpsere, quem motum Caesaris mors diremit.* "Then, when Caligula ordered the Judaeans to set up his statue in their temple, they chose to resort to arms, but the Emperor's death put an end to their uprising."
24. Cf. Philo, *op. cit.,* 31.
25. Cf. *ibid.,* 33.
26. *Ant.,* 18.8.2(258). According to *War,* 2.10(186), Petronius had three legions. Philo said that Petronius came with half of his army, i.e., two legions, since there were four legions in Syria at this time.

27. Cf. *Ant., ibid.* (264); *War*, 2.10.30(192); Philo, *op. cit.*, 31. Cf. also Schürer, *Geschichte*, 1.
28. *Ant., ibid.* (262-270); *War, ibid.* (193). Tiberius is situated S.W. of Ptolemais.
29. *Ant.*, 18.8.4(272-277).
30. Philo, *op. cit.*, 32(232).
31. *War*, 2.10.5(203).
32. Caligula returned from Germany on his birthday, the 31st of August, 40 C.E. Cf. Suetonius, *Caligula*, 49: *ovans urbem natali suo ingressus est.*
33. *Ant.*, 18.8.1(259).
34. Philo, *The Embassy to Gaius*, 35-42(261-333).
35. *Ant.*, 18.8.7-8(289-301).
36. Cf. S. Zeitlin, "Did Agrippa Write a Letter to Gaius Caligula?" in *JQR*, LVI (1965), 22-31.
37. Cf. Josephus, *Against Apion*, 2.76, *quibus nos et imperatores et populum Romanorum dignitatibus ampliamus.*
38. Suetonius, *Caligula*, 23: *ac non contentus hac Augusti insectatione Actiacas Siculasque victorias.*
39. Dio, 59.20.
40. *War*, 2.10.5(199-204).
41. Suetonius, *Caligula*, 58. Cf. Tacitus. *Hist.*, 5.9, "When Caligula ordered the Judaeans to set up his statue in their temple they chose rather to resort to arms, but the Emperor's death put an end to their uprising."
42. *Ant.*, 18.8.9(305-309); *War*, 2.10.5(203).
43. Cf. S. Zeitlin, *Megillat Taanit*, 88.89.
44. *War*, 1.28.2(556).
45. Cf. above, p. 32.
46. *Ant.*, 18.5.5(131-135).
47. *Ibid.*, 6.1(143).
48. *Ibid.* (144-145).
49. Cf. Suetonius, *Tiberius*, 39.
50. *Ibid.*, 61; cf. also Dio, 58.
51. *Ant.*, 18.6.1-2(145-147).
52. *Ibid.* (148-154).
53. *Ibid.*, 18.6.6(181); Dio, 58. Cf. F.B. March, *The Reign of Tiberius*.
54. *Ant.*, 18.6.2-4(149-166).
55. *Ibid.* (167).
56. *Ibid.*, 5(168-169) and (185-204).
57. *Ibid.*, 10(227-229).
58. *Ibid.* (236-237); *War*, 2.9.6(18). Cf. also Dio, 59; Philo, *Flacus*, 5.
59. *Ant., ibid.*
60. See Dio, 59.
61. *Ant., ibid.*, 11(238-239).
62. Philo, *Flacus*, 6.
63. *Ibid.*, 18-21.
64. See above, p. 150.
65. *Ant.*, 18.7.1-2(240-256). Cf. also *War*, 2.9.5(178).
66. Cf. above p. 150.

67. *Ant.*, 18.7.2(252-253).
68. *Ant.*, *ibid.*, 8.2(261-309). Cf. above, p. 185.
69. Cf. Suetonius, *Caligula*, 56-58; Dio, 59; *Ant.*, 19.1.3-14 and (17-113).
70. Cf. *Ant.*, 19.3.4(212-262); Dio, 60.
71. *Ant.*, *ibid.*, 5.1(274); Dio, *ibid.*
72. *Ant.*, *ibid.*(277); Dio, *ibid.*
73. *Ant.*, *ibid.* (276). Later, Marcus son of Alexander married the daughter of Agrippa, Berenice, who, after the death of her husband, married her uncle Herod, King of Chalcis.
74. *Ant.*, 19.6.1(293-294).
75. *Ibid.*, 3(299).
76. *Ibid.* (394). Cf. J.N. Epstein, *Magnes Anniversary Volume* (1938), in Hebrew.
77. *Ant.*, *ibid.* (297).
78. There has been a debate as to the meaning of the phrase, "the Judaeans called Alexandrians," whether it means simply "inhabitants of Alexandria," or implies civic rights, namely, that the Judaeans of Alexandria were citizens of the city. A full analysis of this problem will be given in the volume dealing with the history of the Judaeans in the Diaspora.
79. *Ant.*, 19.5.3(286-291).
80. *Ant.*, *ibid.*, 3(300-301).
81. Deut. 31.10-13. Cf. vol. I, pp. 251-252, and p. 486, n. 114.
82. M. Sota, 7.8.
83. Deut. 7.15.
84. M. Sota, 7.8. Cf. S. Zeitlin, "Herod," in *JQR*, (July 1963), 7-8.
85. Cf. *ibid.*, p. 8.
86. *Ant.*, 19.6.4(312-315).
87. *Ibid.*, 8.1(342).
88. M. Bik. 3.4.
89. *Ant.*, *ibid.*, 5(335-337).
90. Cf. *ibid.*, 9.1(357).
91. See Jones, *The Herods of Judaea*, pp. 210-211; Schürer, *Geschichte*, I, ch. Agrippa I.
92. *Ant.*, 19.7.4(232-234).
93. *Ibid.*, 1(317-325).
94. See Tacitus, *Ann.*, 11.8-10; 12.10-14.
95. *Ant.*, 19.7.2(326-327); *War*, 2.11.6(218); 5.4.1(149-155).
96. *Ant.*, 19.8.1(338-342).
97. Acts 1.6: When they therefore were come together, they asked of him saying, "Lord, wilt thou at this time restore again the kingdom of Israel."
98. *Ibid.*, 5.18-19. With regard to the trial of Stephen, cf. S. Zeitlin, *Who Crucified Jesus?*, pp. 188-192.
99. The Roman historian Dio mentions Agrippa three times (59.8, 24; 60.8). He does not add the name Herod to Agrippa. There is some confusion in the story as given in Acts.
100. Acts 5.33-36.

101. Cf. *Ant.*, 20.5.1 (97-99). See below, p. 208; C. Torrey, *The Composition and the Date of Acts* (1916).
102. *Ant.*, 19.8.2 (343-347).
103. *Ibid.* (349-350).
104. *Ibid.*, 9 (354-355) ; *War*, 2.11.6 (218-220).
105. Agrippa's piety and devotion to his people were sincere. In his early years, while living in Rome, he spent his days in gaiety and debauchery. He resorted to this out of political motives, in order to gain the friendship of the élite of Rome and the imperial family and their hirelings. He possessed the gift of remarkable versatility. His reckless living in Rome was not really in conformity with his character. He indulged in it for the sole purpose of securing the friendship and devotion of the rulers, and thus achieved his goal—to become King of Judaea. Credit must be given to his mother Berenice, whose intimate friendship with Antonia made is possible for her son Agrippa to become an an intimate of the family of Germanicus.
106. Lam. 4.20.
107. *Ant.*, 9.1-2 (357-365).

Chapter 4

1. Cf. *Ant.*, 19.9.2 (362).
2. *Ibid.* (363).
3. *Ibid.*, 20.1.1 (1). Cassius Longinus was a great general and jurist. He belonged to the conservative school of Sabinus. Tacitus, *Ann.*, 12.12; Pliny, *Ep.*, 7.24.
4. *Ant.*, 19.9.2 (364-366).
5. Cf. *War*, 6.2.4 (126). Cf. S. Zeitlin, *JQR*, XXXI (1941), 343-344.
6. *Ant.*, 20.2.5 (51).
7. *Ibid.*, 20.1 (2-4).
8. *Ibid.* (5).
9. *Ant.*, 20.1.1-2 (7-14).
10. *Ibid.*, 3 (15-16).
11. *Ibid.*, 5.1 (97-99).
12. *Ca.* 45 C. E.
13. *Ant.*, 20.5.2 (100). Tiberius Alexander was Procurator of Judaea in the years 46-48. In the year 48, Herod, King of Chalcis, removed Joseph son of Cami from the high priesthood and assigned the office to Ananias son of Nedbaeus. Cf. also *War*, 2.11.6 (220). "Claudius again reduced the kingdom to a province and sent as procurators, first Cuspius Fadus, and then Tiberius Alexander, who, by abstaining from all interference with the customs of the country, kept the nation at peace."
14. *Ant.*, 20.5.2 (102).
15. *Ibid.*, 20.2.5 (51).
16. Cf. below, p. 219.
17. *Ant.*, 20.5.2 (103). According to Tacitus, *Ann.*, 12.54, Cumanus

was the governor of Galilee and Felix was the administrator of Samaria: *cui pars provinciae habebatur ita divisis, ut huic Galilaeorum natio, Felici Samaritae parerent.*

18. *War,* 4.10.6(616).
19. *Satire,* 1.27.
20. Herod died in the eighth year of the reign of Claudius: *Ant.,* 20.5.2(104). His sons were named Aristobolus, Berenicianus and Hyrcanus.
21. *Ant.,* 20.5.3-4(105-117); *War,* 2.12.1(223-227).
22. *Ant., ibid.* (120).
23. *Ibid.* (121) and (161). Cf. also *War,* 2.12.3-4(232-235). Cf. M. Sotah 9.9; M. Kelim 5.10; Tal. Ket. 27; Midrash, Song of Songs, 2.18. Cf. also J. Derenbourg, *Essai sur l'Histoire et la Géographie de la Palestine,* pp. 279-280, n. 3.
24. Cf. *War,* 2.12.4(235).
25. *Ant., ibid.* (123-124).
29. *Ant., ibid.* (134-135); *War, ibid.,* 7(245-246). Tacitus, *Ann.,* of Ananias was one of the delegates.
27. According to *War, ibid.* (241), "to Caesarea."
28. *Ant., ibid.* (130-133); *War, ibid.,* 6(241-244).
29. *Ant., ibid.* (134-135); *War, ibid.,* 7(245-246). Tacitus *Ann.,* 12.54, gives a different account of the strife between the Galileans and the Samarians. "The districts (Galilee and Samaria) had long been at variance, and their animosities were now under the less restraint as they could despise their regents. Accordingly, they harried each other, unleashed their troops of bandits, fought an occasional field, and carried their trophies and their thefts to their procurators. . . . with regard to the Judaeans, who had gone so fas as to shed the blood of regular soldiers, there were no protracted doubts as to the infliction of the death penalty. Cumanus and Felix were answerable for more embarrassment, as Claudius, on learning the motive of the revolt, authorized Quadratus to deal with the case of the procurators themselves. Quadratus, however, displayed Felix among the judges, his admission to the tribunal being intended to cool the zeal of his accusers; Cumanus was sentenced for delinquencies of two, and quietude returned to the province."
30. *Ant.,* 20.7.1(137); *War,* 2.12.8(217); Suetonius, *Claudius,* 28. According to Tacitus, *Ann.,* 12.54, he was previously governor of Samaria. Tacitus, *Hist.,* 5.9, calls him Antonius Felix.
31. *Ant., ibid.,* 7.1(138); *War, ibid.* (294). Cf. *Vita,* 48-52.
32. *Ant.,* 20.8.8(179).
33. *Ibid.,* 7.1(139-140).
34. Suetonius, *Claudius,* 28, "He was equally fond of Felix, giving him the command of cohorts and of troops of horse, as well as of the province of Judaea." Cf. *Ant.,* 18.6.6(182); Tacitus, *Ann.,* 11.29; 12.54.
35. *Ant.,* 20.8.5(162).
36. Tacitus, *Hist.,* 5.9: *Antoninius Felix per omnem saevitiam ac libidinem ius regium servili ingenio exercuit.*

37. Tacitus, *Ann.*, 12.54: *At non frater eius, cognomento Felix, pari moderatione agebat, iam pridem Iudaeae impositus et cuncta malefacta sibi impune ratus tanta potentia subnixo.*
38. Suetonius, *Claudius*, 28.
39. *Ant.*, 20.7.2 (141-143).
40. *Ibid.*, 3 (145-146). Cf. Juvenal, *Satire*, 6 (157-158), *hunc dedit olim barbarus incestae dedit hunc Agrippa sorori.*
41. See below, p. 233. Cf. Suetonius, *Titus*, 7; Tacitus, *Hist.*, 2.2; Dio, 66.15.
42. Suetonius, *Claudius*, 45.
43. Suetonius, *ibid.*, 44; *Ant.*, 20.8.(148); Tacitus, *Ann.*, 12.66-67.
44. *Ant.*, *ibid.*, 4 (158-159); *War*, 2.8.2 (252).
45. Dio, 62.14. Suetonius, *Nero*, 34.
46. Cf. *War*, 2.13 (264)
47. *Ibid.*, 2 (253); *Ant.*, 20.8.5 (161).
48. *Ant.*, *ibid.* (162-163).
49. *War*, *ibid.*, 3 (254-257). *Lex Cornelia de Sicariis* was passed in the year 80 B.C.E.
50. *War*, 4 (258-259); 5 (261-263); *Ant.*, 20.8.6 (169-171).
51. Acts 21.38.
52. Cf. Tacitus, *Ann.*, 13.8, 35.41; 14.23-25; 15.1-4, 15-16; Dio, 62.20-22.
53. Cf. *Ant.*, 20.8.7 (173-178); *War*, 2.13.7 (266-270).
54. *Ant.*, *ibid.*, 8 (179-181).
55. According to Josephus, *ibid.* (181-182), Pallas interceded for his brother Felix.
56. Cf. Dio, 61.3-4; Tacitus, *Ann.*, 13.14.
57. *Ant.*, *ibid.*, 9 (184).
58. Cf. Acts 21.33-34. Paul was born in the city of Tarsus, Cilicia, modern Turkey.
59. Acts 9.1-2; 22.4-5; 26.9-12.
60. The account of the conversion is given in three different places in Acts—chs. 9, 22, and 26, with some variants. Cf. also II Cor. 11; Galat. 1.13-17.
61. There has been considerable debate as to the number of visits made by Paul to Jerusalem after his conversion. The Epistle to the Galatians mentions two visits, while according to Acts, Paul made at least three journeys to Jerusalem (cf. chs. 11, 15, 21). It seems that the account given in Galatians is the more reliable since this Epistle was written by Paul (as is generally assumed), while Acts is a compilation based on a variety of traditions and is full of anachronisms. Cf. F. J. Foakes Jackson and Kirsopp Lake, *The Beginnings of Christianity: the Acts of the Apostles*, pp. 280-290. According to Galatians 1.17, Paul, after his conversion, did not go to Jerusalem immediately, "Neither went I up to Jerusalem to them which were apostles before me; but I went to Arabia, and returned again unto Damascus." He continues, "Then, after three years, I went up to Jerusalem to see Peter, and abode with him fifteen days." Paul made his first visit to Jerusalem in the year 48, three years after his conversion. This corresponds to the account given in Acts 11.29-30 that Barnabas

and Saul (who was still called by his Hebrew name) were sent to Judaea (Jerusalem) with alms to the elders due to the famine which prevailed in the land. The famine occurred in the year 48. Hence the year of Paul's conversion is to be fixed 44-45.

In Galatians 2.1, Paul said, "Then, fourteen years after, I went up again to Jerusalem with Barnabas, I took Titus also." The fourteen years is to be calculated from the conversion, which would place the second visit in 58-59, and on this visit Paul was arrested. This chronology corresponds to the last year of the procuratorship of Felix 59 and the first year of Festus 60.

Between Paul's first visit to Jerusalem in the year 48 and the second in 58, he was engaged in his missionary work and wrote some of his epistles. Cf. S. Zeitlin, "Paul's Journey to Jerusalem," *JQR*, LVII (Jan. 1967).

62. Galat. 1.18-19.
63. Cf. Acts 13.44-46; 14.19-28.
64. Cf. above, n. 61.
65. Cf. Acts 21.21: "And they are informed of thee, that thou teachest all the Judaeans which are among the Gentiles to forsake Moses, saying that they ought not to circumcise (their) children, neither to walk after the customs."
66. Acts 21.20-24.
67. Acts 21.27-29.
68. Cf. above, p. 49.
69. Acts 21.38,39.
70. *Ibid.*, 22.30. Cf. below, p. 222.
71. Acts 23.6-7. Cf. S. Zeitlin, "The Crucifixion of Jesus Re-examined," *JQR*, XXXII (1942), 288-289; Jackson and Lake, *op. cit.*, 296.
72. Cf. Talmud Kid. 43; cf. S. Zeitlin, *op. cit.*, p. 289.
73. Acts 23.10.
74. Cf. S. Zeitlin, *op. cit.*, pp. 289-290.
75. Acts 23.15-24.
76. *Ibid.*, 24.1; cf. S. Zeitlin, *op. cit.*, p. 291, n. 106.
77. Acts 24.5-24.
78. *Ibid.*, 25.
79. Acts 24.26; cf. also 27. "But after two years, Porcius Festus came into Felix's room; and Felix, willing to shew the Judaeans a pleasure, left Paul bound."
80. Acts 25.13-25.
81. *Ibid.*, 26.5-21.
82. Acts 26.24.
83. *Ibid.*, 22-23, 28, 30-32.
84. Cf. *ibid.*, 11-26: "And the disciples were called Christians first in Antioch."

The term "Christians" is found only three times in the New Testament: twice in Acts—in this verse and again in 26-28 when Agrippa said to Paul, "Almost thou persuadest me to become a Christian"; and the third place is I Peter 4.16. Neither the authors of the Gospels nor Paul in his

Epistles ever used the term "Christians." In the Gospels as well as in the Epistles, the followers of Jesus speak of themselves as "brethren," "disciples," "saints," "believers." It seems that the term "Christians" was applied by the pagans in Antioch, as a name of reproach and ridicule, to those who followed Jesus the anointed one, Christ. Cf. also Tacitus, *Ann.*, 15.44, *Quos per flagitia invisos vulgus Christianos appellabat:* "Whom the crowd styled Christians." For the trial of Paul, cf. below, pp. 365.

Chapter 5

1. *Ant.*, 20.8.8(179); cf. *ibid.*, 18.2.2(34). According to Talmud Yoma 9, he served for ten years. Cf. also Ker. 28; Pes. 57, where he was highly praised, calling him a disciple of Phineas. However, in Tos. Men. 13.21, the family of Ishmael son of Fabi, was censured for their oppressive acts. It is stated, "Woe is me from the house of Ishmael son of Fabi, that they are high priests, their sons are *gizbarin* (treasurers) and their sons-in-law are *amarkelin*, and their slaves beat the people with staves." It is possible that there were two high priests with the same name. One held his position in the year 14-15 C.E. (*Ant.*, 18.2.2[34]), while the other was appointed by Agrippa in the year 59 C.E. There is another possibility that, while the high priest Ishmael son of Fabi was a righteous person, his children were wicked.
2. *Ant.*, 20.8.8(181); 9.2(206-207).
3. *Ibid.* (180).
4. *Ibid.*, 11(189-193).
5. *Theosebes*, religious, fearing God; see below, p. 308.
6. *Ant.*, 20.9.11(193-196).
7. *Ibid.*, 9.4(211-212).
8. *Ibid.*, 8.11(196).
9. *Ibid.*, 9.1(198).
10. *Ibid.* (198).
11. *Ibid.* (200). Cf. S. Zeitlin, "The Christ Passage in Josephus," *JQR*, XVIII (1928), 232-234. Origen on three occasions quotes this passage from *Antiquities* with some variation (*Comm.*, Matt. 13; *Contra Celsum*, 1.77; 2.13). He says that, according to Josephus, the execution of James, the brother of Jesus, who was called Christ, caused the destruction of the Temple. We do not find this version in our text of *Antiquities*. The writer of *Chronicon Paschale* also quotes the same passage, not from *Antiquities*, but from *War*. Eusebius in the name of Hegesippus says that James was thrown from the roof of the Temple, stoned and finally killed, and immediately thereafter Vespasian laid siege to Jerusalem (*Ecc. Hist.*, 2.23). Thus Hegesippus also connects the death of James with the city of Jerusalem. From all this it may be assumed that, in the place of this passage in *Antiquities*, there was before the time of Origen and Eusebius a completely different version

of the same event. If, however, the words of the author of *Chronicon Paschale* has historical basis, the execution of James was not recorded in *Antiquities*, but in *War*.

Again Origen wrote, "Though he (Josephus) did not believe in Jesus as the Christ, he none the less asseverates that the calamity of the destruction of the Temple came upon the Judaeans for putting to death James, who was most distinguished for his justice" (*Contra Celsum*, 1.47). If this passage in *Antiquiteis* had the words "James, the brother of Jesus (who was called) the Christ," it is hard to believe that Origen would say that Josephus did not believe that Jesus was the Christ. Cf. further, Ap. IV.

12. *Ant.*, 20.9.1 (202-203).
13. *Ibid.*, and 3 (208).
14. Yoma 18; Yeb. 61; *Ant.*, 20.9.4 (213-214).
15. *Ibid.*, 3 (208-210) ; *War*, 2.14.1 (273-276).
16. *Ant.*, *ibid.*, 4 (214).
17. *War*, 6.5.3 (299-309).
18. *Ant.*, 20.9.7 (219-222).
19. *Ibid.* (222).
20. *War*, 5.1.5 (36).
21. *Ant.*, 20.9.6 (216-218).
22. *Ibid.*, 5 (215).
23. *War*, 2.14.2 (277-279).
24. *War*, *ibid.*, 4-5 (284-292) ; *Ant.*, 20.11.1 (252-258).
25. Cf. Tacitus, *Ann.*, 15.6.
26. Cf. *Ant.*, 20.2.1-4 (17-40). See below, p. 310.
27. Dio, 62.20; Tacitus, *ibid.*
28. Tacitus, *ibid.*, 15.11-24; Dio, 62.20-23.
29. Suetonius, *Nero*, 39, *Ignominia ad Orientem legionibus in Armenia sub iugum missis aegreque Syria retenta.*
30. *Ibid. Dum tendit citharam noster, dum cornua Parthus.*
31. Tacitus, *ibid.*, 25.
32. B. B. 21; cf. S. Zeitlin, *An Historical Study of the Canonization of the Hebrew Scriptures* (Philadelphia, 1933), p. 6.
33. *Ant.*, 20.9.7 (223).
34. Josephus, *Vita*, 3.
35. *War*, 2.14.6-7 (293-300).
36. The fifteenth of the month of Artemisius.
37. *War*, 2.14, 8-9 (301-308).
38. *Ibid.*, 15.1 (309-314).
39. *Ibid.*, 2 (315-317).
40. *Ibid.*, 3-6 (318-329).
41. Cf. below, Ap. I; cf. S. Zeitlin, *Megillat Taanit*, pp. 91-93.
42. *War*, 2.16.1-2 (333-341).
43. *Ibid.*, 3 (342).
44. *Ibid.*, 4 (345-401).
45. *Ibid.*, 17.1.1 (405-406).
46. *Ibid.* (406-407).
47. *Ibid.*, 2 (408).
48. *Ibid.*, 2-3 (409-416) ; cf. Talmud. Git. 57; see below, p. 359.

49. Shab. 17; *Yer. ibid.;* Tos. *ibid.;* cf. S. Zeitlin, "Les Dix-Huit Mesures," *REJ* (1915), 22-36.
50. *Idem, Megillat Taanit,* pp. 93-94.
51. *War,* 2.17.4 (418-419, 421).
52. Tam. 26, "the tenth of Elul," according to the reading of the Munich MS; cf. S. Zeitlin, *Megillat Taanit,* p. 95.
53. *War,* 2.17.5-6 (422-426).
54. *Ibid.,* 6-7 (428-431).
55. *Ibid.,* 7 (430-431).
56. *Ibid.,* 8 (433-438).
57. The sixth of the month Gorpiaeus. Cf. S. Zeitlin, *Megillat Taanit,* pp. 94-96.
58. *Ibid.,* p. 96.
59. *War,* 2.17.10 (449-454).
60. Cf. S. Zeitlin, *op. cit.,* pp. 97-100.
61. Cf. F. W. Madden, *Jewish Numismatics* (London, 1874-76), p. 161. A. Reifenberg, *Jewish Coins* (1947); J. Klausner, *The History of the Second Temple* (in Hebrew) (Jerusalem, 1951), 5, p. 150.
62. *War,* 2.17.9 (941).
63. *Ibid.* (442-448).
64. Cf. S. Zeitlin, "Masada and the Sicarii" in *JQR,* LVI (1965), 290-317.
65. *War,* 2.18.1 (457-458).
66. *Ibid.,* 9 (500-502).
67. *Ibid.,* 9-11 (503-512).
68. *Ibid.,* 19.1.1 (513-516).
69. *Ibid.,* 2 (517-520).
70. *Ibid.,* 3 (523-526).
71. *Ibid.,* "The thirtieth of the month Hyperberetaeus."
72. *Ibid.* (527-530).
73. *Ibid.,* 5 (530-531).
74. *Ibid.* (531).
75. *Ibid.,* 7-8 (541-550).
76. *Ibid.,* 9 (551-555).
77. *Ibid.* Josephus twice refers to the Revolt as beginning in the twelfth year of Nero. He states that the victory over Cestius took place "the eighth of the month of Dius in the twelfth year of Nero's rule." In another passage (2.14.44) he says that the war broke out "in the twelfth year of the rule of Nero, and the seventeenth of the reign of Agrippa, in the month of Artemisius." A critical examination of these two passages shows that the date cannot be placed in one year. For, if the outbreak of the war occurred in the month of Artemisius of the twelfth year of Nero, then the victory over Cestius could not have been in the eighth of Dius of the same year of Nero; for Nero became emperor on the thirteenth day of October, 54 C.E. According to no calculation could Artemisius precede Dius in any one year of Nero's reign. For, if Josephus used the Roman calendar, Artemisius would correspond to May and Dius to November; and if he used the Jewish calendar, Artemisius would correspond to

Iyar and Dius to Heshvan; and if his calendar was Tyrian, Artemisius preceded Dius in the year of Nero's reign. Therefore the war broke out either in Artemisius in the eleventh year of Nero's reign, or else the victory over Cestius occurred not in the twelfth but in the thirteenth year of Nero's reign. This seemingly insurmountable difficulty can be solved. Josephus counted Nero's imperium, not from the day on which he ascended the throne, but either from the beginning of the calendar year (January 1), or from the day of the *Tribunicia Potestas* (December 10). Cf. Unger, "Zu Josephus," in *Sitzungsberichte der Münchener Akademie Philos. Philol. u. Hist. Cl.* (1896), pp. 383-391.

Now, if Nero's reign was dated from the beginning of the calendar year 54 C.E., January 1st, 55 C.E. marked the beginning of his second year. Likewise, if the years of Nero's reign were calculated according to the *Tribunicia Potestas*, then the first year of his reign ended *Trib. Potest.*, December 10th, 54 C.E. According to this theory the seventeenth of Artemisius, which according to the Tyrian calendar corresponds to June 4th, and the 8th of Dius corresponding to November 25th, occurred in the same year of Nero's reign. The twelfth year of Nero's reign began either on January 1, 65 C.E. or, with *Trib. Potest.*, on December 10th, 64 C.E. Thus the revolt which broke out on the seventeenth of Artemisius, June 4th, and the victory over Cestius on the eighth of Dius, November 25th, were both in the year 65 C.E. Cf. further S. Zeitlin, *Megillat Taanit*, pp. 58-60. Cf. *ibid.*, pp. 100-104.

78. *War*, 2.18.5(477).
79. *Ibid.*, 20.2(559-561).
80. *Ibid.*, 18.1(457-460).
81. *Ibid.*, 3(466-476).
82. *Ibid.*, 2(462-463). "For, though believing that they had rid themselves of the Judaeans, still each city had its Judaizers who aroused suspicion." Cf. also *Vita*, 6.24. "This reverse of Cestius proved disastrous to our whole people; for those who were bent on war were thereby still more elated and, having once defeated the Romans, hoped to continue victorious to the end. . . . The inhabitants of the surrounding cities of Syria proceeded to lay hands on and kill, with their wives and children, the Judaean residents among them without the slightest ground of complaint; for they had neither entertained any enmity or designs against the Syrians."
83. Cf. Tacitus, *Hist.*, 5.13, *Pluribus persuasio inerat antiquis sacerdotum litteris contineri eo ipso tempore fore ut valesceret Oriens profectique Iudaea rerum potirentur.* "The majority firmly believed that their ancient priestly writings contained the prophecy that this was the very time when the East should grow strong and that men starting from Judaea would rule the world." Suetonius, *Vespasian*, 4, *Percrebruerat Oriente toto vetus et constans opinio esse in fatis ut eo tempore Iudaea profecti rerum potirentur.* "There had

spread over all the Orient an old and established belief that it was fated at that time for men coming from Judaea to rule the world." Cf. also *War*, 6.5.4(311-312); "What more than all else incited them (the Judaeans) to the war was an ambiguous oracle, likewise found in their sacred scriptures, to the effect that at that time one from their country would become ruler of the world."

84. *War*, 2.18.6(481-486); *Vita*, 11(46-61).
85. *War, ibid.*, 20.1(556).
86. *War, ibid.* (556-558).
87. Cf. S. Zeitlin, *Megillat Taanit*, pp. 105-107.
88. *War, ibid.* (562-563). *Vita*, 38(189-194): Joshua ben Gamala was also chosen as a member of the National Assembly.
89. *War, ibid.*
90. Cf. *Vita*, 7(28-29).

PART THREE

Chapter 1

1. M. B. B., 3.2.
2. Cf. *War*, 3.3.1(35-38); S. Klein, *Galilee* (Jerusalem, 1945) (in Hebrew).
3. *War*, 3.3.4(48).
4. *War, ibid.*, 3(44-47).
5. *Ibid.*, 5(51-54).
6. *Ibid.*, 2(41-43).
7. *Ibid.*, 2.10.2(189).
8. Cf. Tacitus, *Hist.*, 5.7, *At Belus amnis Iudaico mari inlabitur, circa cuius os lectae harenae admixto nitro in vitrum excoquuntur.* "The river Belus also empties into the Judaean Sea; around its mouth a kind of sand is gathered, which, when mixed with soda, is fused into glass." Pliny, *Nat. Hist.*, 36.65 (190-191): "That part of Syria which is known as Phoenicia and borders on Judaea contains a swamp called Candebia amid the lower slopes of Mount Carmel. This is supposed to be the source of the River Belus, which, after traversing a distance of five miles, flows into the sea near the colony of Ptolemais. ... The river is muddy and flows in a deep channel, revealing its sands only when the tide ebbs. For it is not until they have been tossed by the waves and cleansed of impurities that they glisten. ... When the water mingled with the sand on the beach, a strange translucid liquid flowed forth in streams, and this, it is said, was the origin of glass."
9. See S. Klein, *Judaea* (Tel Aviv) (in Hebrew).
10. Cf. *War*, 2.9.1(168). Philip built Caesarea Philippi near the source of the Jordan, in the district of Paneas.
11. *War*, 3.10.7(513-514).
12. *Ibid.* (514-518); 4.8.2-3(451-475); Pliny, *Nat. Hist.* 5.15 (71-72).
13. *Ant.*, 17.6.5(171); Pliny, *ibid.* (72).

14. Pliny, *ibid.* (71-72); *War*, 4.8.4(476-477).
15. Cf. above, p. 118.
16. *War*, 3.3.3(55-56); Pliny, *Nat. Hist.*, 5.15(70). Pliny gives the division of Judaea into ten Teporchies: "The rest of Judaea is divided into ten Teporchies in the following order: The district of Jericho which has numerous palm-groves and springs of water, and those of Emmaus, Lydda, Joppa, Accrabim, Jufna, Timnath-Serah, Beth-lebaoth, the Hills, the district that formerly contained Jerusalem, by far the most famous city of the East and not of Judaea only, and Herodium with the celebrated town of the same name." See A. Shalit, *King Herod*, pp. 111-113.
17. Cf. *Ant.*, 16.9.1(274); 7.3(203); *War*, 1.24.3(479).
18. *Vita*, 63.
19. Cf. *War*, 2.17.1(405).
20. J. Juster, *Les Juifs dans L'Empire Romain* (Paris, 1914), 1, pp. 209-212; S. W. Baron, *A Social and Religious History of the Jews*, I (New York, 1952), pp. 370-372.
21. *War*, 6.9.3(423). A similar story is related in Tos. Pes. 4; Talmud Pes. 64. King Agrippa asked the high priest to count one kidney from each paschal lamb and those counted were 2,200,000.
22. *War, ibid.;* Tos., *ibid.* Josephus gives the number 2,550,000. The arithmetic or the text is at fault. In *War*, 2.14.3(280). Josephus states that when Cestius visited Jerusalem on the occasion of the feast of unleavened bread, the people at that time in the city were "not less than three million."
23. *Vita*, 235. *War*, 3.3.2(43).
24. *Ibid.*, 2.18.1-2(457-464).
25. *Ibid.*, 6.9.3.(420).
26. Tacitus, *Hist.*, 5.13.
27. *War*, 6.9.3(420).
28. Ch. 30 of Seder Olam. Cf. above, p. 242. See S. Zeitlin, *Megillat Taanit*, pp. 58-64.
29. Cf. *Ant.*, 19.9.2(265).
30. Cf. I, pp. 366-370.
31. *Ant.*, 20.5.3(106-107).
32. Cf. above, p. 137.
33. Cf. S. Zeitlin, "The Crucifixion of Jesus Re-examined," in *JQR* (1942), pp. 279-298.
34. Quadratus, the legate of Syria, had authority over Cumanus, the procurator of Judaea; *Ant.*, 20.6.2(132). Similarly Cestius, the legate of Syria, had authority over Florus, the procurator of Judaea; cf. *War*, 2.16.1(333).
35. W. T. Arnold, *The Roman System of Provincial Administration* (1870), p. 64.
36. *War*, 2.14.9(308).
37. Cf. above, p. 222. Acts, 17.7: "Saying that there is another king (one Jesus)"; 24.5: "For we have found this man a pestilent and a mover of sedition among all the Judaeans throughout the world, and a ringleader of the school of the Nazarenes."

38. *Ibid.*, 26.32: "Then said Agrippa unto Festus, this man might have been set at liberty if he had not appealed unto Caesar."
39. *Ant.*, 20.9.1 (200-202).
40. *Ibid.* (199): "He (Ananus) followed the philosophy of the Sadducees, who are indeed more heartless than any of the other Judaeans."

Chapter 2

1. Cf. M. Rostovtzeff, *Social and Economic History of the Hellenistic World*, 1, pp. 295-296.
2. *War*, 5.4.1 (140).
3. Cf. M. Nidah 2.7, "The vine of Sharon"; Talmud, *ibid.*, 21. "The vine of Carmel." Cf. also M. Men. 8.6.
4. *War*, 4.8.2 (454). Cf. M. Suk. 3.1.
5. Cf. above, p. 61. According to Strabo, 16.4.26, the Nabataeans, while rich in gold and silver, had to import iron and brass. "Some things," he wrote, "are imported wholly from other countries, but others not altogether so, especially in the case of those that are native products, as, for example, gold and silver and most of the aromatics, whereas brass and iron, and also purple garb, styrax, crocus, costaria, embossed works, paintings, and molded works were not produced in their country."
6. Cf. I Kings 5.20-23.
7. Cf. I, 306-308.
8. 12.54 (113,118). "The only country in which this plant has been vouchsafed is Judaea, where formerly it grew in only two gardens both belonging to the king; one of them was of not more than twenty *iugera* in extent, and the other less. This variety of shrub was exhibited to the capital by the Emperors Vespasian and Titus; and it is a remarkable feat that ever since the time of Pompey the Great even trees have figured among the captives in our triumphal processions. The balsam-tree is now a subject of Rome and pays tribute together with the people to whom it belongs."
9. Cf. I, pp. 306-307.
10. Strabo, 16.2.45: "At the place called Taricheae, the lake supplies excellent fish for pickling; and on its banks grow fruit-bearing trees resembling apple trees."
11. Cf. above, p. 98.
12. Deut. 21.17. Cf. below, p. 290.
13. Cf. Matt. 21.33 ff.
14. Cf. I, pp. 196-199.
15. Ben Sira, 38.27-31.
16. *War*, 5.8.1 (331); M. Er. 10.9; B.B.K. 82; *Yer.* Ed. 4.1; S. Zeitlin, "Takkonot Ezra," in *JQR* (1917), 17-72.
17. Cf. above, p. 278.
18. *Ant.*, 20.8.8. (181); Pes. 57.
19. *War*, 1.9.3 (508).
20. "Rations for the hands: four *modii* of wheat in the winter, and in summer four and one half for the field hands. The

overseer, the housekeeper, the foreman and the shepherd should receive three. The chain gang (the field hands were chained together and at night kept in an underground prison) should have a ration of four pounds of bread through the winter, increasing to five when they begin to work the vines, and dropping back to four when the figs ripen." *On Agriculture*, 56.

Claudius Caesar issued a decree that slaves who through illness were abandoned by their masters became free, and if they recovered need not return to their masters. He further decreed that any master who preferred to kill such a slave rather than abandon him was liable to a charge of murder. Suetonius, *Claudius*, 25.

The slave owners were in constant fear of uprisings. Indeed, there were many insurrections which were a continuous threat during the last decade of the republic. The greatest insurrection, in 73 B.C.E., was led by Cricus and Spartacus and was crushed by Crassus.

21. Ecclesiasticus 33.23-31.
22. The condition of the slaves in imperial Rome is portrayed by Juvenal. He wrote, " 'Crucify the slaves!' says the wife, 'but what crime worthy of death has he committed?' asks the husband; 'where are the witnesses? Who informed against him? Give him a hearing at least; no delay can be too long when a man's life is at stake.' 'What, you numbskull? You call a slave a man, do you? He has done no wrong you say. Be it so; for this is my will and my command. Let my will be the voucher for the deed.' " *Satire*, 6.219-224. Slaves were regarded as impersonal men, *Cum servus manumittitur, quia servile caput nullum jus habet ideo nec minui potest, eo die enim incipit statum habere.* "A slave who is manumitted, having no rights, cannot lose any, for all his rights date from the day of his manumission." *Digest* 4.5.4.
23. Ex. 21.2, 7; Lev. 25.39; cf. M. Git. 4.6; Tos. Ab. Zar. 3.18.
24. Ex. 22.2. *Ant.*, 4.8.27(272).
25. Gen. 44.17.
26. Cf. S. Zeitlin, "The Halaka," *JQR* (1948), 34.
27. *Idem*, "Slavery During the Second Commonwealth and the Tannaitic Period," *JQR* (1963), 187-188.
28. Cf. I, p. 311. The right of the creditor to the person of the debtor was abolished in Rome by *lex poetelia*, in the year 311 B.C.E. Livy, 8.28. Cf. also Diodorus, 1.79.
29. In *De Virbutibus* 143, Philo wrote, "As for debtors who through temporary loans have sunk into bearing both the name and the painfulness which their cruel situation entails, and those whom a more imperious compulsion has brought from freedom into slavery, he [Moses] would not allow them to remain forever in their evil plight, but gave them total remission in the seventh year. For creditors who have not recovered the debt, or have gained possession in some other way of those who were formerly free, should be content, he again [Moses] says, with six years as a time for their serv-

ice; and those who were not born to slavery could not be altogether deprived of comforting hope, but should pass back to the old independence of which they were deprived through adverse circumstances." The Gospel according to Matthew 18.24-34, gives the story of a man who owed ten thousand silver talents which he did not repay: "His master commanded him to be sold," Matthew relates, "his wife and his children and all that he had, and payment to be made." On the pleading of the servant his master had compassion and forgave him the debt. Matthew continues, "But the same servant went out and found one of his fellow servants which owed him a hundred pence and he laid hands on him and took (him) by the throat saying, 'pay me that thou owest.' And his fellow servant fell down on his feet and besought him saying 'have patience with me and I will pay you the debt.' And he would not; but went and cast him into prison till he should pay the debt." The Gospel continues that when this was told to the master, he called his slave and said to him, " 'O thou wicked servant, I forgave thee all that debt, because thou desiredst me; Shouldest not thou also have had compassion on thy fellow-servant, even as I had pity on thee?' And his master was wroth, and delivered him to the tormentors, till he should pay all that was due unto him."

30. Ex. 21.5-6.
31. M. Kid. 1.3.
32. M. B. M. 1.5.
33. Tos. B. B. 4.4.
34. M. Git. 4.4.
35. *Ibid.*; Yer., *ibid.*
36. Tos. B. B. 9.10-11.
37. M. Git., 4.4; cf. S. Zeitlin, "Slavery During the Second Commonwealth and the Tannaitic Period," *JQR*, LIII (1963), 215-216.
38. Cf. *idem, loc. cit.*, pp. 211-214.
39. *Servus manumissus capite non minuitur quia nullum caput habet.* "A slave by manumission loses no rights, having none to lose."
40. *Ant.*, 15.10.1 (242-243).
41. Ex. 21.20-21.
42. Tos. B. K. 9.24; Ex. 21.26-27.
43. M. Yid. 4.6. Cf. S. Zeitlin, *op. cit.*
44. The Sadducean position, that the gentile slaves were obliged to perform *mitzvoth*, is not a contradiction of their position. It refers only to the Noachite *mitzvoth*, the *ius gentium*. Thus a slave is responsible for homicide, even of a fellow slave; if a slave committed incest, he is culpable. In this regard a slave differs from an animal as the Mishne notes.
45. M. Git. 4.5.
46. Seneca, in his admonition to the Romans, deplored the status of the slaves, "I do not wish to involve myself in too large a question, " he wrote, "and to discuss the treatment of slaves, towards whom we Romans are excessively haughty, cruel

and insulting; but this is the kernel of my advice: Treat your inferiors as you would be treated by your betters. And as often as you reflect how much power you have over a slave, remember that your master has just as much power over you, 'but I have no master,' you say. You are still young; perhaps you will have one. Do you not know at what age Hecuba entered captivity, or Croesus, or the mother of Darius, or Plato, or Diodenes?" *Ep.* 47.

47. Ecclesiasticus 38.27-30.
48. Cf. Talmud, Kid. 82; Tos. Kid. 5.15.
49. Tos. B. B. 5.9. Talmud, *ibid.*, 89.
50. M. B. B. 5.10; cf. also Tos., *ibid.*, 5.5.
51. M. B. K. 9.4-5.
52. M. B. M. 6.1.
53. Varro, *On Agriculture*, 1.17. *De quibus universis hoc dico, gravia loca utilius esse mercennariis colere quam servis, et im salubribus quoque locis opera rustica maiora, ut sunt in condendis fructibus vindemiae aut messis.*
54. Cicero, *De Officiis*, 1.42.150.
55. Cf. Matt. 20.2. Cf. also Tos. B.M. 7.1.
56. Cf. M.B. 7.1, 5.
57. Tos. B.M. 11.23; Talmud B.B.A. The laborers had also the right to organize themselves in order to avoid competition against one another.
58. Tos. B.M. 8.2.
59. Women were expected to rise early and bake bread in order that the poor should have bread in the early morning. B.K. 82; S. Zeitlin, "Takkanot Ezra," in *JQR*, VIII (1917), 70-71.

Chapter 3

1. Tos. Pea 4.9, 15.
2. *Ibid.*
3. Talmud B.B. 8.
4. The term *Heber Ir* occurs in the tannaitic literature six times: once in the Mishne (Ber. 4.7), twice in Baraitot (R.H. 34; Meg. 24), and three times in the Tosefta (Sheb. 7.9; Meg. 4.29; B.B. 6.13). On *Heber Ir*, cf. S. Hoenig, "Historical Inquiries, I, *Heber Ir*," JQR (1957), 123-139.
5. Cf. I, pp. 199-201.
6. *War*, 2.20.5 (571).
7. Talmud Meg. 26; cf. also *Yer., ibid.*, 3-2.
8. See S. Zeitlin, *Religious and Secular Leadership*, I (1943), pp. 12-14.
9. M.B.B. 2.9; 7.
10. M. Toh. 7.7.; Tos. B.B. 3.3; *ibid.*, Maas. Sheni 1.4.
11. Tos. B.M. 11.27.
12. M.B.B. 1.5; Talmud, *ibid.*, 8.
13. M.B.M. 8.8.
14. Cf. II Kings 4.9-11. Cf. also Tal. B.M. 81.
15. Vitruvius (born *c.* 10 B.C.E.), *On Architecture*, 6.7 (2) :*Haec*

pars aedificii gynaeconitis appellatur. The place where men
lived or congregated was called *andron.*
16. Tos. Neg. 1.3.
17. Cf. Tos. Mach. 1.5; M., *ibid.,* 4.
18. Tos. Mik. 2.2; 4.1-2.
19. The pressing of dates, grapes and olives was performed by
    skilled laborers who did the pressing with their feet. Later
    olives and grapes were pressed by wooden and stone presses.
    Oil and wine were collected in tanks and vats. Cf. Tos. Sheb.
    8.1.
20. M. Shab. 2.1-4; Tos. Kelim. (3) 7.11.
21. Tos. Shab. 3.14; Talmud, *ibid.,* 120; Yer. *ibid.,* 3.7.
22. M. Kelim 2.4; Tos., *ibid.,* (3) 7.11. Cf. Talmud Ber. 60.
23. M.R.H. 2.1.
24. Talmud B. K. 59. Cf. further, Y. Brand, *Ceramics in the
    Talmudic Literature* (Jerusalem, 1953), pp. 340-378 (in
    Hebrew).
25. Cf. M.B.B. 3.5; Mark 14.67; Luke 22.55.
26. Tos. Kelim 4.18; Talmud Zeb. 95. Some ovens were made of
    stone. M. Kelim 4.11.
27. Cf. Tos. *ibid.* (1) 4.2; *ibid.,* Pes. 7.11.
28. Cf. M. *ibid.* 5.6; Tos. *ibid.* (1) 4.6; *ibid.,* B.M. 8.29. Cf.
    further Brand, *op. cit.,* ch. 125.
29. Cf. Tos. Kelim (2) 11.10. Usually windows were placed in
    the upper floor.
30. Cf. M.M.K. 1.8.
31. Cf. Matt. 9.6; Luke 5.24. Cf. also Mark 2.9.
32. Tos. Kelim 8.4, 6.
33. Cf. M. Shab. 20.5.
34. Cf. Mark 14.40, 51.
35. Cf. M. Kelim 24.13; Tos. *ibid.* (2) 11.
36. Tos. Kelim 4.12.
37. *Specularis.* Tos. Er. 11.17; Tos. Shab. 13.16. The stucco
    served in some houses as a mirror. The Roman architect
    Vitruvius (flourished during the reign of Herod) in his
    book *On Architecture,* 7.9, wrote, "For just as a silvered
    mirror covered with a thin layer gives back confused and
    ineffective reflections, while one that is made with a solid
    layer takes by its firmness a good finish and reflects images
    which shine to the view and are clear to the spectator, so
    stucco which is spread with a thin mortar soon cracks and
    perishes, while that which is based upon solid sand and
    marble of a suitable thickness, and is worked up by repeated
    polishing, not only shines, but reflects clear images from
    the wall to the spectator."
38. M. Bezah 5.5.
39. *Ant.,* 15.9.6 (340).
40. M. Yoma 5.6.
41. Tos. Ber. 4.15; Yer. *ibid.,* 6.1.
42. M. *ibid.* 7.4; Tos. *ibid.,* 4.3; Talmud *ibid.,* 7.50.
43. M. Bezah 2.1; Talmud *ibid.,* 17; Yer. *ibid.,* 2.1.
44. Cf. Tos. Pea 4.8-9; Talmud Shab. 119.

444 : *Notes*

45. The well-to-do had meat on their table, especially on the Sabbath and the holidays. Cf. Tos. Hulim 5.9; Talmud Bezah 16.
46. M. Ber. 6.5. Cf. Yer. *ibid.*, 6.6.
47. Talmud Pes. 12.
48. Shab. 117-118. It was the custom to invite guests to partake of the Sabbath meal. Cf. Yer. Shab. 16.4.
49. M. Ber. 6.6.
50. M. *ibid.*, 7.1.
51. Tos. *ibid.*, 6.3. During ancient times, as well as in modern, people used toothpicks to remove substances between the teeth. Cf. Tos. Shab. 5.10; Bezah 3.18.
52. M. Kelim 15.1; Tos. *ibid.* (1)2.1-3.
53. Cf. M. Meilah 5.1; Tamid 3.4.
54. Tos. Ber. 4.8.
55. *Ibid.;* Tos. B. K. 10.9.
56. Cf. Tos. B. M. 7.3.
57. Cf. Talmud B. K. 82; S. Zeitlin, "Takkanot Ezra," *JQR* (1917), p. 71.
58. M. Kelim 26.9; Tos. *ibid.* (3)4.5.
59. Cf. I, pp. 419-420.
60. M. Kelim 14.2.
61. *Ibid.*, 17.16; Tos. *ibid.* (2)7.9.
62. M. *ibid.* Staves were carried by magicians and diviners. It was believed that the power to perform miracles was transmitted to the staves. Cf. Ex. 7.9-11, "The stave of Aaron," "The stave of Moses" (*ibid.*, 17.5). Cf. also *ibid.*, 7.11-12. Likewise the magicians of Egypt cast down their staves in order to perform a miracle. Cf. also II Kings 4.29 about the stave of Elisha.
63. Tos. Kelim (2)7.9.
64. M. Shab. 6.3.
65. *Ibid.*, 5.
66. *Ibid.*
67. *Ibid.*, 6. Woman's love of jewels among all the races has not changed throughout the ages. Juvenal complained against women for their extravagance on jewels. He wrote, *Nil non permittit mulier sibi, turpe putat nil, cum virides gemmas collo circumdedit et cum auribus extentis magnos commisit elenchos; intolerabilius nihil est quam femina dives.* . . . "There is nothing that a woman will not permit herself to do, nothing that she deems shameful, when she encircles her neck with green emeralds and fastens huge pearls to her elongated ears. . . ." *Satire*, 6.460.
68. Cf. M. Shab. 6.5.
69. M. Ket. 7.6.
70. Gaius, *Institutionum Iuris Civilis Commentarii Quatuor, De Patria Potestate.*
71. Deut. 21.18-21.
72. *Ibid.*
73. Num. 27.8-9; Ezek. 46.16-17. Cf. S. Zeitlin, "Testamentary Succession; A Study in Tannaitic Jurisprudence," *The*

Seventy-fifth Anniversary Volume of the Jewish Quarterly Review (1967), pp. 574-581.

74. Cf. Tos. B. B. 8.10; S. Zeitlin, *op. cit.*
75. M. B. B. 8.6.
76. Cf. M. Yeb. 13.1-2; Tos., *ibid.*, 13.1-3.
77. M. B. M. 1.5; Ket. 6.1.
78. M. Ket. 4.4.
79. *Ibid.*, 4.9; Tos., *ibid.*, 4.2.
80. M. Ket. 5.5, Cf. Tos., *ibid.* 5.4; M. *ibid.*
81. Cf. I, pp. 417-420.
82. Deut. 22.23-24.
83. Cf. M. Ket. 5.3; Tos., *ibid.*, 5.1; Yer. *ibid.*, 5.4.
84. The groom had no right to her earnings nor had he any right to her findings. Cf. Tos. Ket. 8.1.
85. M. Kid. 2.1.
86. M. Ket. 5.1.
87. Tos. *ibid.*, 4.9; Talmud, B. M. 104.
88. Cf. M. B. B. 9.5; Tos. *ibid.*, 10.10.
89. M. Ket. 1.5; Talmud, *ibid.*, 12.
90. M. Kid. 3.10; Talmud, *ibid.*, 65. Cf. S. Zeitlin, *JQR* (1958), *ibid.*, (1961).
91. Cf. S. Zeitlin, *op. cit.*
92. Lev. 21.13-14.
93. Cf. M. Yeb. 6.4.
94. Lev. 21.7.
95. Cf. I, pp. 417-420.
96. M. B. B. 9.4; Talmud, *ibid.*, 144-145; Tos., *ibid.*, 10.10,8; Yer. Ket. 1.1.
97. M. Ket. 6.5; Tos., *ibid.*, 6.5-6.
98. *Ibid.*
99. Cf. I, pp. 415-417.
100. M. Ket. 8.11; Tos., *ibid.*, 9; Talmud, *ibid.*, 82.
101. M. *ibid.*, 1.1.
102. Ket. 7.
103. Cf. Malachi 2.11-16. Cf. Gen. 2.24.
104. Cf. Talmud, Ket. 7; I, p. 119.
105. Cf. M. Ket. 4.4, 6.1; I. p. 418.
106. Ps. 128.3.
107. Plutarch, *Caesar*, 10.
108. M. Ket. 7.3; Tos. Sotah 5.9.
109. Num. 5.12-31. Cf. M. Ed. 5.4; Sotah 9.9.
110. Cf. M. Sotah 5.1.
111. Deut. 24.1; cf. I, pp. 415 f.
112. M. Gittin 9.10.
113. M. *ibid.*, 4.2,3; 9.4.
114. M. Yoma 8.4; M. Shab. 18.3.
115. Cf. S. Zeitlin, *The Zadokite Fragments* (Philadelphia, 1952), pp. 13-15; *idem*, *The Dead Sea Scrolls and Modern Scholarship* (1956), pp. 62-63.
116. Cf. Luke 2.21-23.
117. Num. 3.45-50.
118. Cf. I, pp. 420-423.

119. See above p. 290.
120. Deut. 25.5-10.
121. M. R. H. 2.5; Er. 4.7; Tos. *ibid.*, 4.9. Cf. S. Zeitlin, "The Takkanot of Erubin: A Study in the Development of the Halaka," *JQR* (1951), 351-361.
122. See above p. 285.
123. M. Eru. 2.6-7.
124. Cf. I, pp. 226-255.
125. Cf. I, pp. 186-187.
126. Cf. M. Shab. 23.4.
127. M. Kil. 9.3; Yer. *ibid.;* Cf. Matt. 27.59; John 19.40, "Then took they the body of Jesus and wound it in linen clothes with the spices, as the manner of the Judaeans is to bury." Cf. Talmud, Ket. 8; Tos. Nidah 9.11.
128. Cf. M. M. Kat. 3.8-9.
129. *War*, 2.1.2(5-6).
130. Cf. M. Ber. 3.1; M. Kat. 1.6. Cf. also Pes. 56.
131. *Ant.*, 17.8.3(197).
132. Among the Judaeans there was always the wish to be buried in the sepulchres of their ancestors (cf. Gen. 40.30). It was believed that if one were not buried with his ancestors he was accursed (cf. I Kings 13.22).
133. See Pliny, *N. H.*, 35.46, "Many people have preferred to be buried in earthenware coffins." Cf. Yer. San. 6.11; Talmud, Naz. 51. Many coffins had holes in the bottom so that the body would have contact with the earth. Yer. Ket. 12.3. Cf. further Y. Brand, *op. cit.*, pp. 46-52.
134. Talmud, M. Kat. 27.
135. Cf. San. 98; see also Tos. Ohol. 10.7.
136. Strangers, without relatives in the community to take care of their burial, and paupers, were buried in a special burial place. Cf. Matt. 27.7. Those condemned to death by the court were also buried in a special burial place.
137. Cf. M. Er. 5.1; Tos. *ibid.*, 10.13; *ibid.*, Oh. 10.7. Cf. also *Ant.*, 16.17.1(182).
138. Talmud, Sanh. 19.
139. Cf. Tractate Shem. 10. S. Zeitlin, "An Historical Study of the First Canonization of the Hebrew Liturgy," *JQR*, XXXVI (1948), 298-303.
140. Plutarch, *The Roman Questions*, 11-13.
141. Cf. Gen. 50.10; *War*, 2.1.1(1); *Ant.*, 17.8.4.(200).
142. Talmud M. Kat. 21.
143. *Ibid.*, 27.
144. *Yer.*, Ber. 3.1.
145. *War*, 2.1.1(1).
146. Tos. Nidah 9.17.

Chapter 4

1. According to the Talmud, Shab. 15, Hillel had a son named Simon, so that Gamaliel was his grandson. It is probable

that after the death of Shammai, the position of *Ab Bet Din* was offered to Akabiah. See also S. Hoening, "New Light on the Epoch of Akibah b. Mahalalel," *Studies and Essays* in *Honor of Abraham A. Neuman*, 1962, pp. 291-298.

2. Cf. S. Zeitlin, "The Titles High Priest and the Nasi of the Sanhedrin," *JQR* (1957).
3. M. Yeb. 16.7.
4. M. Git. 4.2.
5. *Ibid.*
6. M.R.H. 2.5.
7. Acts 22.3.
8. Cf. Galatians 3.16. "Now to Abraham and his seed were the promises made. He saith not, and to seeds (Gen. 29.18) as of many; but as one and to the seed, which is Christ." Here Paul employed rabbinic dialectics. Here, in order to prove that Jesus is the true Christ, he quotes a pentateuchal verse in which is stated that God promised Abraham that in his seed shall all the nations be blessed. Paul argued that, since the word *zara'* has no *yod*, it has the meaning of single "seed" and it refers to Jesus. Of course the word *zaraḥa* as used in the verse covers both. Cf. also Romans 9.3-12.
9. Acts 5.34-39.
10. Cf. above pp. 220.
11. Cf. above p. 220; and Acts 12.1-6.
12. It is true that the word *theomachein*, fighting against God, had already been used by Euripides. He speaks of Pentheus' fight directly with God. Homer in his *Iliad*, relates the story of a king who fought Dionysus, for which Zeus punished him with blindness. It was also used by Josephus in quoting Manetho, *Against Apion*, 1.246. Eusebius in *The Ecclesiastical History* 2.25, wrote "In this way then was he [Nero] the first to be heralded as above all a fighter against God (*theomachos*), and raised up to slaughter against the Apostles." In the Second Book of Maccabees, relating the martyrdom of the seven children, the author states that the sixth child said to Antiochus, "But do not think that you will go free in thus daring to wage war against God." The Second Book of Maccabees was composed in the Diaspora, in Antioch. In both the Second Book of Maccabees as well as in Acts it does not signify fighting directly with God, but fighting the message of God. The conception of *theomachein* in Acts, opposing the message of God, was influenced by the Second Book of Maccabees.
13. Cf. I, pp. 76-93.
14. Dio, 52: "Those who attempt to distort our religion with strange rites you should abhor and punish, not merely for the sake of the gods (since if a man despises these he will not pay honor to any other being), but because such men, by bringing in new divinities in place of the old, persuade many to adopt foreign practices, from which spring up conspiracies, factions and cabals, which are far from profit-

able to a monarchy. Do not, therefore, permit anybody to be an atheist or a sorcerer."

15. *The Embassy to Gaius*, 23 (155-156).

16. Cicero, *Pro Flacco*, 28(69), *Stantibus Hierosolymis pacatisque Iudaeis tamen istorum religio sacrorum a splendore huius imperii, gravitate nominis nostri, maiorum institutis abhorrebat.*

17. Justin (Pompeius Trogus), *History of the World*, 36.2.

18. *Profana illic omnia quae apud nos sacra, rursum concessa apud illos quae nobis incesta* . . . *Sue abstinent memoria cladis, quod ipsos scabies quondam turpaverat cui id animal obnoxium.* Tacitus, *Hist.*, 5.4.

. . . *unde auctae Iudaeorum res, et quia apud ipsos fides obstinata, misericordia in promptu, sed adversus omniss a lios hostile odium. Separati epulis discreti cubilibus, proiectissima ad libidinem gens, alienarum concubitu abstinent; inter se nihil inlicitum. Circumcidere genitalia instituerunt ut diversitate noscantur.* . . .

Iudaei mente sola unumque numen intellegunt; profanos qui deum imagines mortalibus materiis in species hominum effingant summum illud et aeternum neque imitabile neque interiturum. Igitur nulla simulacra urbibus suis, nedum templis sistunt; non regibus haec adulatio non Caesaribus honor. Ibid., 5.5.

Cf. also Quintilian 3.7. *Et est conditoribus urbium infame contraxisse aliquam perniciosam ceteris gentem, qualis est primus Iudaicae superstitionis auctor.* "Founders of cities are detested for concentrating a people which is accursed to others, as for example the founder of the Judaean superstition."

According to Augustine (*City of God*, 6.11), Seneca said, *Cum interim usque eo sceleratissimae gentis consuetudo convaluit ut per omnes iam terras recepta sit; victi victoribus leges bederunt.* "But when speaking of the Judaeans he (Seneca) says: 'Meanwhile the customs of this accursed race (people) have gained such influence that they are now received throughout all the world. The vanquished have given laws to their victors.'" The above text quoted by Augustine is not extant in the writings of Seneca. The expression *sceleratissimae gentis*, "accursed race" (people), was the term employed by the Church against the Judaeans who claimed that before the crucifixion of Jesus the Judaeans were a chosen people. However, after they "crucified" Jesus they became the accursed race (people).

19. Cf. Dio, 57. "As the Judaeans flocked to Rome in great numbers and were converting many of the natives to their ways, he (Tiberius) banished most of them." Cf. also Suetonius, *Tiberius 36*, *Externas caerimonias, Aegyptios Iudaicosque ritus compescuit, coactis qui superstitione ea tenebantur religiosas vestes cum instrumento omni comburere. Iudaeorum inventutem per speciem sacramenti in provincis gravioris caeli distribuit, reliquos gentis eiusdem*

vel similia sectantes urbe summovit, sub poena perptuae servitutis nisi obtemperassent. "He (Tiberius) abolished foreign cults, especially the Egyptian and Judaean rites, compelling all who were addicted to such superstitions to burn their religious vestments and all their paraphernalia. . . ." Seneca, *Epistle* 108: *In primum Tiberii Caesaris principatum iuventae tempus inciderat. Alienigena tum sacra movebantur, sed inter argumenta superstitionis ponebatur quorundam animalium abstinentia.* "The days of my youth coincided with the early part of the reign of Tiberius Caesar. Some foreign rites were at that time being inaugurated, and abstinence from certain kinds of animal food was set down as a proof of interest in the strange cult." Cf. also Tacitus, *Ann.*, 2.85; *Ant.*, 18.3.5 (83-84).

20. *Ne Iudaeus quidem, mi Tiberi, tam diligenter sabbatis ieiunium servat quam ego hodie servavi. . . .* Suetonius, *Augustus*, 76. The Roman historian relates that the grammarian Diogenes used to lecture on every Sabbath at Rhodes. *Diogenes grammaticus disputare sabbatis Rhodi solitus . . .* Suetonius, *Tiberius*, 32, Justin in his history makes reference to the Sabbath: "He (Moses) consecrated the seventh day to be a fast forever, and called it, agreeable to the customs of these people, the Sabbath, because that day put a period to their fasting and wandering." Justin, 36.

21. *Quomodo sint di colendi solet praecipe accendere aliquem lucernas sabbatis prohibeamus, quoniam nuc lumine di egent et ne homines quidem delectantur fuliginc.* Epistle 95. The custom of lighting lamps on the Sabbath was not for worship, but for enjoyment, as lights always provide brightness and enjoyment. Horace also makes reference to the Sabbath. *Hodie tricesima sabbata; vin tu curtis Iudaeis oppedere?* "Today is the thirtieth Sabbath. Could you affront the circumcised Judaean?" *Satires*, 1.9 (69). Ovid also speaks of the Sabbath. *Nec pluvis opta nec te peregrina morentur sabbata, nec damnis Allia nota suis.* "Hope not for rain, nor let foreign sabbaths stay you nor Allia, well-known for its ill luck" (the Romans were disastrously defeated by the Gauls on the river Allia in 390 B.C.E.). *The Remedies of Love*, 218-220. Ovid further wrote, *Nec te praetereat Veneri ploratus Adonias cultaque Iudaeo septima sacra Syro.* "Nor let Adonis bewailed of Venus escape you, nor the seventh day that the Syrian Judaean holds sacred." *Art of Love*, 1.75-76.

22. *Quidam sortiti metuentem sabbata patrem nil praeter nubes et caeli numen adorant, nec distare putant humana carne suillam, qua pater abstinuit, mox et praeputia ponunt; Romanas autem soliti contemnere leges Iudaicum ediscunt et servant ac metuunt ius, tradidit arcano quodcumque volumine Moyses, non monstrare vias eadem nisi sacra colenti quaesitum ad fontem solos deducere verpos, sed pater in causa, cui septima quaeque fuit lux ignava et partem vitae non attigit ullam.* Satires, 14.96-106.

23. *Septimo die otium placuisse ferunt, quia is finem laborum tulerit; dein blandiente inertia septimum quoque annum ignaviae datum.* Tacitus, *History*, 5.4.

   According to Augustine (*City of God*, 6.11) Seneca also attributed the institution of the Sabbath to the laziness of the people. "Along with other superstitions of the civil theology Seneca also censures the sacred institutions of the Judaeans, especially the Sabbath. He declares that their practice is inexpedient, because by introducing one day of rest in every seven they lose in idleness almost a seventh of their life, and by failing to act in times of urgency they often suffer loss." *Hic inter alias civilis theologiae superstitiones reprehendit etim sacramenta Iudaeorum et maxime sabbata, inutiliter eos facere adfirmans quod per illos singulos septenis interpositos dies septiman fere partem aetatis suae perdant vacando et multa in tempore urgentia non agendo laedantur.*

24. Josephus, *Against Apion*, 2(282).
25. Dio, 37.
26. Acts 17.4,17.
27. *Ibid.*, 13.16.
28. *Ant.*, 20.8.11(195).
29. *Ibid.*, 14.7.2(110).
30. *War*, 2.18.2(463).
31. *Ibid.*, 2.20.2(560-561).
32. *Ibid.*, 7.3.3(45).
33. *Ant.*, 20.7.1(139).
34. *Ibid.*, 20.2,3 (35-48).
35. *Ibid.*, 20.2.1-4(17-48).
36. *Ibid.*, 3.4(71).
37. *Ibid.*, 5(49-53). Cf. also M. Yoma, 3.10; M. Nazir, 3.6; Talmud, B. B. 14.
38. *Ibid.*, 4.3(92-96); cf. also *War*, 5.2.2(55), 4.2(147). Cf. also *ibid.*, 6.1(253).
39. *War*, 2.19.2(520).
40. See J. Neusner, "The Conversion of Adiabene to Judaism," in *JBL* (March, 1964).
41. Tacitus, *History*, 5.5.
42. Strabo, 16.2.35.
43. *Primus est deorum cultus deos credere; deinde reddere illis maiestatem suam reddere bonitatem, sine qua nulla maiestas est. Scire illos esse, qui praesident mundo qui universa vi sua temperant, qui humani generis tutelam gerunt interdum incuriosi singulorum. Hi nec dant malum nec habent; ceterum castigant quosdam et coercent et inrogant poenas et aliquando specie boni puniunt. Vis deos probitiare? Bonus esto. Satis illos coluit quisquis imitatus est.* Seneca, *Epistles*, 95.50.
44. Cf. Polybius, 6.56. "But the quality in which the Roman state is most distinctly superior is in my opinion the nature of their religious convictions. I believe that it is the very thing which among other peoples is an object of reproach,

I mean superstition, which maintains the cohesion of the Roman State. These matters are clothed in such pomp and introduced to such an extent into their public and private life that nothing could exceed it, a fact which will surprise many." Cicero, *Laws*, 2.25-26, *Suosque deos aut novos aut alienigenaus coli confusionem habet religionum et ignotas caerimonias nostris sacerdotibus, nam a patribus acceptos deos ita placet coli, si huic legi paruerint ipsi patres.* "The worship of gods, whether new or alien, brings confusion into religion and introduces ceremonies unknown to our priests. For the gods handed down to us by our fathers should be worshipped only in case our fathers themselves obeyed this law." . . . *Iam ritus familiae patrumque servare id est, quoniam antiquitas proxume accedit ad deos, a dis quasi traditam religionem tueri.* "Next, the preservation of the rights of the family and of our ancestors means preserving the religious rights which, we can almost say, were handed down to us by the gods themselves, since ancient times were closest to the gods." Cf. also Dio, 52; *CAH*, 10, ch. 15.

45. The Gospel of Matthew relates that Jesus accused the Pharisees of proselytizing, "Woe unto you scribes and Pharisees, hypocrites, for you compass sea and land to make one proselyte." (23.15).
46. Cf. Tacitus, *History*, 5.5.
47. Cf. *Ant.*, 20.7.1(130); 20.2.1(17); cf. S. Zeitlin, "Mumar and Meshumad," *JQR* (July 1963).
48. *War*, 7.3.3(50); II Mac. 6.24; III Mac. 1.3.
49. Cf. S. Zeitlin, "Proselytes and Proselytism During the Second Commonwealth and the Early Taanaitic Period," *Harry A. Wolfson Jubilee Volume* (1965), pp. 871-881.
50. Cf. S. Zeitlin, "Judaism as a Religion," *JQR* (1944), 193-200.
51. Cf. I, 88-89.
52. Cf. below, p. 358; S. Zeitlin, "L'origene de l'institution du baptême pour les proselytes," *REJ* (1934); *idem*, "The Halaka in the Gospels and its Relation to the Jewish Law at the Time of Jesus," *HUCA*, vol. 1.
53. Cf. Lev. 15.1-18; Deut. 23.14-15. Cf. S. Zeitlin, *op. cit.*
54. Mekilta (Sifre) Mishp.; S. Zeitlin, "Judaism as a Religion," *JQR* (1944), pp. 195-196.
55. Philo, *Flaccus*, 6(43).
56. *War*, 2.20(561).
57. Cf. Philo, *Embassy to Gaius*, 36(281).
58. *Ant.*, 18.9.1(312-317).
59. M. R. H. 1.4.
60. Cf. above, pp. 195-196.
61. *Ant.*, 16.6.2(163-164).
62. Cf. above, p. 54.
63. See below, pp. 355-356.
64. Cf. M. Abot 3.3. "From the sacrifices to the dead." Jubilees 22.17. "They offered their sacrifices to their dead, they worshipped evil spirits, and they ate over the graves"; Augustine, *City of God*, 8.27: "For we do not ordain priests

and offer sacrifices to our martyrs as they do to their dead men."

65. Cf. below, p. 341.
66. Cf. *War*, 2.17.4(388).
67. Cf. above, p. 248.
68. *War*, 2.8.14(166).
69. *Ibid.*, 2.8.1(117-118); *Ant.*, 18.1.1(9-10); 6(23-25).
70. *War., ibid.*
71. See above, p. 251.
72. *War*, 2.13.4(258).
73. *Ibid.* (59-260).
74. Ex. 40.9-15.
75. I Sam. 10.1; 16.13; 26.11; II Sam. 19.22; Isa. 45.1, "Thus said Yahweh to his *mashiah*, to Cyrus."
76. Cf. *ibid.*, 11.1-16; S. Zeitlin, "The Origin of the Idea of the Messiah." *In the Time of Harvest, Essays in Honor of Abba Hillel Silver on the Occasion of His 70th Birthday* (1963).
77. Talmud Meg. 10.
78. Isa. 11.6.
79. The early Church Fathers, to prove that Jesus was the true messiah, *Christos*, maintained that there were references to Jesus as the messiah in the Pentateuch and the other books of the Bible. To combat the views of the Church Fathers, the rabbis interpreted the same verses as containing prophecies of the Jewish *Mashiah*. The verse in Gen. 49.10 reads, "The scepter shall not depart from Judah; Nor the ruler's staff from between his feet, as long as men come to Shiloh." Origen (*Against Celsus*, 1.53) interpreted this passage as referring to the "Christ of God," Jesus. The Targum, according to Jonathan, interprets it as referring to the Jewish *Mashiah*. The verse in Isa. 11.1, reads, "And there shall come forth a shoot of the stock Jesse and a twig shall grow forth out of his root." Justin Martyr (*The First Apology*, 32) interpreted this verse as a prophecy for the coming of Jesus. The rabbis interpreted it as referring to the coming of the Jewish *Mashiah*. In Chapter 53 of Isaiah the suffering of the servant of Yahweh is described. The Church Fathers interpreted it as referring to the Passion of Jesus. Barnabas, one of the Apostolic Fathers, interpreted this chapter as referring partly to Israel and partly to Jesus (*The Epistle of Barnabas*, 5). Origen, in his *Treatise Against Celsus*, 1.55, said that the Jews believed that the prophecies in this chapter referred to the whole people of Israel regarded as one individual. He denied this contention and held that the prophecies and suffering related in this chapter referred to the sufferings and death of Jesus Christ. The Targum according to Jonathan interpreted this chapter as referring to the Jewish *Mashiah*. Cf. Harry M. Orlinsky, "The So-called 'Suffering Servant' in Isa. 35," the Goldenson Lecture, 1964, H.U.C. (Cincinnati, 1964).
80. II Mac., ch. 7.

81. Psalms of Solomon, chs. 17-18.
82. Enoch, 48.10; 49.2; 51.1; 62.14; 69.26.
83. Mark 12.18-27; Matt. 22.23-33; Luke 20.27-40.
84. Mark 2.23-28; Matt. 12.1-8; Luke 6.1-5.
85. Ex. 20.10. Cf. Talmud Yoma 85.
86. Cf. S. Zeitlin, *The Pharisees and the Gospels* (1938).
87. Mark 7.1-5; Matt. 15.1-6. S. Zeitlin, "The Hakala in the Gospels," in *HUCA*, I.
88. Mark 7.10-11; Matt. 15.4-6. Cf. S. Zeitlin, *Who Crucified Jesus?*, pp. 132-135. The word *corban* does not have the meaning of a gift, but of a vow. See S. Zeitlin, *The Pharisees and the Gospels, ad loc.*
89. Deut. 23.24; Num. 30.8.
90. Cf. M. Ned. 11.11; cf. S. Zeitlin, *op. cit.*
91. Matt. 5.3-48; Luke 6.20-49.
92. The *actio furti* can be brought by the person who was injured.
93. Josephus, *Ant.*, 4.8.35 (280): "He that maimeth a man shall undergo the like, being deprived of that limb whereof he deprived the other, unless indeed the maimed man be willing to accept money; for the law empowers the victim himself to assess the damage that has befallen him and makes this concession, unless he would show himself too severe." Cf. also S. Zeitlin, *Who Crucified Jesus?*, pp. 119-121.
94. Matt. 5.17.
95. Mark 10.2-12; Matt. 5.31-32, 19.3-9; Luke 16.18.
96. Cf. M. Gitin 9.10.
97. Matt. 5.27-30.
97a. On the term Gehenna, see below p. 342.
98. Matt. 5.33-34.
99. Matt., *ibid.*, 20-22.
100. Matt., *ibid.*, 43-44. Cf. Luke 6.27-29.
101. The ethical teachings of the sages are far more practical than those of Jesus. Hillel laid down the golden rule when he said, "What thou hatest for thyself, do not do to thy fellow man." Hillel's golden rule may not be superior to the saying of Jesus, but is more in accord with the realities of human nature, and lies within the realm of possibilities.
102. The Testament of Joseph (18.2). Cf. Tobit 4.15.
103. *Epistle*, 95. *Non privatim solum sed publice furimus. Homicidia compescimus et singulas caedes; quid bella et occisarum gentium gloriosum scelus?*
104. Cf. above p. 160; M. S. Enslin, *The Prophet from Nazareth* (1961).
105. When the Samaritan woman told Jesus, "I know that Messiah cometh, which is called Christos; when he is come, he will tell us all things. Jesus said unto her, I that speak unto thee am he." John 4.25-26; cf. also 17.3.
106. Shortly after the crucifixion, Simon, a man from Samaria, who became known as Simon Magus, proclaimed himself Messiah. The author of Acts 8.9-10 referred to him as a

man who "used sorcery, and bewitched the people of Samaria, giving out that he himself was some great one. To whom all gave heed from the least to the greatest, saying, this man is the great power of God." The author of Acts further relates that Peter fought Simon Magus and said to him, "for thy heart is not right in the sight of God. Repent therefore of this thy wickedness and pray to God." Justin Martyr gives a detailed description of the activities of Simon Magus in Rome, "There was a Samaritan, Simon, a native of the village called Gitto, who in the reign of Claudius Caesar and in your royal city of Rome, did mighty acts of magic, by virtue of the art of the devils operating in him. He was considered a god and as a god he was honored by you with a statue, which statue was erected on the river Tiber, between the two bridges and bore this inscription in the language of Rome:

SIMONII DEO SANCTO,

(To Simon the Holy God)

And almost all the Samaritans a few even of other peoples worshipped him and acknowledged him as the first god." *First Apology*, 26.

The Church Father Irenaeus also speaks about Simon the Samaritan . . . *Quippe cum esset sub Claudio Caesare, a quo etiam statua honoratus esse dicitur propter magicam. Hic igitur a multis quasi Deus glorificatus est, et docuit semetipsum esse, qui inter Judaeos quidem quasi filius apparuerit, in Samaria autem quasi pater descenderit, in reliquis vero gentibus quasi spiritus sanctus adventaverit.* "Such was his (Simon's) procedure in the reign of Claudius Caesar, by whom also he is said to have been honored with a statue on account of his magical power. This man then was glorified by many as he was a god; and he thought that he was himself who appeared among the Judaeans as the son, but descended in Samaria as the father, while he came to the other peoples in the character of the holy spirit." *Against Heresies*, 1.23.

Suetonius, *Claudius*, 25, relates Claudius expelled the Judaeans from Rome who made disturbances at the instigation of Chrestus. *Iudaeos impulsore Chresto assidue tumultuantis Roma expulit*. Most probably Suetonius refers to Simon Magus, who declared himself to be the messiah and caused disturbances among the Judaeans. That the Church Fathers named him a Samaritan does not mean that he was a Samaritan by race. He was a Judaean who was born and lived in Samaria, a province of the State of Judaea. Had he been a Samaritan he would not have had followers among the Judaeans who lived in Rome, since bitter hostility prevailed between the Samaritans and the Judaeans. Apparently Simon Magus had great influence upon the Apocalyptists and was a threat to the followers of Jesus. This explains the bitterness expressed towards him by the Church Fathers.

107. The Testament of Judah 21.2; 24.5-6; The Testament of Reuben, 6.7-12; Levi 8.14.
108. Luke 1.5-38.
109. Matt. 10.6.
110. Cf. Acts 21.17-22; Gal. 2.1-9.
111. Cf. S. Zeitlin, "Judaism as a Religion," in *JQR* (Oct. 1944).
112. Galatians 2.16.
113. Romans 3.28.
114. Romans 11.13; Gal. 2.7-10; Acts 18.6. Cf. S. Zeitlin, "The Crucifixion of Jesus Re-Examined," *JQR*, XXXII (1942), p. 280, no. 168.
115. Acts 9.1-18, 26; Gal. 1.13-14.
116. Acts 21.21.
117. Tacitus, *Hist.*, 5.13. . . . *ut valesceret Oriens profectique Iudaea rerum potirentur;* Suetonius, *Vespasian,* 4.
118. *Ergo hi dei sunt habendi mortalibus nati matribus? Quid? Aristaeus, qui olivae dicitur inventor, Apollinis filius Theseus Neptuni, reliqui quorum patres di, non erunt in deorum numero? Quid quorum matres?* "Well then will not Aristaeus, the reputed discoverer of the olive, he who was the son of Apollo, Theseus the son of Neptune, and all the other sons of gods also be reckoned as gods? What about the sons of goddesses?" Cicero, *De Natura Deorum*, 3.18. *Idem, ibid.*, 2.2, "It is the result of the fact that gods often manifest their power in bodily presence."
119. Romans 2.27-29, 4.10-13.

Chapter 5

1. Cf. I, 420 ff.
2. Talmud B. B. 21.
3. Yer. Pea 8.6. Cf. Yer. Hag. 1.7. Those who interpreted the pentateuchal laws and received remuneration were sometimes called sophists. Cf. above, p. 297.
4. See Talmud Hag. 13; S. Zeitlin, *An Historical Study of the Canonization of the Hebrew Scriptures* (1933), pp. 6-8.
5. Cf. *Ant.*, 16.2.4 (43); *Against Apion*, 2.175.
6. *Epistle*, 95, *In rhetorum ac philosophorum scholis solitudo est; at quam celebres culinae sunt, quanta circa nepotum focos iuventus premitur.*
7. Cf. *War*, 1.23.2 (648-649): "There were in the capital two sophists with a reputation as profound experts in the laws of their country, who consequently enjoyed the highest esteem of the whole nation. . . . Their lectures on the laws were attended by a large youthful audience, and day after day they drew together a multitude of men in their prime." Cf. also *Ant.*, 17.6.2 (149).
8. M. Abot. 2.5.
9. Cf. S. Zeitlin, "The Tefillah, The Shemoneh Esreh," in *JQR*, LIV (1964), pp. 208-220.
10. See I, pp. 275-278.

11. *Nil ergo, optabunt homines? si consilium vis, permittes ipsis expendere numinibus quid conveniat nobis rebusque sit utile nostris, nam pro iucundis aptissima quaeque debunt di carior est illis homo quam sibi, nos animorum impulsu et caeca magnaque cupidine ducti coniugium petimus partumque uxoris; at illis notum qui pueri qualiasque futura sit uxor ut tamen et poscas aliquid voveasque sacellis exta et candiduli divina tomacula, porci, orandum est ut sit mens sana in corpore sano. Satire,* 10.346-356.
12. Cf. S. Zeitlin, *op. cit.*
13. Additions to Esther, chs. 13-14.
14. Book of Enoch 84.4-6.
15. *Ant.*, 14.2.1(24).
16. Cf. S. Zeitlin, *op. cit.*
17. Matt. 6.8-13; Luke 11.2-4.
18. Cf. I, p. 429.
19. Cf. above, p. 20.
20. *Ant.*, 20.6.1(293-294).
21. II Mac. 12.43-44.
22. See Introduction, II Mac., ed. Dropsie, p. 84.
23. Sifre to Deut., ch. 20.
24. Ch. 20.
25. The word Gehenna occurs in Bar. 59.10; 4 Ez. 7.36. These books are of a later period. See S. Zeitlin, "The Apocrypha," *JQR*, XXXVII (1947), pp. 239-248.
26. Midrash Tanhuma, Deut. 32.
27. Cf. Introduction, II Mac., ed. Dropsie, pp. 84-85.
28. Cf. I Sam. 1.26; Mark 11.28. The hands were lifted up towards heaven, a custom very primitive and practiced among all peoples. Stretching forth the hands while praying is mentioned often in the Bible. (I Kings 8.54; Ez. 9.5, *et passim.*) Cf. S. Zeitlin, "A Historical Study of the Canonization of the Hebrew Liturgy," *JQR*, XXXVII (Jan. 1948), pp. 296-298.
29. Cf. S. Zeitlin, *op. cit.*, pp. 298-305. Ex. 28.4,40; Lev. 10.6; Talmud Yoma 71. The popes and the cardinals wear mitres as part of their official dress during their ecclesiastical functions. The origin of this may be traced to the high priest's wearing the mitre during the services in the Temple. Although in the Western Church there is no evidence that the mitre was worn by the popes before the ninth century C. E., there are indications that in the East the mitres were worn by the heads of the Church in the early days of Christianity.
30. Epistle of Jeremiah 1.31. See I, pp. 296-297.
31. Plutarch, *The Roman Questions*, 10.13.
32. I Cor. 11.3,4.
33. Cf. Midrash R., Gen. 17.
34. Cf. I, pp. 18-20.
35. Ben Sirah, 49.10.
36. Cf. M. Yad 3.5; S. Zeitlin, *An Historical Study of the Canonization of the Hebrew Scriptures*, p. 37.

37. See I, p. 265.
38. Cf. M. Yad. 3.5; S. Zeitlin, *op. cit.*, p. 37.
39. II Kings 21.2-16; cf. II Chron. 32.12-18.
40. The Hebrew Canon at the time of the destruction of the Temple consisted of twenty-two books: Five Books of Moses, Eight of Prophets—Joshua, Judges, Samuel, Kings, Jeremiah, Ezekiel, Isaiah, The Twelve Minor Prophets; nine books of Ketubim, Psalms, Proverbs, Job, Ezra and Nehemiah, Daniel, Chronicles, Ruth, Lamentations and Song of Songs. The books of Kohelet and Esther were added later.
41. Cf. S. Zeitlin, "Were There Three Scrolls in the Azarah?" *JQR* (April, 1966).
42. M. *Sanh.* 10.1.
43. Pliny, *Nat. Hist.*, 5.16; cf. S. Zeitlin, "The Essenes," *JQR* (Oct., 1954).
44. Psalms of Solomon, ch. 2, verses 30-33, refer to the treacherous death of Pompey: "And I delayed not until God showed to me that insolent one lying pierced upon the high-places of Egypt, made of less account than him that is least on earth and sea; even his dead body lying corrupted upon the waves in great contempt; and there was none to bury him; for he set him at naught in dishonor; he considered not that he was a man."
45. *Ibid.*, ch. 2.7,17; 3.10.13,16; 15.11.
46. *Ibid.*, ch. 17.23, 32-33, 39, 32-35.
47. Ch. 18.6, 8. Ch. 17.36, has *Christos kurios*, the Lord Christ Messiah, probably a mistranslation of the Hebrew. Lam. 4.20, the Hebrew text has *meshiah Adonai*, the anointed of Adonai. The Septuagint rendered it *Christos kuriou*, our anointed Lord. The phrase anointed of Adonai was applied to one who was actually anointed with oil by command of God, like King Saul, King David and the high priests. During the Second Commonwealth neither kings nor high priests were anointed with oil. In these psalms the phrase has a spiritual rather than a literary connotation.
48. Ch. 17.38, 41.
49. See *The Apocrypha and Pseudepigrapha of the Old Testament*, ed. R. H. Charles (Oxford, 1913).
50. Enoch, ch. 58.1, cp. with chs. 91-104.
51. Chs. 1-36. The titles of the messiah given in Enoch are "anointed one," "the righteous one," "the elect one," and the (son of) "man."
52. The book of Jubilees 4.17-18.
53. In the Bible, Enoch occupies a singular position: Like Elijah he was translated from the earth to heavenly spheres. In the dream vision of Enoch 12, where he was transferred to heaven and interceded for Azazel, he said, "And I, Enoch, was blessing the Lord of Majesty and the King of Ages, and lo! the watchers called me Enoch the scribe, and said to me 'Enoch, thou scribe of righteousness, go to the righteous of the heaven, who have left the high heaven, the holy eternal

place, who have defiled themselves with women and have
done as the children of earth do, and have taken unto themselves wives.' " In heaven Enoch interceded for the fallen
angels.

54. The Epistle of Jude 1.14, refers to Enoch. Clement 9
also mentions Enoch, saying that he did not die but was
translated to heaven. Barnabas, *Epistle* 4, wrote that Enoch
said in his writings, "For to this end the Lord has cut
short the time and the days, that his beloved should make
haste and come to his inheritance." The Church Father
Irenaeus, *Against Heresies*, 5.5, wrote, "For Enoch, when
he pleased God, was translated in the same body in which he
pleased Him, thus pointing out by anticipation the translation
of the just."

The early Church Fathers believed that the book of Enoch
was indeed written by him, the great-grandfather of Noah.
Tertullian wrote, *Scio scripturam Enoch, quae hunc ordinem
angelis dedit, non recipi a quibusdam, quia nec in armarium
Iudaicum admittitur. Opinor, non putaverunt illam ante
cataclysmum editam post eum casum orbis omnium rerum
abolitorem salvam esse potuisse. De Cultu Feminarum* 1.3.
"I am aware that the scriptures of Enoch, which has assigned
this order [of action] to angels, is not received by some because it is not admitted into the Judaean canon either. I suppose that they did not think that, having been composed
before the deluge, it could have safely survived that world-
wide cataclysm, the destroyer of all things." Tertullian
attributed the survival of the book of Enoch to his great-
grandson Noah who preserved the traditions and sayings of
Enoch. The Church Father Origen makes frequent references
to Enoch in his writings, stressing that Enoch was translated
into heaven.

55. Onkelos on Gen. 5.24; Midrash R. on Gen. 25.
55a. Cf. Talmud Suk. 5.
56. See Ed. Charles.
57. Testament of the Twelve Patriarchs, ch. 14.3.
58. *Ibid.*, ch. 18.2.
59. *Ibid.*, ch. 8.1.
60. Testament of Levi 18.10; Judah 25.1-5; Benj. 9.7-8.
61. Testament of Benj. 7.4.
62. Testament of Reub. 6.7.
63. Testament of the Twelve Patriarchs, 7.2; 24.1-5; 5.10; 19.11.
64. Cf. S. Zeitlin, *Religious and Secular Leadership* (1943), pp.
4-10.
65. Luke 1.26-44.
66. Testament of Benj. 11.2.
67. Ch. 9.10; 14.6. Cf. Ezek. 44.22.
68. S. Zeitlin, *Megillat Taanit as a Source for Jewish Chronology and History in the Hellenistic and Roman Periods*
(Philadelphia, 1922); G. Dalman, *Aramaische Dialektpro-
proben*, 2nd ed. (1926); H. Lichtenstein, "Die Fastenrolle,"

HUCA, 8-9 (1931-1932); B. Z. Luria, *Megillat Taanit* (in Hebrew) (Jerusalem, 1964). Cf. Appendix I.
69. Cf. S. Zeitlin, *op. cit.*, p. 4.
70. See I, p. 9.
71. See above, p. 247.
72. S. Zeitlin, *op. cit.*, p. 4.
73. M. Tan. 2.8.
74. Cf. S. Zeitlin, *op. cit.*, pp. 2-3.
75. M.B.B. 10.2; Talmud B. M. 104; Tos; Sanh. Yer. *ibid.* Tos. Ket. 4.9; 6; M. *ibid.* 4.12.
76. Cf. Mark 5.41; 7.2; 15.34.
77. Juvenal, *Satire*, 6.187-194.
78. King Agrippa I, who was brought up and educated in Rome with the royal family, addressed the Senate in Greek with the permission of his friend Claudius Caesar. Apparently he did not possess enough knowledge of the Latin language. Cf. Dio, 60.8.
79. Cf. I, p. 443.
80. The development of gnosticism in Judaea after the destruction of the Temple will be discussed in the forthcoming volume.
80a. See above, p. 331, n. 106.
81. Cf. M. Sanh. 10.1.
82. Jesus did not advocate the abrogation of the law, and his disciples followed the laws promulgated by the sages. Paul, who advocated the abrogation of the law, did so in the Diaspora but not in Judaea. When in Jerusalem he conducted himself as an observer of the law, as did James, the brother of Jesus, and Peter.
83. Cf. I, pp. 436-437.
84. Cf. M. Git. 9.8.
85. Deut. 23.2.
86. Cf. Yer. 1.1; S. Zeitlin, "Les Dix-Huit Mesures," *REJ*, (1915), 22-36.
87. *Ibid.* Cf. *War*, 2.17(409); Talmud Git. 56.
88. Yer. *ibid.*
89. *Ibid.*; Talmud Ab. Zar. 36.
90. Tos. Zabim. Cf. also S. Zeitlin, "The Halaka in the Gospels," *HUCA*, 1.
91. Lev. 15.14. Talmud Ker. 9.
92. Cf. Talmud Ab. Zar. 36-37.
93. See I, p. 180.
94. Cf. Tos. Zabim 1.1.
95. Talmud Shab. 17.
96. Cf. M. Yad. 4.6.
97. Cf. Talmud Shab. 17. Cf. above, pp. 109-111.

Appendix I

1. By the side of the Aramaic texts of the Megillah, there exist running commentaries—scholia—in Mishnaic Hebrew, explaining the events which are mentioned in the Megillah text. These scholia are not earlier than the talmudic period. Thus we cannot rely on the scholiast where he gives us what purports to be the historical cause of the event. Cf. further S. Zeitlin, *Megillat Taanit as a Source for Jewish Chronology and History in the Hellenistic and Roman Periods*, Philadelphia 1922, pp. 65-118. (*MT*)
2. Cf. vol. I, pp. 8-9.
3. *Ibid.*
4. *Ibid.*, p. 21.
5. Cf. S. Zeitlin, *MT*, p. 81.
6. Cf. vol 1, p. 143.
7. *Ibid.*
8. Cf. vol. II, p. 235.
9. Cf. vol. I, p. 165.
10. Cf. vol. II, p. 239.
11. Cf. vol. I, pp. 125-126; S. Zeitlin, *MT*, p. 83.
12. Cf. *ibid.*, p. 116.
13. Cf. vol. II, p. 95; S. Zeitlin, *MT*, p. 105.
14. Cf. S. Zeitlin, *MT*, p. 83.
15. Cf. vol. II, p. 242.
16. Cf. vol. II, p. 242.
17. Cf. vol. II, p. 242.
18. Cf. vol. I, p. 102.
19. Vol. I, p. 165.
20. See S. Zeitlin, *MT*, pp. 77-78.
21. Cf. vol. II, p. 142; S. Zeitlin, *MT*, p. 87.
22. Cf. vol. II, p. 247.
23. Cf. vol. I, pp. 164-165.
24. Vol. I, pp. 102-104.
25. Cf. vol. II, p. 252.
26. S. Zeitlin, *MT*, pp. 107-108.
27. Cf. vol. II, p. 185.
28. Cf. S. Zeitlin, *MT*, p. 81; vol. I, p. 111-112.
29. S. Zeitlin, *MT*, p. 117.
30. Cf. ibid., pp. 108-111.
31. Cf. vol. I, p. 116.
32. Cf. the biblical Book of Esther.
33. Cf. S. Zeitlin, *MT*, pp. 89-90.
34. *Ibid.*, pp. 112-115.
35. *Ibid.*, p. 117.
36. Cf. vol. II, p. 95.

Appendix II

1. M. Yad. 4. 7; cf. vol. I, pp. 180-182.
2. M. Yad., *ibid.*; cf. vol. II, p. 277.

3. Tosefta Yad. 2; cf. vol. I, pp. 433-434.
4. M. Yad. 4. 7; Tosefta, *ibid.*, 2. 9; cf. vol. II, p. 359.
5. M. Yad. 4. 8; cf. S. Zeitlin, *Megillat Taanit*, pp. 97-100. See vol. II, p. 140; cf. also M. Men. 65, Tos., *ibid.*, 10. 23; Tos. Suk. 3. 1; Tos. Parah, 3. 7; M. Suk. 4. 9; Tos. 3. 1; Tos. Yoma 1. 8; M. Mak. 1. 6; cf. also S. Zeitlin, *The Sadducees and the Pharisees* (in Hebrew), New York, 1936; vol. I, pp. 176—187.

Appendix IV

1. Cf. the English version of this passage, in vol. II, p. 152.
2. Schürer, *Geschichte* I, pp. 544-549.
3. Niese, De testimonio Christiano quod est apud Josephum antik. Jud. XVIII (Marburgi, 1893-94).
4. Norden, "Josephus und Tacitus über Jesus Christus und eine Messianische Prophetie." *Neue Jarbücher für das Klassische Altertum*, vol. 31 (1913).
5. F. Burkitt, *Teolgish Tijdschrift* (Leiden, 1913).
6. Th. Harnack, *Internat. Monatschrift f. Wissenschaft und Technik* (1913).
7. Th. Reinach, "Josephe sur Jesus," *REJ*, XXXV (1897); cf. also H. St. John Thackeray, *Josephus the Man and the Historian* (New York, 1929), p. 137.
8. Idem, *Judaism and the Beginnings of Christianity*, p. 223.
9. Comment. Matt. 13; *Contra Celsum* 1. 77; II. 13.
10. *Chronicon Paschale*, 1. 63.
11. Eusebius *Ecclesiastical History*, 2. 23.
12. Comment. Matt. 10. 17; *Contra Celsum* 1. 47.
13. *Ecclesiastical History*, 3. 33.
14. *Plinius enin Secundus, cum provinciam regeret, damnatis quibusdam Christianis quibusdam gradu pulsis, ipsa tamen multitudine perturbatus quid de caetero ageret, consuluit tunc Trajanum imperatorem allegans praeter obstinationem non sacrificandi, nihil aliud se de sacramentis eorum comperisse, quam coetus antlucanos ad canendum Christo ut Deo et ad confoederand am disciplinam, homicidium, adulterium, fraudem, perfidiam, et cetera scelera prohibentes. Tunc Trajanus rescripsit, hoc gunus inquirendos quidem non esse, oblatos vero puniri oportere. Apology* II
15. *Ad quae tunc Trajanus rescripti suit auctoritate decernit, ut Christiani non quidem requirantur, si qui tamen inciderint puniantur.*
    (*Die Griechischen Christlichen Schriftsteller der ersten drei Jahrhunderte* [Leipzig 1903].
16. *Plinius Trajano Imperatori*
    Solemne est mihi, domine, omnia, de quibus dubito, ad te referre. Quis enim potest melius vel cunctationem meam regere vel ignorantiam instruere? Cognitionibus de Christianis interfui nunquam. Ideo nescio, quid et quatenus aut puniri soleat, aut quaeri. Nec mediocriter haesitavi, sitne aliquod discrimen aetatum an quamlibet teneri nihil a ro-

bustioribus differant detur paenitentiae venia, an ei, qui omnino Christianus fuit desisse non prosit nomen ipsum etiamsi flagitiis careat, an flagitia cohaerentia nomini puniantur.

Interim in iis, qui ad me tamquam Christiani deferebantur, hunc sum secutus modum. Interrogavi ipsos, an essent Christiani. Confitentes iterum ac tertio interrogavi supplicium minatus. Perseverantes duci iussi. Neque enim dubitabam, qualecunque esset, quod faterentur pertinaciam certe et inflexibilem obstinationem debere puniri. Fuerunt alii similis amentiae; quos, quia cives Romani erant, adnotavi in urbem remittendos.

Mox ipso tractatu ut fieri solet, diffundente se crimine plures species inciderunt. Propositus est libellus sine auctore multorum nomina continens. Qui negabant se esse Christianos aut fuisse, cum praeeunte me deos appellarent, et imagini tuae, quam propter hoc iusseram cum simulacris numinum adferri, ture ac vino supplicarent, praeterea maledicerent Christo, quorum nihil posse cogi dicuntur, qui sunt re vera Christiani, dimittendos esse putavi. Alii ab indice nominati esse se Christianos dixerunt et mox negaverunt; fuisse quidem, sed desiisse, quidam ante triennium, quidam ante plures annos, non nemo etiam ante viginti quinque. Omnes et imaginem tuam deorumque simulacra venerati sunt, et Christo maledixerunt.

Traianus Plinio

17. *Actum quem debuisti, mi secunde, in excutiendis causis eorum, qui Christiani ad te delati fuerant, secutus es. Neque enim in universum aliquid, quod quasi certam forman habeat, constitui potest. Conquirendi non sunt; si deferantur et arguantur, puniendi sunt, ita tamen, ut, qui negaverit se Christianum esse idque re ipsa manifestum fecerit, id est supplicando diis nostris, quamvis suspectus in praeteritum fuerit, veniam ex paenitentia impetret. Sine auctore vero propositi libelli nullo crimine locum habere bebent. Nam et pessimi exempli, nec nostri saeculi est.* Pliny's Letters 10. XCVI-XCVIII. The Loeb Classical Library 1925.

18. Justin Martyr, *Dialogue with Trypho*, 72.

19. The theory that Eusebius was the interpolator of the Christ passage in Josephus aroused some discussion. A. Harnack, who generally did not comment on the writings of Jewish scholars, wrote that he is compelled by my contention that Eusebius was the interpolator to call attention to the fact the word *phulon*, which I adduced as proof that Eusebius was the author, is found in another text, much earlier than Eusebius.

Macht eine kurze besprechung nur deshalb nötig, weil Zeitlin glaubt, den verfasser der Christus—Interpolation im geläufigen text (und bei Eusebius) endeckt zu haben: Eusebius selbst der schuddige (Theologische Literaturzeitung, 1928, No. 7).

The proof which Harnack offered is somewhat surprising. My contention is very clear that the word *phulon* in reference to Christians is not found before the time of Eusebius. Harnack quotes from the fourth book of the Sibylline Oracles, 136, "They shall destroy the guiltless tribe of godly men." The word *phulon* in connection with "godly men" could be used with all propriety so long as it had not been shown that the word *phulon* was used in connection with Christians by the Church Fathers before Eusebius, when quoting non-Christian writers. My theory that Eusebius is the author of the Christ passage stands.

F. J. Foakes Jackson in reviewing my book *Josephus on Jesus*, in *Anglican Theological Review*, 1931, pp. 172-173, wrote, "There is a well-stated opinion of Zeitlin on the *Testimonium Flaviananum* in the *Antiquities*, though it is not easy to endorse the view that Eusebius deliberately invented it." A reviewer in the *Catholic Historical Review*, July 1943, wrote, "Without doubt the problem is nowhere more clearly stated, and there is much plausibility in Mr. Zeitlin's solution—that the Christ passage is traceable to Eusebius."

Appendix VIII

1. See above, p. 6.
2. See p. 197.

Appendix X

1. Book 8.50.
2. Ibid. 75.
3. Ibid. 79.
4. 1.3.
5. 4.2 Cf. also Sophocles, *Ajax* 749, "Leaving the *Synedrou*, Council, of assembled chiefs."
6. 3.16.
7. Cf. Thucydides, 4.22.
8. Book 3.68.
9. Book 2.26, cf. also 6.16; 18.36; 31.2.
10. *Against Neaera*, 83.
11. 14.5.
12. 15.17.
13. 25 (26).4.
14. 3.32; 11.13; 15.22; 22.10; 24.8; 26.26; 27.22; 31.23.
15. 11.19.
16. 23.14, cf. also 42.12. "And sit, *synedreus*, not in the midst of a woman."
17. 6.1; 11.9, cf. also 7.16.

18. cf. 4.1.
19. 5.1, cf. also 17.17.
20. *De Sommiis*, 1.34; *De Sobrietate*, 4; *Quod Omnis Probus Liber Sit*, 11; *De Vita Mosis*, 2.39.
21. *De Praemiis et Poenis*, 5; *Legatio Ad Gaium*, 31.213; *De Vita Contemplativa*, 3.27.
22. *Jewish War*, 1.17, 1 (537).
23. Ibid. 1.29 (571).
24. Ibid. 31.1 (620).
25. Ibid. 2.2.4 (25).
26. Ibid. 6 (38); cf. also *Ant.* 16.2 3 (30).
27. *Jewish War*, 2.6. 1(81).
28. Ibid. 3 (93).
29. *Ant.* 14.5. 4 (91).
30. Ibid. 14.9.3 (167); (168); (172).
31. Ibid. 15. 5 2 (173).
32. Ibid. 20.9. 6 (216); (217).
33. Ibid. 9.1 (200).
34. *Vita*, 12. (62).
35. Ibid. 66.
36. 21.5-6.
37. Cf. Sanh. 3; *Targum, ad. loc.*
38. Ex. 22. 8.
39. Cf. Sanh. 3.
40. 18.13-26.
41. 16.18-20.
42. 17.8-12.
43. 2.18.
44. Judges 4.4-5.
45. I Sam. 8.1.
46. 15.2-4.
47. I Kings 3.9.
48. Ibid. 16-28.
49. II Chron. 19. 6-10.
50. *Politics*, 2. 9 (1285b).
51. Deut. 8-12; 33.10. Cf. also Ezek. 44.23-4.
52. Cf. Volume 1. p. 15.
53. Ezra 7.25-26.
54. Susanna 1.1.49.
55. Ibid. 41.
56. Cf. Ezek. 45.16; S. Zeitlin, "The Titles High Priest and The Nasi of the Sanhedrin," *JQR*, July 1957.
57. Cf. Volume I, p. 279, n.2.
58. Cf. ibid. p. 149.
59. Cf. ibid. pp. 202-212; S. Zeitlin, "The Political Synedrion and the Religious Sanhedrin," *JQR*, 1948, pp. 109-140.
60. On the position of the *mufla*, see S. Zeitlin, *JQR*, 1942, pp. 300-301.
61. Cf. S. Zeitlin, *Who Crucified Jesus?* 1955, pp. 68-83.
62. Cf. *JQR*, 1945, pp. 126-127.
63. Cf. S. Zeitlin, "Synedrion in the Judeo-Hellenistic Literature and Sanhedrin in the Tannaitic Literature," *JQR*, 1946, 414.

64. *Leges Novellae ad Theodosianum*, Lib. XVI, ed. Mommsen, 1905, p. 805.
65. Cf. Deut. 21.19; 22.15; 25.6.
66. Cf. Ex. 21.30; Lev. 24.12; Num. 25.4,7; Deut. 29.9.
67. *Jewish War*, 4. 5.4 (338).
68. See above notes 30-33.
69. A detailed account of the function of the Sanhedrin after the destruction of the Temple will be given in the next volume.

INDEX OF PERSONS AND PLACES

Compiled by Mrs. Evelyn Weiman

A full index will appear in volume III.

467